# The Rowan Rifle Guards

## A History of Company K
## 4th Regiment, North Carolina State Troops
## 1857-1865

*Philip Hatfield, Ph.D.*

Revised 3rd Edition

35th Star Publishing
Charleston, West Virginia
www.35thstar.com

35th Star Publishing
Charleston, West Virginia
www.35thstar.com

ISBN-13: 978-0-9965764-6-8
ISBN-10: 0-9965764-6-0

*Cover Art*: "*The Bonnie Blue Flag*" by Don Troiani.
www.historicalimagebank.com.
Used by permission.
"The Bonnie Blue Flag" depicts the fierce counterassault of Brig. Gen. Stephen D. Ramseur's Brigade (2d, 4th, 14th and 30th North Carolina Regiments) against the Union II Corps at the "Mule Shoe" Salient during the 12 May 1864 Battle of Spotsylvania. The Tar Heels repulsed the Federals and regained the earthworks, protecting Lee's lines from ultimate disaster.

Back cover image: Ambrotype of Meshack F. Hunt, Rowan Rifle Guards, circa 1859-1861. Courtesy of University of North Carolina – Chapel Hill Library, Civil War Photographs Collection. Used by permission.
See pg. 33 for more information on this image.

Cover Design; Studio 6 Sense, www.studio6sense.com

## *Dedication*

This book is dedicated to the loving memory of my friend and fellow researcher, Eric G. Hall, formerly of Salisbury, North Carolina, who departed this life on September 27, 2015. I am forever indebted to him for sharing his expertise in countless discussions, drawn from years of research on the 4th North Carolina State Troops. Rest in Peace my friend.

# Acknowledgements

This project began in June 1998 and is derived from a personal and family interest in the 4th North Carolina State Troops. Much of this research was completed in Salisbury, North Carolina, where the Rowan Rifle Guards originated. Writing their story was both frustrating and fascinating, but I must say that "getting there" was the best part. Not only because of the learning process, but especially the people who made it possible. Everyone who contributed to this book shared two common traits: a love of American history and a desire to accurately preserve the story of these unique soldiers. I am deeply indebted to the following persons for their assistance:

My parents, Calvin and Freda Hatfield for instilling a deep respect for Civil War history and tradition within me. Among my fondest memories is walking the Gettysburg battlefield with them when I was six years old. That is where I began to realize the true cost of freedom. Rachel M. Hatfield, my wife, for her photographic and editing contributions, but more importantly, for patiently supporting my passion for Civil War history. Heather Hanson Conkle, for copy editing and assisting with textual revisions. Rick Holbrook, site manager at Fort Caswell, on Oak Island, North Carolina, for allowing my wife and me to inspect and photograph the remains of Fort Caswell. Chris Fonvielle, Ph.D., historian/author and professor of history at University of North Carolina, Wilmington. Not only is Dr. Fonvielle one of my favorite historians for his work on the 1865 Wilmington Campaign, but he also provided a great deal of assistance in developing the accounts of political and military events on the North Carolina coast in 1861, for which I am grateful. Kaye Brown-Hurst of the Rowan County Museum, Salisbury, North Carolina, for granting access to the uniform and accoutrements of Capt. William C. Coughenhour. Henry Mintz, for research assistance and textual criticism during the early revision process. Author Jack Travis for sharing technical details and some hidden secrets of publishing a Civil War history book. The staff and volunteers of the Rowan County Library, Edith M. Clark History Room, for so kindly assisting me throughout the years when I utilized their excellent holdings for research on the Rowan Rifles. John Coski, Ph.D., Historian at the National Civil War Museum at Richmond, Virginia for allowing access to the Museum of the Confederacy archives as well as artifacts related to the 4th NCST when the original edition was written. Tom Belton, North Carolina archives for feedback on the text as well as assisting with locating flags of the 4th NCST. Robert Krick, Jr., Historian at Richmond National Battlefield Park, for sharing his historical expertise and textual criticism to the author during the early phases of this project. Anyone else who contributed but was somehow overlooked, know that I am grateful but also apologetic for not including your name.

*"The Bonnie Blue Flag"* by Don Troiani.
www.historicalimagebank.com.
Used by permission.

"The Bonnie Blue Flag" depicts the fierce counterassault of Brig. Gen. Stephen D. Ramseur's Brigade (2d, 4th, 14th and 30th North Carolina Regiments) against the Union II Corps at the "Mule Shoe" Salient during the 12 May 1864 Battle of Spotsylvania. The Tar Heels repulsed the Federals and regained the earthworks, protecting Lee's lines from ultimate disaster.

# Table of Contents

# Index of Photographs and Illustrations

# Introduction

The Rowan Rifle Guards formed during an era when young men viewed service in the regular peace-time military as unpopular and unexciting. Extant laws required compulsory service in state militia regiments, but during the 1850's most militia units in North Carolina were little more than a paper tiger. Required to muster only once a year, most such organizations had trouble even keeping reliable officers much less attain skilled instructors for drill and tactics. The disdain toward state militia led a number of youth to organize their own independent military units known as Volunteer companies. Known locally as the Rowan Rifles, this company was certainly not the first of its kind in North Carolina, but it was the first Volunteer company in Rowan County. Typically, these companies were comprised by those youth from more affluent families, and tended to project a sense of elitism. Their uniforms and equipment were certainly expensive enough to preclude membership by most young men whose income was below average. Although a few original members of the Rowan Rifles were wealthy, this proved to be the exception not the rule, as most had very little financial resources or social status, making them something of an anomaly from the outset.

With only a small percentage of the original members having an economic interest in the institution of slavery or wealthy backgrounds, this company was comprised largely of young men motivated by the opportunity company membership provided to advance their social standing. Rather their first three years of service to the community mainly consisted of providing military ambience at parades, ceremonies to honor dignitaries and holiday celebrations. Occasionally, the company would travel to other counties and compete against other Volunteer and militia outfits in drill or target shooting competitions, but rarely did they engage in such hiatus without endeavoring to entertain several young ladies. Such were the fancies of youth until sectionalist tensions began to emerge in 1860.

The Rowan County area was strongly pro-Union during antebellum, with many residual ties to the old Whig party which was strongly nationalist. Yet when Abraham Lincoln was elected by 180 out of 303 electoral votes with only forty percent of the popular vote in 1860, tensions in the Piedmont region began to escalate. State officials began to revamp the dysfunctional militia system in anticipation of armed conflict, and required more regular drill. They also enlisted the help of volunteer companies across the state including the Rowan Rifles who were virtually all better drilled than the militia. Yet the majority of Rowan's citizens resisted Secession, even when Abraham Lincoln was elected in November 1860. As the time for Lincoln's inauguration approached, however, popular opinion on the North Carolina coast felt imminently threatened by Federal invasion, especially after two Federal steamers tried to enter Charleston Harbor in South Carolina only to find resistance by the Corps of Cadets from the state military academy located there. Just barely two weeks before Lincoln was sworn into office, in early January 1861 an agitated band of coastal militia illegally captured Fort Caswell and Fort Johnston in the Smithville vicinity, some thirty miles south of Wilmington. Although rarely discussed in Civil War research, the ensuing political storm between Governor John W. Ellis and U.S. President James Buchanan escalated tensions between North Carolina and the United States, in spite of Governor John Ellis's attempts to reconcile the incident.

But the actions of those zealous militiamen had set the stage for war. Public opinion called for secession afterward as coastal inhabitants were convinced the governor was too passive in their protection. In many ways, events in North Carolina occurring between January and April 1861 suggest the war was already in progress before Lincoln took office. The capture of two coastal forts also correlated with delivery of a questionable shipment some 27,000 arms from Northern arsenals arranged by Secretary of War John B. Floyd to the Fayetteville Arsenal a few days later. Floyd was acting in concert with Governor Ellis, and produced what amounts to a cause and effect sequence that is likely one of the lesser known, albeit direct causes of the Civil War. These factors certainly had an impact on the Rowan Rifles, who were anxiously waiting and pondering what would be their fate as the politicians tried to untangle the complex issues transpiring around them. The series of unfortunate events culminated in April 1861, when Lincoln called for 75,000 volunteers to squelch the uprising among southern states following the attack on Fort Sumpter, South Carolina. Governor adamantly refused to send troops, and instead ordered the militia to again capture the coastal forts near Wilmington. Only a few days later, the Rowan Rifles found themselves onboard a train enroute to Fort Caswell, where they received their first few weeks of army life as a garrison force.

The reader will find numerous original letters and diaries cited herein verbatim; this best articulates the soldier's experiences throughout the war, rather than a second hand narrative. But the question of what motivated the "typical" Confederate soldier is beyond the present work; suffice it to say that for this company at least, careful analysis of their demographic data and other personal correspondence yields a great deal about not only what motivated the officers and enlisted men in the Rowan Rifle Guards to step forward in April 1861, but also we gain a glimpse of what they experienced as members of the 4th North Carolina State Troops in the Army of Northern Virginia during numerous violent and bloody campaigns across the four years of Civil War that rent the very character of America and left most of their families and fortunes desolate. Much of the recent Civil War literature understates those original sources, in particular first person soldier narratives of the war, and relies too strongly on secondary analysis, i.e. the author's opinions and ideologies. Although original soldier accounts are certainly suspect for error or personal biases, one writing from the front lines in the 1860's generally has less reason to distort their story than authors writing about it 150 years later. Even those accounts written for publication in local newspapers (and therefore written with a specific audience in mind), tend to contain more realistic descriptions of camp life and battle events than anything we can construct because the authors participated in the war. Soldier accounts, rather than ex post facto narratives written by those who did not experience the Civil War firsthand, therefore open a window of perspective not otherwise available and are the primary voice speaking on topics such as what they felt about the war, what they experienced in camp and during battle, otherwise unavailable.

By examining their own words, we draw closer to not only better understanding the phenomenon of war, but also recognizing our misconceptions about who they were, what they did, and why they fought. Not unlike thousands of other volunteers in 1861, most of the men serving in the Rowan Rifles grew up together, attended the same public schools, and many worked and lived together. Most were relatives, either directly or by extended family relation, and in most cases they were neighbors before the war. Such common bonds, whether overtly stated or implicit, played a key role in maintaining their commitment to serving for a cause that was ultimately doomed. Most of the original sixty two original members present on the North Carolina coast in 1861 had drilled, marched and trained together for nearly three years as a Volunteer company before the war, and were very closely knit. As casualties from disease and battle increased across the war, we find evidence that both officers and enlisted men, as well as their families and communities at home were profoundly affected by the losses, although it did not defeat them psychologically; it rather served to stir them on, deepening their motivation to fight. This makes them unique in the annals of military history.

With this in mind, the purpose of this study is to consider the military service of one small sample of men serving in the Confederate army, and what they said about the war, themselves and each other. It is not intended to solve problems of racial bias, politics or even consider larger battlefield tactical problems, but hopefully it will awaken a realization that these soldiers were not who we have presumed them to be, and afford us a more personal glimpse into their character, beliefs and motivation for fighting a war that was essentially doomed from the start. In doing so, I hope this work will provide both a detailed analysis of the available evidence showing the trials, hardships the soldiers endured, and also challenge some common stereotypes of this mysterious character we know as "Johnny Reb" especially the notions that he was always starved and ragged during the war, which the evidence contained herein clearly defies. In spite of what amounts to a campaign to do so by some recent academic historians and politicians, we cannot alienate the Confederate soldier from American history. His story is our common history, and it is our responsibility to find the whole truth, not just the parts that seem consistent with current political agendas. On this eve of the sesquicentennial of the American Civil War, we must therefore understand not only why, but how they became products of their culture and society, and not attempt to deny, revise, or re-construct their story with ideology that imposes twenty first century values upon theirs. Instead, we should simply listen to our past in its' native tongue, and learn from it.

Philip Hatfield, Ph.D.
Original edition written in Salisbury, N.C., published 2010.
Revised edition, June 2019.

*"None but the soldiers who enlisted the first six weeks of the war can form an adequate conception of the wild enthusiasm that pervaded all classes at that time. The question of the right of secession in the abstract bothered us but little, the conflict had been precipitated upon us, and North Carolina had taken her stand, and we were with her..."*

*- John Stikeleather, 4th North Carolina Infantry*

Rowan County Confederate Soldier Monument and Inscription, Salisbury, North Carolina

The inscription reads:

SOLDIERS OF THE
CONFEDERACY
FAME HAS GIVEN YOU
AN IMPERISHABLE CROWN
HISTORY WILL RECORD
YOUR DARING VALOR
NOBLE SUFFERINGS AND
MATCHLESS ACHIEVEMENTS
TO THE HONOR AND
GLORY OF OUR LAND

# Chapter One

# Antebellum Era Militia and Volunteer Companies in Rowan County

When the Civil War began, the men of the Rowan Rifle Guards erroneously believed that their only service would be the defense of their home state in a very short conflict. During the antebellum era, they held regular drills and appeared at numerous parades, enjoying a reputation as an elite volunteer company. But those zealous young men filling up the original ranks had little, if any idea as to what malevolence their futures held. Officially designated as Company K, 4th Regiment, North Carolina State Troops in July 1861, (hereafter 4th NCST) the men in this company quickly realized that their service would not be simply protecting their homes and firesides close to home, but rather, on bloody battlefields hundreds of miles from their native state. This unit participated in every major campaign waged by the Army of Northern Virginia and humbly surrendered fifteen survivors at Appomattox on the morning of 9 April 1865, with a ninety-six percent casualty rate across the war. Of those fifteen men, eight members of the original Rowan Rifle Guards were still in the ranks.

The Rowan Rifle Guards were the first antebellum era volunteer company to form in Rowan County. Organized in 1857, its founders' intentions were to provide the community with a company of "minute men" who could respond to any crisis, but prior to the Civil War their service was mainly providing a military ambience. Known locally as the "Rowan Rifles," they were essentially young men from hard working, yeoman farmer and laboring families; only a few hailed from wealthier families. Most youth in Volunteer companies hoped to improve their social standing by serving, as company membership was then considered to be the mark of a young man with a promising future. John J. Brunner, the influential owner, publisher and editor of the *Carolina Watchman* newspaper in Salisbury, the oldest news organ in the state, was an advocate for organizing the Rowan Rifle Guards in 1857. His newspaper business and personal assets were valued at $14,700.00 with four slaves in 1860, making him wealthier citizen, although he was an ardent patriotic supporter of the national government who strongly opposed secession. Brunner was married to the former Mary A. Kincaid and had four children: Clarissa, age 14; Mary B., age 12; Thomas K., age 6; Charles H., age 4 and Anna, age 2. The Brunner's also had a fifth child, William, age 3 who later died of disease.[1]

Evidence of Brunner's influence on the companies' inception is observed in June 1857, just after the Rowan Rifle Guards were formed, when in an editorial he asked for the town business men to cooperate in furthering the object of the Rowan Rifle Guards in celebrating the 4th of July by "...suspending business from 10 until 1..." and was given his wish. James Bowers was age 20 years, and also lived with the Brunner family in 1860. Brunner had taken him in as one of their own after his parent's death left him an orphan, and he was employed at the newspaper office as a "printer's devil" which is akin to a modern day typesetter. Bowers was one of the first volunteers for the Rowan Rifles in 1857 and helped organize the company. He was rewarded by being elected as the company Color bearer, and bore the company flag for nearly five years. Note that in his musings as editor, Brunner often refers to the "Salisbury Rifle Guard" but is actually speaking of the Rowan Rifle Guard since no other company existed by the former name. Before one can understand this companies' experience in the Civil War, a solid grasp of the pre-war militia system and Victorian culture in Rowan County where the company originated must be acquired. Mildly put, the North Carolina militia system was in disarray during the antebellum period, but the social culture was flourishing, and the original Rowan Rifle Guards were decidedly a product of that environment.

The militia system was based on the Federal Militia Act of 1792 which authorized each state to keep a militia for defense purposes. The law also allowed for unaffiliated volunteer companies, a practice that had existed since the early 1780s. All white males aged eighteen to forty-five years were required to enroll in a local company of state militia unless exempted by religion, occupation, or other active military service. Examples of exempt occupations included clergymen, postal employees, doctors, and the sheriff. Each county in North Carolina was divided into militia districts beginning in October 1777, and a militia captain was appointed in each district. The state was divided into six districts, each comprising a brigade reporting to a brigadier general. The brigade commander reported to a major general who, in turn, reported to the governor. In retrospect, the districts appear to have been an arrangement more for the convenience of tax collectors than military objective since militia districts in North Carolina were concordant with those found on state tax rolls.[2]

The enrolled militia in Rowan County from the period following the Revolutionary War to 1861 underwent numerous attempts at reorganization by various military officers, but suffered from frank neglect by the state authorities. In the period between 1780 and 1799 the state militia was largely a paper tiger adorning the adjutant general's office in Raleigh. The Rowan County militia was assigned to the "Salisbury District/Brigade" and included companies from Mecklenburg, Guilford, Montgomery, Anson, Surry, Rutherford, Burke, Lincoln, Wilkes, Richmond, Washington, and Sullivan counties. It rarely drilled. In 1793 the militia was assigned divisions consisting of one to two brigades. The Rowan County militia was placed in the "8th Brigade/Salisbury" of the 4th Division. From 1801-1822 the Rowan County militia was reorganized, and units in the Salisbury area were consolidated with those in Iredell County as 7th Brigade, 4th Division. Essentially dormant for more than forty years following the Revolution, the North Carolina militia was activated for a brief period in 1812 out of fear of another British invasion and again in the 1840s following the Nat Turner Rebellion.* In 1822, Davidson County was added to the 7th Brigade. Again in 1838, North Carolina assigned its militia units numerical designations. The four extant Rowan county companies were assigned to the 63d Brigade but remained in the 4th Division. The 4th Division was absent a major general to command it since Maj. Gen. Bates M. Edney resigned on 4 July 1844.[3] Although the county militia managed to maintain annual muster days during this era, the time invested in drill was "...almost wholly thrown away – skill is not acquired – discipline is not enforced – it remains very problematical whether the training of half a century has added a single item to our stock of military skills...".

---

*Nat Turner's Rebellion occurred on 20 August 1831 in Southampton County, Virginia. Around 2 A.M., Turner and other slaves murdered his master and family. Next they killed several other whites in a house-to-house raid. The local militia caught Turner and hanged fifteen slaves after a lengthy pursuit of six weeks. When Turner was finally apprehended, he was executed by skinning and hanging on 21 November 1831. Kenneth Greenberg, (Ed.). *Nat Turner: A Slave Rebellion in History and Memory.* (New York, NY: Oxford University Press, 2004).

The latter was largely considered to be due to the "innate distaste for discipline" found among peacetime militia members in Rowan County.₄ Two of the four infantry companies in Rowan County were again organized into two regiments: the 63d Regiment (also known as the "Fork Regiment") and the 64th or "Lower Regiment." Their unit nicknames were associated with the area of the county where the member resided.₅ At that time, the militia occasionally patrolled local townships taking the role of a citizen police force.₆ Muster days of the 1840s continued to be inefficiently-managed affairs. As one observer remarked, they were simply "dusty and dry – a poor show." The militia in Rowan County had regressed to the degree that drunken and disorderly conduct was the norm. In 1831 the editor of the *Carolina Watchman* was surprised when the militia finally evidenced some restraint as "not one single person was drunk during the review on Saturday."₇

### Mexican War Volunteers

Ironically, the Mexican War in 1846 had a constructive impact on the Rowan County militia even though they did not actually fight. Gov. William A. Graham called for ten companies of volunteers to form a regiment of infantry on 22 May 1846. Rowan County was the first in the state to respond. A volunteer company, composed mainly of enrolled militiamen, quickly formed under command of Capt. Richard W. Long and offered itself to the adjutant general. By 5 June the town of Salisbury was witness to the muster. Companies aligned in "…a scene of beautiful disorder" and "marched in every direction until finally all were brought into line." The columns eventually marched out of town, erroneously thinking they were headed to war; as it turned out, the twelve-month volunteers were ordered to stay in Salisbury until the government ordered them elsewhere. They began daily drill and formations, and even participated in the Fourth of July parade, although the garrison generally "went about their business in an easy manner."₈ Roughly two weeks later, Rowan County's company was chosen to complete the state's regiment of ten companies, officially becoming "Company A, North Carolina Volunteers." Just days later, the federal government altered its policy excluding twelve-month volunteers, accepting only those who would enlist for the duration. Hence, the disappointed volunteers remained in Salisbury, quartered in local hotels paid for by local citizens and still holding regular drills in anticipation of deployment. In December the governor again called for volunteers, and the volunteer company accepted the call. A flag was flown from the courthouse cupola bearing the inscription "Rowan, Thy Daughters Cheer thee Onward."₉

Orders finally arrived for the company to deploy to Wilmington en route to Mexico, but were quickly remanded. On 31 December they were directed to leave for Charlotte where they arrived 2 January 1847 and "languished" for three weeks without provisions. Disillusioned and angry, the volunteers quickly found their limits and, with the exception of about ten men, simply deserted and returned home. Shortly afterward, amidst great embarrassment and blame for the failure, their Captain resigned. The *Carolina Watchman* editor poked fun at them, publishing the following barb a few days later:

> Company 'A' - - where are you? Echo answers HERE, here, h-e-r-e they answer from every point of the compass, as a sound reverberating among the hills and rocks. Reader, the Rowan Company of Volunteers have disbanded.

In spite of their disappointments, the enrolled militia continued its meager existence; and by mid-1849, muster days were starting to show some facsimile of order. Muster day on 3 May 1849 was held at the old "Race Field" located near the athletic fields at modern Livingstone College in Salisbury, under damp and cloudy conditions. Although these events were frequently chaotic, this particular drill seemed to impress the eyewitnesses. Several area Volunteer companies along with the militia were present that day; newspaper accounts did not identify the Volunteer companies, but did indicate some were from Salisbury. There were a number of volunteer companies then in the area although most did not stay together long. They tended to often disband and re-organize based on internal political allegiances and personality conflicts. Local citizens often gathered to witness the military events and listen to martial airs of the fife and drums in the presence of hundreds of other spectators. Present that day was the 63d Regiment (The Lower Fork Regiment) of the North Carolina Militia commanded by Col. J.M. Brown with Lt. Col. A.M. Rice, Maj. John Verble, Adj. Lueco Bencini, Maj. Shuman, and Q.M. John Rice. One observer recorded that the regiment made a dashing appearance as they marched over to the Race Field in its "gay and beautiful suits" and with officers mounted on their horses. Apparently, early in the 1850s, muster days were sufficient as to create "fuss and feathers enough to satisfy everybody for at least six months."[10]

In spite of some improvements shown on muster days during the late 1840s and early 1850s, several officers resigned due to general dissatisfaction. A number of officers in the 64th Regiment resigned between 1841 to1855, although exact dates were not always recorded. The list of officers included a "Lieutenant Colonel Holshouser" and "Maj. Sam Rebelin" (dates unknown); an individual who was likely Rebelin's successor, identified only as "Lowrey", who resigned on 22 September 1843 due to medical problems; and Col. Richard W. Long, who resigned 15 January 1843.[11] While muster rolls of the 63d militia did not survive, at least one original member of the Rowan Rifles is known to have earlier served in that organization, John Renter. He was a resident of Rowan County, and since he enlisted in the Rowan Rifles in 1859, he was in the 63d Militia prior to that date as state laws required service in only one military organization. By 1850, militia companies were usually designated simply by their township or neighborhood although they rarely (if ever) drilled. In the generally peaceful period after the Revolution through Antebellum, the militia became complacent and slowly decayed. Most members did not even own a firearm, and compulsory attendance at bi-annual musters was only loosely enforced at best. If a soldier failed to attend muster, there were rarely ever any consequences. Yet, muster attendance gradually regained popularity, and the events often lasted up to three days. The bi-annual militia musters were more akin to company picnics than military affairs. Events normally consisted of target practice and -- less commonly -- some drill. Primarily, musters were a time set aside for socializing, dancing, and consuming alcoholic beverages to the degree that problems with carousing and drinking were often reported.[12]

A good example of the frustration felt by militia officers during these years is a letter written by Brig. Gen. C.J. Webb on 9 February 1859. He petitioned Gov. John Ellis for assistance in reorganizing the militia, which he felt was lodged in a catch-twenty two of complacency and blame. His letter encapsulates the state of affairs among North Carolina militia leaders. He complained that annual reports had not been completed for two years and, due to state neglect, there was "no Major General for the 5th Div. The office has been vacated for 3 years…". Webb further pointed out that he had no superior officer to report to, such that he did not know, "...To whom it is my duty to resign: No Maj. Gen., no election ordered for same, - officers wishing to resign as well make their report, but to whom...I do think there is a neglect somewhere that ought to be attended to...the office in the militia is troublesome. A part of the officers deny their duty & complain to their superiors because others neglect theirs."[13] Other factors also contributed to the erosion of the militia during the peaceful antebellum years. The state had only a part-time adjutant general, some changes in extant militia laws made by the General Assembly were not distributed to the various units statewide, and reporting procedures by officers to the state were not standardized. Probably the most significant factor, however, was the change in public perception of the militia's real mission – to protect them from slave insurrection. Insurrection did not even seem a realistic possibility to most citizens until John Brown's raid on Harpers Ferry in 1858. Hence, the upkeep of such a militia force was largely viewed as unnecessary until political events began to alter the course of Southern society in the late 1850s.[14]

### *Volunteer Companies*

With the slowly-fading state militia, another body of militia emerged known as Volunteer companies in the 1850's. In addition to the state militia, these outfits were also authorized under the Federal Militia Act of 1792, but were given a great deal of freedom with regard to their manner of uniform, organization and rules, and weaponry. Such companies typically had their own armories and chose unique -- even gaudy and impractical -- patterns for their uniforms. The variations were permitted as long as they approximated government regulations. Their uniforms were usually paid for by local benefactors or directly out of the officers' personal finances. In contrast to the careless demeanor of most militia, a volunteer company normally drilled more often, took more pride in their military bearing, and was generally better trained than enrolled militia. By the time the Civil War started, some state authorities believed the volunteer companies would eventually replace the enrolled militia as a rapid response force in case of attack.[15] This later proved true for dozens of volunteer companies in 1861, including the Rowan Rifle Guards in 1861 while the Rowan County militia was still floundering.

Membership in a volunteer company was largely viewed as a function of the middle to upper class since the members were primarily young men from the most affluent families in the area. The social status afforded by membership in such a company reinforced a strong sense of elitism, and was looked upon with pride by the general community. Many young men enlisting in an antebellum volunteer company used their membership to catapult aspiring political careers or otherwise advance their social standing. However, this was not especially true for most members of the Rowan Rifles, the majority of whom came from working class families. Most volunteer companies also required a majority vote before accepting a young man wishing to enlist, and helped them avoid having less desirable members in their ranks, which was usually defined as those with less financial resources. One factor contributing to this phenomenon was the cost of uniforms and equipment, which in some cases could be quite expensive. Most of their weapons were privately purchased or issued by the state. The officers were required to provide an acceptable cash bond to the Governor for those arms, and were held responsible for their upkeep and safe keeping, as the guns were property of the state.

Normally, only wealthier young men could participate in Volunteer companies since they had the means to buy their own uniforms and gear. Those young men of a lesser socioeconomic status were usually kept from membership unless the company had made some arrangements to cover the costs for especially promising young men. During the antebellum era the young elite of Salisbury were once described as rather ostentatious, taking "...undue pride in the wealth of their parents, and spurned the society of mechanics for fear their reputations would be spoiled..."[16] Again, that appears to have been the norm in Salisbury, but was clearly not always the case among the Rowan Rifles, whose members were predominantly laborers, farmers, or miners from the northern and southeastern areas of the county. The Rowan Rifle Guards held a high *esprit de corps*, as evidenced by their frequent musters and drill which occurred much more regularly than that of the enrolled county or state militia, who generally viewed drill as a nuisance. In most counties during the antebellum era, militia muster days became the center of the local activity because of the number of influential people involved. Their volunteer companies were mainstays at various political gatherings across the state, such as visits from the governor or other heads of state. For example, in 1857, the Fayetteville Independent Light Infantry, which was the oldest independent volunteer militia company in North Carolina and the second oldest in the United States, provided an escort and honor guard for the Marquis De Lafayette when he traveled to his namesake city in 1820. That company even used lighted candles in the muzzles of their muskets to escort him at night.[17] The "FILI" later became Company H of the 1st North Carolina Volunteers; and they fought at Bethel Church, Virginia, on 10 June 1861.

### The Rowan Rifle Guards Organize

The Rowan Rifle Guards were formed amidst a depressed period in the history of North Carolina's state militia, when militia membership was generally viewed with disdain. The earliest record of the Rowan Rifle Guard's formation was found in a 25 February 1857 advertisement from the *Salisbury Herald*, one of two local newspapers operating in Salisbury at the time. On 3 March 1857 the *Salisbury Herald* published the following announcement appealing to the young men of Salisbury to step forward and fill the ranks of a newly forming volunteer company:

Notice to Young Men

We would very much like to see our young men in Salisbury organize a volunteer military company, believing there are enough to form a very large Captain's command – Besides enlivening the place with their regular drill, they would form a corps of 'minute men' in any emergency – an emergency that might happen at an unexpected moment and for which we would be prepared in advance. Will some of our young readers be inspired by a military feeling and act on our suggestion?

As military zeal captured the community's imagination, the volunteers named themselves the Rowan Rifle Guards. On 11 March 1857 the *Herald* also reported that the company had begun to organize and was then in process of establishing its structure and rules. Typically, a volunteer company was under the command of a captain with two or more junior officers, a first and second lieutenant, serving under him. Twenty-eight year old Williams Brown, a farmer from Davidson County, was elected captain of the new volunteers in March 1857. The ladies of Salisbury quickly rallied to contribute their support by making the new company a flag. The colors were probably made of silk, although the original did not survive.[18] Also on 11 March 1857 the *Salisbury Herald* reported:

> The young gentleman of Salisbury have held 2 Preliminary meetings at the courthouse in furtherance of their laudable subject of organizing a Volunteer Militia Company...and we are pleased to learn that a sufficient number have already enrolled their names to make a good company. They will meet again on Wednesday to adapt a Constitution and by-laws and to elect officers of the corps. The ladies intend embroidering with their delicate fingers a Banner which they will present as a token of their favor and appreciation of the chivalrous young soldiers who hold themselves in readiness to defend the "beauty and booty of Salisbury." We hope the young will attach themselves to the "Guards."

### Rowan County Demographics & Culture

Members of the original Rowan Rifle Guards were primarily residents of Rowan County, North Carolina from the South Salisbury-China Grove area, although some also lived in neighboring Davie, Davidson, Iredell and Cabarrus Counties. A few individuals also hailed from Burke, Gaston, and Montgomery Counties. One officer, Marcus Hofflin, was born in Bavaria, Germany and one of the privates, Henry Williams, was born in England. Salisbury was established in 1755 and was the Rowan county seat. The fifth largest town in the state, Salisbury was known as a "typically proud" little Southern town.[20] A strong farming community, Rowan County had 14,569 residents in 1860, seventy percent Caucasian and twenty eight percent Slaves.[19] The County population then represented descendants of settlers from all across Europe, primarily including German, Irish, Scotch, Welsh, Dutch, French, English, Swiss and Italians. Most of those families' ancestors immigrated to the United States in the 1700's to avoid religious persecution in Europe. As a result, they tended to hold strong religious ideologies in reference to government intervention in their personal lives. The dominant sociological and political context of Rowan County during antebellum can be generally described as affluent, religiously conservative, and strongly pro-Union, but also fiercely self-reliant. The town of Salisbury received an active railroad depot in the 1850's which created a number of jobs, and also led to a more transient, ethically diverse population, yet Salisbury remained strongly geocentric in spite of its diversity.[21]

Although slavery was a cultural norm in the South during the antebellum period, most historians consider it a financially-motivated practice. It did not have widespread practice in Rowan County, as roughly twenty eight percent of population was slave holders in 1860, in contrast to North Carolina's total state population which is estimated to be about thirty seven percent slave holder. Yeoman North Carolinians took pride in their participation in public affairs during this era, although viewed political equality as only intended for non-slaves. Historian William C. Harris has eloquently summarized North Carolina during the antebellum era, noting that the people generally,

> "...disdained aristocratic pretensions and held the elite to a close accounting on this score. Both antebellum political parties – the Whigs and the Democrats – attempted to outdo each other in their professions of support for republican simplicity and values and their hostility to aristocrats, whom they almost invariably associated with their political opponents. The legendary plantation society of the antebellum South existed only on a small scale in North Carolina. The Old North State was primarily a land of yeoman farmers. Fewer than one third of white North Carolina families held slaves in 1860, and

88 percent of these slaveholders possessed only between one and nineteen slaves. By the historian's definition, about 4,000 North Carolinians, owning twenty slaves or more, could be classified as planters in 1860, but of that number only 744 were large planters, holding more than fifty slaves. Few planters in North Carolina had the time, assets, or social proclivity to play the part of the aristocrat assigned to them in the Old South myth.

It is true that planters, or at least slaveholders, enjoyed a preponderant share of public office and influence, but they were divided in the exercise of this power…Artificial class barriers to success did not exist, and all elements of society honored those men who had overcome their "lowly origins" to become prominent in their communities…No part of the cult of equality included blacks, most of whom were held in slavery. Slaves constituted about one third of the total North Carolina population of approximately one million people. Thirty thousand blacks lived in freedom, but it was a freedom carefully controlled by the white community and the law, especially after the sectional conflict over slavery became heated."[22]

Hence, while North Carolina was not without hypocrisy with regards to equality, neither was it ignorant of its own flaws. Because slave ownership was less common in Rowan County than in the larger state population, it was less of a factor in the economic structure of the community. Rowan County was then described as "mild and paternal" in regards to slavery, as one historian wrote that only a handful farmers could afford slaves, and those who could were commonly observed working side-by-side in the fields.[23] Many slaves lived in the same houses as their masters' families, in spite of earlier statewide fears of an armed slave rebellion during the Nat Turner era. Anecdotal evidence of the period suggests that physical abuse of slaves was rare and typically resulted in the overseer's immediate dismissal, often at the behest of children or other family members who had befriended them.[24] Another historian's work on Rowan County during this era reflects that the community was generally glad to see the specter of slavery vanish from their land.[25]

Rowan County was also known as something of a contrast in spite of its religiosity. The town of Salisbury was famous for its problems with alcohol; there was at least two distilleries operating there and numerous public houses (bars). Several historians noted even the more aristocratic citizens frequented "grog" and other public houses that sold alcohol. One author indicated this trend dated back to colonial times when Salisbury was little more than a trading outpost, and men had little to do with spare time but drink alcoholic beverages. The whole of aristocratic society were not as indulgent, however, as many occupied their leisure time with popular horse races, literary and acting societies, but nearly all professed church membership. A large group of young citizens also regularly participated in a phenomenon known as subscription balls. These were essentially dance parties where social class boundaries were relaxed for a few hours and any "respectable man" could participate for a fee of $5. Managers were appointed to arrange social introductions, ensuring no one spent the evening alone. These events usually lasted several hours, and "it was customary…to go to a subscription dance disgracefully drunk…".[26] Conversely there were many Salisbury residents who did not use alcohol, attend public houses, or participate in such parties in that era.

Although the Rowan Rifles were not mainly composed of upper class youth as an antebellum era Volunteer company, membership did seem to provide a political stepping stone for certain prominent young men. Its presence also gave citizens a chance to display their patriotism, and the company quickly became the center of social life as holidays and muster days were often indistinguishable. As no muster rolls from the antebellum era version of the company survived, it is unknown exactly how many men served in the Rowan Rifle Guards between the years 1857-1861. Archival sources including 1861 muster rolls, pension records, and individual service files identified sixty two men who were in the original company on 30 May 1861. This included four officers, seven non-commissioned officers, and fifty one privates. Note that photographic and service records also identified one other man who was an original member of the company, but he transferred out of the unit in 1858. To understand the character, beliefs and behavior of the men who formed this company, the reader should become familiar with not only their military service, but also of the unique socioeconomic and familial backgrounds of the soldiers forming the original Rowan Rifles. This better enables us to form an accurate perspective as to their various political or other motivations for membership in a volunteer company as well as their service in the Civil War.

Therefore, a brief biographic discussion of each man identified as an original member comprising the Rowan Rifle Guards follows. Appendices A and B contain summaries of biographic and military service after June 1861 for both original Rowan Rifles and men who later served in Company K, 4th NCST. Note that two other men are discussed as Non-commissioned officers in the original Rowan Rifle Guards who later received commissions in Company K, Moses L. Bean and Hamilton C. Long. Long did not enlist until August 1861, therefore his biographic information is found among the enlisted men in April 1861. Similarly, Bean was serving as a sergeant in April 1861, and is therefore included as one of the original non-commissioned officers. The following review occurs in rank order, beginning with the officers, then non-commissioned officers and privates in alphabetical order.

### *Officers*

Four officers are identified serving in the Rowan Rifle Guards from 1857-1861, although the first captain, Williams Brown, was reduced to first sergeant in March 1861, and quickly reappointed as a 2d Lieutenant in April. Two of the original officers were reared essentially as orphans or taken in by other families after the death of their natural parents. Two officers then resided with their families, and one was married. Two others were employed in trades independent of their families. Next, two of the men serving as officers in Company K were born outside of Rowan County; Marcus Hofflin was born in Bavaria, Germany, and Frances McNeely was born in Iredell County. Only McNeely came from a particularly influential family, as he worked as an assistant clerk for his father, who was then the Rowan County Clerk of Court. Yet none enjoyed the life of a "gentleman" and none were slaveholders themselves, although McNeely's family did. Williams Brown was a farmer and was illiterate according to the 1860 census, but all other officers attended public schools and could read and write. William C. Coughenhour worked for the railroad as a Conductor, while the entrepreneurial Marcus Hofflin owned his own business, a men's clothing mercantile. The original officers are estimated to have had an average of $8251.00 in personal or family financial assets in 1860, well above the typical amount of personal/family assets (below $2,000.00) reported by males under thirty in Rowan County during the 1860 census. Among the original officers, their average age was 25.5 years. Only one of the original Rowan Rifle Guards officers was married, Williams Brown. Summarily, we find the typical officer serving in the Rowan Rifle Guards to have been age 25 years, unmarried, and from a strongly independent, middle class socioeconomic background, and employed as a tradesman or similar skilled occupation.

**ATTENTION GUARD !**

Meet at Headquarters on Friday evening 21st, at half past 7 o'clock.

By order of the Captain,
WILLIAMS BROWN, O. S.

Salisbury, Aug. 19, 1857

## Williams Brown, Jr.

Williams Brown Jr. was elected captain in March 1857. Born in North Davidson County around 1830, his parents were deceased in 1850, when the census shows him at age 23 years residing near Midway with the family of Elisabeth Burke. In the 1860 census, Brown is reported as illiterate, aged 34 years, and was then married to Ann B.G. Brown and living in Salisbury with no children. He worked as a tinnier and coppersmith and apprenticed 19 year old William A. Weant as a tinnier in 1860, who was also an original member of the Rowan Rifles. There is no evidence that Brown or his family owned slaves. His name appears as the company commander in numerous advertisements in the *Salisbury Republican Banner*, *Salisbury Morning Herald* and the *Carolina Watchman* newspapers 1857 through March 1861. The company held elections in March 1861, and for unknown reasons, Brown was reduced to first sergeant (also known as the "orderly"). He was re-appointed as a 2d Lieutenant at age 32 years in April, with a date of rank 16 May 1861. Although no longer in command, he was still the oldest officer in the company, as newly elected Captain Francis M.Y. McNeely was then only age 21 years.[27] A newspaper advertisement in the *Salisbury Republican Banner* on 19 August 1858 (shown on previous page) announces an upcoming company meeting at "Headquarters." That building was the old Rowan County Courthouse now located on modern South Main Street in Salisbury. Brown was paid $16.00 for service as a 2d Lieutenant from April through June 1861.[28]

### Frances "Frank" M.Y. McNeely

A resident of Salisbury, Rowan County in 1860, Frances M.Y. McNeely was age 19 years. He was the second oldest of five children by Thomas and Margaret McNeely. His father Thomas was the influential Clerk of Rowan County Superior Court. The 1860 census indicates the McNeely family had one slave who worked as a housekeeper, and the 1850 census indicates they then had three slaves, including the same housekeeper. Known as "Frank" to friends and family, McNeely was literate and detail oriented. He worked as an assistant clerk with his father, and also clerked for his brother William occasionally in his mercantile store. McNeely was never married. The McNeely family may have lived in Arkansas at one time, but are known to have lived in New York briefly in the 1850's before coming to North Carolina. Frances formerly resided in Statesville, Iredell County, in 1850. He was familiar with many of the young men there who had attended the Statesville Military Academy, most of whom belonged to the Iredell Blues, another Volunteer company. He was initially elected first lieutenant when the Rowan Artillery organized with a date of rank 18 May 1858.[29] McNeely served in the Rowan Artillery until he resigned in March 1861. He quickly accepted election as captain of the Rowan Rifle Guards on 18 April 1861. McNeely was then working as an assistant clerk with his father and 21 years old. His new commission date of rank in the Rowan Rifles was 16 May 1861.[30] At least twenty seven other officer's commissions (all from Rowan County) were also approved with a date of rank on or about 16 May 1861, including the other Rowan Rifles officers.[31] Although neither the governor's correspondence nor Adjutant General files provide concrete evidence of his involvement, the consistency of commission dates and friendship between Thomas McNeely and Governor John Ellis, may reflect Thomas McNeely's political influence in obtaining commissions. McNeely mustered into twelve months state service on 8 May 1861 while stationed at Fort Caswell near Smithville, North Carolina.[32]

### William Chambers Coughenhour

*From Clark's Regiments, Vol. 1, Courtesy NC Archives.*

William Coughenhour was born in Salisbury in 1836, and educated there. He was the only child of Jacob C. Coughenhour (1800-1844) and Christina Rodgers Brandon Coughenhour (1812-1837). His grandfather was Christian Coughenhour, a German immigrant who settled in Rowan County during the 1780's. William's ancestors were Mennonites, and the family name is believed to have originated in France. They were forced to leave there in 1658 due to religious persecution and settled in Switzerland near the German palatinate. There the family was eventually absorbed into the larger Germanic culture.[33] His mother died when he was one year old, and his father remarried Mary Caroline Monroe and had three more children, two of whom died in infancy. A third child survived, Thomas Adam Coughenhour, William's half-brother. His half-brother Thomas inherited a large sum of money from his father; the 1860 census shows him at age 15 with personal assets at $8,670.00. It is likely that William likewise also inherited a sizable sum, but there was no evidence in census data that he or his family ever owned slaves. Following his father's death, he stayed with his step-mother, Mary Caroline Monroe Coughenhour, for a few years. In 1850, William was 14 years old and a resident of Salisbury and living with her according to the census.

By 1860, his step-mother had remarried John J. Bell, a milliner from Tennessee who settled in Salisbury with seven slaves. Thomas was residing with them, but William had already left home by 1860. William was a strongly independent youth who thrived on autonomy. He carried this trait into adulthood, and he was never married. William was 24 years old and employed as a conductor for the Western North Carolina Railroad in 1860. Typical of young men working on the new railroad, he rarely stayed in one town for very long, and did not own a home. Instead he resided at the Boyden House Hotel located on the Empire Block of South Main Street. This did not reflect a lower income level however, as he held $5991.00 in personal assets in 1860. William was close friends with another tenant at the Boyden House, Edward Neave, who was a member of the Salisbury Brass Band, and later served in the Rowan Rifles as a private. Known as a handsome youth by young ladies in the area, Coughenhour was also a former cadet at the Statesville Military Academy in the early 1850's, where he mastered the intricacies of military discipline and drill.[35] At age 24, Coughenhour initially enlisted in the Rowan Rifles as a private in April 1861. He was quickly elected first lieutenant with date of rank 16 May 1861, when the Rowan Rifles were garrisoning Fort Johnson on Oak Island, North Carolina.[34]

### Marcus Hofflin

Marcus Hofflin was born in Germany in the provenance of Bavaria, sometime around 1835. It is not clear when he came to the United States or Rowan County. In 1850, he resided with Michael Bostian, who held four slaves. Hofflin was 25 years old and unmarried as of June 1861 and living alone in his own home. He then owned a men's clothing store, known as "Hofflin's Clothing" located in Salisbury across from the Boyden House Hotel, where William Coughenhour resided. Hofflin did not have slaves, but had personal assets valued at $10, 25.00 in 1860, revealing that he was in the above average income brackets for the period. He was not always successful, however. Between December 1858 and January 1859 numerous advertisements for "Hofflin's Clothing" store appear in the *Salisbury Republican Banner* reflecting a plea that he "...must have money" and planned to sell out the remainder of his "Fine Stock of Goods...remarkably cheap." He encouraged the interested reader to drop in "with cash and see."[35] His readers took heed, and by 10 April 1860 his fiscal situation had improved, as another advertisement in the "Banner" shows Hofflin had just purchased an entire new fall line of fine (and expensive) gentleman's clothing, including coats, drawers, boots, caps, vests, neckties, hats and imported French ready made shirts.

Such trivia gives us an important hint of Hofflin's shrewd business sense – he earlier persuaded readers to bring cash and get in on a deal couched under the rubric of hard times, but obviously continued to keep his business open the whole time. Numerous other advertisements of the period show he continued to offer "great deals" on clothing into 1861. His frugal personality also later manifest itself in numerous supply and requisition forms serving as a company officer, where he kept detailed records of the various clothing items cost, dates he requested them, etc. from quartermasters. This is not surprising, because as an officer, the fiscally minded Hofflin was held responsible for paying overdrawn clothing items in his company. The 1860 census also revealed that Hofflin was a next-door neighbor to another member of the Rowan Rifles, William Parker, who worked as a Bar Keeper at the age of 17. Hofflin also lived across from the Rowan Rifles former Captain, William Brown and his apprentice William A. Weant. Hofflin was only a few doors away from the Boyden House Hotel and was therefore likely acquainted with both William Coughenhour and Edward Neave who resided there before the war. Hofflin was commissioned a second lieutenant with date of rank 16 May 1861.[36] At 25 years old, Hofflin was then the second oldest officer in the company.

## Non-Commissioned Officers

### 1st Sergeant (Orderly) Addison Newton Wiseman

Addison Wiseman was the original 1st Sergeant or Orderly for the Rowan Rifles, and served in that role until 1862 when he was appointed as a 2d Lieutenant. He was born in 1836 in Davidson County, North Carolina. His parents were Isaac Newton Wiseman, (1787-1836) and Susannah Owen who was born in 1814, but the date of her death is unknown. Addison is shown as a resident of North Davie County in the 1850 census, and was reported as age 14 years and then living with his mother. Addison's father was a farmer who owned several hundred acres of land in Davidson County.[37] There was no evidence that Addison or his father owned slaves in census data. Addison later inherited over 200 acres from his father. He was raised as the youngest of three siblings. In 1860, Wiseman was age 23 years and working as a silversmith in Salisbury. His mother Susan had since remarried Mr. Michael C. Pendelton, a printer with $8,750.00 assets. Wiseman joined the Rowan Rifle Guards in April 1861 at age 24 years as a private, but was appointed as 1st Sergeant/Orderly when former Capt. Williams Brown was re-appointed as 2d Lieutenant.[38]

### 2d Sergeant Wilburn C. Fraley (Frayley)

Both the 1850 and 1860 census lacked information about Wilburn C. Fraley in Rowan or surrounding counties, but he may have been born in 1839 or 1840 in Germany. He was 21 years old while serving as second sergeant in the Rowan Rifle Guards during May 1861.

### 3d Sergeant Moses Locke Bean

Moses Bean was 8 years old in the 1850 Rowan County census, and lived with his parents. His father William was a farmer and owned 187 acres of land valued at $1,000.00, as well as three slaves. Bean, was the only son, and grew up as the youngest of four children. He was unmarried and working as a carpenter's apprentice in 1860. Bean was then shown to be 22 years old although by the 1850 census data he should have been age 18. He was training under Jeremiah M. Brown, who had eight children ages 3 months to 27 years. Bean was also living with the Brown family, who had $200.00 in assets reported on the census, and five slaves. He enlisted as a sergeant, and was age 23 years in May 1861.

*From Clark's Regiments, Vol. 1, Courtesy NC Archives*

### Corporal John James Bowers

John James Bowers was living with his 26 year old mother, Clarissa Bowers in Rowan County during 1850. She had no financial assets or slaves. His father was then deceased, and by 1860 his mother had also passed away. Orphaned, Bowers was taken in by the family of prominent Salisbury newspaper Editor John Brunner, who had four slaves. Bowers worked for John Brunner at his newspaper as a "printer's devil", in 1857, which was an apprentice whose primary role was typesetting and running errands for the editor. Bowers helped organize the original company and enlisted as a corporal in the Rowan Rifles in 1857. At age 21 years, Bowers was the first man to volunteer for three years service or duration of the war at Fort Johnston on 30 May 1861.

### Corporal James (John) Lafayette Lyerly

James L. Lyerly is found on the 31 December 1861 Company K muster roll as a third corporal. However, service records reveal a John F. (Fayette) Lyerly as a member of Company K, 4th NCST, but both names are 27 years old. In 1860, Lyerly was a 29 year old resident of Salisbury working as a day laborer, with $3,650.00 in assets, and no slaves.

### Corporal James Reid Crawford

James Crawford was born on or about 12 August 1836. He grew up in the Granite Quarry area of Rowan County, and worked on his families' farm. His parents were William Dunlap Crawford and Lucretia "Christine" Mull, who were married in 1829 in Rowan County. William was a successful lawyer, and had three slaves in 1850. He died in his early thirties. James had four brothers, and was the second oldest child. After William's death, Christine took the boys to live for a year in Mississippi with her wealthy brother, who owned a plantation with many slaves. They returned to Salisbury, and the 1860 census indicates James was unmarried and worked as a farmer, and held property with assets reported at $14,200.00 and no slaves. When the war broke out, all of his brothers served in the army except his brother Thomas, who instead served in the local Home Guard unit in order to help his mother run the farm. His eldest brother William Henderson Crawford was the first man to volunteer for state service in April 1861 from Rowan County that was not already a member of a volunteer company. He organized Company B of the 42d NCST in April 1862 and served as a captain until his wounding when he was relieved by the surgeons to convalescence. William had also helped organize the 7th NCST before that. William later served in the state General Assembly.40 It is not clear why James did not initially enlist in William's company, but it may have related to the majority of his friends belonging to the Rowan Rifles. George Cauble, also a member of the Rowan Rifles, was his neighbor and boyhood friend. James was 25 years old in May 1861.

### *Rank and File*

*Pvt. Robert D. Beaty*

Beaty was age 18 and residing in Gastonia, Gaston County with his parents in 1860. His father John Beaty was a farmer with $1,618.00 in assets and two slaves. His mother Sophia was born in Cabarrus County which may explain in part how Robert became associated with the Rowan Rifles although he lived nearly 60 miles away in Gastonia. Beaty was recorded as age 22 on 30 May 1861, contradicting the 1860 U.S. Census.

*Pvt. Lindsey Bryant*

In 1860 Lindsey was age 19 and residing in Davidson County with his parents, William L. and Anna Bryant, who were farmers. No financial assets are reported in the census, but his father had seven slaves. His sister Martha Ann was reported as age 19 also, and they may have been twins. Bryant was reported as age 20 years in May 1861.

*Pvt. Alfred C. Carter*

Carter was age 19 and residing with Jesse Thomason, who was his legal guardian. Thomason was a farmer with assets reported at $10,048.00 and no slaves. Carter also had two siblings' living elsewhere whose ages are unknown. His personal assets were reported as $600.00 on 5 July 1860 and he worked on Thomason's farm as a laborer. He was reported as age 21 years in May 1861.

*Pvt. Leroy Carter Colley*

Known as Carter, this member was born in Virginia. He resided with his parents and nine siblings in 1860, and his families assets are not recorded but they held no slaves. Colley was the fourth from oldest child, age 19, unmarried and employed as a carpenter. He is reported as age 21 years in May 1861.

*Pvt. William W. Cummings*

Cummings was age 19 years, residing in Iredell County, but his financial or slaveholding status is unknown. He was age 20 years in May 1861, and later Pension records show that Capt. W.C. Coughenhour testified Cummings was neither a widow or married in 1861.

*Pvt. John C. Deaton (Denton)*

John Deaton's ancestors immigrated to Virginia from England in 1651, and eventually settled in western North Carolina in the early 1800's. Deaton was unmarried and apprenticed as a carpenter by Green Cauble, who lived near Addison Wiseman in Salisbury. Deaton's financial assets are not listed in the census. He held no slaves. He was reported as age 23 years in May 1861.

*Pvt. William A. Durrell*

Nothing is known of Durrell's activities or financial status before the war. His name did not appear in the 1860 Census as a slave owner. Col. Edwin A. Osborne of the 4th NCST wrote after the war that he was a "Northern man" but remained loyal to North Carolina "on principle."[41] The *Carolina Watchman* newspaper published his obituary on 23 September 1886, indicating he died in Chicago Illinois on 4 August 1886. He may have came to Rowan County as one of hundreds of gold miners or railroad workers in the 1850's. Durrell was age 18 years in May 1861.

*Pvt. Jacob Adam Eddleman*

In June 1860 Eddleman was age 25 years, unmarried, and living on the farm of Tobias File, where he also resided. File was not a slave holder and his financial assets are unknown. He appears to have been an adopted father to Jacob Eddleman.

*Pvt. Nelson A. Eller (Ellar)*

In June 1860, 19 year old Nelson Eller was unmarried and living on the farm of Paul Misenheimer in the south Salisbury area. Misenheimer's assets were then $3,460.00 and he had two slaves, but Eller had none. The farm was near the home of the Rendelman, Casper and File families, who also had members in Company K. Note his surname was misspelled as "Ellar" in the 1860 census. Eller was reported as age 20 years in May 1861, and is shown in a post-war photograph at left.

*Courtesy Linda Hanabarger*

*Pvt. Jacob L. Fraley*

Frayley was age 39 years, residing in Iredell County with his wife and six year old son in 1860. He reported $1,500.00 in assets and worked as a merchant. Frayley had one slave, age 26 years old identified as "Ann" who worked as their housekeeper. Fraley was then the oldest man in the company.

*Pvt. John L. Hendricks*

In 1860 Hendricks was age 21 years, unmarried, and owned his own farm in the area of Rowan County north of the rail road. He had four slaves, but his financial assets were not recorded.

*Pvt. George Horah*

Horah was age 19 years, unmarried and residing his father, W.M.H. Horah, Sr. in Salisbury in 1860. His father's assets were $44,139.00 and he had nineteen slaves. His mother had passed away before 1860, and he was raised the sixth of seven children. Horah was unemployed, and seems to have enjoyed the life of a "Gentleman." He was reported as age 20 years in May 1861.

*Pvt. Daniel C. Johnson*

There was no information reported for this name in Rowan or surrounding counties 1850-1860. Johnson was age 20 years old in May 1861.

*Pvt. Robert G. Kyle*

Kyle was born in Lynchburg, Virginia and resided in Greenville, North Carolina in 1860. His financial assets were not recorded, and he did not own slaves. Kyle and his family were close to Capt. Frank McNeely and was a noted "favorite" of both the men and officers. He was reported as age 21 years in May 1861.

*Pvt. Benjamin Lanier*

Lanier was born in Virginia during 1840. He resided in Salisbury in 1860, but his asset values are unknown. He was not shown as a slaveholder. Lanier was age 21 years old in May 1861.

*Pvt. Alfred A. Lowrence (James M. Lawrence)*

Lowrence was age 27 years, unmarried and resided alone in Salisbury with no property or slaves in 1860. He was promoted to corporal sometime before July 1861.

*Pvt. John B. Locket*

John Locket was 5'4" with grey eyes, brown hair and a light complexion in 1861. He was not a slaveholder. He was age 24 years on 30 May 1861.

*Pvt. Lewis Mahaley*

Born in 1834, Mahaley worked as a carpenter before the war. No financial assets are recorded, and he is not shown as a slaveholder in 1860. Mahaley was reported as age 27 years in May 1861.

*Pvt. William McQueen*

McQueen was a resident of Montgomery County, North Carolina in 1860. Then age 22 years, he resided with his parents. His father, Alexander McQueen, worked as a laborer and had seven slaves on his farm. William was the oldest of six children and had attended public school, and on 30 May 1861 was reported as age 23 years.

*Pvt. Francis Mills*

Mills was born in South Carolina, but his family moved to Salisbury during the 1850's. The oldest of three children, he was age 16 years and residing with his parents in Salisbury in 1860. His father, W. J. Mills, was owner of a local dry goods store with $1,900.00 assets and no slaves. He worked for his father as a clerk until he left for active service in April 1861 at age 17 years, the youngest member of the Rowan Rifle Guards.

Pvt. *William A. Moose*

Born in 1843 at Catawba County, North Carolina, Moose was the eldest of nine children. He resided with his father in the Rowan Mills area, a farmer with $2,684.00 in assets and no slaves. Moose was also a member of the Salisbury Brass Band. The town of Salisbury had a fancy horse drawn bandwagon made for them, used during parades and other ceremonies. One can only imagine the ire directed at Moose and his musician cohorts on particularly hot days when the infantry company was engaged in long parades or drills, and their "dual-membership" comrades comfortably rode along in the band wagon.

*Pvt. William Morris (Morras)*

Morris was unmarried, worked as a laborer, and owned his own home in 1860, with $20.00 in assets. He was not shown as a slaveholder. Morris was reported as age 26 years in May 1861.

*Pvt. Andrew Mowrey*

Andrew was employed as a buggy maker, unmarried and owned his own home in 1860. His brother, George, and his wife and son also resided with him. Mowrey's assets were $1,700.00 with no slaves. He had another brother, John Mowrey, who also later enlisted in Company K in July 1861. Andrew lived next door to Hamilton Long, who served as both a sergeant and lieutenant in Company K. Mowrey was 24 years old in May 1861.

*Pvt. William G. Mowrey (William C.)*

William was 23 years old when he married 16 year old Barbara C. Gallimore on 11 October 1856, and they had a two year old son, Thomas, in 1860. At that time William was working as a brick mason, and reported $50.00 in personal assets and had no slaves. He was age 24 years in May 1861. William and his brother Andrew may have been twins as their ages are concordant.

## Pvt. Daniel Moyer

Moyer was age 25 years in 1860, and married to 19 year old Maria with two children. He worked as a buggy trimmer. His assets are not reported and he is not shown as a slave owner. He lived four houses from William C. Coughenhour's half-brother, Thomas Coughenhour, and five doors away from William H. Thompson, who was also in the Rowan Rifle Guards. He was age 26 years in 1861.

## Pvt. James W. Neely

Neely resided in Davie County at Mocksville in 1860, as an unmarried farmer with one slave. His assets are not recorded. Neely was age 20 years in May 1861.

## Pvt. Edward Patterson

Little is known about this soldier. He resided in Rowan County in 1860, and was illiterate. His assets are not recorded and he is not shown as a slaveholder.

## Pvt. William Parker

Parker was age 19 years in 1860, unmarried, and owned his own home in Salisbury. He resided in the same vicinity as Marcus Hofflin, and was two houses from Williams Brown, William Murr and William Weant, all members of the Rowan Rifle Guards. Parker worked as a barkeeper, although his assets are not recorded. He owned one slave, and owned shares in a local gold mining interest at Gold Hill, North Carolina. Parker was one of twenty-five similar shareholders who leased their slave out to the mining company as a laborer.[41] He was age 20 years in May 1861.

## Pvt. John T. Peden

Peden was a resident of Rowan County in 1860. His assets are not recorded and he is not shown as holding slaves. Peden was age 21 years in May 1861.

## Pvt. Lawson M. Rendleman (Randleman)

Rendleman resided with his widowed father on their farm in 1860. His father George had $11,688.00 in assets and reported two slaves lived in the house with them. His father also employed a non-slave female housekeeper. Lawson was age 20 years in May 1861.

## Pvt. James W. Roberts (Robberts)

Roberts grew up as the eldest of eight children. He was age 22 years and residing near Lexington with his family in 1860, where he worked as a transportation clerk. His father, Robert Stephen, worked as a section-master and had one slave, identified as seventeen year old David Sears. His father was conscripted (drafted) into Company K. James was age 23 years in May 1861.

*Pvt. Michael W. Rowland*

Rowland was unmarried, and employed a laborer with $25.00 assets and no slaves in 1861. He lived with his cousin, John Rowland and his family who was not a slave holder. Rowland was age 26 years in May 1861.

*Pvt. William Smithdeal*

Smithdeal was age 19 years and employed as a clerk at J.J. McConnaughy's Dry Goods store in Salisbury during June 1860. His assets are not recorded but was not identified as a slaveholder. He lived with McConnaughy's three sons in a room located above the store. He was age 20 years in May 1861.

*Pvt. Samuel Strayhorn (Stighorn, Strayham)*

This soldier is identified by the two surnames noted above in the 1860 U.S. Census and service files respectively, although signed his name on later muster rolls as Strayhorn. In June 1860 he resided in Salisbury, and was apprenticed as a mason by William H. Tunstall, a master mason from Virginia. Neither Strayhorn nor his mentor held slaves. Assets were not recorded for either man. Strayhorn was reported as age 21 years in May 1861.

*Pvt. John F. Thompson, Jr.*

Thompson resided with his family in Salisbury during the 1850's, where he was raised as the eldest of seven children. His father, John Thompson, Sr. was a shoemaker with two slaves in 1850, but in 1860 had no slaves. After his father died, his mother worked as a milliner, making hats and clothing. In 1860, they lived beside of Thomas Coughenhour, the half-brother of Capt. William C. Coughenhour, and five houses from Daniel Moyer, also a member of the Rowan Rifle Guards. Thompson was age 19 years in May 1861.

*Pvt. Joseph F. Thompson (Thomson)*

Thompson was age 16 years in 1850. His father, Thomas L. Thompson, owned a farm with 101 aces valued at $300.00. His family did not own slaves. In 1860, he was unmarried and residing with his father. Although he worked as a laborer on his father's farm, Thompson was also mechanically inclined.[43] He was reported as age 26 years in May 1861.

*Pvt. Matthew J. Weant*

Matthew was age 12 years and residing with his parents in Rowan County during 1850. His father, George then worked as both a farmer and shoemaker, and held $300.00 in assets with no slaves. Matthew also belonged to the Salisbury Brass Band as a coronet player. He was age 23 years in May 1861. He proved to be an effective soldier until transferring to the 4th NCST regimental band in 1863.

*Pvt. William A. Weant*

William was Matthew Weant's younger brother. He was age 10 years in 1850 and residing with William Brown, who apprenticed him as a tinnier and coppersmith. Weant was age 19 years and still working for Brown along with William Murr, also a member of the Rowan Rifles, in 1860. The Brown family lived next door neighbor to Marcus Hofflin, and two houses from William Parker, another original company member. Weant was age 21 years in May 1861.

*Pvt. Richard D. Williams*

Williams was born in England, and his family migrated to the United States during the 1850's. They resided in Davie County prior to 1860, when they lived in the mining district of Gold Hill. His father, John Williams, had $425.00 in assets with no slaves. He and his sons worked as miners. William and his siblings attended public schools and were literate. Records conflict as to his age in May 1861 when the company was at Fort Johnston; the census indicates he was but age 13 years in 1860, while his enlistment papers show him as age 24 years. The census taker may have made an error, or Williams may have simply used deception, and added 10 years to his age in order to enlist. Since he was already in the Rowan Rifles, it is possible no one questioned his age. His brother Henry, age 20 years, later enlisted in Company K in September 1861. Service records note that he enjoyed good health before the war.

### Original Members Identified in Other Sources

As mentioned earlier in this chapter, there were also fifteen members of the antebellum Rowan Rifle Guards whose names did not appear on the 31 December 1861 Company K muster rolls, but who were identified in Compiled Service Records or other documents. A discussion of their biographical history and service through June 1861 follows.

*Corporal John F. Renter*

Renter was age 23 years, unmarried and a resident of Rowan County in 1860. He did not own slaves, although his occupation and financial assets are unknown. Renter was a member of the 63d North Carolina Militia Regiment in Rowan County before 1859 which may explain why he was enlisted as a corporal in the Rowan Rifles during 1861.

*Pvt. Paul Barger*

In 1850 Barger was recorded as age 7 years and attending school. His father was a farmer who then had 530 acres of land valued at $2,500.00 and thirty slaves. In 1860 he was described as age 19 years, unmarried, and 5'8" tall. He then resided with his widowed father and two siblings in Salisbury. His father reported $36,147.00 in assets and twenty five slaves in 1860. Barger was age 20 years in May 1861.

*Pvt. John W. (A). Basinger*

Basinger resided with widowed mother in 1850, Sene Basinger, who was unable to read or write. Raised as the second youngest of four children, in 1860 he was age 17 years, unmarried and working as a day laborer with no assets or slaves. He was then living an uncle, also named John Basinger who was a stone cutter with $750.00 in assets and no slaves. At that time Basinger was next door neighbors with his cousin, George H. Basinger, who later served in Company K. He was age 19 years in May 1861.

*Pvt. Michael N. Beaver*

Beaver was age 21 years, married, and employed as a farmer in June 1860. He resided in the South Salisbury area, and did not own slaves. His father Alexander was a blacksmith with $375.00 in personal assets and no slaves in 1850. Michael was the second oldest of four children. Only his brother R. E. Beaver was shown as a student in 1850, and Michael was likely illiterate. He married Sarah Ann Mowrey on 24 November 1857, at ages 18 and 15 years respectively. Their only son was born in April 1860, Robinson L. Beaver. The North Carolina Roll of Honor indicates he enlisted in the Rowan Rifle Guards on 12 January, 1861 at age 21 years. His next door neighbor, William H. Glover, later enlisted in Company K. Glover's wife, Malvina E., was close friends with Sarah Beaver. Both couples had a fifteen month old son in May 1861.

*Pvt. Henry W. Crooks (Crook)*

Crooks was born in 1847 at Ohio, and in 1860 resided with his parents at Silver Hill in Davidson County. His father, John Crooks, was a miner with $25.00 in assets and no slaves. Henry was a fan maker until age 23 years, when the Rowan Rifles deployed to the North Carolina coast and he mustered into Confederate service.

*Pvt. William H. Huff*

Huff resided in Rowan County in 1860, but his financial assets or slaveholding status was not recorded. He was skilled as a Ferrier (shoes horses), and was age 24 years in May 1861.

*Pvt. Meshack Franklin Hunt*

Hunt served in the Rowan Rifle Guards from 1857-1861 and is probably the most visible member of the company in modern times because he is the only one known to have made a photograph (shown on following page). Hunt was age 21 years and living with one of the wealthiest people in the area in 1860, M.A. Macay, a single woman age 24 years whose occupation was reported as a farmer in the 1860 census. Her personal property and financial assets are then shown as $96,475.00, decidedly one of the wealthiest people in the state. She also had thirty four slaves. Hunt's occupation was not shown but there was also a man named D.P. Clark residing there, who worked as an overseer for the slaves so it is likely Hunt simply enjoyed the life of a Gentleman. His service file is sparse for records of his time in the Rowan Rifles, but there is a document notating he received pay from April-June while the company was at Fort Johnston in 1861.

Ambrotype of Meshack F. Hunt, Rowan Rifle Guards, circa 1859-1861.

Hunt is wearing the antebellum uniform worn by the Rowan Rifles. Patterned after the 1858 U.S. Army Regulars, the dark blue wool frock coat was a very popular style throughout the state during antebellum. It has nine buttons and a gold tape-trimmed collar, and what appear to be three functional cuff buttons. There is also gold trim or stripes on his shoulders, but their significance is unknown. Enlargement of this image using compression techniques shows the buttons are large, U.S. pattern "Eagle" type with a block letter "I" in the middle, signifying infantry service. Hunt is also holding a Sharp's Rifle, which the Rowan Rifles received in 1859. The date of this image is unknown, but the rifle precludes earlier dates. The Salisbury Republican Banner newspaper ran an advertisement on 5 January 1859 for "Clark and Henderson" who ran an Ambrotype business located opposite the Mansion Hotel, and would strike one's image for the price of fifty cents. A perusal of other organs from the era, including the Carolina Watchman and Salisbury Morning Banner suggest that to be the only such establishment in town, and was likely where Hunt had this image made. Courtesy of University of North Carolina – Chapel Hill Library, Civil War Photographs Collection. Used by permission.

*Pvt. William T. Lilly*

Lilly hailed from Cabarrus County. His financial assets or occupation are not recorded, although he was not shown as slaveholder. He was age 18 years in May 1861.

*Pvt. William Lillycross (Lillycrop)*

Lillycross was born in England during 1837. His family migrated to the United States in the 1850's. He was 5'6" tall, with brown eyes, black hair, and a sallow complexion in 1861. Although he was employed as a miner at Gold Hill before the war, the value of his assets is unknown. He was not identified as a slaveholder in 1860, and in May 1861, was age 24 years.

*Pvt. Isaac P. O'Neill*

O'Neill was born in Burke County, North Carolina during 1836. He relocated to Rowan County where he worked as a master mason in 1860. He was unmarried, with no financial assets or slaves, and resided at Mary Minor's Boarding House in Salisbury. O'Neill was 25 years old in May 1861.

*Pvt. Solomon Plowman*

Information was sparse for this soldier. Muster rolls notate that he was age 22 years, and present with the Rowan Rifle Guards at Fort Johnston on 30 May 1861.

*Pvt. Allison H. Rowzee*

Rowzee resided at the Boyden House Hotel in Salisbury. His father, William Rowzee, was the hotel owner and reported having twenty three slaves who were leased to a mining company in Gold Hill in 1860. William C. Coughenhour also resided at the hotel. Employed as a marble cutter in 1860, Rowzee left that lucrative occupation when Coughenhour swore him into service in April 1861 at age 21 years.

*Pvt. Hiram Adam Trexler*

In 1850 Trexler was age 14 years, and residing with Ben Blackwell in Salisbury who worked as an overseer. Blackwell also had two slaves and eighty acres of land, valued at $500.00. Trexler was reared there as an orphan, along with his five siblings of whom he was second eldest. During May 1861, he was reported as age 25 years.

## A Former Rowan Rifle Guard

*Pvt. William L. Saunders*

Another well known member of the antebellum era Rowan Rifle Guards, albeit only briefly, was William Laurence Sanders. The son of a prominent and influential Episcopal Minister, Joseph Hubbard of Raleigh, William attended the University of North Carolina from 1850-1854. The highly literate Saunders graduated with honors and next took up the study of law. He was admitted to the bar in 1856 and completed an LLB degree in 1858 and later gained an LLD degree from the university in 1889. Saunders came to Salisbury in 1857 and became co-owner of the *Salisbury Republican Banner* newspaper, a strongly pro-democrat organ and secession voice. Saunders served with the Rowan Rifles until 1859, when he joined the Rowan Artillery as a lieutenant. When that company became Battery D of the 10th NCST, he was commissioned therein as a 2d Lieutenant on 16 May 1861. Saunders served there until his receipt of a "recruiting commission" as a captain from Governor John Ellis on 11 January 1862, and he raised his own company. That unit became Company B, 46th NCT, where he eventually rose to the rank of Colonel.

Saunders was wounded several times, including two dangerous wounds in the mouth. The story of his first wounding at Fredericksburg on 13 December 1862 became something of a legend among Civil War Veterans, and was later told as "...it was related by those near the major, that during a lull in the firing, he was enjoying a hearty laugh at some remark when the minie (ball) entered the wide open mouth, making it's exit through the cheek. It was said to have been the most abruptly ended laugh heard during the war." He was again wounded in the mouth at the Wilderness on 5 May 1864, but survived to surrender at Appomattox on 9 April 1865.[44] The wounds permanently disabled Saunders voice to the degree that he was no longer able to argue legal cases in court after the war. He married Florida Cotton in 1864, who died eighteen months later following the still birth of their only daughter. After the war, he settled in Pitt County. In 1871 Saunders was summoned before the Congressional Joint Select Committee due to popular belief he was affiliated with a secret group who many thought was part of the Ku Klux Klan, although he never publicly admitted or denied membership.[45] In 1872 he became editor of the *Wilmington Journal* and in 1876 he established the *Raleigh Observer* newspaper. Whatever his affiliation with secret organizations may have been, it did not stop his political career as he served as Clerk of the North Carolina Senate from 1870-1874 and also served as Secretary of State from 1879-1891. Saunders died in 1891.

*Ambrotype of Lt. William Saunders, Rowan Artillery, circa 1858.*

William Saunders is holding an officer's sword and wearing a white buff leather belt, and leather gauntlets. These suggest that this image struck shortly after Saunders accepted the nomination as a lieutenant in the Rowan Artillery. The cloth and trimmings for the flashy uniforms worn by the Rowan Artillery was acquired from A. Meyer's Dry Goods store in Salisbury according to a 30 June 1858 advertisement in the Salisbury Republican Banner. The advertisement admonished members to "…march forward" and select their cloth and trim, so as to "be ready for the Fourth of July." The presence of volunteer companies in Rowan County had obviously become a significant factor in public celebrations and ceremonies. A. Meyers Dry Goods regularly sold cloth and other supplies to local military companies throughout antebellum and during the Civil War, including the Rowan Rifle Guards. Ambrotype image Courtesy University of North Carolina Chapel Hill Library, Civil War Collection. Used with Permission.

Typical of larger towns in antebellum, Salisbury had its own brass band that originated in 1852. Unlike most during antebellum, it was led by professional musicians and half-brothers, William and Edward Neave. Sons of a failed Scottish textile manufacturer, they came to Salisbury with the circus early in the 1850's. William established a successful music school. William was an expert trombonist although mastered several instruments, while Edward was a noted e-flat coronet player. The band first performed as a military unit with the Rowan Rifle Guards in 1857, and routinely accompanied them during parades and other ceremonies until 1861. The Salisbury Brass Band was paid $50 a day to accompany Col. Charles Fisher with his 6th Regiment, NCST, to Virginia in June 1861, but was sent to a hotel in Staunton, Virginia while Col. Fisher fought at the 21 July battle of Manassas.[46] Both Neave brothers surrendered at Appomattox on 9 April 1865 -- Edward as leader of the 4th NCST band and William as the bandmaster of the Army of Northern Virginia. There was also a popular, but unproven anecdote in Salisbury after the Civil War. Some residents quite fancied that one of their own, William Neave, had led the band a farewell musical salute to General Robert E. Lee after he surrendered at Appomattox.[47] (*Note:* The incident is discussed further in Chapter 10.)

Another Salisbury Brass band member who later served in Company K (but not the original Rowan Rifles) was Charles Heyer. Other members of the original Salisbury Brass Band who became the 4th NCST regimental band were John Y. Barber, Thomas Gillespie, John T. Goodman, James C. Steele, (known to his friends as "JC") and Nathaniel J. Raymer, (known as Nat) who both of Iredell County, and each also left detailed written accounts of their wartime experiences. Also Green Austin, E.B. Stevens, R.L. Patterson and R. Brawley were members of the brass band. The Salisbury Brass band later became the regimental band for the 4th NCST, and as non-combatants, most of its members served as stretcher bearers or nurses in hospitals during the war.[48] As part of the town's Fourth of July festivities in 1857, the Salisbury Band gave a concert, and the "Guards" were ordered to "proceed to Fisher's lawn* for target practice at 4 o'clock." In spite of their zeal and musical accompaniment, the young militia company still required more training in live firing weapons. Three days later, the *Carolina Watchman* reported that the Guards' marksmanship on 4 July had been "terrible" although it kindheartedly blamed the deficit on the company's weapons. The *Salisbury Herald* kindly blamed their poor shooting on the "...fault due to breach-loading Hall's Rifles" and reported that Lieutenant Aldridge had won the prize with at least some "skill." The following sections will discuss the uniforms and weapons used by the company during antebellum as well as provide a chronological review of the company's activities from available sources, primarily local newspapers and archival documents.

---

The "Fisher" home referred to on 4 July 1857 was that of Col. Charles Frederic Fisher, a native of Salisbury whose home was located at the northwest corner of modern North Fulton and West Innes Streets in Salisbury. Fisher's grandfather was a militia officer in the Revolutionary War. Fisher attended Yale but did not graduate. He later served as a representative to the state legislature from 1854 - 1855. Fisher quickly raised a company of volunteers in 1861 and was commissioned colonel of the 6th NCST shortly afterward. He was killed at Manassas in July 1861 trying to rally his regiment to capture an artillery battery. His body was returned to Salisbury for burial. Robert W. Iobst, *"The Bloody Sixth: The Sixth North Carolina Regiment, C.S.A."* (Raleigh, NC: Division of History and Archives, 1965).

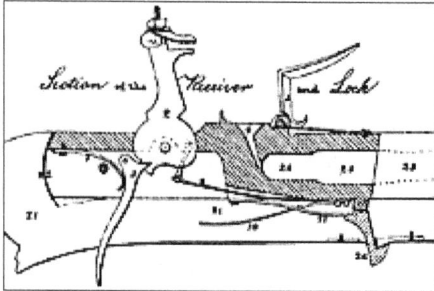

Sketch of Hall's Rifle. U.S. National Archives.

## Early Weapons & Uniforms

The Rowan Rifle Guards carried Hall's Rifles in 1857, although it is unknown whether they were privately purchased or acquired from the state arsenal. North Carolina received 680 Hall's Rifles between 1808 and 1861 under the Militia Act of 1808, which required the U.S. government to provide weapons to state militia.[49] This was not the first breech-loading military rifle, however. The Ferguson rifle was also breech loaded and was used briefly by the British Army in the Revolutionary War.[50] Breech-loading rifles remained overshadowed by common flint lock muskets and muzzle-loading rifles in the early to mid-1800s, when most were converted to percussion ignition. Those weapons were more complicated to operate than standard muzzle-loaders, as the Rowan Rifles experienced on their 4th of July target practice. The M1819 Hall's rifle was made at the Harper's Ferry Arsenal, and was a single-shot breech-loading rifle, using either flint-lock or percussion cap ignition systems. The ball and charge were loaded similarly to the process of loading a cylinder on a percussion revolver.[51] By 10 November 1857, the Rowan Rifle Guard wore dark blue uniforms patterned after those of the United States Army regulars with some minor variations, including trimming on the collar and cuffs. (cf. Ambrotype of Meshack F. Hunt). The "Guards" now also held regular muster to drill and conduct company business affairs including the one held on this date. Their ornate uniforms were noted by John Brunner, editor of the *Carolina Watchman* newspaper, who also took opportunity to barb the young men who had yet to volunteer for service in the new infantry company: "...Salisbury Rifle Guard on parade duly equipped. It is a very handsome company. The dress is simple but neat and substantial The exercises upon the whole were well performed. We were surprised to find so few of our young men in the ranks."

## 1858: Musters & Parades

The first record of the Rowan Rifles' activities in 1858 is an 18 May article in the *Carolina Watchman*. Note that during Antebellum it was considered a status symbol among both militia and volunteers to have an attached artillery battery. The newspaper proudly reported, "Military Spirit Reviving. But a few months ago the Rifle Guard organized and at Newbern vied with the oldest companies in State in respect to drill and soldierly accomplishment. And now we have an Artillery Company forming. Dr. J.W. Hall* elected Captain, E. Myers, 1st, Wm. S. McNeely 2nd, and W.R. Darby 3rd Lts. Company to take part in celebration of Fourth of July."

---

*Dr. Josephus W. Hall was a surgeon, and resigned in April 1861 so he could serve as Chief Surgeon at the Salisbury Prison in 1862, where he remained until the end of the War. The Rowan Artillery disbanded for a few months in 1860, and re-organized in April 1861. There was a long history between the Rowan Artillery and the Rowan Rifles. Later designated as Battery D, 10th NCST (Artillery) on 3 May 1861, it was known as "Reilly's Battery" after its commander, James Reilly. The Rowan Artillery departed Salisbury for Garysburg on 27 May, carrying their new flag, but the Rowan Rifles were then at Fort Johnston and did not depart until 2 June. The Rowan Artillery then had only one older smooth-bore field artillery piece deemed unfit for service. As a result, when Battery D arrived at Camp of Instruction in May, 1861 was briefly assigned to the 4th NCST and by mid June was drilling as infantry for a brief period with the Rowan Rifles, likely made easier by their close affiliation in the antebellum era. Capt. Frank McNeely of the Rowan Rifles was a formerly 1st Lieutenant in the Rowan Artillery. Sources: Jordan and Manarin, Vol. 10, 40-42, 74, and Brawley's Index, 23 April & 15 August and 1861.

*The Weekly Union* newspaper in New Bern reported on 27 May 1858 that they were enroute to the coast for a drill competition with several local volunteer companies, and decided to stop the train as they passed by the gravesite of former North Carolina Governor Richard Caswell. The troops formed ranks to the sound of "muffled drums" and fired a three volley salute over his grave, and quickly returned to the train. One observer stated that this incident spoke "highly for the good taste and warm and appreciative patriotism of our citizen soldiers." On 6 July 1858, the Rowan Rifles received their second company flag, made by several local ladies who began working on it in 1857 just after the unit was formed. Creating such a banner was both difficult and time consuming as most were very ornate and completely hand-sewn. This flag did not likely survive and its inscription remains unknown, however. The new flag was presented in a gala ceremony reported by John Brunner, revealing further that not only were the Rowan Rifles well-drilled, but they were also well-versed in the old militia tradition of occasionally indulging in heavy drinking, as were the other volunteer companies:

> Ladies of town presented a beautiful satin flag with appropriate emblems and inscriptions to the Rowan Rifle Guard. The honored corps was accompanied by the Rowan Artillery. Miss Mary McHorie presented the flag in front of F.E. Sober's at six o'clock in the evening. Capt. Hill responded in gallant style. Military display was most attractive feature of 4th celebration despite dusty streets and oppressive heat. There was three full companies and a small delegation of a fourth on parade consisting of the Salisbury Rifle Guards, The Rowan Artillery, the Hornet's Nest Rifles, and an Iredell Blues delegation. At the dinner nothing was lacking but a little more room and a little more order. Perhaps we ought not to expect men who had been orderly for eight hours, marching and counter marching with military precision to go through the ceremonies of a late dinner amidst the popping of corks as if they were burying a deceased brother-and we so did not let that pass.

Several men in the Rowan Rifles befriended those in the Hornets' Nest Rifles as well as the other company from Statesville present that day, The Iredell Blues.* They often drilled and served in parades or other functions together afterward. Volunteer units often traveled around the state, showing off their military skills and challenging other companies to drill or shooting competitions. It is not known whether the Rowan Rifles were aware of a pending visit from the New Bern Light Infantry, who were under the command of Col. John D. Whitford, a former mayor of New Bern who later served a term in the state legislature in 1865.[52] Whatever the case, they received a visit from this established volunteer company on 12 July 1858, as reported by the Carolina Watchman the next day. The following account demonstrates the Rowan Rifles could muster on a moment's

---

*The Hornets' Nest Rifles became Co. B of the 1st NC Volunteers and fought at the Battle of Bethel Church, Virginia, on 10 June 1861. The Iredell Blues were chartered in 1842 by the North Carolina Assembly, and was affiliated with the state militia as "Captain A.K. Simonton's Company, 52d Reg't. N.C. Volunteer Militia." The "Blues" were so named for the bluish-gray tint of their woolen uniforms. This company was composed mainly of cadets from the Statesville Military Academy where Capt. Absalom K. Simonton and his friend 1st Lt. John Barr Andrews were drill instructors. The "Blues" became Co. A, 4th NCST in July 1861. Simonton was killed waving the regimental colors atop enemy earthworks at Seven Pines on 31 May 1862. Sources: Jordan and Manarin, Vol. 4, 13. See also Diary of Elle Andrews, April 1861.

notice, confirming John Brunner's 1857 characterization of the company as "minute men." The event was described as follows:

> New Bern Light Infantry arrived here last Thursday afternoon on a flying pleasure excursion to this part of the state. Upon arriving they fired a salute from a Spanish cannon taken from Mexicans by Gen. Scott. In not time the Rowan Artillery roared in answer to the greeting and the Rowan Rifle Guard in full uniform with music were marching to the Veranda to welcome the visitation. After mutual greetings they marched through the principal streets. Local company got together ladies for the evening for a dance. Next morning they moved off to Charlotte with drums rolling.

### New Weapons

In August the Rowan Rifles replaced their Hall's Rifles with Sharps rifles, but from whom they procured the coveted new arms is unknown. On 17 August, supported by the Rowan Artillery, the company paraded through the streets of Salisbury, showing off their new weapons for the first time.[53] These weapons made quite an impression among local volunteer and militia companies, as shown by a letter written to North Carolina Governor John Ellis on 15 December 1859 by John Kerr of Yanceyville, who was jealously soliciting the same arms for his own company, stating, "...says a volunteer company just formed, and are anxious, to procure a supply of Sharp's Rifles, if they can be obtained by the state for them. Whether we are entitled to such firearms, I know not, but I am informed that a company in Rowan has been supplied with them."[54] Sharps Rifles, made by the Sharps Rifle Manufacturing Company of Windsor, Vermont, were popular arms in the antebellum era, and the 1851 version employed a primer system that pulled an explosive pellet under the hammer when the trigger was pulled. The second (1853) version of the rifle used a Maynard tape primer system similar to a modern toy cap pistol, and was probably the type acquired by the Rowan Rifles given the 17 August 1858 date.[55]

North Carolina's militia arms were limited in 1858; arsenals then held primarily only older flint lock muskets, with a few of those that had been altered to percussion. At that time, a limited number of M1842 .69 caliber U.S. Percussion Muskets (smoothbore) were stored at the Fayetteville Arsenal and were still available to the militia. Yet, rifles were highly coveted by nearly all military organizations as they were considered state-of-the-art, especially the Sharps breech-loading rifles. On the other hand, it is odd that the Rowan Rifles had only recently petitioned North Carolina Governor Thomas Bragg* for new rifled muskets who was at that time denying all such requests.[56] Bragg approved the request for the muskets just days before the company received the Sharps rifles. Records do not show what circumstances emerged to cause the shift or how the purchase was funded. Perhaps the officers paid for the weapons themselves or the rifles were

---

*Thomas Bragg (9 November 1810 - 21 January 1872) was an attorney from Warren County and the thirty-third governor of North Carolina from 1854-1859. He was also in the state legislature from 1842 and was elected to the U.S. Senate in 1859. Bragg withdrew in 1861 when North Carolina seceded, and he was appointed attorney general of the Confederate States by Pres. Jefferson Davis, where he served until 1863. Bragg's Confederate service literally cost him his livelihood -- bar membership for lawyers who served in the Confederacy was forbidden by the Federal government during the Reconstruction period. *The National Cyclopedia of American Biography Being the History of the United States.* Vol. 9, (New York: James T. White and Co. 1899), 276-280.

purchased by local benefactors who would have nothing less than the best for their premier volunteer company; the same benefactors may have also put political pressure on Bragg, but evidence is unclear. Neither Ellis' correspondence nor the North Carolina Adjutant General's records contain evidence of a bond posted by officers of the Rowan Rifles 1857-1860, so it is uncertain how they were acquired. Meanwhile, the U.S. political scenario was intensifying as the Lincoln - Douglas debates of 1858 were occurring, causing many Southerners to fear Lincoln's election and ultimately leading to stronger interest in secession in the South.[57]

At least one generalized effect of increased rumors of secession in Rowan County was an emerging sense of sectionalism; but Union sentiment remained the dominant view until the spring of 1861. The Rowan Rifles were aware of the changing politics, continued to drill regularly throughout the early fall of 1858, and was often accompanied by the Rowan Artillery. The town of Salisbury received a visit from the entire student body of the Concord Female Academy in Statesville on 5 October. Those young ladies came from the most prosperous of local families and were at the apex of antebellum era society and culture; and, as can be easily imagined, their presence created quite a stir..[58] Whether the event was impromptu or not is unknown, but the young ladies received escort from both the Rowan Rifles and Salisbury Brass Band on their return to Statesville. A few days later, Gov. John Ellis and his wife visited his hometown of Salisbury and were honored by the Rowan Rifles, Rowan Artillery, and the Salisbury Brass Band in a ceremony. On 19 October 1858, the *Carolina Watchman* reported the Rowan Rifles, the Rowan Artillery, and their friends from Charlotte -- the Hornets' Nest Rifles -- had met in Salisbury that morning and boarded a train. They traveled to Statesville via railroad for a celebration. When the Hornets' Nest Rifles arrived in Salisbury, the brass band played "a lively air" and the artillery "boomed away" firing salutes in the background.[59]

The celebration in Statesville included a day of parades, speeches, and military business meetings. Muster days nearly always ended in a late evening celebration with dancing, alcohol consumption, and much fine food. In the presence of many from Statesville's upper society, including young women from the Statesville Ladies Academy, the three companies enjoyed such an event at the home of Iredell Blues commander, Absalom K. Simonton. Dancing was reportedly "...kept up until after midnight." The year 1858 had brought not only more members and experience to the Rowan Rifles, but also a new artillery company. The Rowan Artillery added to the Rowan Rifles' status and military presence. Another new addition was their second company flag, again made of satin, which they proudly carried at each parade and muster although it is unclear what inscriptions or insignia adorned the banner. The Rowan Rifles continued to hold regular monthly drills and frequented similar gala events, in spite of their reputation for somewhat unruly behavior and tendencies toward the excessive use of alcohol. They trained more regularly when public ceremonies or holidays required their presence. These seemingly innocent hours spent on parade would have a significant impact in coming years, as the young soldiers with a great deal of discipline and knowledge of drill and tactics would have a faster adjustment to army life when civil war fell upon the land.

## 1859 - "Mustering enough for one day"

Often during this era, membership in volunteer infantry and artillery companies became somewhat enmeshed. Troops learned to drill in both artillery and infantry manuals of arms and tactics. A few days before 25 January 1859, the Rowan Artillery was out "on Sat. last in all their gay and dashing trappings for parade and target firing" and conducted target firing at a range of "800 yds" with cannon, but also had target practice with their muskets, according to Brunner.[60] Their training was quite diverse. On 13 January, the Rowan Rifles and Rowan Artillery combined into one unit and appeared on the streets of Salisbury as a cavalry company. Brunner described the officers as thoroughly "posted" in a wide range of military tactics and remarked the Rowan volunteers "rarely ever fail to comprehend and perform with facility and precision all his orders."[61] The practical affiliation of the Rowan Artillery and Rowan Rifles led to an integration of infantry and cavalry tactics in their regular training, and artillery training was similarly reciprocal for infantry members on muster days but oddly, not required of artillery officers to learn infantry tactics. On 15 Feb 1859 the Rowan Rifle Guard was still under the command of Capt. Williams Brown, who continued to drill the company on that cold, windy day. The blustery weather wreaked havoc on the officers' tall black felt hats which were quite ornate and plumed with long feathers, according to eye witnesses. The Rowan Rifles were continued to drill, and were even cheered by the Salisbury Brass along with the Rowan Artillery while on parade on the last Saturday of April. Both units continued to maintain high turn-out rates for their regular parades and drill, and the local citizenry had "unabated interest taken in the maintenance of this company."[62]

### The Militia's Quest for Improved Weapons

Rowan County had two regiments of state line militia in 1859, the 63d Regiment, also known as the "Fork Regiment," and the 64th or "Lower Regiment." Both were part of the 63d Brigade, 4th Division, who were essentially loathed by the volunteer companies in Rowan and Iredell counties.[63] By early spring, state authorities were beginning to take more interest in upgrading the organization, arms, and training of the enrolled militia as well as for volunteer companies. For example, Gov. Ellis had been corresponding with Henry K. Craig who was a U.S. Ordnance Department officer that Ellis felt was unfairly shorting North Carolina on her due annual allotment of arms. Craig wrote Ellis on 18 March stating that the governor's former request of "Colts' arms" (referring to 120 Colt's Rifles) would reduce the previously promised "392...Long range rifles" (referring to M1855 pattern U.S. Rifles) to 37." He also stated that North Carolina would get only "197 sets of Long range accoutrements" instead of the requested 552 sets. Craig further advised Ellis the state could also have three 6-pound cannons, equivalent to two 12-pound Howitzers, with proper carriages and implements. When the Rowan Artillery and Rowan Rifles heard of this, Rowan County's political wheels began turning in hopes of acquiring one of the shiny new brass cannons and long-range rifles. Unfortunately, neither the Rowan Rifles nor the Rowan Artillery received new arms from Ellis at that time.[64]

With pressure for new arms mounting from not only Rowan County but several other militia units around the state, Ellis realized that dealing with the U.S. Ordnance Office was not going to yield satisfactory results. Hence, the North Carolina governor took the state's case for improving militia arms a step higher. He petitioned the U.S. Secretary of War, John B. Floyd. Floyd was a Virginian well known for sectionalist tendencies and to be an ardent supporter of states' rights on issues such as taxation and slavery. Ellis wrote to Floyd on 22 June, advising him the North Carolina armory was full of "flint lock muskets which are wholly useless to us from the fact that the militia are unwilling to use them."[65] "The percussion musket and rifle are the only kind of arm in requisition," Ellis also wrote. He indicated further that the Fayetteville Arsenal had recently established works to begin "altering the old style of gun," the outdated flint and steel muskets of 1816 and 1822. Ever the realist, Ellis also knew this would take a great deal of time to accomplish. He further petitioned Floyd to allow the state to gradually exchange her outdated arms for newer rifles and percussion muskets with the United States Arsenals. The savvy Floyd knew that civil war was imminent; he responded in late December and ordered 25,000 M1842 Percussion Muskets and 2,000 .54 Mississippi Rifles from the U.S. arsenals at Springfield, Massachusetts, and Watervilet, New York, respectively -- be shipped to the Fayetteville Arsenal immediately. He also simultaneously ordered thousands of arms shipped to other southern arsenals such as Baton Rouge, Louisiana and Columbus, Georgia.[66] The latter would prove to have much significance in the series of events leading up to the onset of civil war in 1861.

On 25 October, Col. B.R. Moore, commander of the 63d Regiment of North Carolina militia (with whom the Rowan Rifles were affiliated), ordered local militia officers to meet at Salisbury for a dress parade on 15 November.[67] Considering the political events which had transpired since the 1858 Lincoln-Douglas debates, an increase in state-government involvement in North Carolina's militia organizations is not surprising. As the political climate intensified, the state Adjutant General sent notice to Governor Ellis that enrolled militias were to begin training with the volunteer companies. Hence, in addition to their monthly muster for drill and parade on 1 November 1859, the Rowan Artillery and Rowan Rifle Guards under Capt. Williams Brown held a full military parade on 22 November which was described by John Brunner in the Carolina Watchman.[68] Brunner wrote there were several hundred other soldiers present, but did not offer any praise for their military performance. The relatively untrained enrolled militia companies from Rowan County must have created a pathetic contrast to the better drilled and motivated volunteer companies such as the Rowan Rifle Guards. This event had "about 1500 men under arms on regimental parade in Salisbury in obedience to the call by B.R. Moore, Colonel" who was their commandant, according to Brunner. He noted the number of participants was several hundred more men than usually took part in parades there and "they were under arms from 9 o'clock until 4 in the afternoon and doubtless got mustering enough for one day."

The enrolled county militia had been quite inactive for "several years past" and had held musters to drill only infrequently, if at all, until then. The effect of years of neglect on the enrolled militia, who had little-to-no training in contrast to the well-trained Rowan Rifles and Rowan Artillery, was striking. The enrolled militia were described by the editor of the Carolina Watchman as "quite awkward" due to years of "…no musters of the country militia of any sort…".[69] As Brunner observed the inconsistent evolutions of the various militia companies attempting to complete their maneuvers, he opined, "2 drills a year at 2 hours each not enough for a good militia and officers should have more practical experience rather than reading how to drill out of a book and men need more practice, too. There was a great contrast between the two volunteer companies and the county militia. The former did a good job and reflect credit upon the community."[70]

### 1860: "Long live this spirited Company"

The year of 1860 began with rather routine and benign circumstances for the Rowan Rifles. The Rowan Rifles took a railroad trip to Newton on 7 February with the Rowan Artillery and the Iredell Blues from Statesville. At Newton, the companies gave the citizens a parade and drilled. All the soldiers then boarded the railcars and returned to Statesville, where the units parted ways and the

Rowan Rifles rode the train back to Salisbury.₇₁ Martial spirit in North Carolina, like many other Southern states, was beginning to accelerate, triggered by John Brown's attempt to take over the U.S. armory at Harper's Ferry, Virginia in 1858. This expanded the role of the enrolled militia and volunteer companies in some states although North Carolina was rather slow to join the trend of using various militia and volunteer companies as "citizen police forces." Such was commonly done during the Revolutionary period, and now communities once more used armed citizen patrols in order to prevent armed slave insurrections the authorities still feared might occur. In 1860 fears in Salisbury must have reached a fever pitch as the *Carolina Watchman* remarked on 15 May that the Rowan Rifle Guards had been "out on patrol" just a few days before.₇₂

The Rowan Rifles, now conducting regular muster for drills, performed "their maneuvers…in the most exact and beautiful style" and had a reputation for being quite "spirited." Their presence had even altered the traditional celebration of Independence Day. The Rowan Rifles and Rowan Artillery led the annual celebration in 1859 and now regularly included the Salisbury Brass Band in their parades. The band now marched in cadence with the infantry and artillery and was viewed as an integral part of the muster. The 4th of July celebration in 1859 was "ushered in by firing of cannon and ringing of bells" and "The day was hot and dry" according to the *Carolina Watchman*.₇₃ Brunner wrote of the day's festivities, "At an early hour the military was on parade – the Guards and the artillery headed by the band…at 5 O' clock the military was again out in their gay costumes with flashing arms and went through many beautifully and exciting exercises closing their part of the exercises with a salute of 13 guns." By the fall, however, the country was beginning to show more signs of upheaval. Political divisions were becoming more evident. On 16 October a "Great Union Party Mass meeting" was held at Salisbury, with more than 6,000 people present and over 30 counties represented. John Brunner described the rally as the "Greatest since the 1840 Whig meeting." While citizens struggled with political matters, the militia was also undergoing a transition. In November, the state militia and Adjutant General held a military convention in Salisbury in response to what they viewed as growing threats of coercion spurred by comments Lincoln made during his presidential election campaign.₇₄

The much anticipated reorganization and increase in military training among the state militia and network of volunteer companies became a reality. The first convention to revise the existing militia laws was subsequently held on 11 July 1860 at Goldsboro prior to Lincoln's election. Following the national election, the state held another meeting on 14 December at Salisbury to again update state militia organization and establish plans to step-up training. There were twenty-seven companies of North Carolina militia were represented at Goldsboro in November, and the attendance nearly doubled in December. This likely reflects the increased concern following Lincoln's election.₇₅ The conventions had a dramatic impact on North Carolina's military preparedness for war. First, one of the new laws stated that no arms or equipment would be provided by the state to any volunteer company (thus minimizing political pork-barrel influence) unless it affiliated with the regular enrolled state militia. The new law also pointed to a more coherent structure, in that a member of a volunteer company would be exempted from other compulsory state militia service. The minimum number of recruits needed before the state would recognize a new company increased from 32 to 100. The latter was likely decided in anticipation of hostilities in an effort to standardize regimental organization.₇₆

But the volunteer officers voiced concern about having to drill with the relatively untrained and undisciplined militia. Locally, such reluctance stemmed from the awkward experiences of having to drill with the militia since November 1859. The editor of the *Carolina Watchman* along with

Capt. Williams Brown and the other company officers of the Rowan Rifles were present in both meetings and expressed similar concerns over drilling with line militia, whom the obviously viewed as inferior soldiers. Their hesitation was not due to an elitist perception of the militia's "unsavory" character and alcohol usage since the majority of volunteer company members were likewise well known to attend Subscription balls and regularly consume more than their fair share of alcohol alongside the same young men who participated in annual militia musters, but rather due to the militia's lack of discipline and precision in drill and tactics.[77]

As noted, John Brunner held considerable political influence as a newspaper editor. That occupation was also exempt from compulsory military service by the new militia law. In the period between 1 July 1860 and 12 February 1861, the Rowan Artillery disbanded and reorganized as war approached. It is unknown whether internal conflicts arising from differences of sectional allegiance or political views may have influenced the decision to disband or if there were other reasons for the parting of ways. *Carolina Watchman* did not mention the artillery for several months in the interim. The year 1860 ended with a great deal of uncertainty in Rowan County, and the Rowan Rifles were beginning to feel the pressure and excitement. Rumors of war started to thicken following Lincoln's election. As a result, North Carolina increased military requirements for both enrolled militia and established volunteer companies, most of whom were already well-organized and well-disciplined. The unfortunate series of political events would climax in 1861; and, in spite of strong Unionist sentiments statewide, several North Carolina communities began taking matters into their own hands. The anxious volunteers would soon realize, however, the lessons of the drill field and parade ground do not always apply in a real war.

# Chapter Two

## 1861
## North Carolina Minutemen
## Draw The Sword

Early 1861 brought political turmoil and a growing number of secession supporters although the general sentiment in Rowan County was still strongly pro-Union. Gov. John W. Ellis was inaugurated for his second term on 1 January, and he was rightfully concerned the situation in North Carolina could easily escalate into violence. A series of events were about to unfurl on the southern coast of North Carolina that would dramatically contribute to the onset of Civil War. At first glance, the following incidents may seem irrelevant to the Rowan Rifles, who were then located some two hundred miles away in Salisbury. But a solid grasp of the tense situation in then occurring on North Carolina's southern coast is crucial to understanding the Rowan Rifles first experiences as state volunteers, as they would soon find themselves stationed in the same region in April. Ellis was also a native of Salisbury and friends with Capt. Francis McNeely's father, Thomas, who was then the Rowan County Clerk of Court. As a result of their friendship, Capt. Frank McNeely was able to closely monitor coming crisis, and the company stepped up both the frequency and intensity of their drill and discipline in anticipation of an armed conflict they perceived to be looming on the horizon. Ellis was decidedly loyal to the Union and deeply concerned about risk of a Federal invasion, especially in the coastal areas where the shipping trade produced a significant revenue for his state. But he was also in poor health, and the stressors he faced in the coming six months ultimately contributed to his demise, as he died on 7 July 1861.[1]

Indeed, the larger population of North Carolina was still considered to be of Union sentiment, but shortly after Lincoln's election rumors circulated in North Carolina's seaboard counties that he planned to place a large force to occupy the local coastal fort system, including Fort Caswell and Fort Johnston near the port of Wilmington, bastions located some twenty-five miles to the north on the Cape Fear River. Fort Johnston was the oldest fortification in the area, but it was not considered a strong defensive location.[2] Some four miles south was Fort Caswell, which was built in 1825. This was a large, pentagonal masonry fort intended to protect the entrance to the Cape Fear River as well as command shipping lanes in the ocean for several miles with long-range cannons. It was thought to be one of the strongest in the world, although had gradually deteriorated over the years due to neglect.[3] In spite of capacity for sixty one channel bearing guns mounted "en-barbett" [on an earth mound atop the walls],[4] the fort's only two cannons were mounted on rapidly decaying wooden carriages rendering them useless.[5]

In spite of their strategic locations, Fort Johnston and Fort Caswell were both earlier placed on "caretaker status" by the government meaning it was now occupied by only one soldier each. Their primary duties included little more than supervising civilians who used the beaches in front of the fort to fish, and with little else to do, the bored garrison soldiers regularly ensured that he received his "cut" of their catch.[6] But local citizens were well-aware that controlling these forts was crucial to preventing the Cape Fear River from being sealed off from the Port of Wilmington, and were incensed by Ellis's reluctance to ally with neighboring Southern states such as South Carolina loudly speaking of secession. Locals also knew that it would be nearly impossible to retake these garrisons if Lincoln actually took steps to fully occupy these forts. A delegation from Wilmington had even approached Governor Ellis immediately after he was sworn into office and asked him to approve seizure of the two forts. Ellis refused the request on the basis that North Carolina still remained in the Union and such an act would be taken as overt hostility, frustrating them even further.[7]

The residents' fear was based on an ostensibly reliable source from Washington D.C. who told the *Wilmington Daily Journal* on 9 January that the U.S. Revenue's cutter *Forward* had left Wilmington, Delaware, armed with four 12-pounders and forty soldiers, under "sealed orders" to take possession of Fort Caswell. Another presumably accurate dispatch quipped on 8 January that yet another U.S. ship, the *Harriett Lane*, was inbound to help strengthen Fort Caswell and was thought to be carrying "50 men and 8 guns" but like the former, turned out to be mere rumour.[8] Growing political unrest combined with inaccurate news reports led to a strong sentiment on the coast that Ellis wasn't listening to the people, making it particularly easy for citizens to take matters into their own hands. The already agitated residents quickly polarized this belief, and on 9 January 1861, anxieties peaked in a mass meeting held at the New Hanover County Courthouse in Wilmington. In response to the perceived ambivalence by the state authorities, the citizens established a "Committee of Safety" and called for volunteers to immediately organize a home guard to deal with the crisis. This new group of volunteers was a combination of recruits and enrolled militiamen who were acting without state authorization.

Col. John L. Cantwell of Wilmington, commanded the 30th Regiment North Carolina Militia, which was then part of the 3d Brigade, 6th Division, North Carolina Militia under Brig. Gen. John Cowan.[9] The 30th Regiment was a something of an anomaly in comparison to other militia, as it was then thought to be the only organized regiment in the state. The Committee appointed former militia captain John J. Hedrick as a major and placed the volunteers under his immediate command.[10] This new ensemble deemed itself as the "Cape Fear Minute Men," viewing itself as "a band of patriots" and were armed mainly with shotguns and other private arms when they boarded a small schooner from Wilmington to Smithville (modern day Southport) early on the morning of 10 January. Once landed at Smithville, the hastily formed band marched toward Forts Caswell and Johnston.[11] U.S. Ordnance Sgt. James S. Reilly was the only soldier garrisoning Fort Johnston. He was awakened around 4:00 A.M. to find the Minutemen standing at his quarters' doorstep demanding surrender. He wrote, "They came to my door...and demanded the keys of the magazine of me. I told them I would not give up the keys to any person with my life. They replied it was no use to be obstinate, for they had the magazine already in their possession...I considered a while and seen it was no use to persevere, for they were determined to have what ordnance stores there was at the post. I then told them if they would sign receipts for me for the ordnance...I would give it up to them..."[12]

Later that afternoon, Major Hedrick also met the "The Smithville Guards" and together with another group of roughly twenty-five men from Smithville who was "acting as civilians only" crossed the bay to Fort Caswell. They met the lone ordnance sergeant there, Frederick Darlingkiller, and demanded he surrender the fort which was promptly done. Although unharmed, neither of the sergeants was allowed to communicate with his chain of command.[13] The Minutemen were prepared to hold the forts at all costs, and immediately began to strengthen their new position by improving the earthen works, and spent several cold nights standing guard along the parapets and patrolling the beaches. At face value, it would appear Governor Ellis was faced with a classic Catch-22. He could either appease the irate citizens of the region, or seek to maintain amicable ties to the United States. Ellis wrote that he was deeply distressed by the affair, but simultaneously believed their actions were "...actuated by patriotic motives." He clarified that "...in view of the relations existing between the general government and the state of North Carolina, there is no authority of law, under existing circumstances, for the occupation of the United States forts situated in this state....[I] am compelled by an imperative sense of duty to order that Fort Caswell be restored to the possession of the United States."[14]

Upon receipt of the governor's orders to withdraw on 12 January, Cantwell went to Fort Caswell, where Major Hedrick was located. After several delays from obstinate Smithville citizens who were aware of their intentions to return the forts, Cantwell's entourage arrived at Fort Caswell after dark and encountered more resistance from sentries. After arguing a while, Cantwell's party finally accessed Hedrick who asked to consider the matter overnight. He conceded the next morning, responding, "...we as North Carolinians will obey the command. This post will be evacuated tomorrow at 9 a.m."[15] Ellis afterward wired his apology to Pres. James Buchanan in an attempt to explain the militia's actions and maintain a civil relationship with the United States. Ellis also advised in a polite but clear fashion, that "the forts in this state have long been unoccupied, and their being garrisoned at this time will unquestionably be looked upon as a hostile demonstration and will, in my opinion be certainly resisted." Buchanan replied on 15 January, applauding Ellis for taking quick action, but made it clear that he would make no promise of restraint should "any future takeover or similar hostile action" occur.[16] One historian later concluded this was a veiled threat that should North Carolina secede, it would be sufficient to justify invasion of the coastal region.[17]

Apparently no one noticed how the inaccurate news reports and political posturing had led to the treasonous act, as the entire affair was triggered by ungrounded rumors. The two steamers presumably headed to the North Carolina coast from Washington were actually headed to South Carolina, where they attempted to quietly reinforce Fort Sumpter. While Ellis publicly denounced the incident, what he did after the forts were surrendered is most telling. Although their actions amounted to treason under extant laws (before secession), the men responsible received little more than a public scolding. No charges were ever filed against them. It is also significant that not only was capturing the forts outside of law, but the military organizations including the "Cape Fear Minutemen" and 30th North Carolina Militia received no consequences from Ellis. Most their officers later received commissions in the Confederate army, including Colonel Cantwell who commanded both the 51st North Carolina Troops and 59th North Carolina Troops.[18] Given the already strained relationship with the national government, one could easily conclude that it was this group of North Carolina citizens who caused political tensions to escalate into actual war even before Lincoln took office. Although there was of course other complex factors involved beyond the scope of this study, such was the result of rumors generated by inaccurate news reports and public hysteria, causing "...much chafing among her people in the eastern counties..." who now adamantly desired secession. Afterward, the ranks of the state militia and volunteer companies across the state began to swell as secessionist fever grew. North Carolina's citizens had thus drawn the sword.

### *Ironic Events Escalate Tensions*

Another critical incident occurred at Fayetteville, North Carolina only a few days later that affected the Rowan Rifles. On 15 January the Fayetteville Armory received 15,480 M1842 Muskets by order of Secretary of War John B. Floyd, who was an ardent fan of Secession. In addition, Floyd also sent 9,520 altered to Percussion Muskets and 2,000 .54 Mississippi Rifles from the U.S. arsenals at Springfield, Massachusetts, and Watervilet, New York, couched under the rubric of improving the southern coastal defenses in case of foreign attack.[19] Governor Ellis earlier wrote to Floyd in June 1859, requesting to exchange the state's outdated flintlock arms for newer ones and began a series of communiqués with him intended to increase the state supply of arms, but mentioned nothing of such a large quantity.[20] In spite of the obvious appearance of correlation, no evidence exists to prove conspiracy on part of Floyd or Ellis, but the arms were quickly issued to volunteer regiments formed between April and June 1861 after North Carolina's secession. Of particular note is the fact that both the capture of Fort Johnston and Fort Caswell as well as the "arms negotiation" with Floyd occurred prior to Lincoln's inauguration, a point that did not escape the attention of the Rowan Rifles who now attempted to inventory and collect all outdated arms and equipment, as shown in the *Carolina Watchman* on 22 January. This small blurb reveals one of the effects of Floyd's arms delivery was to prompt them to seriously ponder the prospect of war, as Frank McNeely, who was a lieutenant in the Rowan Artillery during 1858-1859, is herein identified as the Rowan Rifles new captain, although he had not been formally voted in. While those circumstances are yet unclear, McNeely was obviously privy to the inside track regarding Floyd's arms delivery in less than a week after arriving at Fayetteville.

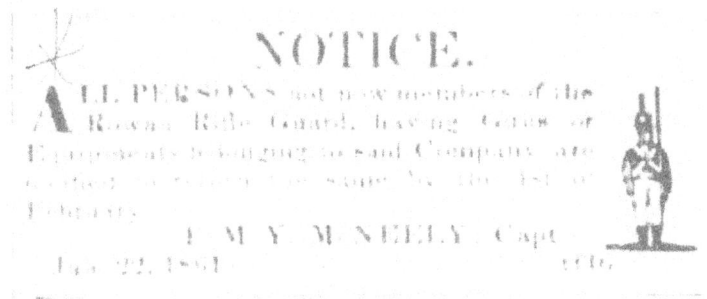

A few days later, on 29 January 1861, the *Carolina Watchman* reported a mass meeting of "Union Men of Rowan" at Murphy's Hall in Salisbury. The gathering was held at the request of the state legislature to "Consider secession." Delegates were nominated to inform state lawmakers of local sentiments. Several officers of the Rowan Rifles and the Rowan Artillery were present at this meeting, and on 12 February the Rowan Rifles planned election of their officers for the ensuing year.[21] Following the recent events at Fort Caswell, the sense of conflict was spreading throughout the state. The Rowan Rifles were now aware that their company elections scheduled for March would have serious consequences on their lives, and company membership was no longer viewed merely as a tool for acquiring social opportunity. March 1861 was a time of change and, despite a somewhat ominous political forecast, the Rowan Rifles continued to drill and support various community events. On 5 March the results of the secession meetings were announced, and it was clear that in Rowan County, the "Union prevails." The *Carolina Watchman* reported an event just after the announcement of the convention results which on the other hand, demonstrates that mixed sentiments existed; clearly the entire county was not in favor of remaining in the Union:

> Disunionist's disgruntled over defeat hoist disunion flag over Mansion Motel. This strange bunting consists in the center of a cross, seven well defined and seven or eight outlined stars filling the four prongs of the cross. It has little beauty to attract and we trust will never become the standard of those who have lived so prosperously and happily beneath the protection of the stars and stripes under which our liberty was gained by the fathers of the Revolution.

In a virtually prophetic statement, John Brunner also described a flag variant he opined would become the Confederate battle flag, having a red field, with a large blue cross and a single white star in the middle. Yet Brunner adamantly encouraged citizens to "stand firm and work like patriots" to preserve North Carolina's place in the Union. He wrote on 19 March that "future historians will award highest praises to those who held out the longest..."[22] Frank McNeely resigned from the Rowan Artillery to become captain of the Rowan Rifles in mid-March.[23] The Rowan Rifles drilled more earnestly in concert with current events, and traveled to Greensboro with two other companies on 25 March to help celebrate the eighty-fifth anniversary of the battle of Guilford Courthouse with their host company, the Guilford Grays.* The sight of these companies drilling together was construed by one observer as a show of military force in favor of secession because each of these companies hailed from strongly pro-Union or "No Convention" counties.[24] The *Carolina Watchman* reported on the same date, erroneously so, that one "R.C. Jones" was promoted to captain of the Rowan Rifles.

Capt. William Brown was reduced to First Sergeant sometime between January-March when McNeely took command. The circumstances of Brown's removal are unknown but it was by a majority company vote. It isn't clear how long Capt. R.C. Jones had command of the Rowan Rifles or if that was merely reported in error. Jones may have been an interim commander since Brown was voted out, however the antebellum era muster rolls did not survive and Jones' name does not appear on any records later associated with the 4th NCST. Brown was soon reappointed as a second lieutenant in April.[25] William C. Coughenhour was then elected first lieutenant. One historian suggested the company was commanded by "Capt. Hamilton Jones" but he was then a sergeant in the Rowan Rifle Guards.[26] With a newfound sense of urgency, the Rowan Rifles drilled more frequently along with the Rowan Artillery and even shared officers for several drill sessions during this apprehensive period. This cooperation and recent changes in leadership were likely responsible for the historic confusion as to who was in charge of the company. The last days of training in peacetime were near their end, however, as the winds of war blew fast across the Carolina countryside.

---

*The Guilford Grays were an antebellum era volunteer company formed in 1855 who later became Company B, 27th NCST. Source: Clark, Vol. 2, 435. The name 'R.C. Jones' is not found in the Adjutant General's letter books from 1846-1861, Co. K Muster Rolls, or the 1850 or 1860 Census for Rowan County. This name may have been confused with 1st Lieutenant Hamilton Long who was in the Rowan Rifles at that time and is elsewhere misquoted as commanding the company at Fort Johnston in May 1861. For detailed studies of coastal North Carolina in 1861-1862, see James S. Reilly's, "Wilmington Past, Present and Future", originally published in Wilmington in 1894, and James Sprunt's, classic "Chronicles of the Cape Fear."

## Coastal Forts Recaptured-The Die is Cast

In response to the surrender of Fort Sumter on 13 April, President Abraham Lincoln issued a call for 75,000 volunteers on 17 April 1861. He also dispatched the Secretary of War to inform Governor Ellis that North Carolina was required to provide two regiments to suppress the rebellion. Lincoln's request offended all of Ellis's sensibilities, and he flatly responded, "You can get no troops from North Carolina." Several Southern states were already pushing for immediate secession, and this event locked the wheels in motion for North Carolina's withdrawal from the Union on 20 May. When Lincoln's demand was announced in Salisbury, the secessionists "made the event the subject of rejoicing by firing cannon."[27] In an ironic twist of circumstance, Ellis wasted no time retaking the coastal forts on 15 April, defying the earlier warning from President Buchanan. He ordered the Col. John Cantwell's militia to retake Forts Caswell and Johnston without delay, "...in the name of the state of North Carolina." His message also admonished them to "...observe a peaceful policy" and to "act only on defensive."[28] Cantwell took the 30th North Carolina Militia plus another 120 men from four companies, the Wilmington Light Infantry, the German Volunteers, Wilmington Light Infantry and the Cape Fear Minutemen along with the recently formed Cape Fear Artillery,* and hastily boarded two steamers toward Smithville.[29]

Upon landing, the unit marched roughly a half-mile to Fort Johnston, where militiamen found the U.S. garrison again consisted of only one man, career army ordnance sergeant James Reilly. The fort contained the stores of artillery ammunition and powder which had been "captured" along with the same sergeant in January 1861. Much to his chagrin, Reilly listened once more as the militia demanded the surrender of his garrison, only this time he was argumentative, but eventually begrudgingly surrendered.[30] Meanwhile, the Cape Fear Artillery were detailed to hold the fort, while the militia departed for Fort Caswell. They arrived there in late afternoon and once more found Sgt. Frederick Darlingkiller and two other men. One man identified only as "Sgt. Walker" made several attempts to contact his officers resulting in close confinement, but no one was harmed. Once again, the mason forts guarding the entrance to the Cape Fear River were in the hands of North Carolina militia.[31] After hearing the news about Lincoln's demand for troops, Governor Ellis immediately alerted the state militia and volunteer companies around the state, including the Rowan Rifles. Meanwhile, four days later, some 1,000 men of the 4th Brigade of North Carolina Militia, comprised of the 33d Regiment North Carolina Militia and the Fayetteville Light Infantry, captured the Federal Arsenal at Fayetteville with over thirty thousand muskets and other ordnance.

---

*The German Volunteers and the Wilmington Light Infantry predated the Rowan Rifles, as each formed in 1853. Along with the Wilmington Rifle Guard, these companies also served in the 8th North Carolina Volunteers later as Companies A, G, and I respectively, of the 18th NCST. The 18th NCST carried a heavy burden after the May 2 1863 Battle of Chancellorsville; many scholars believe soldiers in this regiment fired the musket volley that mortally wounded Lt. Gen. Thomas "Stonewall" Jackson. The Cape Fear Artillery was organized by Maj. John Hedrick and became Battery C, 36th NCST. Adding to the irony, Fort Johnston was similarly captured from the British by angry citizens in 1775. Seventy-seven years later, Sgt. James Reilly became a case study in military irony by his two-fold capture at the same location. Reilly had fifteen years of artillery experience in the regular army, but then left the army and was commissioned a first lieutenant in Company A, 10th NCST. He transferred into Company D, formerly the Rowan Artillery, who had recently elected John A. Ramsey as captain. Governor John Ellis was apologetic over the capture of coastal forts, and likely had Reilly promoted to captain on 28 June not only due to his experience, but also to compensate for his troubles at Fort Johnston. He was captured at Fort Fisher in 1865. Sources: Jordan and Manarin, Vol. 6, 267, and Vol. 10, 218, and Angley, 23-24, and Herring and Williams, 1999, 24.

Once the news of the captures reached Salisbury, the Rowan Rifle Guards immediately volunteered their service to Governor Ellis, who quickly accepted their offer, and the Rowan Rifles received orders to Wilmington on 20 April. That evening, as the governor's call for volunteers was announced at the courthouse, a foreboding quiet gripped the town. All understood that North Carolina had taken a stand and civil war was imminent. As evidence that many young men likely had to "see it to believe it," one young man volunteered "there and then" who had apparently doubted it would actually happen.[32] The silence was broken as the Rowan Artillery boomed out a celebratory battery in the unusually empty streets later in the evening.[33] Capt. Frances McNeely stated the companies' mission was to "assist the militia in forming a garrison of Fort Caswell in Brunswick County."[34]

Rumors of war had the Rowan County-Salisbury area buzzing with excitement. Observing the transition from Unionist to Secessionist loyalties in Salisbury, pro-Unionist John Brunner later reflected that when the townspeople finally recognized that "war was inevitable" he felt burdened to persuade them to "wholeheartedly" support the war effort.[35] Citizens quickly mobilized to support the war effort, as one group of ladies began making "caps of North Carolina cloth" for the soldiers.[36] The Rowan Rifles were now going to war. Ellis readily accepted McNeely's offer of service, and the company received its orders to proceed to Wilmington on 20 April. As the Rowan Rifles prepared to depart, the ladies of the Salisbury Methodist Church made a new flag for the company. In 1858 the company received a satin flag with unknown inscriptions. A crowd gathered in front of the Methodist Church (located on modern Innes Street in Salisbury) on the warm, balmy evening of 21 April. The Rowan Rifles were under arms and formed for parade. As their families and friends watched in silence, the new flag was presented to the company. Onlookers began to grasp the impact of a divided Union and realized this could be the last time they would ever see many of the young men. The *Carolina Watchman* covered the spectacle:

### FLAG PRESENTATION

The Rowan Rifle Guard received a very pretty company flag last Friday evening, got up and presented to them by Mrs. A. Meyers. It consists of the Confederate stripes and a single star. We do not know the interpretation, unless it be secession and the Southern Confederacy. We were too far off to hear the address which accompanied it and the response by 1st Lieut. H.C. Jones, Jr.* The Salisbury Band contributed their invaluable services on this occasion, as also on several others during the past week. The incident was an interesting one. The hearts of some of our friends were wrung to see our sons marshalling under the folds of a strange flag; but since the stars and stripes now cover those who wage war against us, it can no longer be our ensign.

---

*The Carolina Watchman here refers to 1 Lt. Hamilton C. Jones, but was likely referring to 1 Lt. Hamilton Long who later commanded Company K. The 1860 Census for Rowan County indicates Abraham Meyers lived in Salisbury and owned a Dry Goods Store. Meyers supplied the Rowan Artillery and other area Volunteer outfits with uniform cloth and other military items. He was later commissioned as a captain and served as an Assistant Quartermaster for North Carolina. Mrs. Myers does not appear on the census with Abraham Myers.

*Courtesy North Carolina Museum of History. Used by permission.*

This small flag is now held in the North Carolina Museum of History, and was donated by a private individual in 1977. It is 14" x 18" and made of satin; the flag is completely hand made, and was believed to have been reconstructed of scraps from the original that the ladies of the Methodist Church presented to the Rowan Rifles in April 1861 just before they left Salisbury. The flag is double-sided, and since it resembles the Army of Northern Virginia battle flag varieties, was likely constructed after 1861.

Just after sunrise on 21 April, the Rowan Rifles were joined by two companies from neighboring Cabarrus County, who earlier heard the martial sound of fife and drums calling them to muster as they left their homes. The Cabarrus Guards and Cabarrus Black Boys Rifles tendered their services to the state on 18 April, and later became Companies A and D, respectively, 20th NCST.[37] Once in Salisbury, they met with the Rowan Rifles who were already preparing to board trains for Wilmington, with Pvt. James Bowers proudly bearing their new silk flag. It must have been an imposing sight to seem them falling into formation to move out, in their fancy dress blue uniform coats and tall, feathered caps. The *Carolina Watchman* recorded their departure on that crisp morning of 23 April:

## DEPARTURE OF TROOPS

The Rowan Rifle Guard, accompanied by the Cabarrus Guard, and the Cabarrus Black Boys, and the Iredell Blues, left this place on Sunday morning for Fort Caswell, below Wilmington. An immense concourse of citizens assembled at the depot to witness the departure. It was an impressive scene. The men seemed resolute and determined, and will no doubt give a good account of themselves when service is required of them. By appointment the Rowan Rifle Guard assembled at the Methodist Church Saturday evening for prayer, and also at the Presbyterian Church, at 7 o'clock, Sunday morning. After the services at the latter place, they marched to the music of the Salisbury Band to the depot. There they took leave of their friends; and being joined by the above companies, all proceeded on the same train.

As the troops deployed, secession fever pitched in Salisbury as evidenced on 23 April when the *Carolina Watchman* announced, *"Our position: "The die is cast! Civil War is Upon Us, beyond a doubt and we are called upon to take a position in response to it"*. Elsewhere in the same edition, it was announced that the Rowan Rifles had "promptly responded to the Governor's call and as soon as they could make necessary preparations, departed for Wilmington..." Amidst a flurry of political rhetoric, the *Salisbury Banner* also covered the departure of the Rowan Rifle Guards and other volunteers from the Salisbury train depot on 23 April:

## EXCITING TIMES

Our town has been in unusual excitement for the last week, which has resulted in unity of feeling, unity of heart, and firm determined purpose and unwavering spirit of resistance against the Huns and Vandals of the North, who have dared menace our Liberty and domestic peace. Our people are one in sentiment, in interest, and all agree that the time has come, when we should rally as one man in defense of our liberty, our homes, our firesides, our wives and our children. And not only here, but the people of the county— the State, so far was we have been able to hear, have caught the contagious flame and are elamorous to be led forth to vindicate their ancient honor and the glory of their cause. Lincoln may raise his millions of blood-thirsty mercenaries, but this Spartan spirit of resistance to an unholy, ungodly, and unlawful disposition of power, that animates the hearts of our brave, united people, will never be crushed until he shall have gained such a victory...-Yea! it will be crushed when the brave sons of North Carolina and of the South shall have been silenced by the cold hand of death and found a soldier's grave. But Sunday was, however, the solemn day. The lovely morning was ushered in by martial music and the gathering of men clad in the panoply of war.

At an early hour our streets were crowded with anxious spectators and rarely, if ever has there been so much excitement and bustle in our town since the days our fathers struck for their freedom and threw off the tyrannical yoke of George the III. About 6 o'clock the Rowan Rifle Guards formed in rank, on the old Courthouse hill, and marched to the Presbyterian Church for prayer. After which they repaired to the depot here the train was in readiness to bear them to the scene of strife. A large concourse of people had gathered here to bid them God speed in so noble a cause and utter silent prayers that they might soon return victorious to the bosoms of their families. The cars moved off amid the loud booming of cannon, the shouts of the multitude, and waving of handkerchiefs, and hats. The number of soldiers in all that left on the train form Rowan, Iredell and Cabarrus, were two hundred and thirty-five. All went off in fine spirits prepared to do their duty

Once en route, the young men, several of whom had never traveled too far from their homes, found that the excitement had spread statewide. They also learned that the prospect of war could also mean a great deal of attention, especially from young ladies. This attention was much different than the sort they had previously experienced at dances or other social functions where they seemed to have to work much harder and display more self-control. One soldier observed while riding on the train, "...the wildest and most intense greeted us a every point. The waving of handkerchiefs, the smiles of ladies, the throwing of bouquets and the continuous cheering made the scene a grand ovation all along the route, and was well calculated to inspire us with unbounded enthusiasm."[38] Truly, the new volunteers were then being "embued with the spirit of war that filled the land and few understood its' tragedy..." according to one young lady who was deeply saddened as she watched her brother depart.[39]

### "I am now a regular soldier..."

The Rowan Rifles, and other four companies all arrived at Fort Caswell on 22 April. The *Carolina Watchman* reported on 30 April 1861 that the "Rowan Rifle Guard are posted at Fort Caswell, for the present. Packages for them, left at McCubbins' and Fosters' Store, will be duly forwarded." Local supporters and concerned citizens routinely collected foodstuffs and blanket for the Rowan Rifles while they garrisoned Fort Caswell. Although originally ordered to Fort Caswell, the Rowan Rifles and two Cabarrus companies were quickly re-directed to nearby Fort Johnston at Smithville in May, although the date is unknown. Local newspapers in Salisbury often misreported their assigned location as Fort Caswell after they relocated to garrison Fort Johnston. The Rowan Rifles and the Cabarrus Guards were the first two companies to reach the fort, and the garrison commander, Capt. J.B. Jones, ordered the Rowan Rifles to set pitch their tents along a brick walkway underneath the shade of several cedar trees near the water. Meanwhile, the Cabarrus Guards made their quarters inside the enlisted men's barracks, while the other Cabarrus company was housed in the government hospital located only a few blocks away at the corner of Nash and Howe streets, which was leased for "one ear of Indian Corn" per year.[40]

Those early days on the North Carolina coast illustrate not only the enlisted soldiers' naïveté but also, on occasion, their officers. In their time on the North Carolina coast in 1861, the Rowan Rifles, along with the other volunteers, learned that camp life and soldiering was to be a great deal more work than colorful parades and the cheers of adoring young ladies. Many of the officers, including Captain McNeely, were only recently elected and knew little of drilling an infantry company. McNeely had served in the Rowan Artillery, but now spent most of his time studying the infantry drill manual, written by General William Hardee in 1858 to give the proper commands to his men.[41] There was much more discipline and physical labor to endure in the early coastal garrison than is normally presumed, and because it preceded even the Camps of Instruction later established at Garysburg in July 1861, we may conclude that the era is relevant for study as it was is in fact where many volunteers first tasted the rudiments of army life.

Early garrison life at Fort Caswell and Fort Johnson in 1861 more closely resembled a "plebe system" at one of the military academies, only with more manual labor. A "Plebe" system is a traditional basic indoctrination program for new cadets at a service academy such as West Point or Annapolis. It typically lasts a year and is quite rigid and requires several hours of physical, academic and disciplinary training each day. Some of the men wrote home complaining which promoted their families to write appeal letters to Governor Ellis, but most kept it to themselves, as the majority of these volunteers were so enamored with whatever naive concepts of war they had formed by listening to grandparents who were veterans of the Revolution and War of 1812 or simply reading books that many of them would do anything to prove themselves worthy of being called soldiers. For example, many of the young men from wealthy families had never worked a day of hard physical labor in their life; they were now required to provide 8-9 hours a day of manual labor, hauling sand and dirt onto the parapets of the forts or otherwise strengthening the defenses. One private was shocked at his new lifestyle, and wrote from Fort Caswell that their daily routine was to awaken around 5:00 A.M., report to roll call on the parade field, return to their quarters and wash up; that is, if they could find an open basin -- a process that he complained could take up to thirty minutes, then return to roll call on the parade field again.[42]

The troops serving in early garrisons at Fort Caswell and Fort Johnston were required to answer roll call once more before marching to the "mess," or dining area, for each meal. Even their meals were regimented with each unit sitting together at designated tables. If they were late, the troops simply missed their chance to sit at a table and eat. Instead, the latecomers had to "sit on the bricks" outside and wait their turn. The fare was acceptable, usually consisting of rice, bacon, and bread. Quite possibly, the men were so hungry that even such simple food seemed a delicacy. As one volunteer noted, "Our work gives us a good appetite." The hard physical work performed by the volunteers all day ended with yet another roll call on the parade ground, then"such scrambling to get to sleep you never saw."[43] Literally, their entire day was fully accounted for. When they weren't performing manual labor, the volunteers generally drilled throughout the day. The volunteers were also required to learn both infantry and artillery manuals of arms, something many of the Rowan Rifles had done throughout much of the antebellum years while drilling together with the Rowan Artillery, although not all of them, as noted some of the officers struggled learning their new system of drill and tactics. One private described the daily regimen as "At 8 after breakfast we are drilled until night, resting at short-times every hour or so. If we are not drilled at the cannons, we are drilled at the sea beach with our muskets." He reflected both his pride and naiveté when he wrote home, "I am now a regular solider…wishing to fight for the south & old NC in particular, I gloried in shouldering my rifle. I belonged to my company for a month."[44]

Also as more volunteer companies poured into the garrison, conditions also became crowded at both facilities. By mid-May, there were five companies stationed at Fort Johnston including the Rowan Rifles, the two Cabarrus companies, and also the Sampson Rangers, the Columbus Guards, and the Duplin Grays, making the garrison over 350 men strong. The Rowan Rifles officers, Capt. Frank McNeely, 1st Lieutenant W.C. Coughenhour, 2d Lieutenant Marcus Hofflin, and 2d Lieutenant Hamilton Long had not received official notice of their commissions when they arrived on the coast. They waited several weeks to receive notice they were officially recognized as state officers, which was attained by 27 June while in camp elsewhere.45 Col. B. R. Moore, the 63d Militia commander from Rowan County, went to the coast to visit the Rowan Rifles and reported to the *Carolina Watchman* on 30 April that "the troops sent to Forts Caswell...are dependent upon Rowan for bacon, meal, flour, corn, peas, etc. These articles are being gathered at store room of McCubbins and Foster and will be sent Rowan Troops free of charge." Moore also noted, "the troops at that place are all in fine spirits and are very alert in the performance of their duties" A "Ladies Aid Association" for the volunteers was also organized in April by the ladies of Salisbury to make blankets and coats for the soldiers. They elected one of the members, Miss K.H. Rice, to correspond with Captain McNeely in order to ascertain the soldiers' needs. Later, this committee raised $50,000 to be spent on soldiers' needs, prudently including aid for their families.

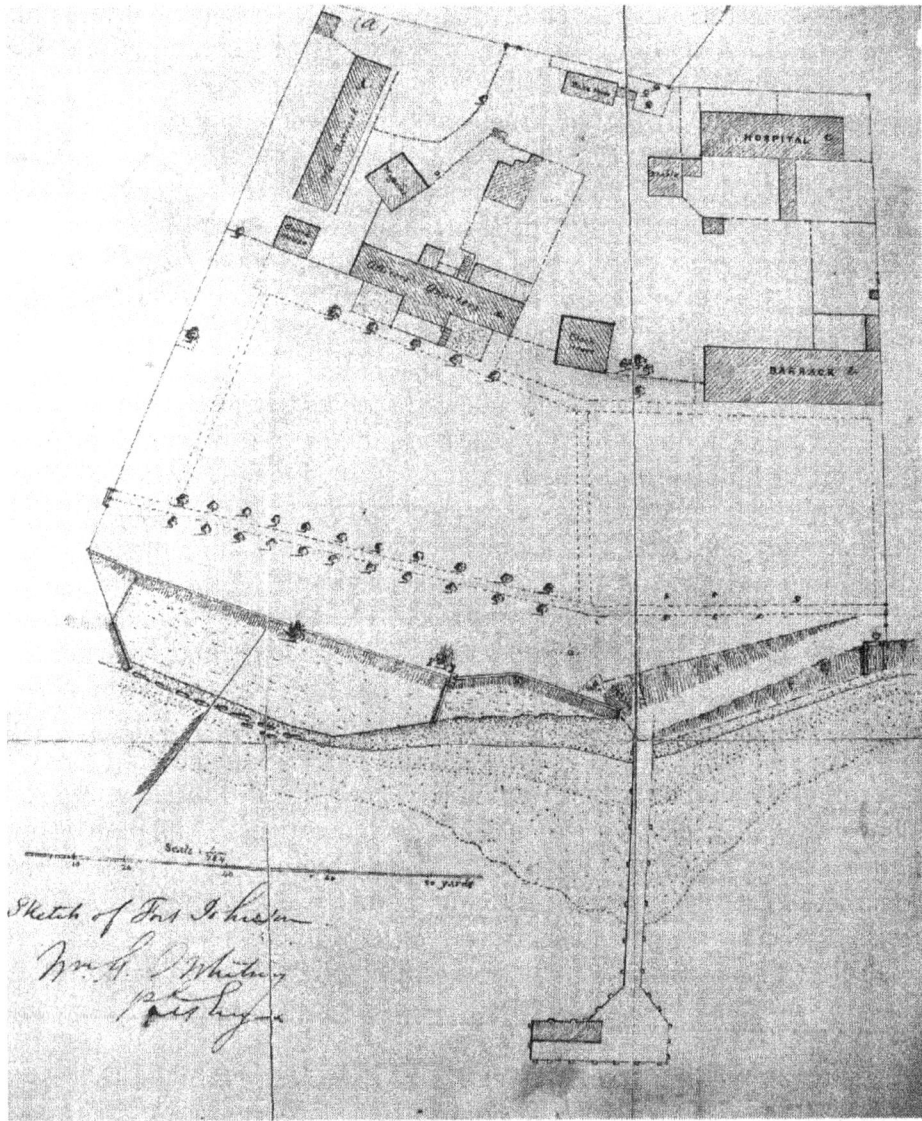

Sketch of Fort Johnson, circa 1856 by Lt. William Whiting. Courtesy City of South Port, NC.

As over 300 troops had already departed Salisbury, and the citizens had little, if any confidence in the militia, the city council formed a "Vigilante Committee" whom they tasked to "patrol anywhere they please." This posse's mission was to patrol streets after dark, carrying one gun, with authority to arrest "suspicious characters" that may be lurking about. By 1 August 1861 this somewhat extreme reaction was curtailed by more reasonable city leaders, and the group was disbanded.46 The routine of garrison life was occasionally interrupted by visitation from wives and children of soldiers who commonly traveled to and from Smithville on various steamers to see their loved ones in these early weeks of the War.47 As the volunteers were learning about army life, frequent formal military ceremonies and an officious demeanor was the order of the day. An unidentified member of the Rowan Rifles published a letter to the citizens of Salisbury on 1 May 1861 describing their activities at Fort Johnson. The new company flag with a single star was hoisted on the garrison flag pole, and the ceremony was led by Capt. "Frank" McNeely, a former member of the Rowan Artillery. He took command of the artillery battery as follows:

Fort Johnson
Dear Watchman:

I suppose you would like to hear occasionally from the Rowan Rifle Guard. Of course our time for correspondence is quite limited, but I steal a few moments to inform you of the high distinction conferred upon our beautiful flag. This being 1st of May, at ten minutes before nine o'clock, our battalion was paraded upon the green in front of the barracks, where a pole, eighty feet high, had been erected by order of our commander, Capt. J.P. Jones of the Confederate Army. A 9 o'clock, precisely, the flag of the Rowan Rifle Guards was ordered to the front where it was received by Mr. J. Mc L. Turner, who bored it to the pole, the battalion presented arms, and when our boys saw it floating high in the breeze, proudly waving above them, they stood gazing upon it in silent admiration, every heart was swelling, every eye was beaming, and every thought was of home, of Rowan, lovely glorious old Rowan, her green hills and her greener forests; above all, they thought of those fair hands that combined that beautiful Sabbath morning when they bade them farewell.

There was no mistaking that common feeling, it was written upon every face, eloquent in every eye, they were proud of their flag, proud of their kindred, their country, and their cause. But if the sons of Rowan were proud of their flag, their comrades in arms were not less so; the brave sons of Cabarrus, our kindred and our neighbors, were there to do homage to our flag, theirs ere not the sisters not that wrought it, but theirs was the cause. They saw there the star they worshipped, that single star, the emblem of North Carolina's untarnished fame. It was an inspiring sight. All combined to heighten the effect. In the distance the eye traced the white beach, girt with those terrible breakers, whose foaming crests can never permit the advancing mermindons of Lincoln to invade the hallowed soil of North Carolina, while upon the point of the beach that borders the channel, Fort Caswell frowned, jealous and watchful—the advancing tide with its measured cadence swept along the shell strewed beach. The sun shone brightly as we have so often seen the May sun brighten the green hills of Rowan. And this was all part and parcel of North Carolina—our own loved State. And few were the hearts in that line of volunteer soldiers that did not swell with devotion to her honor and her interests.

The flag lingered awhile aloft, its beautiful folds reflected from the restless waters of the Cape Fear, then slowly descended. As it neared the earth, the artillery belched forth its thunders, Capt. McNeely of our company firing the first gun, nine guns were fired when Capt McNeely received it and returned it to the Ensign. Thus was our flag honored. Many times again I trust we will honor it, should Lincoln ever dare to invade our beloved State, or her sisters of the sunny South. Her sons are brave and determined—they cannot forget, tis the Anglo Saxon blood that never warmed the loathsome carcass of a slave. Today the boat brought us a quantity of tents, provisions clothing &c, from our considerate friends at home, and as long as they display this spirit of liberality and tender regard for the welfare of the company, we were the worst of ingrates did we not strive to reflect credit upon our country. We are well provided for in every way and all our men are cheerful and contented; sternly determined to see the close of the dawn. We see the Watchman occasionally and I assure you it revives many tender memories of home.

R.R.G.

But having exceptional zeal does not make one a skilled soldier as one seventeen-year old private soon learned. A lack of knowledge could be equally as dangerous as a lack of heavy artillery at Fort Caswell, where the following event occurred as the volunteer companies were streaming into the fort on 22 April, "To illustrate the utter ignorance of us all, officers and men, of what we most needed to know at the time, Company A was ordered to assist in mounting some guns in Fort Caswell. The first one we attacked was an eight-inch Columbiad a huge piece of metal which we were to roll up to the nearby perpendicular embankment to the parapet and lift to its place on the gun carriage. With our crude devices and inexperience it was a Herculean task, but at last we accomplished it and were very proud of our job. The next morning at sunrise our squad was detailed to fire the morning gun from our piece, the only one at that time mounted in the fort. The gunner pulled his lanyard, the great piece belched forth its thunder and for an infinitesimal moment we were much delighted with its great noise. But the recoil that always follows a firing caused the gun carriage to tilt up and the infernal thing went end over end to the foot of the embankment. No one bethought them to place where it belonged, the "prop" (an integral part of the gun carriage then in use and designed to prevent just what had happened)..."[48]

Typical of inexperienced soldiers, rumors of a coming assault on their position abounded. Some soldiers reacted with ridiculous impetuosity and rigidity -- although, in fairness, none but those who have tasted war can truly grasp the heightened perception and anxiety that accompanies the possibility of attack. Another incident illustrative of the young volunteers' inexperience was recalled by a young private, which happened in his first few days after arriving at Fort Caswell in April. The reader should bear in mind, however, that he wrote about the occurrence years after the War. At that point, the early coastal events seemed ridiculous given the horrors of combat and four years of privation he subsequently experienced on active campaigns. Yet, he shows us that to most of the new soldiers, the perceived threat on the North Carolina coast was quite real:

---

An eyewitness to the above mentioned flag ceremony , Pvt. Fred Foard of Cabarrus County, wrote that "Capt. Hamilton Jones" was in charge of the Rowan Rifles at the flag ceremony. As there was no one by that name in the company, he likely confused the name of 1st Lt. Hamilton Long who was a member since 1858, or Capt. J.B. Jones, who was then commanding the garrison at Fort Johnston. Long probably had temporary command of the company while Captain McNeely led the artillery; but other records rule out Long as an elected company commander at this point. Captain J.P. Jones is mentioned in Clark, Vol. 1, 713, and The North Carolina Convention and Military Board Report of 27 May 1861 noted that a Capt. J.B. Jones of Cabarrus County was in command of the garrison at Fort Johnston, but is not otherwise identified.

*Courtesy North Carolina Baptist Association. Photo by R.M. Hatfield.*

This photo shows the remains of Fort Caswell located on Oak Island, North Carolina. This view faces north and shows what was once the parade ground. On the right are the remains of one of the fort's four causeway entrances; the former is likely the same entrance area where the militia confronted the U.S. Army garrison troops in 1861. Much of the original structure has been lost to damage and deterioration over the years. On the interior of the causeway to the left center in the foreground was a powder magazine. There were also barracks and officer quarters lining the field during the 1861 garrison. Just to the left (out of view) is the Cape Fear River water (no more than 100 meters), where the young volunteers daily "made a break" for fishing duty after morning roll call.

"At Fort Caswell we remained for some four weeks, drilling and perfecting our organization. We western boys enjoyed the scenery along the seacoast with a keen zest; the broad expanse of water east of us, the shells along the seashore, the turbulence of the waves today and their placid shimmer at sunrise tomorrow, the bathing in the vast Atlantic, the hurrying away from an imaginary shark, the drilling, picketing, and watching out for an incoming war steamer and other things not necessary to mention, were well calculated to prevent an attack of ennui for a few weeks at least. Some four or five other companies besides ours were at the fort similarly engaged. An incident or two illustrative of the ludicrous side of a soldiers life occurs to memory here, by the way how fortunate it is that there is a ludicrous side to war, but for the fact, many now at home, useful citizens, a comfort and support to their friends, never would have survived the terrible ordeal through which they passed in the late war. One of the incidents occurred on picket.

A heavy guard was required to picket the seacoast for several miles below the fort day and night to warn the garrison of the approach of a war steamer or anything else of a suspicious nature. False alarms were frequent as might have been expected of an inexperienced soldiery. The shooting of a star, the firing of a musket, and such like occurrences resulted several times in arousing our soldiers from their peaceful slumbers, much to their chagrin after they became satisfied the alarm was false. I very well remember being on picket one night on the coast. The line of pickets that night was perhaps two miles long, and the number of pickets in charge of a commissioned officer about thirty. My beat was near the water's edge on hard white sand from which the tide had receded but a few hours before. Our respective beats were about one hundred yards each, and the instructions were, that should anything suspicious be seen or heard, the one making the discovery was to immediately fire off his gun as an alarm to the entire line, which was to be at once followed by the firing of every picket on duty.

Then the pickets were to leave their beats and assemble at the point where the first gun was fired to ascertain the cause of the alarm, and arouse the garrison. On the night alluded to an Irishman was on the beat on my immediate left; as we passed back and forth we frequently accosted each other to help wile away the hours. Just before midnight I noticed a light appearance in the east, and was congratulating myself that I was about to witness what I had never seen before, namely, a moonrise on the Atlantic. As the brightness increased in the eastern horizon and I was getting ready to break forth in exclamation of delight at the beautiful, and to me, unusual scene of a moonrise on the water, my friend the Irishman just on my left, called to me to fire off my gun. I asked him why, pointing to what I had supposed was the rising moon, he said Look at that war steamer coming in, she will open fire upon the fort in a few minutes, I told him my impressions were otherwise, but he said he had been there long before and knew the difference in a war steamer and a moonrise after night.

I was still somewhat skeptical in regard to his theory of the phenomenon being correct, and was loath to relinquish the idea of witnessing a moonrise on the ocean, but thought I might possibly be mistaken. However, I remarked to my friend the Irishman, that was we were together that I would save my load, and if he was sure the light we saw was the blaze and smoke of a war steamer to fire off his musket, and he did so; pop, pop, pop, up and down the line, and the pickets in a few moments with the officer of the night came running up fro right and left to find the cause of the alarm. The chagrin of my friend the Irishman can be imagined when I state that the moon (for moon it was) had got clean up out of the water and was hanging there in all its silvery brightness almost before any inquiry could be made by the officer of the pickets at all in regard to the alarm. By this time the garrison of the fort had been aroused and were out on the parapet awaiting an immediate attack. My gun was loaded, the only one loaded on the line after the alarm till the pickets reloaded. In a little while everything resumed its former status. Paddy discovered no more war steamers during our stat at the fort."[49] Other than the anxieties of overnight sentry duty and sore backs from drilling all day, there were not a significant number of medical problems experienced in the first days of active service among the Rowan Rifle Guards. However, many acquired bad habits as a popular -- albeit erroneous -- belief was that in order to ward off sickness one had only to take up smoking, but tobacco was also quite difficult to acquire at that location."[50]

The war caused many things to change at home also, including loss of the popular Salisbury Brass Band that disbanded when members volunteered their services to the army. On 7 May, the Carolina Watchman indicated, "In its present state of advancement of musical science, it is an ornament to our town and state; and many of our citizens will regard its destruction as a sad event. Some of its members desire that the whole corps shall offer their service to accompany our army. It is a capital idea. We verily believe this Band would be of more service in the army than ten times their number with muskets in their hands. Among the sad events of the times, we regret the probability that the Salisbury Brass Band will be dismembered and broken up. This company of amateur musicians has no equal in many miles around, and no superior in the Southern States. It has been training for six or seven years; and for the last three years, and a half under the direction of one of the best instructors in the Country." Another significant event soon occurred on the coast, as the Rowan Rifles mustered into twelve months' service as state volunteers on 8 May at Fort Caswell.[51] One day later, the *Carolina Watchman* indicated the morale of the company was strong and that the Rowan Rifles were still at Fort Johnson. Notice the author also provides us with more insight as to the identity of the post commander, Capt. J.P. Jones:

## FROM THE CAPE FEAR

It is gratifying to watch the rapidity with which the martial spirit of the Old North State is developing. But a few weeks ago all was quiet within her borders; now, from mountain to ocean, we hear the onward tramp of thousands of her devoted sons, who have left their homes to meet the invaders of her hallowed soil. But more especially, do we listen with eager interest for tidings from the mouth of the Cape Fear, here are stationed our kindred and friends, and we are gratified to announce upon the authority of a gentleman just returned from Fort Johnson, that the troops, stationed at that place, are rapidly improving, and will soon reach the point of efficiency, when it will be dangerous for the hirelings of the North to encounter them.

Our informant represents the men as contented and light hearted, but at the same time resolute and determined. Many of them, we know well, for among them, we recognize the sons of Cabarrus, descendents of the first champions in the first war of independence. They are now side by side with the Rowan Rifle Guard, and side by side may they stand till the great work is accomplished. The commander at Fort Johnson is Capt. J.P. Jones, an officer of considerable experience, having held commission in the United States Army.

Upon the commencement of the difficulties between the two sections, he resigned and accepted one in the Confederate Army. He was in command of a batter at the bombardment of Sumter. He is, we learn, a strict disciplinarian, but at the same time highly popular with his command, both officers and privates. We already have a strong force at the mouth of the Cape Fear, and recruits are daily pouring in. Let Mr. Lincoln send some of his holiday soldiery around by that way and take our word for it, they will open their eyes as to the men they have to deal with.

On 9 May 1861 Rowan County appropriated $50,000 in assistance monies toward feeding and clothing the volunteers garrisoning the coastal defenses. And on 10 May the *Carolina Watchman* indicated all was status quo with the Rowan Rifles, although it erroneously reported the company was at Fort Caswell when in fact, the company was still garrisoning Fort Johnson:

### ROWAN RIFLE GUARD

A letter from a member of this Company now in Fort Caswell, informs us that all are well and in fine spirits. Nothing of special interest. The vote of the Company was taken for delegates to the convention. Craige and Jones received a majority of the whole number cast, though the vote was very much divided between the other persons.

Another article appeared in the *Carolina Watchman* on 13 May 1861 regarding a recent general militia muster at Salisbury, and showed that the state of political affairs contributed to the "...full turn of the militia" suggesting their participation and military bearing had improved from former accounts. That muster day was described as "...pleasant and the people seemed to have a proper appreciation of the state of the country and about 65 men enrolled their names as volunteers. These together with the Rowan Rifles, Rowan Artillery and Rowan Grays numbered about 300 men." Doubtless, this was an error as the Rowan Rifles were yet encamped at Fort Johnson where they held elections for the state convention on 16 May. There was also a special meeting on 18 May 1861, when they gratefully acknowledged support of their friends and families at home, and even boasted of their devotion to their state on 23 May 1861:

Dear Watchman,

At a meeting of the Rowan Rifle Guards, held at this camp on Saturday the 18th of May, 1861, Capt. F.M.Y. McNeely was invited to take the chair, and H.C. Long was to act as Secretary, when the following resolutions were read and unanimously passed.

Resolved 1st. That we hereby tender the citizens of Rowan County our earnest acknowledgements of the debt of gratitude which we owe them for the promptness and liberality with which they have contributed to relieve the wants of the Company, called upon in an emergency when the forms of the State government could not be exercised with sufficient dispatch, the generous sons of Rowan have responded nobly to the voice of patriotism, and are making sacrifices that we behold in a people whose ardent devotion to liberty, stands paramount over any other passion. Wisdom hath another lesson for those that would conquer them.

Resolved 2d. That in the Ladies of the county we recognize invaluable friends, Judicious in imagining the wants of the Company, they have been as active in relieving them; brave, magnanimous spirits! The recollection of their sacrifices, of their anxious solicitude, and their zeal in the cause of freedom, has inspired within us new pride for our kindred, and thrown an additional tenderness around the memory of home. To them we tender our thanks and venture the hope, that the sequel may prove that they have not bestowed their kindness upon soldiers less resolute then themselves.

Resolved 3d. That a copy of these resolutions be sent to the Carolina Watchman, the Salisbury Banner, and the President of the Salisbury Ladies Association.

F.M.Y. McNeely, Pres't.
H.C. Long, Sec'y.

Just two days afterward, on 20 May 1861, the state of North Carolina formally seceded. A few days earlier, there was a crisis near Smithville, when an unknown cargo ship crept up the Cape Fear River, and the soldiers formed up a boarding part to capture it. An article appeared in the *Carolina Watchman* on 20 May, that was taken from the *Charleston Courier* on 18 May, indicating the "N. Carolinians became excited and they have reason to believe she is a government transport..." The mysterious ship turned out to be the *Thomas Watson* from New York, but her purpose there remained "not yet ascertained" for several days. The article reported that four Rowan Rifles members were involved the capture party, including Capt. Williams Brown, and the names "Reaves, Pearson and Davis" were reported as present with him. This likely contains several errors, as Williams Brown was then a 1st Sergeant, not captain. Later muster rolls do not confirm anyone named Reaves or Pearson in the company during 1861, although Michael Davis was later a private in Company K, but did not enlist until 1864. Therefore it appears only one member of the Rowan Rifles was actually involved. Fifty one privates, seven non-commissioned officers, and four officers are identified who formed the original company who deployed to Fort Caswell on 22 April 1861. The following is a discussion of company strength as well as their demographic make up, allowing us to gain further perspective on their socioeconomic as well as personal characteristics.

### Company Demographics in 1861

The North Carolina Revised Militia Code of 1854 did not require volunteer companies with less than sixty four men and officers to file an annual muster roll with the state adjutant general's office, although officers requesting weapons from the state arsenal were required to post a bond "of sufficient security" for the weapons in the governor's office.[51] Ironically, if the company was ever mustered into state service, that law provided the governor an option of filling gaps in the volunteer companies ranks with men from the county militia – those same undisciplined fellows who saw drill and muster only as a social event. On 27 May 1861, Col. John F. Hoke, then the Adjutant General of North Carolina, reported to Governor Ellis that he was aware of the "...the number of volunteers that have tendered their services to the State, and that have been accepted. I also send you a statement of the number of troops stationed at each post in the State." However, Hoke also told the Governor that, "The exact number of men belonging to each company, except those mustered into service, cannot be ascertained. The companies tendered have each sixty-four men rank and file. Muster rolls have been forwarded to the different places where troops have been ordered to assemble, and the complete muster rolls will be forwarded to this office." According to Hoke, the Rowan Rifle Guards had not forward a muster roll back to his office on 27 May.[52]

Another letter written the same date by Warren Winslow to the Hon. Weldon N. Edwards, chairman of the 1861 North Carolina Convention, shows that the Governor was virtually uninformed of the actual whereabouts of the volunteer companies, although several were already under orders to the coastal areas. Except for some companies already assigned to the 1st, 2d, 4th, 5th, 6th and 7th NCST regiments who were then forming in camps near Raleigh, most volunteer companies were in a kind of limbo during this period, and left little, if any official records of their activities. Winslow indicated those units whose location and activities were known by the state were only ascertained by inference from general correspondence, not from actual muster rolls in the Adjutant Generals office. Winslow, like Col. John F. Hoke, also reported that he could not yet accurately report the rendezvous location or strength of the volunteer companies deployed to the field, as he had no muster rolls or even enlistment documents for any officers, non-commissioned officers or enlisted men yet on file.

Winslow was dependent upon Hoke's office for information, but was clearly not indulging himself in intradepartmental politics but rather practical necessity, when he further complained on 24 May 1861 that "...Until all the troops are mustered into the service, the number of privates and non-commissioned officers, the latter of whom are appointed by the Colonels respectively, cannot be ascertained...Not a single commission has been issued to any officer of a Regiment."[53] There had simply not been enough time to gather the needed information from the various garrisons on the coast of North Carolina where hundreds of new volunteers were pouring in each week. But a lack of time was not the only reason the Rowan Rifles did not file a muster roll; Hoke again wrote to Governor Ellis on 24 June 1861 with a composite report of the location, officers and number of men in each volunteer company then deployed to the field from North Carolina.

In this report, Hoke indicated that the total garrison at Fort Johnston then contained five volunteer companies, with 18 officers, 38 non-commissioned officers, and 324 privates inside the fort, including the Rowan Rifle Guards. Two other volunteer companies stationed there had already completed and returned their muster rolls, including two from Cabarrus County, who were reported as then part of the "10th Regiment NC Militia" along with the Rowan Rifle Guards and other companies.[54] If taken at face value, this information may appear trivial, but it is relevant to ascertaining the number of men in the Rowan Rifle Guards present when the Civil War began. Hoke stated further to Governor Ellis that "...no record is kept of companies not having the full complement of men..." referring to the militia law of 1854 that did not required volunteer companies with less than 64 men (including commissioned officers) to file muster rolls in the Adjutant General's office. The Rowan Rifles were ordered to the coast on 22 April, and by 24 June Capt. McNeely had still not filed a muster roll with the Adjutant General.[55] Therefore it is doubtful that a muster roll was ever completed in that early deployment to the North Carolina coast, largely because it does not appear that the company had enough men to require a roll.

As noted earlier, the Rowan Rifle Guards likely had sixty two men aggregate on 30 May 1861. This is below the required number of sixty four men by the Revised North Carolina Militia Law of 1860 and potentially explains the absence of official muster roll or other records from this formative era. This assertion is supported by several sources, including 1861 muster rolls which identified thirty nine privates, six non-commissioned officers, and four officers present at Fort Johnston on 30 May 1861 when the company mustered into Confederate service.[56] Also, other archival information such as military service records and payroll receipts identified another non-commissioned officer and twelve privates who were also there on 30 May 1861, but are not found on the muster roll. There were no deaths due to illness, wounds, or accidental injuries reported at

Fort Caswell or Fort Johnston during April – June 1861, so those factors did not affect the number of men reported present. There is yet some ambiguity about their actual strength, however. Captain McNeely's post-war pension application states that he had 115 men in the Rowan Rifle Guards at Fort Johnson on 30 May 1861, but is discordant with the numbers found in other sources.[57] Since McNeely's pension application was written several years post war, it is possible that he failed to question their enlistment dates, and simply referred to the aggregate number of enlisted men shown in compiled service records which contain similar data both original members and men later serving in Company K throughout the war. It could also mean that a significant number of men were present whose records are missing, but the latter seems reasonable.

Both individual military service records and muster rolls contained numerous demographic factors such as age, height, eye color, complexion, occupation, etc. which are summarized herein for fifty eight men of the sixty two men. Such information enables a reasonable sketch of the Rowan Rifle Guards' physical appearance in 1861. The enlisted men present on 30 May 1861 had an average age of 22.6 years, with forty nine percent between ages 17-21, thirty three percent between 22-25 years, and only one man above the age of thirty. The typical soldier in the company was unmarried, 5'8" tall with light colored eyes such as blue or grey, dark hair and a light complexion. All were of European descent, and there were two Englishmen as well as one German immigrant in the group. Thirty-three percent of the original company was born in Rowan County; thirteen percent were born in other North Carolina counties, such as Cabarrus, Davidson and Iredell and elsewhere. Four men also hailed from Virginia, and one from South Carolina. Several men had a direct family lineage to a Revolutionary War veteran. The most common occupation was a farmer or farm laborer, although there was a wide range of occupations identified including miner, brick mason, carpenter, clerk, and tinnier. Only two men, one officer and one enlisted among the Rowan Rifle Guards were identified as illiterate. In addition, the 1850 and 1860 U.S. Census provided a great deal of information about the original members. For example, thirteen percent of the enlisted men were orphans either living with a guardian or other family members following the death of their parents. Although twenty eight percent continued to reside with their natural families in 1860, the majority were living independently. Forty-five percent were either apprenticed in a trade, residing in another family home, or acting as head of their own household whether married or single. The most common state of personal assets was valued well under $1,000.00 among enlisted men in the antebellum Rowan Rifles, (thirty two percent) but there were clearly exceptions. Eighteen percent indicated their personal or families' assets were valued between $11,000 and $50,000.00 but most of those were familial not personal assets.

There were only three men identified whose circumstances could be construed as the stereotyped "Gone with the Wind plantation" lifestyle as stereotyped in popular folklore, and unfortunately, the work of several historians. It is ironic that most research on the Confederate soldier consistently contends that the enlisted men were poor and unable to afford slaves, as it was not the case in this company. In such portrayals, it is typically the officers who are portrayed as "Gentleman" who were slave holders, but herein there was eight privates who had slaves, including one of who leased the slave to work in the local gold mines, and none of the officers did so. Twenty five percent of the company members had parents who owned slaves, or they had lived with someone else who did, but over half had no connection to the practice. Considering the majority of men was working independently of slave labor when the Civil War began in 1861, these findings make it difficult to conclude that the average soldier in the original Rowan Rifle Guards was motivated by an economic or other personal interest in slavery. Table 1 demonstrates the range of slave holder status among officers, non-commissioned officers and privates in 1860.

Table 1 Original Rowan Rifle Guards Slaveholder Status

| STATUS | Privates (52) | NCO (7) | Officers (4) | Percent |
|---|---|---|---|---|
| Slave Holding | 8 | 0 | 0 | 12.5 |
| Non-Slave Holding | 29 | 3 | 1 | 51.5 |
| Family/Other Held Slaves | 9 | 3 | 4 | 25 |
| No Data | 6 | 1 | 0 | 14 |

NCO is an abbreviation for Non-Commissioned Officers. Note that the family / other data is exclusive of the officers, NCO and enlisted men. Sources: Compiled Service Records, 4th NCST, Co. K, and 31 December 1861 Co. K Muster Roll, NC Archives.

Once mustered into Confederate service and awaiting new orders, the officers were almost certainly aware they would soon be reassigned into one of the new state regiments then forming near Raleigh. Captain McNeely and the Rowan Rifles appear to have returned to Salisbury on or about 1 June ostensibly for recruiting duties, but McNeely was observed "trying to procure a position for Rowan Rifles in one of the newly forming State Regiments."[58] McNeely's efforts to obtain a regimental assignment for the Rowan Rifle Guards did not go unnoticed, and was likely also fraught with political strings from his father's influence. *Carolina Watchman* Editor John Brunner confidently quipped, "We understand they will go into the 4th Regiment." McNeely did not have to recruit very hard however, as dozens of men were stepping forward from Rowan County to enlist in several new companies. Those men who enlisted after 30 May 1861 are referred to herein Volunteers, except for nine Conscripts who came into the company after March 1862. Not surprisingly, the Volunteers shared many demographic characteristics as the antebellum Rowan Rifle Guards with few exceptions. There were thirty nine other men identified as Volunteers who enlisted from May-September 1861, and service records show an aggregate 147 men identified as members of Company K from 1861-1864. The reader is cautioned that ten men were also identified whose names were either not found on Company K muster rolls or who were documented as members of other units. One of the latter men belonged to Company C, NCST, not Company K. Col. E.A. Osborne, an officer in the 4th NCST, estimated after the war that Company K had 129 privates after June 1861. Therefore, it is believed that between 129-137 men actually served in Company K throughout the war.[59]

The ages of volunteers after 30 May 1861 ranged from 18-30 years, with an average age of 22.6 years, identical to the antebellum Rowan Rifle Guards. However there is more to the story than averages; fifty three percent were between 22-25 years, and thirty seven percent were between ages 18-21, and ten percent were ages 26-30 years. These data indicate the later Volunteers who tended to be slightly older than the antebellum Rowan Rifle Guards. Of men who enlisted in Company K after 1 June 1861, whether as a Volunteer or by Conscription (draft), twenty-eight percent were from other North Carolina counties, mainly Davidson, Iredell and Montgomery, and fourteen percent were from other states, primarily Virginia and South Carolina although there were also men from Illinois and New Jersey in the ranks. Further illustrating the diversity of this company, Sixteen percent were born outside the United States, mainly in Germany, Ireland and England, although there were also men from Scotland and Switzerland also serving. Among men serving after 1 June 1861, the most commonly reported value of personal or family assets in 1850 or 1860 was valued under $1,000.00, similar to the antebellum Rowan Rifles, although as expected, there were exceptions. Twenty-five percent had assets between one thousand and three thousand dollars, while fourteen percent reported assets between three and ten thousand dollars. One soldier who enlisted in 1862 came from a family with assets valued at $98,000.00 and there were two "Gentlemen" identified who later enlisted in Company K who were from families or living with someone who had incomes well above average and did not work. Of the later volunteers, eight cases of illiteracy were identified, and six of those were conscripts.

While this trend indicates the later Volunteers and Conscripts generally held more financial worth than the antebellum Rowan Rifle Guards, the overall implication is that nearly all of the soldiers were of average-below average financial means, and only a small number, roughly eleven percent, had any direct financial interest in slavery. While conclusions are obviously limited with so much information lost or missing in original sources, there is yet enough information about them available to allow a reasonable inference of the Volunteer demographics and financial status. About Forty-four percent of the later Volunteers were either farmers or farm laborers in 1861, and seven percent were carpenters, miners or clerks. There were also men who worked as blacksmiths, two musicians, a brewer, a school teacher and a railroad engineer and rail road agent, and one doctor who enlisted as an infantry private.

Typical of young men far from home serving in the military, many sought to engage in various activities to find relief from boredom, stress or were perhaps motivated by simple self-indulgence, but there were also six cases of sexually transmitted diseases identified in the ranks that required hospitalization. This hardly agrees with the prudish image of Victorian era men and women as is so often projected by popular media. Summarily, the reader is again cautioned not to over-generalize this finding, but certainly such cases existed. Another caveat is to avoid over-interpreting company level statistics, as it may not generalize to the larger army. There were several errors found among some original sources such as names, age, dates, in military records as well as census data, etc. In addition, much of it is incomplete, so obviously, there are limitations to how well this research may represent the actual company. Yet, in spite of drawbacks, analyzing such information from archival sources helps us form a more broad view of not only who they were, but also what the soldiers looked like across the war period 1861-1865. As spring faded into summer in 1861, the men of the Rowan Rifle Guards were anxiously awaiting their next experience as soldiers. The naïve impressions of war formed in those early experiences of soldiering in a safe coastal garrison, not far from their homes were about to change.

# Chapter 3

## June 1861
## Volunteers Step Forward

Editor John Brunner wrote on 10 June 1861, "The earth is almost vibrating with the troops of men marching to battle…Since our last edition; we know not how many troops have passed through this place [Salisbury]…" Hundreds of volunteers were trying to make their way to the camps near Raleigh where new regiments were forming, and most passed through Salisbury where the large train depot provided a main access route. Brunner's earlier words were prophetic, as the Rowan Rifle Guards received orders to board trains and move toward Weldon, North Carolina on 2 June to join the five other companies of the newly forming 4th NCST at Garysburg, North Carolina, who were already drilling. They would not arrive until 24 June due to overcrowded railroads.[1] Rather than leaving town enmasse, only small groups could leave intermittently over the next few weeks. Captain McNeely attested that on 2 June, "…that Nine men, rank and file, have this day been transported over the Seaboard & Roanoke Rail Road from Weldon to 3 mile camp…"[2] McNeely also noted their fare was two and a half cents per man. 2d Lieutenant Williams Brown remained behind on recruiting duty through September. He did not return to the company, resigning on 30 October.[3]

When the Rowan Rifles arrived they were directed to "Camp Three Mile" then located about three miles outside of town. By 18 June, North Carolina had twelve regiments of volunteers enlisted for twelve months' state service and five regiments of "state troops." The distinction was found to be confusing and caused a great deal of misidentification of regiments in early months of the war. When the war erupted, North Carolina had to rely on pre-secession laws to organize its troops. Governor Ellis realized he needed more than a few volunteer companies in the field to garrison coastal forts, but he had to operate according to extant laws requiring the state Adjutant General, then Colonel John F. Hoke, to organize new volunteer regiments and muster them into twelve months state service. However, Ellis soon found that the state would need men in the field for longer than twelve months, because the Confederate government was quickly organizing a national army to be composed of troops from various states mustered in for three years or duration of the war.

In anticipation of the eventual takeover of state military forces by the Confederate government, the legislature authorized Ellis to raise ten regiments of State Troops on 1 May 1861 for three years state service in anticipation of the eventual transition to Confederate service. The new state regiments were numbered consecutively as they were mustered into State service for twelve months, regardless of branch of service. Cavalry and artillery regiments were also numbered consecutively according to their branch. For example, the Ninth Regiment State Troops was also designated the First Cavalry Regiment, and the Tenth Regiment State Troops was designated the First Artillery Regiment, making discernment of volunteer units very difficult. Since volunteer regiments were required to be organized independently of the ten regiments of State Troops, they were designated as "North Carolina Volunteers" or "N.C.V.". By 18 July Col. Hoke had fourteen Volunteer regiments mustered into the state service for three years or duration of the war. Shortly afterward, Hoke resigned as Adjutant General when he was elected Colonel of the Thirteenth Regiment of North Carolina Volunteers. The legislature named James G. Martin, a West Point Graduate then serving as a cavalry officer, as Hoke's replacement. Upon appointment, Adjutant Martin was ordered by the state convention to take charge of both State Troops and the Volunteer regiments, in the interim until the Legislature could meet again.

This act consolidated the previously independent state troops and volunteer regiments under one command. When Martin assumed his new office, there were ten regiments of State Troops designated First through Tenth, and fourteen regiments of Volunteers designated First through Fourteenth. The duplicate set of numbers, First Regiment State Troops through the Tenth Regiment State Troops and the First Regiment Volunteers through the Tenth Regiment Volunteers created confusion in the field, at Richmond, and at Raleigh. North Carolina and Confederate government authorities collaborated to design Special Order Number 222, which specified that the State Troops would retain their designations of one through ten, while the Volunteer regiments would simply add ten to their existing numerical designation. In other words, Volunteer regiments one through fourteen would be re-designated starting with the number eleven. The order was made effective on 14 November, 1861 per the Adjutant and Inspector General's Office, Richmond. Thus, the fourteen volunteer regiments were re-designated the Eleventh through the Twenty-Fourth Regiments North Carolina Troops. Regiments organized afterward were numbered consecutively beginning with the Twenty-Fifth Regiment. The first ten regiments were officially designated State Troops, and the Volunteer regiments, (re-designated Eleven through Twenty-Four), were now officially designated "North Carolina Troops." All regiments organized afterward used both designations, (State Troops and North Carolina Troops), interchangeably without official designation.[4]

### *Arms and Equipment Issued*

The Rowan Rifles once more soon received new muskets, accoutrements and other supplies upon arrival at Camp Three Mile. The circumstances as to why they received new arms when they already carried the highly coveted Sharps rifles are unclear; but once the Rowan Rifles arrived at camp, they were issued eighty new percussion muskets from the Fayetteville Arsenal. Ordnance Department records indicate Captain McNeely signed for receipt of their new arms and equipment, but nothing was mentioned about what became of their former accoutrement sets worn during their militia years.[5] The company received 80 muskets, 80 bayonets, 80 cartridge boxes, 80 cap boxes, 80 bayonet scabbards, 80 waist belts, 20 spare cones, 4 ball screws, 4 spring vices, 80 screwdrivers, 80 wipers, 3,000 cartridges, and 5,000 caps in this initial supply. Although the date was unrecorded, the new arms were received between 2 and 5 June, as reflected in the following letter written on 5 June by North Carolina Secretary of Warren Winslow to Colonel Bradford, commander of the Fayetteville Arsenal. Winslow stated: "I do not see you report any Flint & Steel, when I left Fayetteville, there were at least 1,500 in the state arsenal…you report 4,347 Percussion Muskets; is this the number after supplying Col Tew [2nd NCST], McRae [5th NCST], Anderson [4th NCST?]"[6]

The term 'Percussion Musket' found routinely in ordnance records refers to the M1842 .69 U.S. Percussion Musket made at the Springfield (Massachusetts) Armory. It is routinely distinguished from another common identifier, 'Altered to Percussion Muskets', which was used to denote the old 'Flint & Steel' or flintlock arms, many of which were later converted to a Percussion ignition system. The M1842 pattern was made specifically with a percussion cap ignition. A comparison of the number of new arms issued with muster roll data also suggests their number increased in June, as the Rowan Rifles had sixty two men at Fort Johnston, and the company received twenty new recruits between 14 and 29 June 1861, making the company census roughly eighty two men at that time, and explains the need for eighty new arms although two men remained unarmed.[7] The question why they drew new weapons when they already had Sharps Rifles is potentially explained by the ordnance department's tendency to arm an entire company with the same weapon, but this seems conflicted with Col. Warren Winslow's note to Col. Bradford suggesting that North Carolina was short on percussion muskets in June 1861. Between 1808 and 1859, North Carolina received 10,363 Flint & Steel Muskets from the war department under the Militia Act of 1808, primarily the U.S. M1808, 1816, and 1822 pattern flintlocks. The state also obtained 519 M1841 and M1842 U.S. Percussion Muskets between 1841 and 1859, as well as 1,950 .50 muzzle-loading hunting rifles or "Common Rifles" also commonly referred to as "Country Guns" in ordnance receipts. The Fayetteville Arsenal also received 645 M1855 U.S. "Long Range" Rifles, and 479 U.S. M1841 "Mississippi Rifles" from the U.S. Ordnance Department in 1859.[8]

Recall that in June 1859 Governor Ellis wrote to U.S. Secretary of War John B. Floyd, requesting the War Department authorize an exchange of outdated flintlock and altered to percussion weapons with North Carolina for newer models, primarily the M1842 .69 smoothbore U.S. Percussion Muskets from the Springfield Armory.[9] Interestingly, on 12 November 1859, the Fayetteville Arsenal reported to the U.S. War Department that the inventory consisted of 4,817 Altered to Percussion Muskets; 2,861 M1842 U.S. Percussion Muskets; 0 "Altered to Maynard" Muskets; 0 Rifles; 0 Altered to Percussion Rifles, for a total of 7,678 arms that had not been issued to state militia. Original sources do not clarify why the arsenal reported no rifles, considering 1,124 rifles were delivered in 1859, but there were also 23,894 Flint-lock muskets and 652 Flint Lock Rifles "still remaining unaltered" in the arsenal's inventory, many of which were eventually sent to various contract gunsmiths for rifling later in 1861-1862.[10] Therefore including the arms delivered to the Fayetteville Arsenal in 1860 by former Secretary of War John Wise, as of 21 January 1861 there were roughly 36,362 muskets (percussion and altered to percussion) and 3,636 rifles in serviceable condition and available for issue.[11] Hence, it is estimated that sixty-eight percent of the guns held by North Carolina in early 1861 were M1842 U.S. percussion muskets, twenty-four percent were the older flintlock muskets that had been "Altered to Percussion" and nine percent were rifles, the majority of which seemed to be .54 "Mississippi Rifles." Hence, the quantity, if not quality of weapons available from April to June 1861 was adequate to arm the volunteers and first five state regiments then forming in camps near Raleigh, but North Carolina continued to complain of depleted weapons stocks due to the influx of new volunteers pouring into camps during June and July.[12] Yet on 22 August 1861, the state Adjutant General's office estimated that there were twenty five regiments comprised of 8,255 state troops and 12,315 volunteers in the field (20, 570 aggregate).[13]

Warren Winslow even wrote on 22 August to Capt. John C. Booth, the government ordnance officer in charge of the Fayetteville Arsenal and Armory, admonishing him to hasten the production of altering the Flint & Steel muskets to percussion, as the state was literally "scouring" to locate old militia arms stored in local armories.[14] Considering the number of troops reported by the Adjutant General's office, it is not clear why Winslow complained of early shortages, as there should have been roughly 15, 792 arms still available given the number of troops reported before September 1861. The number of serviceable weapons may have been over-stated in early reports, as malfunctioning firearms were delivered to the field from the armories, but the initial thirty volunteer companies formed in North Carolina during 1861 generally received an adequate supply of .69 caliber smooth bore muskets and a few hundred rifles. However, by September 1861 the state had twenty eight regiments armed and in the field, with roughly twelve or thirteen more forming across the state. The Ordnance Department soon realized that the Confederate Government was not going to supply arms and other supplies to the twelve month volunteer regiments, leaving North Carolina to fend for itself for arms to supply the new regiments.[15] When the Fayetteville Arsenal was relinquished to the Confederate government on 27 July, it was then used primarily to convert old Halls Rifles into Cavalry Carbines until November 1861. Most regiments mustering in late September-October 1861 were sent to the field before they were adequately armed. Most of the twelve month regiments afterward received either the outdated flintlock muskets or none at all for several months.[16]

Despite Warren's earlier plead to quickly alter the old flintlocks, the task proved arduous and the state was "greatly pressed for arms" during the winter of 1861-1862. North Carolina did not receive its first shipment of altered flintlocks from contract armorists until January 1862, and she did not receive bulk quantities of newly converted rifled muskets from contract armorists in the state until March. These arms did not make their way to regiments in the field until April 1862, but the 4th NCST did not receive any of those weapons. On the other hand, other sources indicate the regiment conveniently rearmed several companies during the Peninsula Campaign with U.S. Springfield rifles confiscated from the battlefield.[17] Governor Zebulon Vance later reported that North Carolina had issued 21,140 muskets; 6,831 rifles; and approximately 1.4 million cartridges with nearly 1.6 million percussion caps to troops in the field between 30 June 1861 to 30 Sept 1862, so it is clear that a shortage existed later in 1861, (with over 30,000 troops in the field by December 1861) but records do not appear to support the notion of an early arms shortage in North Carolina before September 1861.[18]

### Rowan Rifles Become State Troops

The Rowan Rifle Guards were officially designated as "Company K" and assigned to the 4th Regiment, NCST, while they were at Camp Three-Mile on 2 July 1861. Shortly afterward, the 4th NCST took their new weapons and relocated to Camp Anderson, located at Weldon in Halifax County. This camp was close to the town of Garysburg, in neighboring Northampton County. There they drilled until 13 June. On this date the regiment received orders to move to Richmond, Virginia.[19] Pvt. James C. Turner of Company C, like the many young men in the army, regularly wrote to a young lady at home. Turner grew quite fond of Miss Emily Cain whom he eventually planned to marry. Turner was killed in 1864, however, and never saw her again. He wrote on 30 June from Camp Anderson and referred to the paucity of females around their camp and described the appearance of some women he had seen which was less than attractive. This was likely a ploy to persuade "Miss Emily" that he was trustworthy of her affections, and possibly stir up her jealousy, "I think we are in a healthy place...I would like to stay here splendid were it not for one thing and that is there are no ladies here. I have not seen but one since I have been here and she looked like she had been raised up in a cellar or some other filthy place."[20] While stationed at Camp Anderson, the 4th NCST was formally organized into ten companies on 2 July 1861 by John Martin, North Carolina's adjutant general. A brief description of the nine other companies in the regiment follows. Note the Rowan Rifles' old friends, the Iredell Blues, were mustered as Company A. The regiment now consisted of the following Companies:

### Company A: Iredell County

The Iredell Blues were chartered in 1842 by the North Carolina Assembly. This militia unit was designated as the 52nd Regiment, N.C. Militia, on 18 April 1861. The unit enlisted for the duration of the war on 29 May 1861. The "Iredell Blues" were so nicknamed because of the bluish-tint in their uniforms. A noted opponent of secession, A. K. Simonton, was elected captain. Simonton was killed at the Battle of Seven Pines in 1862.

## Company B: Rowan County

Known as the Scotch-Irish Grays, this pre-war militia unit was the second Rowan County unit to volunteer for state service in 1861. They wore U.S. pattern blue frock coats and were armed with Mississippi rifles. Formed in 1858, the Scotch-Irish Grays mustered into state service 3 June 1861 while encamped at Rowan Mills near Salisbury. The men elected James Wood as captain and were ordered to Camp Hill near Garysburg a few days later.

## Company C: Iredell County

Capt. John Barr Andrews, who in 1858 co-founded the Statesville Military Academy, also formed this unit, nicknamed the "Saltillo Boys." Captain Andrews was the brother of Miss Elle Andrews, who kept a detailed diary of life during the civil war in Iredell County. Company C mustered into Confederate service on 7 June 1861 for three years or the duration of the war. This company included a large number of recruits from the Statesville Military Academy.

## Company D: Wayne County

The "Goldsboro Volunteers" were formed 15 April 1861 under Capt. Junnius P. Whittaker. Initially mustered in for twelve months' state service, this company transferred to the 45th Regiment, NCST, on 28 June 1861 for the duration of the war.

## Company E: Beaufort County

The "Southern Guards," commanded by Capt. David Carter, were formed 3 June 1861 and mustered into Confederate service for three years or duration of the war.

## Company F: Wilson County

Mustered into state service 18 April 1861 for twelve months' state service, the "Wilson Light Infantry" later mustered into Confederate service for three years or duration of the war on 28 June 1861. This unit was commanded by Capt. Jesse Barnes.

## Company G: Davie County

The "Davie Sweepstakes" mustered into Confederate service 4 June 1861 for three years or duration of the war. William F. Kelly was elected captain, and both he and his brother were killed at Sharpsburg on 17 September 1862 at the Bloody Lane.

## Company H: Iredell County

The "Iredell Independent Grays" were composed largely of cadets from the Statesville Military Academy. Formed in 1858, this unit mustered into Confederate service 13 June 1861 for the three years or duration of the war. Capt. Edwin A. Osborne, a former cadet under Capt. John B. Andrews, was elected company commander. The academy was also known as the Statesville Military Institute and initially used space at the Buena Vista Male Academy. Capt. Osborne would later become colonel of the 4th NCST. His second lieutenant, Franklin Weaver, was also a cadet there and would be the last officer to fall mortally wounded carrying the colors out of the Bloody Lane at the Battle of Sharpsburg.

## *Company I: Beaufort County*

The "Pamlico Rifles" were mustered into Confederate service 25 June 1861 for three years or duration of the war. Company I was commanded by Capt. William T. Marsh, who was mortally wounded at Sharpsburg.

### *Early Camp Life*

Just as life at Fort Caswell was a culture shock for many members of the Rowan Rifles, so was life in a larger regiment while in a large army garrison encampment. An enlisted private solider had to deal not only with his company's officers but also the officers of nine other companies and the regimental staff. Thousands of young men were away from their homes for the first time in these early camps of instruction, and they quickly took to indulging in vices such as card playing, swearing, or otherwise neglecting their common moral values learned at home, which created significant value conflicts between many of the men. Military leadership of the day typically encouraged soldiers to turn to Christianity, and the 4th NCST recruited four ordained ministers to attend to spiritual needs in the camps. On 24 June, the *Carolina Watchman* reported the following from a letter received from the *North Carolina Presbyterian* newsletter:

### FOURTH REGIMENT

There are four ministers of the gospel attached to this Regiment. Sabbath before last, a most solemn raiment of the Lord's Supper was administered to the Christian professors of the Regiment. The services were conducted by Rev. Capt. Miller, aided by several other clergymen. The thought that it would probably be the last time in which some would participate in the ordinance, and that before another opportunity occurs, they might be on the field of battle, affected every mind, and gave-great tenderness to the meeting.

In stark contrast to the gala events of Independence Day of 1860, in 1861 the Rowan Rifles were in camp drilling while the 4th NCST was forming. This day was also the advent of a new phenomenon in Salisbury, the War Correspondent. A member of the Rowan Rifles who identified himself only as "Scribbler" regularly wrote letters to the editor which Brunner faithfully published in the *Carolina Watchman*. Scribbler's identity remains obscured by history, although his musings became a regular offering in Salisbury newspapers in the early part of the war. Scribbler sent word home of the companies' activities from 29 June through 4 July 1861 in the following letter written from Camp Anderson near Garysburg:

Mr. Bruner We traveled all day, Saturday, and that night, at one o'clock, found ourselves in Weldon. Everywhere along the road we were cheered by all. Old men, young men, matrons and fair maidens, all gave us a hearty God speed. At Greensborough, while the cars stopped some young ladies presented our officers with beautiful bouquets. Our journey from Goldsboro to Weldon was in the night time, yet at every station there were crowds collected to see us pass. At Wilson, the ladies stood close to the road and showered flowers upon us. Long live the ladies of Wilson. On Sunday morning, we took the train for this camp, which is situated about four miles from Weldon, on the Seaboard and Roanoke Rail-Road.

The Companies of this Regiment, (The 4th, of the N.C. State Troops) now in camp here are the following: The Iredell Blues, Capt. Simonton; Rowan Rifle Guard, Capt. McNeely; Davie Sweepstakes, Capt. Kelly, Southern Guard, Capt. Carter, Saltillo Boys, Capt. Andrews; Scotch Ireland Greys, Capt. Wood; Iredell Independent, Capt. Dalton; Pamlico Riflemen, Capt. Marsh. Our camp is situated in a beautiful grove bordering on the drill ground. The water, which is obtained form wells sunk on the border of the Camp, and therefore convenent, is very good.

There are about five thousand troops in the village, Col. Tew's and the eight companies of our regiment at this Camp. Those at Garysburg are, I believe, mostly volunteers, while those here, are regular State Troops. All are in good spirits; the Camp presents a lively scene in the intervals of drill exercise. Fiddling, singing, wrestling and jumping are carried on to a considerable extent. The Camp is comparatively healthy and the officers are making every exertion to keep it in that condition.

SCRIBBLER

On 9 July 1861, Pvt. George Battle wrote, "We arrived here about night...having raised our tents prepared to get supper, which we got about 9 o'clock. We are encamped in an old pine field, which is very hot, but the other companies...have a very pleasant oak grove on a hill. Our Col. Anderson is a fine looking man, about six feet high, large and muscular, but not corpulent; a high, broad and intellectual forehead, bold face, and whiskers...about a foot long. It is different with us here to what was in Fort Macon and Newbern, as we are now the same as regulars. We have to come under the general regulations of war. I do not think that we will leave here for some time yet, as the whole regiment has to be uniformed with state dress. We have not received anything, and have only drilled this morning...only two are in the hospital."[21]

*Col. G.B. Anderson*
*Image is public domain*

The *Carolina Watchman* reported on 15 July 1861 that the Salisbury Band "has elicited much praise in Virginia, for their admirable musical performance." It also noted that the Salisbury Band accompanied the 6th NCST (commanded by Col. Charles Fisher of Salisbury) "forward" to Manassas, Virginia. There, large forces of both Union and Confederates were gathering in the area with expectation that a large battle would occur soon. However, the Salisbury Band did not participate, but were rather sent to a hotel courtesy of Col. Fisher until after the battle. Pvt. William Adams of Company C wrote on 15 July that the regiment had not yet received its state uniforms griping, "I have not seen a lady cince I been here that I ever seen before and they sand hill gals and I tell you they don't took Iredell girls something take a dozen here...Tell pa that here is more men here than he ever saw...Our company is near the largest of any of them. I suppose in all there is 2500 men in the two regiments...We have not got our uniform yet. There was a man here last Sunday as a week taking our measures. Sunday is no more than Monday here. We go out on dress parade every evening at 6 o'clock. Sunday not except. We drill battalion drill now every day."[22]

North Carolina Adjutant General John H. Hoke had issued General Order No.1 on 27 May 1861 establishing the regulation state uniform. This outfit consisted of a five- button sack coat with black, sewn-down epaulettes on the shoulders; matching trousers with a half-inch black stripe down the seam, and a cap. The Confederate government was using a commutation system for clothing at this time, so volunteer companies purchased their own uniforms and were reimbursed by the government. The Raleigh Clothing Depot was established on 20 September 1861 when the Quartermaster Department was reorganized under Maj. John Devareux. There was also several assistant quartermasters including Capt. W.W. Pierce, whose name appears on numerous supply forms throughout the war from various North Carolina regiments, including Company K.[23] Pvt. Jacob H. Hanes of Company G, the "Davie Sweepstakes", wrote to his wife on 17 July stating, "Lt. Sam Davis started to Charlotte this morning, to get our state uniform. He will be here in about 7 days." There are quite a number of ladies turn out every evening to witness the display of military tactics on dress parade. It is quite an incentive to the soldiers to think they attract the attention of the ladies by there skill in the management of arms."[24]

On 21 July 1861 the Rowan Rifles were at Richmond, Virginia, with Companies A, C, F and G of the 4th NCST. They camped at Howard's Grove until 25 July, then relocated approximately one-and-a-half miles away to Camp Pickens. The regiment remained there until 8 August, and their primary activity was drilling. Meanwhile, Companies B, D and E stayed at Camp Hill until 28 July when they were ordered to join the regiment in Richmond to prepare for the anticipated attack on the Confederate capital. As Companies A, C, F, G and K arrived in Richmond a few Company K received their new state uniforms with the rest of the regiment while located at Camp Hill near Raleigh. Pvt. George Battle of Company F again wrote home to his mother on 22 July, describing not only their new uniforms, but also some new and unpleasant experiences all faced. A few days later they went into camp some two miles from the city at Howard's Grove.[25]

His brother, Walter Battle, also wrote home that day complaining about not having all of his equipment yet. Soon however, the soldiers would learn that carrying anything but their weapon on the long, arduous campaigns ahead was truly something worth complaining about, instead of having less equipment. Battle said that his regiment, "...arrived here yesterday [21 July], and had to walk about four miles to our camp, without knapsacks on our backs, and everything necessary to soldiers. Before we left Camp Hill, we got our state uniforms, blankets and all the accoutrements. We were nearly worn out after having walked four miles to our encampment, the knap sack straps hurt our shoulders, besides the weight..."[26] On 22 July, just one day after the Battle of Manassas or Bull Run, Pvt. William Adams of Company C described the difficulties of adjusting to living in camp with thousands of men from such diverse backgrounds. It was a culture shock, as the majority of volunteers were farm boys who had never traveled more than a few miles from home.

---

Pvt. Jacob H. Hanes was a student before the war, and age 21 years at enlistment on 4 June 1861. Assigned to serve on the brigade provost guard from 20 December 1861 until 1 August 1863, he was promoted to corporal on 1 October 1863. He was killed at Spotsylvania on 12 May 1864. Source: Jordan and Manarin, Vol. 4, 79. See Richard Warren, "Uniforms of the Confederacy, Journal of the Confederate Historical Society, Plate No. 72, Vol. 17, (Summer, 1990), 45-52, for a detailed analysis of early NC uniforms and regulations. Also, see Greg Mast, "Tar Heels", Military Images, Vol. 28(2), 6-31, for photographic examples and discussion of early NC uniforms.

Adams also mentions sending his civilian clothing home, now that the regiment had received its state uniforms while reporting, "We are going to leave this place this evening for Manassas Junction, we are at Richmond yet, it is a very large city and a very prity place...Ask me how many live in my tent. There is 5 in there now...White and Brady, Carpenter and J. Gibson. Brady is one of the lazy fellow in our camp. He won't do any thing, only what he can't get round. I (bore) him over it every day. He is always complaining he can eat as much more as I can...I sent my Rock & Janes (coat). I sent two pair of pants, my coat my best, one shirt that is all. I have to some of my cloths at Richmond. We all are going to leave some of our clothes there. They are going to box them up put them under the care of some person till we need them...Ma don't send me any more prevision for I don't expect to get it. Some of our mess just lived of me while it lasted. That was Brady. Don't say anything about it. He is that stingy he won't buy one thing as we came down. He would beg anyone he would see eating."[27]

Notice that Adams also mentioned that many soldiers were storing their clothing in Richmond. North Carolina, along with several other states, rented warehouses as storage facilities for boxes of personal items that the soldiers could not carry. The depot for North Carolina was located on Main Street, between 8th and 7th Streets, opposite Spotswood Hotel.[28] In spite of the many personality conflicts and persistent rumors of the large battle near Manassas Junction (Bull Run) that shocked both North and South alike, members of Company K found time to write home and describe their experiences in Virginia to John Brunner, who published an early account on 25 July in the *Carolina Watchman*. Notice Brunner's reaction to the soldiers' complaints of missing a meal; in coming years, privation would become the norm not an exception:

## ROWAN RIFLE GUARD

The Company, with the Regiment to which it belongs, is now at Richmond, Virginia. Their destination, as we learn by a private letter from a member of the Guard is Manassas Gap, where they expect to arrive in a few days. Our correspondent says the regiment faired pretty badly between Garysburg and Richmond for want of something to eat. That they spent a night in a large brick-house in Petersburg, upon their blankets, supperless; took up the line of march to the depot next morning without breakfast where they stood until two o'clock before the train was ready to convey them to Richmond. This is pretty severe, and it is fortunate for the cause of the South that patriotism of our volunteers can bear it so well.

On the same day this letter was published, Companies A, C, F, G and K of the 4th NCST boarded trains for Manassas Junction, Virginia, from Richmond. This was very exciting for the green troops, the equivalent of being sent "forward" or "to the front" in military parlance.[29] After their arrival, however, the eager members of Company K and their comrades in the 4th NCST quickly discovered that camp life at Manassas, Virginia, would be dull, boring, and often lethal due to disease. Records show this encampment to be the worst camp experience for sickness and death due to illness they would suffer throughout the war, largely because it was their first one and their bodies immune systems had not adapted to the unhealthy conditions of thousands of men huddled together in such an austere environment. Sgt. Ashbel Fraley of Company A penned in his diary on 25 July that the regiment had "Arrived at Manassas (Tudor Hall) where we remained drilling and performing garrison duties till March 8, 1862."[30]

Another member of the Iredell Blues, John Stikeleather, offered more detail about their new situation, stating, "While at Manassas Junction our troops were constantly employed in garrison duty, Col. George B. Anderson in the meantime acting as commander of the post. The 4th North Carolina and the 49th Virginia, commanded by Col. Wm. Smith, "Extra Billy", the 27th and 28th Georgia did the garrison duty at Manassas Junction until our evacuation of the place the next spring. Our stay at Manassas was somewhat monotonous. Our visits to the battlefield soon after our arrival at camp were occasions of much interest to us, but in a little while we settled down in to the regular routine of camp life with plenty to do in the way of drilling, guard duty and fatigue duty. The saddest feature connected with our stay was the great amount of sickness in the regiment. Numbers of our best soldiers fell victims to disease...Rations were plenty during the first summer of the war; our soldiers wasted as much the first year of the war as they consumed the fourth year."[31] Company K also spent time at Manassas serving as Provost Guard, as various companies of the regiment were rotated for this tedious duty. Samuel Marshbourne of Company F, indicated that "We guarded prisoners and all the arms and provisions for about eight months."[32] During the long summer months at Manassas, Scribbler found time to write home again with a synoptic account of their time in Virginia through 8 August 1861:

> It has been so long I wrote to you, that to give you a full account of our doings since then, would take up more space than you could spare. I will, therefore, merely give a synopsis of our movements for the benefit of our friends among your readers. Five companies of our regiment, viz: Iredell Blues; Rowan Rifle Guards; Davie Sweepstakes; Saltillo Boys and the Wilson Light Infantry, accompanied by the Rowan Artillery, left our Camp near Gareysburg, N.C., on Saturday evening, July 29th, bound for Virginia. We went by way of Petersburg and arrived at Richmond, Sunday, about noon. We went by into camp below the city, within a quarter of a mile of the river James, where we remained for four days. On Thursday night we took the train for the seat of the war. At Gordonsville, where we arrived the next morning by sunrise, we were, for some cause or other, detained until nearly night.

> However, we did at last get off, and that night, about three o'clock, found ourselves at Manassas Junction. We encamped about a mile and a half north of the Junction, where we yet remain. We did nearly all of our traveling by night, either on account of the bad arrangement of the trains or to baffle any lurking spies, who might be along the road. Be the cause what it may, it was quite unpleasant to us, for it not only kept us from seeing the country through which we passed, but deprived us of much sleep. The next day after our arrival here, many of us visited the scene of the late battle. The field, of course, did not present as shocking an appearance as it did immediately after the fight, yet, we saw enough to give us an idea of the real horrors of a bloody battle. Dead horses filled the air with a sickening odor, rendering it almost unbearable to go near the points where the hardest fighting had taken place. Numerous graves-or rather imitations, for they could scarcely bear the name of graves-were scattered all over the field. In many places limbs lay exposed, and in several instances, the naked skull was visible, so shallow was the covering of the body. Those, thus buried, however, were Northerners, to whom a descent burial was refused by their own friends, and who were left to the care of their more humane enemies.

> The Southerners, of course, attended their own dead at first, and consequently, by the time they came to the Yankees, they were much decayed. It was, therefore, impossible to re-move them or remain long enough to give them a decent burial. The ground around the graves was blackened by the life blood of the occupant, and in many instances,

84

showed marks of the death struggle. Despite of hatred towards the invaders of our soil, we could not but pity the fate of those who lay around us. To a person of refined feelings, there is something very repulsive in the thought of being thus buried, out of the reach and knowledge of relatives and friends. Many of those buried on this battle field doubtless left the bosom of families and started on this expedition, allured by the thoughts of wealth and renown. Unfortunately enough for them, instead of their expectations being realized, they have scarcely enough of earth to cover their dead bodies, and those, against whom they came to wage a war of extermination, had, by the unnatural con-duct of their pretended friends, to give them such a burial as they have received. This is war! this is glory with all its brightness. Thus may be it be to all who came threatening upon the people of the South barbarities worthy of the most bloodthirsty savages. Would to God that those more quietly,--the Greelys Sumners and Beechers—should meet with such a fate rather than the miserable dupes they have deluded.! The health of our Regiment is not very good just now. The measles have got into camp and many are down with them. One man in the Iredell Blues, (James Sprinkle,) died with them night before last. I know of no other very serious case now in camp.

And on 23 August, Captain McNeely reported to the *Carolina Watchman* that the Rowan Rifles had suffered some deaths due to typhoid and measles, the latter of which became epidemic at Camp Pickens near Manassas. McNeely also wrote that there were then ninety men in the Rowan Rifles, showing the effects of the massive influx of volunteers between their tenure at Fort Johnston and Camp Pickens in June. He offers a glimpse of hope that things might improve, in spite of the rampant disease in camp as well. McNeely wrote on 2 September 1861:

Mr. J.J. Bruner—Dear Sir: I have the very sad duty of informing you for publication for the benefit of their friends, the deaths of three of my gallant little band, viz: John W. Bassinger, of Rowan, aged 20 years; James L. Hendricks of Forsyth, aged 24 years, who died on the 20th instant of Typhoid fever, caused from measles and exposure; also on the 21st Henry W. Crooks, of Ohio, who lived in Salisbury for several years, and was engaged in the Fan Making business-he died of the same disease, aged 26 years. I do not know their friends, or I would write to them. I had them decently buried with military honors. There is a good deal of sickness in our camp—no serious cases that I know of now. My Company did number 93-now 90. There is no news of importance. We are ready for the enemy, only waiting for orders. Very wet, which causes all our sickness.

While the soldiers at Manassas were often bored to the point of insanity and terrified of diseases in their camp, some young men back home still held romanticized notions of becoming soldiers. Twenty-five year old Hamilton C. Long traveled from Salisbury to Manassas to enlist on 17 August 1861, and found army life to his liking. He was soon appointed a second lieutenant in November.[33] In September 1861, North Carolina reorganized the state militia (not to be confused with volunteer companies or state troops). The men staying at home in Rowan County eligible for militia duty were assigned to the 76th Militia Regiment, 19th Brigade, under Col. John A. Bradshaw. Several men who served in the 4th NCST were later assigned to key positions in the local militia following their discharge from Confederate service.[34] Amidst the doldrums of camp life and sickness, the 4th NCST soon received good news. A large sum of money was received on 7 September 1861 to pay for the new state uniforms, and the soldiers could finally be reimbursed. A payment voucher signed by Capt. Thomas M. Blount, assistant quartermaster for the 4th NCST, indicates that

$19,600 was received from the Confederate States Treasury Clothing Fund, signed by one Capt. I. Rand in Richmond.₃₅

Under the process known as the "Commutation System," soldiers first paid for their uniforms and the government reimbursed them. Considering that the regiment had received their uniforms roughly a month prior, the timing was not poor at all. Sunday, 8 September 1861 proved to be a fair and pleasant day, and Lt. Col. John A. Young, of the 4th NCST penned in his diary that there was a shortage of shoes in spite of the unit's new uniforms. Young also indicated there were still 314 men out due to illness, which seems contradictory to Captain McNeely's earlier observation that there were no serious cases of measles in the camp. Young was also the inspecting officer on the very first regimental inspection held at Manassas. He penned the following description, "It was the first review the regiment had passed. After review we submitted the regiment to a Brigade inspection of arms and of uniform, which developed a very great deficiency in shoes. Every company is in bad condition for essential article of apparel...two men actually appeared in line barefooted. I wrote...to forward us by express one hundred pair of shoes if he could purchase them in Charlotte and to make contracts at once for four hundred pair more and send these forward as fast as he could 50 or 100 pair ready. I also ordered A.J. Orr to have our coats made for our men out of Rock Island goods, and forward as early as possible. The Confederate Government having determined to pay the troops $21.00 each six mo. With which they shall furnish their own clothing, making soldiers unprepared for the rapidly approaching winter. We regard it as a mistake in the government, but as far as our regiment is concerned Rock Island makes us safe, provided we can get the shoes. The whole duty of providing clothing devolves upon the field officers, who certainly have much less opportunity to look after the provisions of these necearies that the officers of the Quartermasters..."₃₆

With winter approaching, the soldiers often wrote home requesting personal items such as overcoats, new blankets and other warmer clothing be forwarded to them to the camps via rail ways and couriers through Richmond. There were shortages on several important items including candles, wax, flour, and certain textiles, and prices skyrocketed. But citizens at home also did a great deal to assist them, by compiling supplies and forwarding them to the camp. On 9 September 1861, the Ladies Soldiers Aid Society of Rowan held a meeting to arrange to provide for the soldiers' winter needs by taking up a collection of blankets, clothing, etc., and even socks knitted by a "lady with one arm" according to the *Carolina Watchman.* Two local men visited the camp, and took along three "fine three year old North Carolina Bacon hams" as a present for General Beauregard. The Salisbury Brass band is mentioned on 12 September, and by that time, two more soldiers from the regiment had died, in spite of reports that the regiment's overall health was improving. The *Carolina Watchman* reported:

> A private letter from a member of the Rowan Rifle Guard, of Sept. 5, speaks of the Salisbury Brass Band, now in the service of the 4th Regiment. Mentions the death of two men, one from Capt. Andrews Company and the other from Capt. Whitaker's Goldsboro Company. Says the health of the Regiment is rapidly improving. We quote from the letter as follows: "We were paid off yesterday, for the time we were at Fort Johnston, and for one month since we were sworn in as regulars and they promised to pay all that is due us the first of next month. This is what we call tardy work. How the men have got along without their pay is wonderful."

By the end of September 1861, many units were transferred away from Manassas near Fairfax, Virginia, while the 4th NCST remained with a few others in that garrison. The Salisbury Brass band performed frequently, doubtlessly to help morale. Scribbler found time to write the folks at home again on 19 September and again mentioned numerous illnesses. He also described an accident that caused a great deal of alarm when the inexperienced volunteers realized how powerful their "Minnie ball" bullets were. Scribbler's letter appeared as follows in the 30 September 1861 *Carolina Watchman*:

We are still stationed where we first camped near the Junction. Nearly all the other regiments that were encamped so thickly around here, have been moved towards Alexandria. Our regiment is left almost alone, though we are daily expecting marching orders. Gen. Beauregard has moved his headquarters from this place to Fairfax, some sixteen miles further on. This removal of so many troops in the direction above mentioned, gives reason to believe that something important will take place in a few days. When the report of the Cape Hatteras disaster reached here, it created considerable excitement. Every man seemed to burn with the desire to aid in driving the invaders from the soil of the Old North State. Several companies of this regiment are from the counties which would be exposed to the depredations of the Yankee, should they get out on a stealing expedition consequently, they feel a lively interest in the movements of both friend and foe in that section. The health of the regiment has been very bad since I wrote before. Not less twenty have died.

Eight have died out of Capt. Andrew's company alone, among them our excellent Orderly Sergeant, James E Summer. At times, so many of our company have been sick, that when details for guard, garrison or fatigue duty were taken out, scarcely six men could be found fit for drill. But I am happy to say things have taken a better turn. Deaths are now less frequent, and the sick are improving generally. Our excellent surgeon, Dr. King, and his corps of assistants, deserve great credit, for their unremitting endeavors to stop the ravages of disease. A very sad accident happened in the regiment last Monday evening. One of the Wilson Light Infantry shot another through the head killing him instantly. The skull was literally crushed, showing the effects of the minnie ball. The man did not know his gun was loaded, some one through mistake having taken it on guard duty, where the pieces are required to be loaded, and in taking it out of his tent for drill, it by some means went off with the above sad results. A portion of the Salisbury Brass Band is now here and delights us with its good music. Mr. Neaves, their accomplished leader, is training a regimental band and is, I understand, much encouraged by his success so far.

SCRIBBLER

Pvt. William Adams of Company C wrote home again on 1 October suggesting the soldiers were beginning to feel the strain of winter's approach and the unresolved shortage of shoes. Adams mentions that at least part of his own need was self-inflicted. At least he received some blankets and socks, but the desperate tone of his request may have also been a plea to the family's heartstrings rather than actual want when he wrote, "...I received my blankets and socks on Sunday...Ma I received my socks which you sent...ten thousand times oblige to you for those socks. Pa you said you were going to get me a par of shoes made. I am needing them as soon as I can get them...have them made very high and a half sole...tacked on for we can not get our shoes half soled without paying $1...boots would be much better in the winter than shoes, they will cost more I know. I told you to send me shoes. I change my notion. It snows a great deal here, if we have to stay this winter I will have to buy boots, a pair cost $15, that is two much.  If you can get them made and sent I would like to have them. I have got know shoes since I left home. I lost my new shoes in Richmond or some one stole them…If you get me boots Pa, have the soles tack on for it cost $1 dollar to get a pair of shoes half soled and they not done better than I can do myself and you know that is bad. I will be glad to get either shoes or boots."[37]

As clothing, blankets, and shoes began to arrive from home in October, the troops still needed new munitions. Col. George Anderson, a West Point graduate, signed an ordnance requisition for the 4th NCST, indicating their weapons were still largely smoothbores.[38] The original document reveals his request to the Confederate Ordnance Department in Richmond for 1,530 musket caps and 1,900 Smooth bore musket Cartridges. By 24 October, the regiment had received some overcoats from the North Carolina clothing manufactory in Raleigh, which were mentioned in a letter written by Walter Battle, who also noticed that winter had definitely arrived, as he penned, "We have had frost for several nights and it is already beginning to turn very cold, but we have not suffered any yet.  I wear two pair of socks in my boots and they do very well, for it keeps the cold wind off my legs…We have got thick overcoats from the government, with capes reaching below our elbows. They are of great service to us in standing guard."[39] Scribbler indicated in his next letter, written on 16 October, that the regiment had moved to a new location. Many seemed to blame the location of the former camp for the high level of sickness amongst them, but no mention was made of any skirmishing with enemy forces yet. Surely there were rumors and high expectations for a battle that never took place. Scribbler's letter was published in the 28 October *Carolina Watchman*, as follows:

> We have moved to a new camp but are still in close proximity to the Junction. Our move was made at the direction of the doctors for the health of the regiment. The sickest men were sent to a station some twenty-five miles up the Manassas Gap Railroad. Many of these have returned to duty and report the remainder as rapidly improving. Our men have had new spirits infused into them by our move. It had become a settled conviction among them that it was the next thing to an impossibility to get well at the old camp, when once taken sick. This belief has been dissipated by the change and great improvement is visible among the men. Col. Chipley, of Iredell, arrived here the first of the month with three car loads of "good things from home." He brought an abundance of potatoes, cabbage, apples blankets, clothes, honey, wine vinegar, molasses, and numerous articles of comfort and of luxury.
>
> This is the second visit Col. Chipley has paid us. We are under lasting obligations to him for his self-sacrificing exertions in our  behalf. Since he has been here he has been building a depot at the Junction for this regiment. The good people of Rowan and Iredell need not, therefore withhold their hands, lest their sons should be overburdened with clothing or other necessaries. Many will not send things, fearing that they would be left behind and destroyed should the regiment be ordered to march. This will be the case no longer. Whatever is of any value can be boxed up and left in this depot where it will be safe until called for. Thanks to Col. Chipley, thanks—a thousand thanks—to the folks at home for the abundance of good things sent us. Thanks for past favors we sincerely hope for a continuance of the same.—News is scarce here, that is reliable news.
>
> Rumor after rumor has come until, we no longer pay attention to them. Somehow or other the great battle, which everybody is and has been expecting for some time, does not take

place. The Yankees will not advance—they are not ready. We hear cannon nearly every day, but it is said to be the artillery practicing. Two such bodies of men, however, cannot long remain so near each other without some action. The soldiers are anxious for prompt, decisive and final action. They are sick and tired of this inactive camp life, with its dull routine of never ending and laborious duties. We have rumors of another action on the N.C. coast in which our men were victorious. May this report prove true. Let the cowardly rascals be driven from the Old North State.

SCRIBBLER

Pvt. William Lillycross of the Rowan Rifles, who must have been quite confused, wrote to Captain McNeely on 30 October 1861 while encamped near Manassas, Virginia, and requested a transfer to the Rowan Artillery. His Letter of Appeal indicates he unknowingly enlisted in the infantry company, thinking he was going to serve in the Rowan Artillery. Early in the war, it was considered an honor for an artillery unit to be attached to a specific infantry company or regiment. Many similar arrangements were made statewide between infantry and artillery companies in 1861, but it caused a great deal of confusion in this instance. North Carolina authorities seemed to indulge in this practice until the state troops mustered into Confederate service that summer. Another common practice was for volunteers to be assigned to units with other family members, and many officers made this a priority for their men. Lillycross' father-in-law was in the Rowan Artillery, and he wanted to transfer to serve with him. His letter of appeal states, "Sir, I respectfully request that I be transferred to Light Battery D NCS Troops. My reason for applying for the transfer is that my Father-in-law is serving in that Battery and the Captain Commanding it is willing to accept me. I would be a great satisfaction to me to be with - I always desired to be in the same company with him. My (Father-in-law) and I enlisted under the impression that his company belonged to the 4th Reg but on my arrival at Manassas I found it was detached therefore, I hope my request will be granted."[40]

Col. William N. Pendleton, chief of artillery for the Confederate army, approved the transfer based "…upon the declaration of Capt Reilly, that he knows the facts & that he desires the transfer alike for the good of the service, & for the sake of justice to the applicant who was separated from his company by mistake." Yet Lillycross may not have transferred; his name later appears on hospital records identifying him as a member of Company K as well as later muster rolls in 1864 link him to service in this unit. Otherwise, 2d Lt. William Brown, former captain of the Rowan Rifles resigned on 30 October 1861.[41] Captain McNeely wrote to "Miss Beard" on behalf of Company K on 13 November, and his missive was published in the *Carolina Watchman* on 2 December:

I have the pleasure of answering your note of the 4th, and also of acknowledging the receipt of all the articles mentioned in it, for which you will give to the society my companys, and my own, highest thanks—they came when most needed—and we shall ever feel grateful to the Ladies of Salisbury and vicinity, for their kind consideration for the men who have left their homes and friends to suffer the toils which fall to the lot of soldiers for their own, their friends and their Countries protection. I am glad that I can say my Company is getting along very well, but little sickness, none of a severe character, and all perfectly contented. We shall soon into winter quarters, (if the enemy does not attack us soon). We shall always be glad to hear from our friends, and to think, they take such an interest in us. We only hope that your confidence will not be misplaced.

## *Regimental Quartermaster Arrested*

The boredom of the stagnant winter encampment led to a number of disagreements between the soldiers, and as noted, officers were no exception. A conflict occurred on 19 November 1861 between 33-year old Maj. Brian Grimes, a former member of the state secession convention in 1861, and later commander of the 4th NCST. Grimes did not fare well with Capt. David Carter, commander of Company E. In a rather malicious move, Grimes sparked a quarrel with Carter's close friend and the regimental quartermaster, Capt. Thomas M. Blount, by accusing him of insubordination over an incident involving an order to remove a wagon of firewood. Blount responded to Grimes in a manner that was deemed "unbecoming" of an officer, although it was Grimes' own malicious and manipulative behavior that caused the incident. On the other hand Blount's actions seemed based on his belief that he was somehow entitled to special treatment due to his social status before the war, even though he was now a junior officer to the cagey Grimes.[42]*

As their first Christmas spent at war approached, members of Company K continued to battle cold weather, stagnancy, and disease. Some men were assigned to serve in the provost marshal's police guard, including Jacob Fraley and Charles Jones. Jones was from Iredell County, but had enlisted in the Rowan Rifle Guards in April. After the Civil War, Jones was quite influential, and founded the *Charlotte Observer* newspaper. The provost marshal was Henry A. Chambers, and the two worked as part of Gen. Joseph E. Johnston's staff.[43] Hamilton C. Long, who for unknown reasons stayed behind in Salisbury when the company left in June, traveled from Salisbury to Manassas in August to muster in. He was appointed second lieutenant on 23 November 1861.[44] The 4th NCST also received a new silk battle flag on 8 December 1861 from the Army of Northern Virginia. George Battle wrote on 9 December that he felt like "The enemy knows our national flag and had already tried to deceive us by hoisting it at their head. Now I guess we will deceive them next time."[45] Many volunteer regiments also continued to carry their original company flags showing their pride as original volunteer regiments, which only added to confusion in battle.[46]

As winter settled in at Camp Pickens, military activities seemed to slow down, if not stop altogether for the 4th NCST. Many men died in the warmer months from measles and typhoid, but as Capt. E.A. Osborne of Iredell County, who later became colonel of the 4th NCST, noted "But when the winter came, the men regained their health, and having become inured to camp life, and accustomed to taking care of themselves, they were soon in fine spirits.".[47] Not surprisingly, boredom and restlessness soon hallmarked their first winter encampment, although most of the men were quite pleased with their log hut accommodations, most of which had stone chimneys. John Stikeleather, now a sergeant in Company A, left a humorous account of how many enlisted men dealt with their need for entertainment – practical jokes. However, this one is particularly mischievous, and the comrades who cooked up the diabolical scheme to humiliate a love-sick friend were anxious when their plan almost backfired. Their angst was justly deserved.

---

*Blount's official response stated he felt entitled to the same level of courtesy as any other gentleman, and that Grimes' rude conduct had nothing to do with a rank disparity. Grimes did not agree and filed charges of insubordination. Blount challenged Grimes to a duel, demanding the "usual satisfaction of gentlemen." Grimes responded by tendering his resignation. Fortunately, both ideas were refused. Lt. Col. John Young promised to have each of them court-martialed if the matter could not be settled. The situation even grabbed the attention of Maj. Gen. P.G.T. Beauregard, who later wrote that if only a "competent" quartermaster could serve directly under Col. George Anderson, the situation would be easily remedied. Grimes finally later agreed to settle their differences. Blount was literally shot out of the saddle and killed only days later at the battle of Gaines Mill, while carrying the colors of the 30th NCT and riding ahead of the battle lines. Source: OR, Series I, Vol. 11(2), (1884), 629-630.

It is not known whether the boys in the Rowan Rifles knew about this incident, but there was surely camp gossip about it later so it is highly probable. Stikeleather corresponded,

"While in winter quarters many practical jokes were deployed upon each other, and, as a rule no class of men take jokes more gracefully than soldiers. Bob L. like many others had a correspondent back in Iredell, whose letters he greatly prized; her letters were always signed "Libbie." No relation stronger than that of friendship existed between them. But, at times, Bob saw in Libbie's letters, expressions, that led him to hope that at no distant day the relation between them might be a stronger and dearer one. Such as letter had a very enlivening effect upon Bob; he would take a regular chicken fit, lie down, roll over, kick up his heels, and in various ways give expression to his feelings of joy, much to the amusement of his comrades; and finally the appearance of Libbie's signature along at the bottom of a page was sufficient to produce one of the paroxysms of joy just described even before the letter was read. After a time Andy K. and myself messmates of Bob concluded that we would see if we could not cure him of his 'fits.' Fixing up a letter, dating it back, counterfeiting Libbie's handwriting and getting it into Bob's hands was more easily accomplished than might be expected. The contents of the letter were very respectful, but Bob was made to understand that friendship between them was the border beyond which he must not presume to go.

As soon as the letter was handed him, before reading it seeing Libbie's signature at the close, he took on one of his chicken fits; but alas! the reading of but a few lines of the missive showed him that in this instance at least he had counted without his host. Bob was artless in his ways and before he read the letter half through he turned to his friends, several of whom were near by, and with a woebegone countenance said, 'Boys, I thought that I had two strings to my bow but now I am not sure I even have one.' In a short while he told Andy K. in all seriousness he felt like hanging himself. Many such remarks fell from his lips before he retired to rest that night. Of course he had the sympathy of his comrades. He turned to Andy K. and myself a short time after the letter was read and said, "Boys, I want you to help me send her a hell jolter." That night a little after dark he absented himself from camp for nearly two hours, and, some of us grew uneasy lest he might be meditating self destruction sure enough, and, we felt quite relieved when he returned. The evening passed with sadness to Bob but with much suppressed enjoyment to several of his messmates. After all had retired to their bunks save Bob and myself, I determined to relieve him of the suspense from which he was suffering. I broke the facts to him as gently as I could, expecting probably an angry outbreak on his part. For a moment he was silent, but there was too much joy in his breast that it was all a joke to give room for any anger whatever. After remaining in a dazed attitude for a few moments, his first words were, "Sold for a sixpence, but lookout, remember, retaliation is the word." In a short time he retired and no doubt slept the sleep of the innocent. It completely cured him. From the time to this he never has attempted retaliation, nor did we ever again hear from his lips the name of Libbie. I am glad to say that Bob L. survived the war...but he never married "Libbie."[48]

Company K muster rolls covering 31 December 1861 through 28 February 1862, and includes a detailed statistical summary of the company census.[49] Subsequent muster rolls 1862 through 1864 are discussed chronologically throughout the following chapters. The present roll was completed at Camp Pickens, Virginia, by Capt. McNeely, who wrote that 2d Lieutenant Hamilton Long and

1st Sergeant Addison Wiseman and four privates were under arrest, but did not specify the circumstances. Each subsequent table herein is transcribed from the original and shows both the "aggregate" total i.e. total number of enlisted men and officers noted on the muster, and the actual number of enlisted men and officers available for duty:

| Captain | 1 Lt | 2 Lt | Brevet Lt | Sgt | Cpl | Musicians | Privates | Total Enlisted | Aggregate |
|---------|------|------|-----------|-----|-----|-----------|----------|----------------|-----------|
| 1 | 1 | - | - | 4 | 5 | 1 | 45 | 52 | 85 |

Capt. William F. Kelly of Company D inspected the regiment and found Company K in good condition with regard to their discipline, arms and general military appearance, but were wanting in the area of uniforms. Capt. McNeely assigned fourteen privates extra daily duties elsewhere in the camp including Robert Beaty was serving in a most unusual capacity – he was sent to the Confederate Balloon Corps.* Also Michael Rowland was detailed as a teamster; and James Roberts was serving as a clerk in Maj. Gen. Daniel H. Hills office, while Lewis Mahaley was detailed as a Carpenter working on "Mountain Cannon" carriages. John F. Thompson was likewise on Extra Daily Duty serving as a courier for the regimental commander. 2d Lieutenant Marcus Hofflin was sick in camp, and musician Edward Neave was also sick in camp. There were four other privates in Richmond Hospitals at the time the roll was made. Company strength decreased from May 1861 due to deaths from illness and attrition (some had resigned or transferred into other units). Summarily, the year 1861 had altered forever the course of this young, zealous local militia unit. The Rowan Rifles were now mustered into three years Confederate service or duration of the war, and would soon face the long and bloody campaigns of 1862.

---

*The Civil War had many firsts, but the advent of aerial observation via gas filled balloons was dramatic. The Union Army first employed balloons, then the Confederates in 1862 amidst myths such as the belief that southern ladies sacrificed their silk dresses to help make the balloon. The balloon was actually made of varnished cotton. It was filled with hot air, because the Confederacy did not possess the technology to make hydrogen in the field. Their balloon first launched over Yorktown, Virginia on 13 April 1862 and made two flights, enabling important aerial observation sorties but broke free and was captured. See L.T.C. Rolt: *The Aeronauts: A History of Ballooning - 1783-1903*. N.Y.: Walker and Company, 1966 for more discussion.

# Chapter 4

# Winter encampment,
# Spring Campaigns of 1862

**"... A marching army is a mass of the grandest confusion I ever saw"**

The doldrums and relative comfort of their first winter encampment was suddenly broken in early March, when a strong Federal force encroaching on the Manassas lines. On 5 March, the Confederates at Camp Pickens near Manassas were ordered to have all excess baggage packed away, and be prepared to evacuate on sudden notice. A few days later, the order came to move out, and the army hastily relocated to new camps near the Rapidan River some twenty five miles away. But practically all was lost upon retreat, as one frustrated private recalled on 14 March, "When we camped for the night, everything that we could not carry on our backs was burned up, and I can tell you that you cannot imagine how much we suffered on the march, which consisted of three days' traveling, loaded down with our baggage and equipment, sleeping on the hard, cold ground, feet sore, half fed on hard dry crackers and meat. Out lot was not to be envied...We have no tents here to sleep in, but we have made ourselves shelters out of cedar bushes...The night we left Manassas it was all burnt down and I expect there was a million of goods consumed on that night, all the soldiers clothes they could not carry with them and everything that could have been expected to be at such a place ...all was burnt."[1]

Early 1862 brought much tragedy into the lives of the Rowan Rifles. During the siege of Yorktown, Virginia, in March and April they were exposed to heavy shelling from Union gunboats, but the company did not see its first sustained combat action until the Battle of Seven Pines in May. The losses suffered at Seven Pines were immediately followed by the Seven Days Battles around Richmond, causing more casualties, and the idealistic youth became hardened veterans. The Rowan Rifles also endured privation and casualties on the long Maryland Campaign in September. Those early winter months after the battle of Sharpsburg were hallmarked by lack of clothing and supplies, and made an indelible mark, as evidenced in the testimony of several soldiers' years after the war. Truly this was a year of shock and loss; the majority of soldiers had never traveled outside of North Carolina, much less faced combat. On 27 January 1862, the 4th NCST obtained supplies from the ordnance department at Richmond, including 98 cartridge boxes, 175 cap boxes, 59 shoulder belts, 143 waist belts, and 8 bayonet scabbards. Cartridge boxes were prescribed to be worn on a leather shoulder belt.[2]

### Peninsula Campaign

In April 1862, shortly after the Confederate defeat in the west at Shiloh, Union commander Maj. Gen. George B. McClellan, a West Point man, amassed a large Union force at Fort Monroe in Hampton, Virginia. McClellan's troops began a slow movement northward up the peninsula, intent on capturing Richmond. As the Union forces advanced, they soon encountered Confederate defenders under Maj. Gen. John Bankhead Magruder who stubbornly resisted near Lee's Mill, just south of modern Newport News. Magruder's men were spread out along miles of earthworks running from Yorktown behind the Warwick River and southward toward the James River across the peninsula. He bluffed the Federals, constantly relocating and force marching his troops back and forth across the peninsula to create the illusion of a larger force than he had. The trick worked for a while. McClellan significantly overestimated Confederate strength (a tendency he exhibited throughout the war) and hesitatingly moved toward Yorktown. The long rows of earthworks along the Yorktown - Warwick line served their purpose, but was problematic to the Confederate troops, who suffered from disease and unhygienic living conditions in the trenches.

Brig. Gen. Daniel Harvey Hill, a North Carolinian, commanded the division to which the 4th North Carolina was assigned.* The division arrived at Yorktown in late April and took positions on the left flank of the Yorktown - Warwick line in the trenches near redoubts 10-12. Many earthen works there were built on the remains of the trenches their colonial ancestors used against the British during the Revolution. The Confederates were well aware of their historic location as they were making their own chapter of history.₃ At Yorktown, the Rowan Rifles heard enemy gunfire for the first time, while the regiment was on picket duty. The Federal Navy was attempting to proceed up the James River on their right flank, but the ironclad *C.S.S. Virginia* slowed that portion of the Union advance. On 6 April intense skirmishing was reported along the Yorktown-Warwick line as McClellan began looking for weaknesses in the Confederate defenses. Heavy rains ensued, making most roads nearly impassable; McClellan decided that a direct assault was not practical. Instead, he resorted to siege tactics. Confederate soldiers in the trenches faced daily shelling and the whining of minnie balls around them during their defense of Yorktown. During the rainy month of April, field conditions became increasingly difficult as there were but very few tents available. Most were still packed in wagons for the first eight nights that the 4th NCST was in the trenches, and Maj. Bryan Grimes recalled that "my best covering has been a few branches of pine thrown up to cover myself from the rain."₄

Grimes also noted that officers and men alike slept on arms wearing their boots because of the threat of battle on a moments notice. Grimes reported that at one point, the Federals even encroached within "one-half mile…shooting at us upon all occasion whenever we show ourselves." The constant bombardment took a significant psychological toll on the 4th NCST. Even the stoic Major Grimes reflected anxiety about the shelling. He reveals a glimpse of his uncertainty, "not since my arrival here on the 10th of April has there been two consecutive hours without their firing into our camp and sometimes at the rate of 50 shells a minutes. But Sunday night at about two o'clock we all thought the battle was opened, such a hailstorm of iron and lead I never conceived of… If you wish to imagine how a bomb or shot sounds at it comes whizzing through the air, get …a whirl-a-Gig that children often play with, and whirl it around a few times and the noise that it makes somewhat resembles the sound, except that you can hear the ball that is the larger one a half-mile and have to drop behind the breastworks for protection."₅

Original company muster rolls in the Confederate army were written on a document known as a "Form 28." This was a standard military form and contained a section called "Record of Events," normally used by the reporting officers to make a few comments about the unit's recent activities and contains many important comments and descriptions about their physical appearance and activities; the 1862 winter and spring campaigns were laden with hardships and losses, primarily illnesses, poor camp conditions and death of friends from disease, although there was one combat death at Yorktown, where the regiment was heavily involved in daily picket duties in the trenches.

---

*Brig. Gen. Daniel Harvey Hill was well-known as a strict disciplinarian and staunch Presbyterian. As he required drill three times daily in camp, he often prayed and read Scriptures aloud to the passing troops from his tent door. Hill admonished the men to refrain from common "soldier" vices like prostitution, gambling, cursing, and alcohol. Douglass S. Freeman, *Lee's Lieutenants: A Study in Command.* (New York: Scribner Books, 2001), 19-21.

Captain McNeely wrote that he was completing the updated muster roll literally as the company was encamped "in the trenches" there under "heavy naval bombardment" by Union gunboats harbored in the Chesapeake Bay. This second known Company K Muster roll covers the period from 28 February to 30 April 1862 and reveals that Company K increased its numerical strength to forty six privates and eighty-eight men aggregate, and received twenty two new recruits since 31 December 1861, several of whom only briefly survived in the austere trenches with poor sanitary conditions.[6] The table below is transcribed from the original muster roll and summarizes statistical data provided by Capt. McNeely, including the total number of men available for actual Duty on date roll was taken, and the Aggregate or cumulative number men shown on the paper muster roll.

| Captain | 1 Lt | 2 Lt | Brevet Lt | Sgt | Cpl | Musicians | Privates | Total Enlisted | Aggregate |
|---------|------|------|-----------|-----|-----|-----------|----------|----------------|-----------|
| - | 1 | 1 | 1 | 4 | 4 | 1 | 46 | 84 | 88 |

This roll further indicated roughly seven months had lapsed since their first pay receipt, and Captain McNeely was ill and staying inside his tent. He did not drill the company for several weeks, but managed to compose the document. Company K then had one private under arrest or in confinement but McNeely did not identify him. His notes indicate one private died from of wounds sustained in battle at Yorktown on 11 April 1862 at the hospital near Rapidan Station, 38 year old John Mowrey. James "Frank" Dorsett was sixteen years old when he enlisted on 16 March 1862 at Salisbury, and when he arrived at Yorktown deserted exactly one month later on 16 April 1862. Several other recruits arrived in the winter-early spring 1862 period, including four brothers, Alex and Daniel McQueen and Henry and Tobias Wise. There were also two men who were cousins, Lewis and Crawford Holshouser who arrived from Rowan County in late March. Crawford Holshouser was a former 2d Lieutenant in Company E, 76th NC Militia in Rowan County. George Basinger, John Campbell, Ambrose Casper, Jeremiah Eddleman, James Mauldin, James Soloman, William Peeler, Henry Severs, Noah Troutman, Levi Turner, Wallace Josey and Rego Lancherry also reported. Lancherry was born in Italy and worked as a miner before the war in Gold Hill, but could not tolerate the diseased conditions and died one month after his arrival.

Both Edward Fulk and John Caster also found the unhealthy environment too much for their bodies immune systems to adapt with, and became so severely ill only days after their arrival that both required transfer to Richmond hospitals. Caster remained there until August 1864. Samuel "Frank" Gardner also arrived in April, only to serve about six weeks before his death at the battle of Seven Pines on 30 May 1862. Two corporals received promotions to 2d Lieutenant and transferred into other regiments as officers on 27 March 1862, John Lyerly and James Crawford who went into Company B, 42d NCT. Crawford's elder brother Capt. William Henderson Crawford commanded Company B, and had helped organize not only the 42d NCT but also the 7th NCST in 1861 in Rowan County. He was a man of significant political influence so it is not surprising that his younger brother James and his friend John Lyerly managed to attain commissions in his company. Both survived the war, and James Crawford lived until 1906.

Francis Mills was one of six privates and one sergeant sent to Richmond hospitals in March with unspecified conditions. This would not be the only time he was hospitalized, as he contracted Gonorrhea in 1864 and spent several months in Richmond Hospitals. Four men remained detailed for extra duties carried over from the former roll, including Michael Rowland as a teamster, and Lewis Mahaley who remained detailed as a carpenter for the artillery. James Clark served as one of Gen. Daniel H. Hill's clerks, and John Thompson daily worked as a courier. Robert Beaty remained attached to the Balloon Corps, and another private, George S. Winters was also then detached to the same service, totaling two Company K men serving with the fledgling aeronauts.

Another significant event occurred in early 1862; Lt. Addison Wiseman took leave to return home on 2 March, where he married his sweetheart, twenty-two year old Sarah Antoinette Brown of Rowan County on 6 March 1862. They conceived their first child during a brief honeymoon, William Wiseman, who was born in November 1862.[7] Sarah Brown was born on 7 October 1840 and died 19 September 1898, on the thirty-fourth anniversary of Addison's death at the third battle of Winchester on 19 September 1864. Brown was the granddaughter of John Brown and Catherine Miller Brown, and Great-Granddaughter of pioneer Michael & Margareta (Miller) Braun, who built the "Old Stone House", now a national register historic building in Rowan County, North Carolina. Sarah and Addison later had two more children, Addison Moses Wiseman and William Wiseman. After Addison's death in 1864, Sarah later remarried Reuben Jasper Halton of Rowan County had several children with him, but only two survived into adulthood.

When General Joseph E. Johnston assumed command of the Confederate Army of the Potomac in May 1862, he quickly realized that holding the Yorktown - Warwick line was no longer practical. Largely due to the continued massive Federal bombardment, the siege of Yorktown resulted in a massive Confederate withdrawal towards Richmond. Confederates quietly withdrew from their positions on the Yorktown lines during the night of 3 May and began their march up the peninsula. This was good timing, as Federal commander General McClellan later reported he planned to open fire with his heavy artillery on 6 May. When the Confederates withdrew, Brig. Gen. D.H. Hill's division was ordered to remain in the trenches to provide a cover fire to mask their retreat throughout the night, and then withdraw just before dawn. It was raining heavily, and the muddy roads bogged down hundreds of wagons, making the movement arduous and slow. The 4th NCST held its picket line until the rest of the division had left the lines as ordered, and then slowly withdrew toward Richmond. They caught up with Hill's division late on the afternoon of 4 May near Williamsburg and camped there for the night.

On 5 May Gen. Joseph Hooker and Gen. William F. Smith's Federal forces attacked Gen. James Longstreet's division in the center of the Confederate line at the small hamlet of Williamsburg, a few miles north of Yorktown. Here, the Rowan Rifles witnessed their first real infantry engagement of the war; but although Brig. Gen. Joseph E. Johnston decided to halt and make a stand at Williamsburg, this engagement was brief and of mild consequence to the 4th NCST. and Company K was described as only "...held in readiness but did not join the battle of Williamsburg" by Captain McNeely.[8] When Longstreet's center began to deteriorate late in the fight, Brig. Gen. D.H. Hill launched a counterattack, but the 4th NCST was only held in reserve, all sources reviewed indicate the 4th NCST never fired a shot at Williamsburg. Hill's counterattack was a rather piecemeal affair; fighting became more sporadic and confusing until nightfall brought the action to an end. A bitter, freezing rain ensued, further complicating the retreat from Williamsburg toward Richmond. Maj. Bryan Grimes described the regiment's condition on the evening of 5 May as "...one of the most disagreeable of my Army experience, a heavy, penetrating mist, nearly freezing the men to the bone, all would huddle together for the natural warmth of their bodies, and when my horse became the centre for the regiment, around which they collected, the first few attracted by the animal heat from the horse's body, until they formed a complete mass of men."[9]

Grimes further wrote that the 4th NCST literally waded in knee-deep mud and each man received an ear of hard corn for his supper that night. Pvt. Arthur Evans, Company E, "The Wilson Light

Infantry" wrote to his wife Rebecca on 11 May also commenting on both the bitter rainstorm that occurred on their retreat from Williamsburg, as well as the regiment's orders to drop their heavy knapsacks, "At Williamsburg comnsed on Sunday we campt their at night Monday morning we left very Early we travel about three miles when we got orders to march Back they were fighting hard at Williamsburg We turn back and came on at Doublequick three miles through the mud from half leg to nee deep to the Burg  If you could of bin to see us when we got the word to unsling napsasks you would bin suppres the pile  as some carry apples from the groves  when it is shuck we run through the turn to the field of battle we continued their until night  their was but no man hurt in our company…We stood on line of battle all night after the fight was over in mud and water…"[10]

After the exhausting march toward the Chickahominy River, the 4th NCST went into camp on 13 May near the river. The land was swampy, and troops were beginning to realize that General Johnston had retreated from Yorktown within a few miles of Richmond without a major engagement or other damage to the enemy. Pvt. Joseph F. Gibson, Company C, 4th NCST wrote to his brother John Gibson of Catawba County on 23 May and described their march to Richmond in the heavy rains two weeks earlier. Fatigued, cold and wet, Gibson had been quite sick for four or five days, but continued to march. He too was frustrated with the stop and starting of the large force, with no clear objective to the common soldier. He wrote, "…We had a very heavy march we marched about 60 miles we march from Yorktown to Richmond …This marching through the mud there is no fun in it certain and sure. We haven't any tents and our blankets is all the shelter now. I lost all my close and was not able to carry my napsack and it was put in the wagon and the roads was so muddy that they had to throw the napsacks out."[11]

On 21 May ye another driving rainstorm hampered McClellan's troops as they began their attempt to cross onto the south side of the Chickahominy River. Sgt. Ashbel Fraley and his comrades in Company A spent most of 22 May performing drill in ankle-deep mud. He was not pleased, and penned several humorous anecdotes hallmarked by his blithe and sarcastic style of capturing his observations of army life. Fraley indicated that at least some of the soldiers had recovered their cumbersome knapsacks, much to his chagrin, as he quipped on 29 May 1862, "By some fool command we carry our knapsacks with us -- it is seldom that a sensible order comes round. Yet one did last night, - That was to leave our knapsacks in Camp and go unencumbered. But the discovery was made (unfortunately) that it was sensible, and revoked this morning."[12] As tensions mounted around Richmond, the 4th NCST continued to maintain regular discipline and camp duties such as hours of daily drill. Fraley was furious with it all, and penned an embittered diary entry of daily life in the camps around Richmond on 22 May 1862:

"Brigade Drill.  Regular humbug!  Intolerable nuisance. It's General uses.

(1)  To keep the men from enjoying a little rest, which they so much need.
(2)  To take out the sick men that the surgeon alway refuses to excuse from duty (tho' they are scarcely able to walk) that our Cols & General's may have the gratification of seeing them faint and fall in the boiling sun.
(3)  To make the men careless in drill that the officers may have the pleasure of speaking to them as to Negros.
(4)  To exasperate the men beyond the endurance of patience, that they may curse and swear so the Devil will reap the greater harvest in eternity.

(5)  That the General. and his aides may show their uniform suits; and (tho' they know it not) their ignorance, O' was some power the gift to gi' us, To see oursel' as others see us; It was from many a blunder free us, And foolish notion."

This day will also be ever memorable on account of Gen. Hill's humane order to shoot southern men for losing their guns and accoutrements, and buck them for straggling. Thus they treat the southern army.[13]

President Jefferson Davis was very concerned about the army, and rode out to see the vanguard approach during the latter part of their retreat from Yorktown to a spot on the Chickahominy Bridge just below Richmond. Although the exact date is not known, Pvt. Daniel Carpenter, Company C, 4th NCST had opportunity to meet President Davis on the bridge. His friends, James .C. Steele and T.M.C. Davidson of the 4th NCST left an anecdotal account of Carpenter's meeting, "President Davis asked him many questions about his fare, etc., in the Army and asked him what state he was from. Dan told him he was from North Carolina and asked him what state he was from and he said from Mississippi."[14] By the end of the May, Davis' hopes were heightened as McClellan's Army was divided into two unequal segments by the flooded Chickahominy River. Maj. Gen. Joseph Johnston had a chance to systematically destroy the Army of the Potomac, and soon found opportunity at the small and unsuspecting village of Seven Pines just a few miles east of Richmond. There, Company K would have its first taste of a general engagement, and see the brutal effects of their weaponry. Known in army parlance as "seeing the elephant", the coming fight would indelibly mark their conscience that no longer was war a thing to be envied, or gloried in, as the young soldiers were well on their way to becoming hardened campaign veterans with an emptiness from which many would never recover.

### Seven Pines "...A victory, but dearly bought."

On 31 May 1862, one of the most intense single actions of the entire War was fought at the small village known as Seven Pines (called "Fair Oaks" by many Northerners, named after a small railroad depot located nearby). The 4th NCST was then assigned to the brigade of Gen. Winfield Featherston, along with the 49th Virginia, 27th and 28th Georgia Regiments. They were reassigned to Maj. Gen. D.H. Hill's Division, in Longstreet's Corps at Seven Pines, with Maj. Bryan Grimes commanding the regiment. The latter changes occurred because Featherston had become ill a few days before; and Col. George B. Anderson, who then commanded the 4th NCST, was placed in command of Featherston's brigade just before Seven Pines. Hill was well-known for his strict discipline and sharp battlefield tactics, and he also kept a close eye on his men's moral and physical condition. On the evening of Friday 30 May, violent thunderstorms raked the area, once again raising the Chickahominy River into wildly rushing muddy waters. McClellan's army was forced to separate although two Federal corps managed to establish positions fortified with earthworks and *abatis* (sharpened tree limbs stuck in the ground) near the village of Seven Pines. The works extended roughly one mile northeast toward Fair Oaks as well.

Maj. Gen. Joe Johnston had initially planned for D.H. Hill's division to spearhead the attack along the Williamsburg Road which divided Hill's divisional front. Brig. Gen. Samuel Garland's brigade was deployed on the left side of the road and in front. They were supported by Featherston's (Anderson's) brigade about one-quarter mile in its rear. On Hill's right was a thirty-three year old Alabamian, Brig. Gen. Robert Rodes, whose brigade formed the right wing. Johnston's intentions were to begin the fight early in the morning of 31 May. As the battle opened, the 4th NCST simply waited; Hill's division stood on arms from 8 A.M. until nearly 1 P.M. without firing a shot. Anderson had his regiments aligned as follows, from left to right: 27th, 28th Georgia (left wing) and the 49thVirginia and 4th NCST (left wing), respectively. Anderson's brigade was held in the rear on Hill's left originally, but when the fighting came, the 4th NCST had moved in front of even other regiments in Anderson's brigade. Thus, Grimes men were slightly ahead of the general advance with both flanks exposed when Hill ordered his division forward around 1:30 P.M. His men quickly moved through the woods as artillery began to boom and rounds exploded around them. Making their way through heavy foliage, Grimes and other officers barked commands to keep their alignment as shells exploded in their midst tearing off limbs and grinding into the ground.

As the ranks moved forward over the boggy ground, the terrain was difficult, wet, and covered with thick growths of trees. Recent rains had left large puddles and in some places, waist-deep water, according to both Grimes and Capt. E.A. Osborne of Company H. In spite of obstacles, the 4th NCST was the first regiment from Hill's division to "see the elephant" (face hostile fire), and the regiment made its first full scale advance as a "splendid picture of manhood."[15] Soon the 4th NCST advanced too far ahead of the supporting brigade on the right, which was too slow coming up, and Grime's men found themselves in an open area within range of Federal artillery and musket fire, and the regiment began taking heavy casualties. While waiting for supporting brigades to move up, Grimes managed to briefly stop the regiment inside a small body of woods to give them time to realign. The tension was nearly unbearable as men nervously leaned forward in anticipation of getting outside of the incoming artillery rounds while other companies hastily dressed their ranks for the coming advance toward the Federal earth works, held by Brig.Gen. Silas Casey's Division consisted of green, untested troops.

Casey's Division was in Maj. Gen. Erasmus D. Keys IV Corps, Army of the Potomac. Brig. Gen. Henry M. Naglee commanded Casey's First Brigade of infantry, including the 52d and 104th Pennsylvania regiments, 56th and 100th New York, and the 11th Maine Volunteer Infantry. His second infantry brigade was commanded by Brig. Gen. Henry Wessells who had the 85th, 101st, and 103d Pennsylvania and the 95th New York regiments. Casey's Third Infantry Brigade was led by Brig. Gen. Innis N. Palmer, who commanded the 81st, 85th, 91st, and 98th New York regiments. Casey's artillery was commanded by a regular army officer, Col. Guilford D. Bailey, who had present batteries A and H of the 1st New York Light Artillery, 7th and 8th New York Independent Light Artillery, none of whom had any combat experience, but would be veterans after the fight they were experiencing on that day. Grimes quickly ordered his men forward again; the regiment quickly emerged from the woods at the quick-step roughly one-half mile from the federal artillery redoubts and earthworks where heavy cannon and musketry opened up on them. Shells plowed up the ground all around.

As Grimes men stepped outside this small wood line, they quickly found the edges lined with hundreds of felled and sharpened trees, known as *abatis*. Abatis were felled trees with branches shaved one to three feet or more and sharpened to delay advancing infantry as much as possible. The barriers successfully impaired Grimes' advance to the Federal earthworks, where the 4th NCST eventually found the center of Casey's line laden with artillery redoubts flanked on both wings by the 101st and 85th Pennsylvania and the 81st and 85th New York Infantry regiments, who were well concealed and protected by another hundred yards of *abatis*. Pvt. James Bowers of Company K was the original regimental color bearer at Seven Pines and was ironically both the first man to volunteer for the duration of the war and the first color bearer killed. He died in the initial assault "with the Regimental Colors in his hands." His last request was to inform his adopted father, John Brunner, that he died "...with my face to the enemy." Brunner had raised Bowers and his sister from a very young age, and was terribly affected by the loss evidenced by numerous epitaphs and editorial reflections afterward. According to the nineteenth-century military mindset, dying with the unit's colors in one's hands was considered the highest attainable honor on the field of battle.[16]

As Grimes men stepped from the small woodlot and worked their way through the *abatis*, they came under more intense fire, and Grimes soon realized that the field closest to the redoubts contained even more obstacles, and that the muddy terrain was having a significant effect on his men's ability to maneuver. Another federal battery hidden in the woods on their left began to pour enfilade fire into them (from the side), and Grimes identified a small ditch nearby as a potential shelter area. He ordered the regiment to move at the right oblique toward the ditch line to take cover. Once inside the ditch, the regiment remained there for some time under heavy artillery fire. Colonel Anderson wrote later that he observed the 4th NCST "under fire, but completely exhausted and very badly cut to pieces." Soon, Grimes ordered them forward again, only to return to the ditches when they failed to gain the Federal works.[17] Pvt. Sumpter A. Hoover from Company C summarized events he recalled from the time the North Carolinians initially stepped out from the wood line and saw their enemy in direct front, "...there we met the Yankee's behind their breastworks - we had to charge their batteries through a piece of cut down forest, which was cut and thrown in every direction. The limbs cut off from two to four feet from body of trees in order to keep us from advancing rapidly, so they would have a better chance to cut us down, but we got through that thicket and got their battery but lost lots of good men lay on battlefield all that night."[18]

By the third assault, two color bearers had been killed, and another artillery battery had opened on the brigades' left wing, raking them with enfilade fire. Along with the abatis and rough terrain, Grimes had little opportunity to fire en masse' into the Federal lines. The persistent constant whizzing of mini balls and explosions while entangled simply prevented formation firing. The large number men knocked down by grape and canister rounds from the artillery fire were appalling, but eventually the other two Georgia regiments and the Virginians in Anderson's (formerly Featherston's) brigade managed to make their way to the tree lines behind the ditch where the 4th NCST had taken cover. But they were not aligned on Grimes' left flank when he ordered the Tar Heels forward again, although Grimes managed to finally lead the regiment in its first experience of returning mass (volley) fire on the Federals in the next assault. Capt. E.A. Osborne said they "Opened fire upon the enemy with such deadly effect as the cause a momentary lull in the storm of deadly missiles that were assailing us, but again the enemy renewed his fire with redoubled fury." The Volley shocked but failed to overwhelm the Federals, and the Tar Heels had to retreat back to the ditch to regroup for another attack.[19]

The 4th NCST made several attempts before getting close enough to breach the Federal lines. Each time they charged, Major Grimes, who was commanding the regiment, was observed "in the thickest of the fight." After a brief respite in the ditches, Grimes managed to get the regiment moving forward again, only this time their sister Georgia and Virginia regiments moved in concert on his left flank. As the 4th NCST steadily advanced under fire, they encountered a small rail fence where they briefly halted to await more support on their right where the artillery was taking a heavy toll. Unfortunately, more support on the right or extreme left wing never came, and as their position was continually exposed, Capt. E. A. Osborne explained "It was evident that the regiment could not remain there without being utterly destroyed."[20] Osborne had enough, and decided to persuade Grimes, who seemed to be sitting on his horse pondering their situation, to charge again due to their vulnerable position, which was still pounded by artillery. Osborne reasoned to himself that while charging again was dangerous, it had to be better than sitting still under heavy fire, and approached Grimes and insisted that he order a charge. He found Major Grimes "sitting calmly on his iron-gray horse, with one leg thrown over the saddle bow, as afterwards so often seen on the battlefield." Their position proved to be no safer than the former wood lines at that point, as Federal artillery had attained site on their position and were tossing heavy shell and rifled musketry causing even more casualties.

Osborne was not totally disdained with Grimes however, as he later opined that Grimes then appeared as an "angel of war." Other studies of the battle at Seven Pines have discussed this event; one contrasting opinion suggested that Grimes was probably wondering just what to do next at this point.[21] Before the war, Bryan Grimes was a wealthy planter rather than a professional soldier, and although would later rise to become the last major general in the Army of Northern Virginia in 1865, he was anything but a seasoned officer at this time, truly a neophyte in terms of both general military and combat experience. Seven Pines was his first real test in battle and sitting on his horse thinking may well have been as much as he could do at that moment –certainly the gallantry he mustered to lead the former charges had not been successful. He remained pensive until Captain Osborne seized his leg and implored over the din, "Major, we can't stand this! Let us charge the works!" His awareness was suddenly shifted back to the matter at hand. Grimes quickly conceded and yelled "Charge them! Charge them!"[22]

Grimes again led his North Carolinians in another attack, which this time came within roughly one hundred yards of the Federal redoubt, only to stall when Grimes' horse was shot out from under him, sending him tumbling to the ground. The horse's head was torn off by a Federal artillery projectile. Grimes noted in his official report that, "The regiment seeing me fall, supposed killed for wounded, and began to falter and waiver, I waived my sword and shouted 'Forward! Forward!'and the regiment moved forward…Some of the men came to my assistance and pulled the horse off…"[23] Grimes was not the only one to lose a horse out from under him. Sgt. R.A. Best of Company D, 4th NCST was a courier on Col. George Anderson's staff during the battle, and had two horses shot out from under him but reportedly managed to keep his composure and acted well. Grimes watched while the attack swept past him until it was thwarted roughly thirty or forty yards from the redoubt. Realizing their plight, Grimes ordered his regiment to fall back toward the ditch midway between the redoubt and *abatis* entangled wood line which the previously passed through.

As the regiment retired it kept reasonably good order until their third color bearer became confused and in spite of Grimes orders fell back to wooded areas some 250 yards the initial lines of *abatis*. As men already in the ditches supposed they were to retreat even further when they saw their flag moving in reverse direction, they followed suit to the rear. When Grimes caught up with them, he quickly ordered the regiment to halt, but they were then approximately 450 yards from the Federal lines. Although a bit disoriented from his fall, Grimes hastily reorganized his ranks, and took a brief account of the state of his regiment. He observed the gruesome effects of their previous assaults, "…in evidence of the severity of the fire of the enemy while in front of the battery 46 of my men were found killed within an area of one acre."[24] Grimes was likely still feeling the effects of his fall minutes later, as he remained in the rear during their next assault which ironically came closer to breaching Federal lines than any previous attacks that morning.

Accounts vary, but eyewitnesses indicate their next assault came within 20-40 yards of the redoubt before being repulsed in this attack, as close range Federal canister and musket fire intensified until the regiment was unable to advance further. Another problem was that although the Georgia and Virginia regiments had come up before, they were not properly aligned with the 4th NCST, who remained unsupported on both flanks when Grimes realized "we were 200 yards in advance of any other regiment."[25] Once more, the fire remained too strong and Grimes' men retreated, but this time again stopped in their former haven, the ditch some 200 yards from the Federal earthworks. The North Carolinians had become psychologically shaken and nearly physically exhausted by this time and Grimes allowed them a brief respite. But while taking cover in the ditches, Grimes' men witnessed a Confederate battery unlimber on their left and begin to fire into the Federal lines, greatly bolstering their courage. Grimes then prepared his men for what would be their final and only successful assault on the Federal lines of the day. Moments later, exhausted but determined to take the works, 4th NCST burst out of the ditch and made its last and most furious assault of the day. Capt. E.A. Osborne relayed that "…we rushed with such impetuosity and determination that the enemy abandoned everything and retired."[26]

As they approached the edges of the federal redoubt, Grimes saw his third color bearer killed, and he and Capt. Absalom K. Simonton of Company A, the Iredell Blues, raced to raise it once again. Simonton was killed instantly just seconds after giving Grimes the colors, and young 2d Lieutenant R.D. Funkhouser of the 49th Virginia regiment observed Grimes picking up the colors as the third color bearer fell. The lieutenant implored the major to give him the flag instead. Grimes refused and reportedly stated, "Lieutenant, your life is worth as much as mine."[27] Grimes later described the incident when his third color bearer was killed, "After allowing my men time to recover from their fatigue, just then I saw my third color-bearer shot down. Captain Simonton and myself rushed to raise the colors. Captain Simonton reaching them first, placed them in my hands, raising them aloft, calling upon my men to rally around their standard. It was done with alacrity, and together with    several other regiments, we reached the redoubt, the enemy fleeing."[28]

MAP Of 4th NCST Movements at Seven Pines 31 May 1861

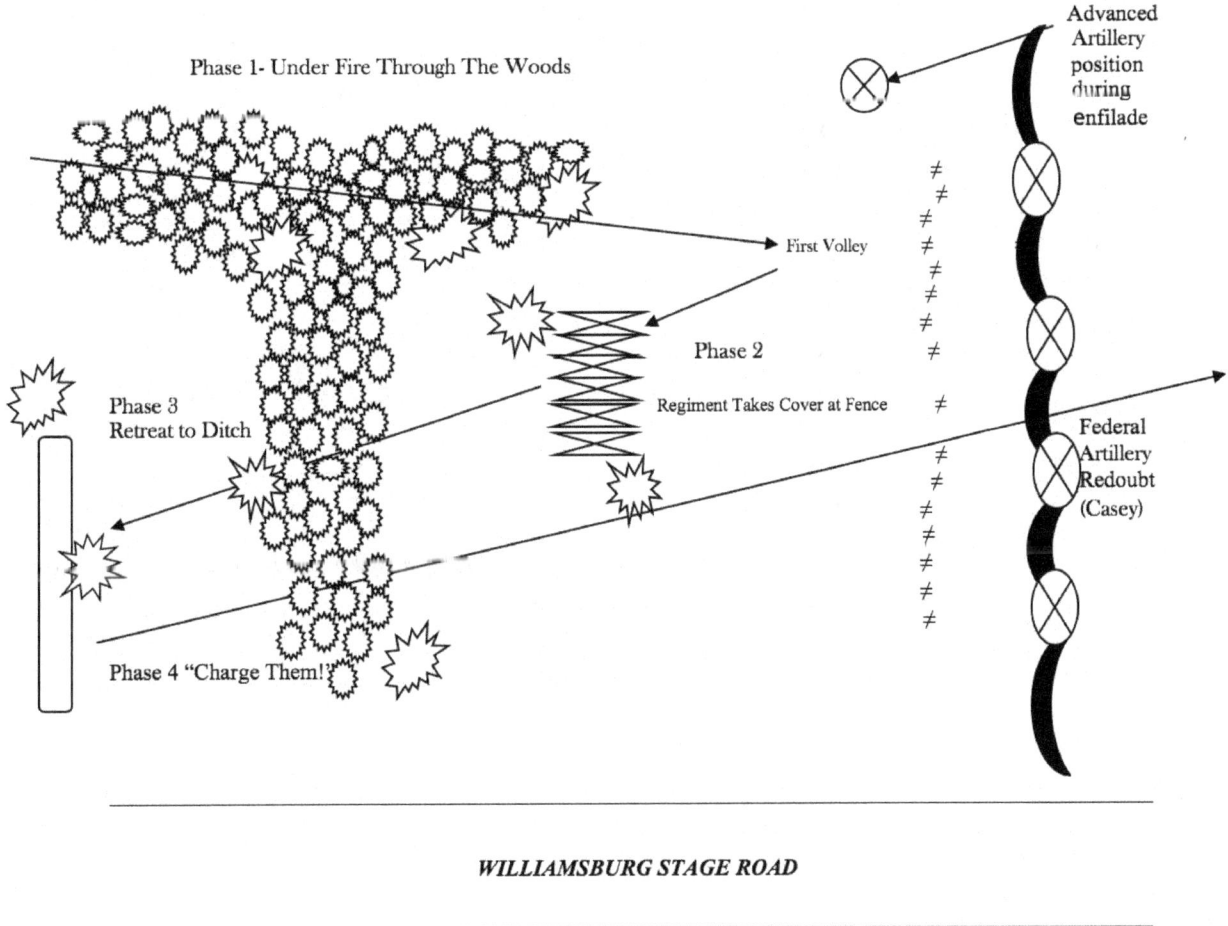

North

Advanced
Artillery
position
during
enfilade

Phase 1- Under Fire Through The Woods

First Volley

Phase 2

Phase 3
Retreat to Ditch

Regiment Takes Cover at Fence

Federal
Artillery
Redoubt
(Casey)

Phase 4 "Charge Them!"

WILLIAMSBURG STAGE ROAD

**KEY:**

≠          ⊗          ✹          ⋈          ✺

**Abatis    Artillery  Explosions   Fence    Woods**

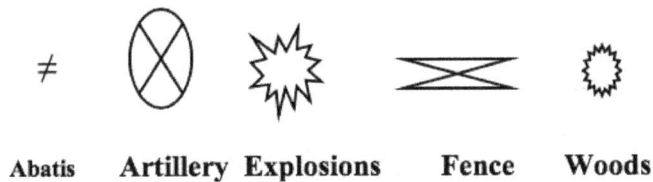

Map is not to Scale. Distance from Stage Road to 4th NCST position roughly a quarter mile. Distance between fence and redoubt was estimated to be over 200 yards. Distance from fence to ditch was estimated to be over 500 yards to the rear of the tree line. This map may not be copied or duplicated in any form without express written consent by the author.

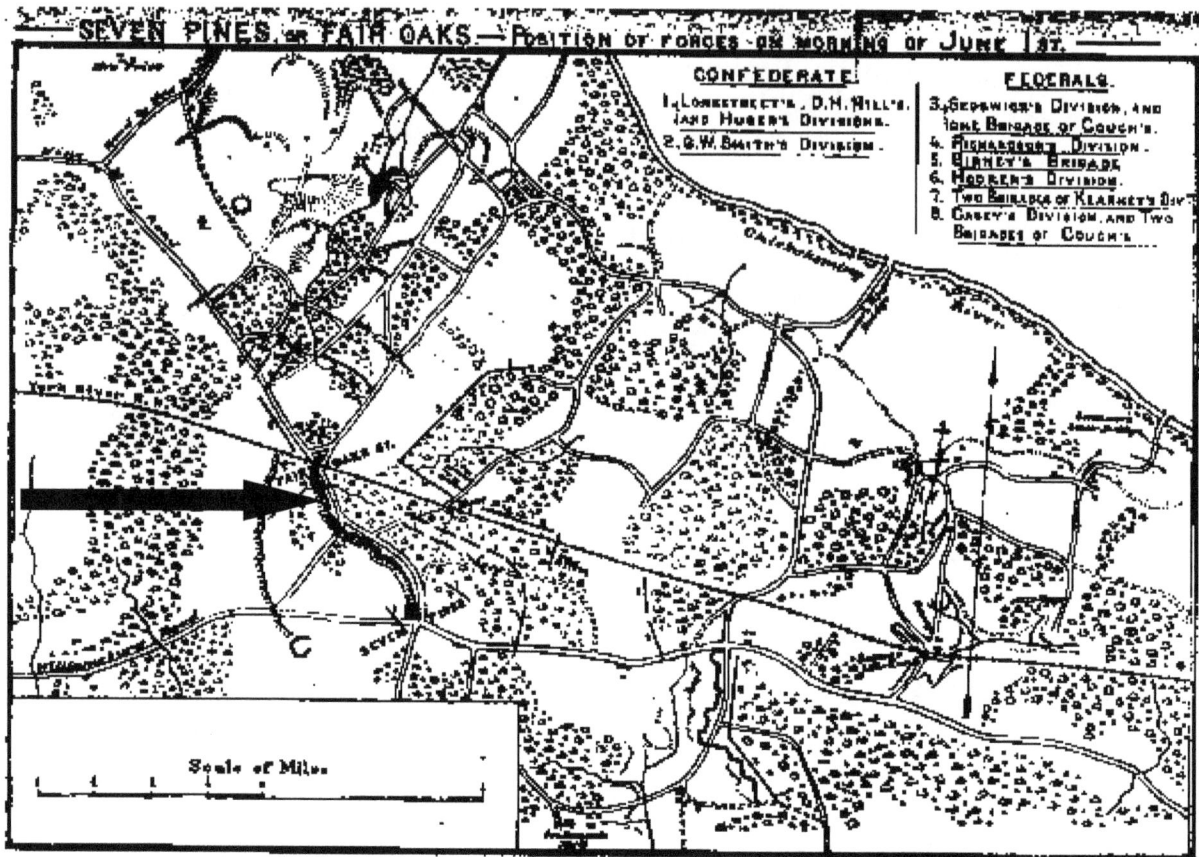

Source: The Battle of Seven Pines May 31-June 1, 1862. G.W. Smith, Confederate War Papers. 1884. The large black arrow shows the general path of the 4th NCST and is superimposed on the original.
Map is public domain.

Cpl. B.B. "Bob" Ross of Company I recorded his wounding during the final advance in his diary; he managed to survive, but was in a great deal of pain afterward and stated, "…I was within twenty yards of the breastworks when I was struck in my left breast. I had on my overcoat with twenty rounds of cartridges in my left breast-pocket. The ball went through all of these, into my uniform coat - pocket, and made holes through about 20 letters in my coat, several holes in my handkerchief in that pocket and lodged in there. When I regained consciousness, I felt that death would claim me in a few minutes, for I was sure the ball had gone through me. Our company was ordered to fall back, but I remained where I was to die. But after seeing the havock played in our regiment when they did fall back as many killed as when going forward, for the Yankees kept pouring it into them…While lying there, I summed up courage to examine my wound, and found that the ball, which I thought had gone through my side, had lodged in my pocket. My side was badly bruised but I felt relief to find the bullet, and although I was suffering dreadfully, I went into camp."[29]

Lest the opinion form that Federal resistance during the last charge was somehow less stubborn and lethal, note that Grimes also said the artillery fire was so intense during that final attack that it was essentially "…a fearful storm of shot, shell, grape and canister tore through the trees, plowing up the ground of every side and cutting down the branches and saplings around us." Yet even with heavy defenses, and an experienced regular artillery officer in command of the Federal batteries, his calm demeanor could not steel the Federal gunners when they witnessed the onslaught of North Carolinians storming the center redoubt, killing, wounding and capturing their cohorts, and they simply ran. Several officers including 1st Lieutenant W.C. Coughenhour of Company K were wounded, and during the second assault Capt. E.A. Osborne observed the ground was already "literally covered" with dead and wounded of the 4th NCST attesting to the deadly struggle in this otherwise serene Virginia countryside. By the end of the day, the entire color guard was killed or wounded and the flag was shot "32 times" according to Grimes. Pvt. James Carter of Company C, wrote to his father on 4 June 1862 suggesting that not three as suggested by Major Grimes, but four color bearers shot down at Seven Pines, "Our flag was shot down four time but was picked up and carried in the Yankey batery waving though the staf was broken by a bum shel and the flag shot to pieces."[30]

After the battle, John Stikeleather of Company A approached Bryan Grimes and volunteered to bear the regimental colors after seeing his friend Capt. Simonton die carrying them.[31] Stikeleather wrote some years after the war that he was also motivated by an incident occurring just as the battle was pitching at Seven Pines. Stikeleather indicated while he was in ranks moving toward the battle field that morning, and passed a Georgia soldier whom he estimated to be about sixteen years old, who was only slightly wounded in the arm and yet "boo-hooing right out" while walking to the rear. Someone asked how the battle was going, and in between sobs, Stikeleather heard him say "They are whipping us like hell" and then decided that the response was so "ludicrous" he would never allow himself to lose his fortitude in such manner.[32] He kept his promise to Grimes to bear the colors with…credit to himself and the regiment so long as strength and life lasted" and he carried the regimental colors for the remainder of the war.

Seven Pines was the first real test of Company K and it lost several killed and wounded. Captain McNeely's post-war pension application testified to the human damage of this fierce battle, although there are discrepancies in testimonial reports and data found within the most recent muster roll prior to the battle on 28 April 1862. McNeely's witnesses stated "…that his regiment stood the brunt of the battle of Seven Pines, that his company went into that engagement with 64 privates, and 3 Lts, that he and 3 Lts together with 27 privates were wounded and 10 privates killed."[33] Although anecdotal accounts of the 4th NCST strength before the battle of Seven Pines vary between 540 and 678 available men, 369 casualties are identified in Grimes' official report.[34] He later indicated that sadly, he had but fifty-four men answer roll call along the Williamsburg road late that evening.[35] The 4th NCST suffered a sixty-eight percent casualty rate at Seven Pines, and would never fully recover its former numerical strength at any point in the war afterward. Recall that the 28 April 1862 muster roll indicated Company K had eighty-eight men aggregate, with forty-six privates, four sergeants, four corporals, three officers and one musician for perspective on the impact of this fierce battle, which strangely has received little if any attention from modern historians.

Records of Seven Pines casualties show that Company K lost ten men killed in action (27 percent), three mortally wounded (one percent), and seventeen were wounded (forty six percent). Of those wounded, seven (nineteen percent) were later discharged or removed to the Invalid Corps. Appendix F summarizes wound types in Company K calculated from service files, muster rolls and anecdotal correspondence, and notes a significant trend of wounds received below the waist (twenty nine percent) and extremities (hands, feet and fingers-twenty two percent) in this battle. This may have been due to the heavy use of artillery which contained canister rounds, i.e. shotgun like projectile blasts of multiple small round balls which tended to travel at lower trajectories than larger rounds. The *Carolina Watchman* gave the following account of the Rowan Rifles' engagement at the Battle of Seven Pines just two days earlier with casualties on 2 June 1862:

> List of killed and wounded, Captain McNeely's company, 4th N.C. at Richmond. Wounded. Lt Coughenhour, slightly in the head, and many, many more. Ten killed, including Pvt Bowers, 31 wounded including Paul Heiling and James W. Neely.

Typically after large battles in the Civil War, only fragmented information was available at home for weeks and sometimes months afterward. The initial account printed by the *Carolina Watchman* was bolstered on 16 June 1862 after more grim statistics had trickled back to Salisbury:

> "List of killed and wounded of Company K, 4th N.C. Regiment.

> Regimental officers: 12, privates 65 killed, 37 officers and 245 privates wounded." "Those in Company K, 4th N.C., who distinguished themselves at battle of Seven Pines were: Sgt M.L. Bean, Privates W.A.M.S.F.., W.R. Josey, W.D.C. Peeler, W.A. Glover, A.C. Carter, S. Solomon, A.W. Miller."

Not only did the battle cause many casualties which altered the composition of Company K, but there were also several important changes in rank and leadership occurring as a result of this battle. On a larger scale, Maj. Gen. Joseph Johnston was wounded by both a bullet and an artillery fragment that knocked him from his horse and required roughly six months convalescence to heal before he could return to command. In the interim, President Jefferson Davis briefly placed Maj. Gen. Gustavas Smith in command who quickly asked to be removed on 1 June when he realized he was not fit for the duty. Davis then appointed Gen. Robert E. Lee in command later that afternoon, whose first action was to order a general withdrawal of Confederate forces back to their original position after Smith's attempt to re-engage hostilities in the area along their lines between the railroad and the Williamsburg Road had failed miserably on 1 June.[36]

At the regimental level, there were also changes in command and rank order. Bryan Grimes received news of his promotion to lieutenant colonel while still on the battlefield on the evening of 31 May, although the commission was dated 1 May 1862.[37] In spite of a head wound, 1 Lt. William C. Coughenhour was promoted to captain on 31 May after Capt. McNeely resigned. McNeely was literally ordered to return home on account of a medical problem reported as "phthisis pulmonalis and single reducible hernia" a type of respiratory illness from which he had suffered for several months. McNeely's resignation was officially accepted on 22 June 1862. He had requested to stay in the army and share his experiences with raw recruits, so he was re-assigned to light duty at Camp Stokes, a camp of instruction for conscripts (draftees) held near Greensboro, where he served until March 1865.[38] 24-year old First Sergeant Addison N. Wiseman was slightly wounded at Seven Pines, but continued to serve and was later appointed a second lieutenant on 26 June 1862 during the battle at Gaines Mill.[39]

On the evening of 31 May following cessation of fighting, forty-six men killed in front of the Federal redoubt were moved to an unrecorded location on the Williamsburg Road along with twenty-four others from the regiment killed elsewhere in the battle for burial. Sgt. Ashbel Fraley allowed an uncharacteristic glimpse of his compassion when he recorded a stirring event conducted by Lt. Col. Bryan Grimes several weeks after the battle. Grimes had the seventy-two bodies removed, but did not have time to give them due military honors; when the regiment passed through the battle field area at Seven Pines on 2 July 1862 he halted the regiment, which was marching right in front, and gave the command, "On the right by file into line—march!" while Fraley was inwardly cursing him for the awkward placement of regimental guide markers during the evolution, unknowing as to what Grimes was planning.

Fraley left a touching description of the next few minutes events, as he wrote, "But my unpleasant feelings toward him were suddenly stopped and changed to the warmest and most solemn affection, by a very unexpected and solemn scene. We were then fronting to the grave of the killed from our regiment on the 31st of May, 74 all buried together. The Col. commanded, 'Present arms.' Then taking off his hat he said, "Fellow soldiers! There is no more fitting place to render thanks to almighty God we have been spared to avenge their death's than by the graves of those who fell by our sides fighting so gallantly for their country's rights. Let each one silently within his own heart return thanks to God that we have been permitted to live, to again see the last solemn resting place of our companions and friends." A solemn peace ensued. The Col like the remainder of the regiment was not a religious man; but it made the scene more affecting. 'Shoulder Arms' and 'Left Face' was commanded and we proceeded toward Richmond. Went into camp two miles from the city."[40]

As in all wars, sometimes the casualties were not only physical, but as Pvt. Walter Battle revealed, the experience of watching his brother George die on the battlefield at Seven Pines could also leave deeply imbedded psychological scars. He told his mother in a letter written two weeks later that "...In fact I don't believe I am the same thing I was two weeks ago, at least I don't think as I used to and things don't seem as they did. I don't believe I will ever get over the death of George. The more I think of him the more it affects me, and unless I am in some battle and excitement I am eternally thinking of the last moments of his life. How he must have suffered, if he was conscious of it. I shall never forget it."[41] Ashbel Fraley left the most fitting epilogue to the battle of Seven Pines, all the while complaining that in spite of their heavy losses and grief at the loss of so many comrades, the regiment had returned to the usual camp rigors of daily drilling and picket duties in the weeks following the battle of Seven Pines. Fraley, who referred to Seven Pines as a "...victory, but dearly bought" also growled about how privates were then sneering at their new officers only recently promoted on the battlefield, many of whom had no experience in command as officers. But he again reveals his humanity in the following epitaph, "But blame not the 4th N.C. once the pride of the state. Once the praise of all. 'Tis a sad story that tells what reduced it to this. It is written in blood, and may be read on the battlefield of Seven Pines, and those of the 26th and 27th June - a story that has made bleed harder hearts than mine. Then; - be kind to the sad relic of the 4th N.C."[42]

As in all large engagements, ambiguity surrounded early casualty reports. However in several cases at Seven Pines, even official records later contradicted themselves. For example, Pvt. Benjamin Lanier, age 21 years, was supposedly killed at Seven Pines according to the North Carolina Roll of Honor, which derived its' information from Company K Muster Rolls. Yet, Lanier survived as he appears on later muster rolls and also turned up in the 1880 census as a resident of Rowan County at age 40 years, unmarried and employed as a distiller.[43] Another private, identified as Alfred A. Lowrence in Company K muster rolls, was supposedly killed at Seven Pines, and his name is even found on later muster rolls as present through 1864. But Lowrence transferred into Company B of the 42d NCT as a second Lieutenant in March 1862, although was identified as "James M. Lawrence" who transferred from Company K, 4th NCST. Possibly his name was misspelled on the muster rolls, but clearly one must interpret casualty reports with caution.[44]

Pvt. Robert Kyle was promoted to corporal before the 31 May 1862 battle of Seven Pines, where he was killed. Capt. McNeely was close to Kyle's family, as evidenced by a letter written to her after Kyle's death on 18 June 1862. McNeely eulogized, "I can only say that your Son Robert died in a good cause, and while charging nobly – the Enemy batteries in his front. You lose a good son, I a friend, and the country as noble a soldier as ever marched to the defence of his country...I did not see any of our dead being buried that night at the foot of the batteries which we fought for and won. I think he was killed instantly; he made no requests at any time before his going into the fight. I found on his person two dagerotypes, one of yourself, and one of his younger brothers which I send by mail. He had nothing else having lost everything in our rapid march but some old clothing which is not worth possessing...Robert was loved by all his companions, he was faithful in his discharge of his duties, never being sick or out of place, he was a particular favorite with all his officers." His father wrote to the paymaster, A.W. Taylor, on 29 August 1862 from Lynchburg, Virginia, requesting that he settle the matter of pay and uniform allowance due, but there was no evidence that his father ever received it.[45]

you with any information
that I have omitted don't hesitate
to write — with much respect
I am Madam

Your very Obt Servt
F. M. Y. McNeely.

Salisbury N.C. June 18th 1862

Mrs. Kyle—

Madam— Your letter
of the 10th was received this morning
having been delayed by going to
Richmond— I left Richmond on
the 8th on account of my health
which has been very delicate for
several months In answer
to your inquiries I can only
say that Your Son Roth died
in a good cause and while charging
nobly the enemy's batteries lost
his life upon three a good son
& a friend and his Country
as noble a soldier as ever risked
to the defence of his Country—

Source: Compiled Service Records of Capt. F.M.Y. McNeely

111

The following tables show casualty figures in both Company K and in the 4th NCST at Seven Pines. These data are a sad testament to the desperate charges the young regiment made capturing the Federal earthworks but it is not known in which phases of the battle that the majority of casualties occurred.

### *Co. K Casualties at the Battle of Seven Pines 31 May 1862*

37 Aggregate, 87 Men present for Duty as of 30 April 1862 Co. K Muster Roll, 43% Casualties

Table 1

Aggregate Company Losses

|  | No. | Percent |
|---|---|---|
| KIA | 10 | 27 |
| Mortally Wounded | 3 | 1 |
| Wounded Returned Duty | 17 | 46 |
| Wounded Discharged/Invalid Corps | 7 | 19 |

Table 2

| Wound Type | No. | Percent | |
|---|---|---|---|
| Shoulder | 8 | 17 | |
| Knee-Thigh-Feet | 15 | 29 | (3 amputations) |
| Head-Face-Eye | 7 | 12 | (2 eyes lost) |
| Arm/Hand/Finger | 10 | 22 | (5 fingers lost) |
| Chest / Side | 6 | 13 | |

Sources: Company K Muster Rolls, 30 June 1862, CSR, 4th NCST.

Note: Some men received more than one wound.

# 4thNCST Casualties at the Battle of Seven Pines, 31 May 1862

Table 3

Killed in Action

| Captains | 1st Lt | 2d Lt | Sgt | Cpl. | Pvt. | Aggregate |
|----------|--------|-------|-----|------|------|-----------|
| 2 | 1 | - | 4 | 6 | 64 | 77 |

Wounded in Action

| Captains | 1st Lt | 2d Lt | Sgt | Cpl. | Pvt. | Aggregate |
|----------|--------|-------|-----|------|------|-----------|
| 5 | 7 | 9 | 10 | 14 | 241 | 286 |

Missing in Action

| *Privates* | *Aggregate* |
|-----------|-------------|
| 6 | 6 |

Following the battle of Seven Pines, the 4th NCST spent most of the month of June strengthening their defenses around Richmond and serving on picket duties and preparing for their next major engagement, which would be to meet Maj. Gen. George B. McClelland's forces in series of battles known as the Seven Days Battles around Richmond. Col. George B. Anderson was promoted to Brigadier General on 9 June, and his brigade was re-organized into the 2d, 4th, 14th and 30th North Carolina regiments. The Confederate army seemed to refit itself with every kind of Federal blanket, rubber cloth, tent flask, haversack and canteen available on the field at Seven Pines. One source noted there was so much loot that entire companies spent hours on the fields plundering hundreds of knapsacks and thousands of rifles and other items. Grimes' men also stuffed themselves with fresh beef, hardtack, and coffee which were captured in large quantities. Even with a sixty-eight percent casualty rate, the exhausted survivors of Seven Pines would still have more fiery trials to face in coming weeks as a major campaign around Richmond was now brewing.

# Chapter 5

## Seven Days Battles, Maryland Campaign 1862

Confederate commander Gen. Joseph Johnston was wounded at Seven Pines when an incoming shell exploded nearby and hit him on the shoulder as he sat on his horse. Johnston also received a slight bullet wound there, but tried to laugh it off. His recovery would require nearly six months, however, and President Jefferson Davis realized he had to make a decision. Consulting with the soon-to-be legendary Robert E. Lee on the afternoon of 1 June, Davis and Lee rode together to the house of a person named Hughes located on the Nine Mile Road, where Brig. Gen. Gustavas Smith had set up his temporary headquarters. President Davis quietly informed Lee of his decision to place him in command of the Confederate Army, which then had roughly 75,000 men in the lines around Richmond. Immediately, Lee began to reorganize and even rename the Confederate forces in the eastern theater. At roughly two o'clock in the afternoon that day, the Confederate Army became known as the Army of Northern Virginia.₁ Lee's initial plan was to build a serpentine line of entrenchments, including gun emplacements, along more than twenty miles of the James River which ran through Richmond to strengthen their stronghold, and seize the initiative from General McClellan.

Meanwhile, Col. George B. Anderson was rewarded for his conduct during the battles of Williamsburg and Seven Pines with a promotion to brigadier general on 9 June 1862 and command of a new brigade. Lt. Col. Bryan Grimes was promoted to colonel and given command of the 4th NCST on 19 June. Anderson's new command was one of many formed by General Lee who, at the urging of President Jefferson Davis, tried to consolidate the troops from each state into brigades and divisions as it was generally believed they would fight better together. Anderson's brigade became the 2d, 4th, 14th, and 30th North Carolina State Troops and would remain so until late 1864. After the battle of Seven Pines on 31 May 1862, Gen. D.H. Hill's division was encamped a couple of miles from Richmond, not far from Seven Pines for about three weeks serving on picket and other garrison duties until fighting finally erupted near the small village of Mechanicsville north of Richmond on 26 June.

Lee's goal was to remove the Federal threat from Richmond and regain the initiative from the hesitant McClellan, who was slowly retreating along the Chickahominy River. McClellan had left only one Corps just north of their position to cover the retreat movement, the V Corps commanded by Maj. Gen. Fitz Hugh Porter. Porter's V Corps was deeply entrenched northeast of Mechanicsville, although as Lee discovered on 26 June, the Federal extreme right was wide open to a dangerous flank attack. Lee also knew McClellan was intensely worried about Jackson, whose reputation had become larger–than-life following his recent series of victories in the Shenandoah Valley, and devised a complex and daring plan to have Gen. Thomas "Stonewall" Jackson march around the Federals and execute a thorough flanking movement at that location, taking advantage of McClellan's indecisiveness and frequent delays in movement. Lee's plan was to attack the exposed right flank held by Porter's V Corps with roughly 50,000 men massed on that exposed area. Jackson's 18,000 man army, however, had just returned from the Shenandoah Valley, and was delayed getting into position on 26 June. D.H. Hill's division was placed to the right of Longstreet's division, facing the Federal V Corps on Old Cold Harbor Road when they received orders to advance shortly after daybreak.

At D.H. Hill's command, the 4th NCST advanced toward Mechanicsville along the Mechanicsville Turnpike. The 4th NCST was eventually placed in reserve to support of Gen. A.P. Hill's troops, and several hours delay passed while A.P. Hill waited for Lt. Gen. Thomas "Stonewall" Jackson to begin the assault, but he didn't arrive. A.P. Hill became impatient and Jackson failed to communicate his location to A.P. Hill, so he finally ordered his division to attack around 3 PM on 26 June. This proved costly, as the well entrenched Federals repeatedly butchered the poorly supported Confederate attacks until well after dark. Porter eventually retreated from Mechanicsville to the east towards Beaver Dam Creek where he had earlier prepared much heavier earth works for protection in anticipation of a retreat. D.H. Hill's division, including the 4th NCST, was held in reserve throughout the fight, as A.P. Hill threw brigade after brigade recklessly into the attack which continued into the evening after dark.

On 26 June, Sgt. Ashbel Fraley of Company A wrote in his diary that he had been "aroused at 2 a.m. and marched toward the left of the lines near Mechanicsville. Battle commences in the evening. Company A, having been detailed as skirmishers are detached from the regiment. Lie down on the damp ground in line of battle and remain all night."[2] The 4th NCST listened to skirmishers popping and rattling throughout the night. D.H. Hill reported that he received Lee's orders around 9 PM, which essentially said to cooperate with Jackson eastward along the Cold Harbor Road. Hill's division left shortly after 2 AM, marching eastward by way of Bethesda Church on the Old Church Road from Mechanicsville. Hill arrived roughly three miles south off the Old Church Road near Old Cold Harbor near daylight, but could not locate Jackson. He quickly discovered the area near Cold Harbor was "held by the enemy in force" with strong entrenchments lined with artillery.[3]

### Gaines Mill

At Old Cold Harbor, Hill decided the Federal force was larger than Lee had anticipated and decided to wait for Jackson before attacking, especially since the Federals in their retreat from Beaver Dam Creek had concentrated behind earthworks behind Boatswain's Swamp, with the center being a small stream some two miles southeast of Gaines Mill that was not reflected on Hill's map. His map only mentioned an area known as "Turkey Hill" below the Boatswain's Swamp. The fighting renewed there in earnest early on 27 June, but Jackson had still not arrived by 10 AM, when the weather was described as "hot, hazy, and still" and the still-rising sun suggesting the day would become even hotter as it slowly drew on. By this time, Federal commander George B. McClellan had discovered that the Confederates assaulting his extreme right at Beaver Dam Creek were not, in fact, Stonewall Jackson's men. This led him to conclude that the Confederates still dramatically outnumbered him, and he decided to retreat further down the peninsula.

A.P. Hill's division was now on the right of D.H. Hill, just northeast on a plateau which curved around to the northern and western side of the area where the Boatswain's Swamp emptied into the Chickahominy River. This slow, marshy stream was heavily overgrown with trees and underbrush and was treacherous to navigate, especially under fire. A.P. Hill here began to push the Federals out of their entrenchments, and D.H. Hill was ordered to send two brigades out to try and get behind the federal artillery. He sent the brigades of Brig. Gen. Samuel Garland Jr., and Brig. Gen. George Anderson, consisting of the 2d, 4th, 14th and 30th NCST. Hill wrote in his report that Anderson and Garland soon gained the rear, and the "Yankees abandoned the works."[4] Jackson finally arrived that afternoon, and D.H. Hill was ordered to support the extreme left of the Confederate lines next to Gen. Richard Ewell's division. Just to their right, A.P. Hill's division was now in the center, and Longstreet's division was on the right following the road along the aforementioned bluffs near the Chickahominy River. Not far to the north, Jackson's 18,000 men finally engaged the Federals near Walnut Grove Crossroads. D.H. Hill was still tying to locate

Jackson, and although his troops had already made a rapid march that morning, and were exhausted in the dry, engulfing heat, continued to push them.

While moving to meet Jackson, D.H. Hill found the road was blocked by yet another battery of Federal artillery located behind the Boatswain's Swamp near Gaines Mill. Hill decided to remove the guns through an infantry assault. Hill ordered Grimes' 4th NCST to charge the battery, but Grimes relayed that he only had around sixty men with no officers in his regiment. Hill decided to hold Grimes in reserve, but advised him to be prepared in case those who were ordered to charge a second time "failed to take it." Although held in reserve, the 4th NCST still found itself "under a terrific infantry fire" according to Col. Bryan Grimes. Combined with the frustration of waiting under heavy fire, there was also concern that A.P. Hill's men to their front may not move forward when ordered to do so, and in response Grimes put his regiment into line of battle and ordered them to "fire on upon any of these troops who failed to move forward in the charge."[5] Grimes did not have to act, however, as Hill decided to withdraw and continue their march via a circuitous route around the artillery.

Meanwhile, A.P. Hill engaged numerous failed attacks against Maj. Gen. Fitz Hugh Porter's V Corps., who were now heavily concentrated around Gaines Mill. Jackson's division was marching to the northeast along the Old Cold Harbor Road around the headwaters of Powhite Creek where he planned to meet D.H. Hill as Porter was gradually being dislodged and starting to retreat. There Jackson, supported by D.H. Hill, would begin a turning movement on the Federal right flank, which Lee hoped would draw the Federals from behind the creek. As D.H. Hill approached Cold Harbor, however, he encountered numerous artillery batteries, with one in particular facing his front. He was unsure whether the battery was Jackson's men or not, and ordered Col. Bryan Grimes to wave a flag to ascertain their identity. Grimes said that D.H. Hill "...ordered a flag forward to be waived, when I took the flag of the 4th Regiment and galloped my horse towards the battery, the enemy opening with the whole battery on the line in column in my rear. I was on the extreme left of the long continuous line of battle and kept the enemy in check, until late in the afternoon there came an order to charge! And forward they went. My horse was killed, and I continued on foot, driving the enemy from his breastworks, through his camps, taking his artillery and supplying myself with another horse."[6]

If taken at face value, the impetuous Grimes' actions here may appear careless, but his men knew he would risk his own life to save their own and respected him for it. John Stikeleather of Company A, later described it as a "chivalrous act" and that it had endeared as a lifelong admirer and friend of Grimes.[7] As Jackson's division engaged Porter's V Corps, supported by D.H. Hill's brigades they crashed into the right wing of Maj. Gen. George Sykes' division of U.S. Army regulars. The terrain was wet and swampy, and E.A. Osborne later described that fighting at Gaines Mill as "very heavy and incessant" with the battle lasting almost twelve hours that day.[8] Once, when the 4th NCST was reloading their weapons, Grimes stopped in front of an unidentified company and admonished them, "Do your duty, men" with a heavy face expressing the "gravity of the situation." Anderson's North Carolina brigade soon advanced in line of battle through an open field to a small swampy, heavily wooded area, where a Federal regiment of Sykes U.S. Regulars was waiting and immediately opened fire. Anderson's North Carolinians quickly fired back causing the Federals to give ground briefly. D.H. Hill wrote that Anderson's men "...met the Yankees on the edge of the swamp, and was first engaged. The contest was short but bloody, and the woods were entirely cleared of Yankees, who fell back behind a fence and ditch at the brow of a hill."[9]

Col. Bryan Grimes allowed his regiment to rest for a few minutes then found a slight ridge parallel to his line of battle, and pushed the 4th NCST across an open field near the crest of the ridge where he could observe the Federals taking shelter in an old road on the opposite bank. Grimes again ordered the regiment to charge. The Carolinians advanced with a shout, moving across the field into a "face of a furious fire," according to Capt. E.A. Osborne, who saw it as "terrific beyond description…the yells of men, the roar of musketry, the thunder of artillery, the shrieks of the wounded and dying, the screaming of shells, with the loud commands of the officers, all combined to excite and stimulate the men, who rushed across the field, closing up their ranks as their comrades fell, cut down by the enemy's fire…"[10] Osborne also wrote that the Federals stubbornly held their ground until they were almost near enough to cross bayonets with them, providing another glimpse at the severity of combat around Gaines Mill. The North Carolinians' assault prevailed, however, and the Federal lines gave way in confusion.

During the battle, Grimes had another horse shot out beneath him near Boatswain's Swamp. Around 7 P.M. the sun hung low on the western horizon, glowing a dull red through the haze of the battle smoke. With dusk approaching, the battle climaxed as the entire Confederate line advanced, although in fragments, starting, stopping, then rushing again, and finally, the Federal lines collapsed in the twilight. D.H. Hill's five brigades immediately became entangled in the Boatswain's Swamp, losing all alignment. Regiments came out of the trees intermixed, piled up behind one another, many unable to return fire. There was no counterattack and darkness quickly fell, ending the fighting at Gaines Mill except for desultory skirmishing during the night. The 4th NCST spent the night in the Boatswain's Swamp marshland with water "up to our ankles," according to E.A. Osborne. The regiment entered the fight at Gaines Mill with fewer than 150 men and suffered 11 killed and 54 wounded.

In addition, the 4th and 5th North Carolina regiments were detailed to bury the dead that night. Although Colonel Grimes lost his knapsack in the capitulation of the Federal breastworks, he made a new friend. Grimes wrote, "Here I Captured a fine St. Bernard dog, which was protecting a corpse of Col of a Pennsylvania regiment, who, upon inspection was found to have on steel breast-plates which had protected him so long as his face was to the fire, but upon retreating, had received a mortal wound in the rear. This dog (General) became the pet of the regiment and remained with it for over two years, when in pursuit of Hunter in the Valley of Virginia in 1864, he succumbed to the hard marching, broke down and was lost, not having the endurance of the men."[11] Grimes later managed to meet and even have dinner with Stonewall Jackson that evening who informed him the enemy had crossed the Chickahominy, putting the 4th NCST out of immediate danger. They dined from a captured mess chest Grimes acquired from a union sutler's wagon that day, and Grimes later noted in postwar memoirs that he kept the chest as a memento of the occasion.[12] The next two days were relatively quiet for the regiment, as other units from the Army of Northern Virginia began to pursue McClellan in a southeastwardly direction down the peninsula on 28-29 June 1862. E.A. Osborne was wounded in the action, and took convalesce at the home of George S. Palmer near Cold Harbor. He and several other wounded men from the regiment stayed at the Palmer house for a several days, trying to recover.

1st Sergeant James W. Shinn of Company B wrote on 28 June 1862 shedding further light on the 4th NCST experience at Gaines Mill, "At early morn on the 28th we were all up again and eat our crackers, examined our cartridges and received a full supply and about nine o'clock we marched on toward the Chickahominy, which was but a short distance, when we came to the swamp. We halted and lay there all day having skirmishers or pickets in front expecting to march every hour through the day. We divided a wagon load of good things among the boys, of butter, ham, eggs, and c., and c., which was relished very much as we fought the mosquitoes. By and by night came and we went back to bivouac, drew some crackers and meat, broiled the latter and had a first rate supper. Slept on arms as usual, rained a little through the night, but not enough to make us uncomfortable."[13] William Gorman was a regimental band member who left a compelling and shocking account in his diary describing the awful scenes he witnessed serving as a litter bearer on the Richmond battlefields after the fighting on 28 June. Of particular relevance is the account of a conversation he had with Pvt. Paul Barger whom Gorman erroneously identified as a member of Company C, when he was actually in Company K. Barger predicted his own death, which Gorman recounts as a matter of fact:

"About four o'clock on Saturday we found the hospital of D.H. Hill's division. Though I had my feelings wrought up mutilated dead on those bloody fields; yet that feeling was nothing to what I saw and heard, when I saw the wounded, and heard the dying groans of those devoted braves. I shudder while I write about it. I am going to tell you a tale of horror which was true, and may God forbid that I ever have to witness the like again! The dead, none being there to bury them, lay among the suffering and dying, from which arose the most sickening stench. Their lifeless bodies were almost in motion with the myriad of maggots that infested them. Oh! It was horrible! Too awful to think about. Nor is this all. I myself did a task there that makes my flesh crawl to think of. A man from Company C, 4th Regiment, told me something hurt him under his arm. He was shot through the right breast, breaking his collor bone. When I looked, horror of horrors One thousand maggots were working there. I borrowed a pair of scissors and went to work, and it took me a half hour to remove them. Such as grateful look did he give me that I could have done anything. Those three days were days of horror-a "reign of terror" indeed. Our regiment lost about 60 killed and wounded. One of the killed in that company, one young man, Paul Barger,* gave me his pocket book before we started, stating that possibly he might be killed and did not want a Yankee to have his money. That was the last I ever saw of him."[14]

William Gorman's military career didn't last much longer as he died on 24 May 1863 following an illness which lasted seven months. The Carolina Watchman reported on 15 June 1863 that he died at home in Concord, North Carolina while on convalesce from the army and that "He was about twenty-six years old and before the sickness, which terminated in death, he ever enjoyed the most robust health. Many weary days have we marched side by side, but he is gone, gone, gone!" A less serious anecdote was discovered from another private soldier who, in spite of the awful carnage massed in the Seven Days campaign, found a way to amuse himself in a hospital in Richmond. Pvt. Daniel Carpenter of Company C recalled the story some years after the War in an impromptu meeting with two other veterans, J.C. Steel and Capt. T.M.C. Davidson. The story was described as follows: "Dan tells the story of seeing our old friend R.E. Patterson when he was wounded on the end of his finger. Bob spun around on his heel and used words not suitable for a Sunday School lesson. His wound was painful but not serious. When Bob got to the hospital at Richmond, there was a beautiful girl who was doing all she could to relive the wounded. She heard Bob say, Oh Lord! And she meaning to reprove him, said to him I heard you calling on the Lord. I am his daughter. Is there anything I can ask Him for you?, and he said, "Yes, I thank you, will you please ask him to make me his son-in-law?"[15]

---

*Pvt. Paul Barger was not in Company C as Gorman asserted, but rather Company K. Source: Company K Muster Roll, 31 December 1861. NC Archives.

On the morning of 30 June 1862, D.H. Hill's division was on the move again, and this time crossed the Chickahominy River toward the White Oak Swamp via Savage's Station, where a bloody fight had occurred on 29 June as McClellan continued his retreat. In the Confederate advance that included Hill's division, over 1,000 prisoners and as many weapons were captured. At this point, the 4th and 5th North Carolina regiments were detailed by General D.H. Hill as rear guard to secure the cache, and they encountered only minor skirmishing near Frazier's farm, Charles City Crossroads, New Market Crossroads, and Willis Church on June 30, 1862.16 During the 1 July 1862 Confederate debacle at Malvern Hill, the 4th NCST remained detached, guarding Federal prisoners and supplies near Savage Station. The battle at Savage Station is often referred to as "Glendale" by the soldiers who fought there. The last major engagement of the Seven Days culminated when McClellan gained a series of bluffs and small hillsides south of Savage Station and massed the federal artillery there. Eager to gain a decisive victory, Lee ordered his army to attack the position. Anderson's Brigade suffered heavy losses from Federal artillery fire in the subsequent assaults on heavily fortified Malvern Hill, although official casualty statistics for Company K were not specified. Brig. Gen. George B. Anderson suffered a severe hand wound during the battle at Malvern Hill, but continued to command his brigade.

Having ended the weeklong series of bloody engagements to be forever known as the Seven Day's battles, Anderson's exhausted brigade returned to camp near Richmond, where they garrisoned until late August. Several men suffered an outbreak of typhoid fever acquired in the local swamps surrounding Richmond, including Col. Bryan Grimes, forcing him to return to Raleigh to convalesce in August.17 Company K also lost Pvt. James Solomon killed, and James McCanless, William Morris and John F. Thompson wounded at Gaines Mill 26-28 June. During Grime's leave, the Army of Northern Virginia was ordered northward following General Lee's recognition that a large Federal army was gathering near Washington under Maj. Gen. John Pope. The *Carolina Watchman* editor mentioned the regiment's status on 14 July, "Compliments of the 4th N.C. Regiment which went to war with one thousand men and now only 160 left. It needs a rest and rumor has it that 4th will return home to recruit."

At this time D.H. Hill's division stayed near Richmond to protect the capitol from another potential attack by McClellan's army, which was lurking nearby along the James River. The 4th NCST stayed on rear guard north of Richmond until mid-July 1862, then joined Anderson's brigade and returned to their camp life near Richmond. Amidst the dull camp routine, Arthur Evans of Company E wrote to his wife on 18 July noting that "There is nothing of much importance transpired since I last wrote you, times is very quiet now, there seems to be but little life among the soldiers but still the members of this regiment are very well...I wish that I had something to write that would be worth your perusal but it is so very dull in camp...".14 The *Carolina Watchman* posted the obituary notice of Pvt. Samuel Gardner, who died in camp a few days before 18 August, indicating he passed away from "heart dropsy" at age 26 years. The account noted Gardner was thought to be improving at the time of his death, but had been unwell for several weeks. He apparently felt well enough to attempt taking a walk, when he suddenly "fell dead."

On 8 September, just a few days before the Battle of Sharpsburg near Antietam Creek, Maryland, the *Carolina Watchman* then ran a brief but humorous account of an accident suffered by Capt. W.C. Coughenhour while he was on medical leave from wounds he had received at Seven Pines; recall that he and several other soldiers convalesced at the Palmer house for several weeks afterward. Although the story did not specify the date or what he was doing when the accident occurred, it does ironically suggest that things at home could be equally dangerous as things on the front, particularly after one had sustained a "slight head wound" in battle. The byline stated, "Captain Coughenhour recovered after a fall from a second story window at Morganton."

## *Uniforms and Weapons after the Seven Days*

The muggy, miserable summer heat smothering Richmond brought not only many infectious illnesses, but the violent campaigns of May-July also exposed a significant weakness in Confederate quartermaster services and ordnance supplies, making no small impact on their fighting capabilities. During the battle at Gaines Mill, the 4th NCST nearly ran out of ammunition on the field. Col. George Anderson later said that the fighting there was so intense that there was barely a man without an empty cartridge box at the end of the day, and they had started out with sixty rounds per man. A North Carolina Ordnance Department receipt signed by George B. Anderson on 25 July 1862 reflects that the regiment was outfitted with 1,000 new bayonet scabbards, Cartridge boxes, Cap Boxes, Shoulder Belts, Waist Belts, and also drew 1,000 rounds of rifled musket ammunition that day. There was also an odd acquisition by Company K, a "Gunner's Level" which was a device used to sight artillery pieces in the field.

While it is not clear why this device was issued, short of an error by the Ordnance Department, the device could potentially serve to stabilize a sharpshooter's rifle or may also have meant that someone had plans to capture an enemy artillery piece and make good use of the level in an upcoming battle. Whichever the case, Anderson's ordnance receipt correlates well with numerous sanguine soldier anecdotes from the bloody Seven Days campaign, who routinely described witnessing entire regiments confiscating hundreds of U.S. Springfield rifles from dead Federal soldiers lying on Richmond battlefields. The 4th NCST acquired several hundred new rifles in this process, of .58 calibers in lieu of their former .69 caliber smoothbore weapons.[15] Considering that many of the Rowan Rifles were well drilled on the artillery manuals of the day before the war, the latter seems realistic. The Rowan Rifles stayed with the Army of Northern Virginia throughout the summer and eventually encamped near Orange Courthouse.

Not only did Company K getting its first taste of combat and receive new weapons and accouterments during spring and summer of 1862, their uniforms were also altered. Some important changes occurring at the Quartermaster Department in North Carolina during the winter and summer of 1862 had a direct impact on the men of Company K at Richmond. North Carolina Quartermaster Maj. John Deveraux wrote to a uniform contractor on 10 February 1862 requesting new uniform jackets be cut in an effort to save both money and cloth: "I will be obliged…if you will cut no more coats, but cut all jackets, a sample will be sent you in a few days."[16] The North Carolina "sack coat" was modified initially in February 1862 by removing the skirt, and turning it into a six-button jacket with a falling collar. Known as the first pattern Shell-Jacket, this garment retained the black shoulder trim.[17*] The North Carolina quartermaster again altered their jacket pattern in mid-July by eliminating the black shoulder trim and the falling collar to a more orthodox shell jacket with five buttons. This style was issued until end of war.

Yet Deveraux's request can be deceiving, as North Carolina was far from facing a shortage of uniform cloth at that point in the war. North Carolina's former governor Clark had previously arranged a rather loosely-worded agreement with the Confederate quartermaster in Richmond in 1861, allowing North Carolina to supply its own troops serving in Virginia. The agreement also specified that the Confederate government could also purchase any surplus from North Carolina if any was available, and that policy remained in effect throughout the war.[18] By the end of 1862

North Carolina Gov. Zebulon Vance told the state legislature that North Carolina was well stocked, and actually selling her surplus uniforms and supplies to the government, while her troops received "nothing at all from the Confederate Government" in Richmond, largely because of "our agreement to furnish themselves." This statement tends to dispel any myths that North Carolina troops were drawing clothing from the Confederate manufactory known as the "Richmond Depot" including the jackets so commonly attributed to troops serving in the Army of Northern Virginia in 1862. Rather Vance's writings confirm they wore state manufactured uniform garments throughout the war.19 Vance's profit making policy of stockpiling excess supplies also led to price gouging by local industries such as textile mills who quickly realized they could cause the state and central Confederate governments to compete for their products as the war intensified.

Vance wrote several angry letters to North Carolina textile manufacturers in response; one firm in particular that drew his ire was that of Henry Fries, proprietor of the Fries Woolen Mill & Salem Manufacturing Company in Forsyth County. Fries was one of the largest suppliers of cloth to the Raleigh Clothing Depot, yielding thousands of yards of cotton jeans cloth, gray wool, and other products throughout the war. In conflict with his public support of States' Rights focused economic policies, however, Vance seemed to privately contradict himself in these letters with veiled threats of hostile military takeover of all the mills in North Carolina, albeit he claims a higher moral ground: "I have seen with regret and mortification...you say you cannot comply with the provisions of the Exemption Law requiring manufacturers to furnish goods at 75 percent profit over the cost of supplying the wants of our brave soldiers in the field. It is melancholy in every sense. If the Standard of patriotism was no higher in the great mass of people, we might treat with the enemy tomorrow and consent to be slaves at once and forever. Poor men, with large and often helpless families, go forth to bleed and suffer at $11 per month, supporting their wives and children God knows how, with flour at $20, shoes and cotton at fabulous prices and yet men who stay at home in protected ease to reap a harvest of wealth, which might truly be called a harvest of blood, from the necessities of the Country, cannot afford to take 75 percent above the cost for the garments in which his protectors stand guard & do battle for his liberties? What per cent, gentlemen, do you suppose the solider is reaping, with a half starving family, a shattered constitution, ragged and barefooted, sleeping on the bare earth or languishing with gaping wounds or raging fever in loathsome hospitals?

If he can incur personal and pecuniary ruin for his country's sake, cant you afford to eat good food, sleep in a warm bed every night on 75 percent clear profit for the country's good also? Alas, Alas, that such a state of things should exist in North Carolina I will not pursue the subject. Suffice it to say that without the assistance of manufacturers the State cannot clothe the troops & they must brave the severities of the coming winter naked. When men of intelligence and public spirit take such a position, we may expect suffering & ruin to overwhelm our country. There is only one remedy to arrest the evil which threatens us: and that is for the civil authorities to permit the military to put forth its strong arm & take what it wants. The Confederate authorities have desired my permission to seize the Mills of N.C. and work them for the benefit of the Army; should it be

---

*An example of a variant of the first pattern N.C. Shell Jacket is found in an image of the brothers Seaton G. Durham, and John R. Durham, Company E, 12th North Carolina State Troops. Their jackets vary from regulation by having black trim on the cuffs and eight buttons. Greg Mast, *State Troops and Volunteers: A photographic record of North Carolina's Civil War Soldiers*, Vol. 1, (Raleigh NC: 1995), 303 (No. 5.3.29). Note that the Confederate government officially abandoned the commutation system in October and no longer reimbursed states for purchasing their own uniforms, and officers had to privately pay for their own garments.

formally asked of me again I shall withdraw my objection & permit to do as they wish, unless they will make reasonable contracts with the State. I should state as a matter of justice that you have been quite as liberal & perhaps more so with the State, as any others, but no amount of company can render extortion justifiable or respectable."[20] During the summer months, with an excess of uniforms soldiers tended to store their winter clothing or ship it home. Like many states, North Carolina kept the troops' boxes of clothing and other personal items in a rented warehouse located on "Main Street between 7th and 8th Streets opposite the Spotswood Hotel" in Richmond, although it "…sometimes took several weeks for delivery and many items were found missing upon receipt."[21]

## The Maryland Campaign

Pvt. Walter Battle of Company F wrote home on 11 August with a brief description of the regiment's activities during August and early September, just as the army was about to move northward. Lee planned to invade Maryland in hopes of providing a tactical win as well as a psychological edge by causing a general panic among citizens and the United States government in Washington when he advanced. Battle shares some insight as to the living conditions the brigade was enduring and also the incessant heckling from veterans that the new conscripts (draftees) received who had only recently reported to the 4th NCST, "…We have a very pleasent place for our quarters, a large two story house with plenty of shade, in an open field, where we have the breezes from every direction. I don't know yet, but I may come up here to mess and sleep, though I thought I would wait a while. I haven't slept in a tent since I've been in camp, but once. That was last night. It rained yesterday morning, and the ground was wet, and the air rather cold, so I thought I would go in the tent, as it was convenient. I shall go in bathing tonight to cool off, and sleep out doors. We have an excellent place for that purpose that is bathing. It's been awfully hot here today. I believe it is warmer here than at home. General G.W. Smith was to-day assigned to the command of our Division. I understand he is an excellent officer. Some of our regiments in this brigade have received their conscripts. They are a very good looking set of men seen drilling in a field as they were this morning. It looks right funny to see men so green, but I suppose all of us were so at first, and we ought not to make fun of them…P.S.…I forgot to tell you that our whole brigade was throwing up breastworks every day, about two miles from here, that is the only duty they do now, no guard duty."[22]

During August, while Col. Brian Grimes was stricken with typhoid fever, the Army of Northern Virginia issued a stunning defeat to Federal forces at Second Manassas on the 29th and 30th. Grimes returned to the 4th NCST a few days too late to participate in this fight. However, he noted in a letter to his wife, "My command did not participate much in the battle of Second Manassas, but were in the field and assisted in driving the enemy beyond Centerville, when the line of march was taken up from Maryland."[23] After the Second Battle of Manassas, D.H. Hill's division reached the Army of Northern Virginia near Chantilly, Virginia, on 2 September 1862. The victory at Second Manassas apparently convinced General Lee that similar success would be possible north of the Potomac River. The regiment suddenly found itself on the road to Maryland beginning on 5 September. As they crossed the Potomac River at White's Point near Edward's Ferry, Grimes was seriously injured when a horse kicked him in the groin; he apparently did not do well with horses considering his former experiences at Seven Pines and Gaines Mill! He maintained command for about two weeks, until he found himself unable to continue after receiving another fall from his horse during the battle at South Mountain. Although he minimized the affair, it was serious enough to require traveling in a wagon afterward until Brig. Gen. George B. Anderson learned of it and ordered Grimes to again convalesce, causing him to miss the battle at Sharpsburg.

On 7 September, the Army of Northern Virginia encamped near Frederick, Maryland, as Lee continued moving his army northward. Confederate forces faced a great deal of uncertainty as they entered Maryland, considered a border state between North and South, and one that political and military leaders hoped to win over to the Southern cause. However, Confederate soldiers quickly learned that not all Marylanders were aligned with the Confederacy; many broke ranks to stop and beg at farms along the roadside only to be turned away and occasionally harassed by the citizens.[24] An unidentified field correspondent described the appearance of the men in Anderson's brigade, particularly the 4th NCST, during this campaign in an article published in the *Daily Charlotte Observer* on 8 March 1895: "The men had nothing to eat from Saturday night, the 13th until Wednesday night of the 15th; were in battle all of the 14th; marched all night; in line at Sharpsburg Monday and Tuesday; in battle Wednesday. After the battle was over they received a half ration of bread and meat. They were barefooted, ragged and dusty. On the 14th the fourth was detached from the brigade early in the morning and sent to General Garland. As the message was urgent they threw off their knapsacks by the roadside, leaving a guard with them. At night they left the mountain and came down the opposite side, and at Sharpsburg the men rested. Mother earth was their downy couch, cartridge boxes their pillows, and the blue sky a covering. A soldier in battle sees very little of the field. What occurs around him is about all…"

A number of Confederates thought to offer citizens their "script" (confederate money) for items such as eggs, crackers, cheese, and even tobacco or salt, but most citizens were quite skeptical of tendering the Confederate bills.[25] However, across the lines, the average Federal soldier was quickly losing faith in the army, and morale was poor at that time. On 2 September, Gen. George B. McClellan was named commander of the newly reorganized Army of the Potomac which greatly improved the attitude of soldiers in the Federal ranks. On 6 September, skirmishing between Lee's rear guard and vanguard began with elements of Federal cavalry patrols near Frederick, Maryland. Meanwhile, the Confederates generally waited for orders and continued to look for food. Soldiers in Anderson's brigade strongly resented what they perceived as a condescending attitude from the Maryland citizens who seemed better advised about the location and movements of the Army of Northern Virginia than the Federals. While historical analysis has corroborated the Confederates perception of the civilians' attitudes toward them, the citizens were also in shock at the appearance of Lee's troops on this campaign. One observer said the Confederates looked "…horrid; clothed in rags, "half of them are barefoot; have not even dirty uniforms…" as yet another observer agreed, and also quipped "…but just look at their guns, ain't they bright and polished, and don't they glisten in the sun?"[26]

The Army of the Potomac began to move toward western Maryland when word reached Washington of Lee's invasion of the North. Soldiers began to suspect another large battle was looming. Orderly Sgt. James Shinn of Company B wrote to his father on 11 September, and opined, "We left camp with the rising sun for parts unknown to us. The Confederates had moved from Monocacy Junction and entered Frederick where they received a rather cold reception from the citizens, who simply peeked out of windows which had been shut…generally, I thought the people looked rather long-faced to have much sympathy with the South."[27] However, no small disaster was soon impending. Lee's now infamous Special Order No. 191 was dated 9 September 1862 and addressed to Maj. Gen. D.H. Hill, and detailed his plans for the upcoming invasion. It was somehow lost by a courier along the National Turnpike just north of Crumbs Ford on the Monocacy River, giving the Federals plenty of insight and time to prepare for Lee.

Meanwhile, word was beginning to circulate back at home in North Carolina of the Confederate invasion of the North. Miss Ellie Andrews, sister of Captain John Barr Andrews of Company A, wrote in her diary just a few days before, "Our news from the army in Va is startling-our Generals are assuming the offensive and are pushing forward Baltimore-it is said they have already crossed into Maryland. We await with anxiety and the developments of another week."[28] The Confederate juggernaut continued toward Hagerstown on 13 September when Elle Andrews again updated her diary, this time stating, "To day I had another hasty communication from the camp telling me they were in all the confusion attended upon moving. The Reg. was ordered to proceed immediately to its destination and I suppose by this time they are fairly on their way."[29] D.H. Hill's Division (including the 4th NCST) was deployed at South Mountain that day, along the western edge of South Mountain. Hill's orders were to guard the two main gaps in the mountain range, known locally as Fox's and Turner's Gaps, to prevent the Federals from passing through them while Lee's army was still divided. Once Lee decided to hold the pass near Boonsboro until Stonewall Jackson could Capture Harper's Ferry, he ordered D.H. Hill's division to defend the area near Fox's Gap. The Rowan Rifles soon found themselves posted along Wood Road, not far from the National Turnpike, and heavily engaged.

### South Mountain

On 14 September 1862 at roughly 3:30 A.M., the 4th NCST began its march down the National Turnpike toward Boonsboro with Anderson's brigade and other elements of Hill's division. Most of D.H. Hill's division had already moved forward through the gap and taken up defensive positions on the eastern slope of the mountain by the time the 4th NCST. By 9 A.M., the 14th and 30th NCST of Anderson's brigade were detached and quickly engaged the Federals who were beginning to mass near the base of the mountain. Around 1 P.M., the rest of Anderson's brigade (the 2d and 4th NCST) along with the 13th NCST was dispatched to support them. They began their uphill trek through the rough and wooded terrain toward the rocky summit at the double quick. D.H. Hill was adamant they hold Fox's Gap because the Army of Northern Virginia's ammunition train was slowly advancing near the western base of the mountain along that route, and disaster would be certain if it was captured. As fighting on nearby Wise's farm intensified, it seemed as if the Federals wanted possession of every inch of Wise's one-acre plot of farmland. The 4th and 2d NCST advanced northward in an effort to reach a more secure position near Pelham's artillery position. Orderly Sgt. Jonathan Shinn of Company B later wrote of the advance, "The fight now became a bushwhacking affair. The Mt was very rugged & the Laurel & other bushes very thick.  We fell back but little at a time..."[30]

The 2d and 4th NCST finally rallied at Bondurant's Alabama artillery, just north of the Wise farmhouse. The 2d, 4th, and 13th NCST tried to align with General Garland's left, with the 2d and 4th NCST positioned to the left of the 13th NCST, where fighting was becoming desperate. Hill had originally directed Anderson to align his right flank on Garland's brigade's left flank; however, the Federals had already positioned themselves between the two brigades and began enfilade fire. This caused some fragmentation among the 14th and 30th regiments as they tried to out maneuver Federals on the right with little effect. Col. Bryan Grimes ordered his 4th NCST to position itself behind a low, stone wall running parallel to the road on a slight brow of the ridge. This point was held for roughly half an hour, and 4th NCST sharpshooters were soon posted forward and began to impede the Federal advance. Another interval soon formed of roughly 300-400 yards between Garland's left wing, allowing the 30th Ohio infantry to exploit the gap and flank the 4th NCST on the left. In response, Col. Grimes crossed the fence and formed his battle line into right angles to hold his position near Wise's farm.

Along Anderson's line other units were taking a beating, such as the 14th NCST who was nearly fully enfiladed on each flank by the 12th and 36th Ohio Regiments. Anderson continued to push the Federals in his front for nearly an hour; these units included the "Kanawha Division" (11th, 12th and 23rd Ohio Regiments) so named because of their former service in the rugged mountains of western Virginia during the Kanawha Valley campaigns of 1861-1862. The Kanawha Division was commanded by Maj. Gen. Jacob Dolson Cox, a stern leader and former attorney from Ohio whose military career ironically peaked in 1865 when he led Union forces in capturing Fort Fisher and the port of Wilmington on the North Carolina coast, not too far from Fort Johnson where the Rowan Rifles had earlier garrisoned. The 23d Ohio was also commanded by future U.S. president Rutherford B. Hayes, and his troops were intensely loyal to him. Hayes' Federals were campaign-wise veterans and stubbornly resisted Anderson's North Carolinians who eventually had to pull back to reform lines. The fighting dwindled for a while until just after noon. Both sides seemed to be re-establishing their positions north and south of the Old Sharpsburg Road.[31]

During the morning action, Col. Brian Grimes found himself in the midst of yet another horse crisis when he was again tossed off his animal as it was shot out from under him. Grimes stayed on the field; but he was limping and weak that night and had to ride in a wagon. He eventually encountered Colonel Anderson, who ordered him to the hospital. Grimes recalled the scenario, "On the 14th the command was called upon to proceed down the turnpike toward Middletown, ear the pass over South Mountain, when, seeing an engagement with the enemy was inevitable, I had myself placed upon my horse and took the command of my regiment, and was first sent with the command to the left of the turnpike and subsequently withdrawn and ordered with another regiment to proceed to the assistance of General Garland, then engaged on the right. In advancing, was met by the corpse of that gallant officer being brought off the field. Here the fight continued all day. Here my horse was killed under me on the mountain, and to my own and the surprise of my men, I commanded my troops in the battle until nightfall, when I threw myself down to rest by my brigade commander, General G.B. Anderson."[32]

It wasn't long after noon when Lee's artillery began shredding Federal troops with canister as they attempted to reorganize on the mountainside below Wise's cabin. The fighting soon began to escalate again, and Gen. George B. Anderson brought the 14th and 30th regiments back into line. The 30th NCT was sent to make reconnaissance of the Wood Road, located just north of the Old Sharpsburg Road where the 30th Ohio was already in position and fired into the 30th NCT as they advanced; the North Carolinians retired to the safety of the woods beyond the mountain crest. Anderson regrouped his brigade along Wood Road, aligning the 14th and 30th Regiments on the left of the 2d and 4th NCST respectively, all occurring around 1 P.M.[33] The 13th NCT was on their right at this point. The Confederates began to move westward on Wood Road, unaware that several New York units, including the 79th Regiment, had taken position behind a low stone wall lining the road. As D.H. Hill sent more troops from Georgia into line along the old Sharpsburg Road, he extended his lines from Ripley's brigade to the west, reforming the Confederate line. Both armies continued to feed more troops into their line of battle. Sometime around 4 P.M., George B. Anderson's left flank lost contact in the woods. The brigades were halted on the western slope, and the 4th NCST was detached to recon to the south.[34]

Company H under Capt. E.A. Osborne was detailed in front as skirmishers near a cornfield along Wood Road. Ordered to probe the mountainside cautiously and silently as possible, Osborne noted, "Our progress was necessarily very slow, as the woods were very dense and the ground very rugged and mountainous."[35] As they moved slowly to the south along Wood Road, the Federal IX Corps was quickly climbing into position on the eastern side of the mountain. Soon, the 4th North Carolina had a good view of the Federal left flank. They were close enough on the Wood Road to see the cornfield on the southern end of the Federal line and the adjacent plowed field north of it. Captain Osborne saw the standing corn and the casualties littering the field. He noted the Federal artillery contained four 10-pound parrot rifles, all facing north, which made a "tempting prize".[36] West of the Wood Road, skirmishers from the 48th Pennsylvania "blundered" into Captain Osborne and his skirmishers who were screening the approach of George Anderson' brigade. A few rounds were exchanged, and then the Carolinians took cover. However, this quick round of fire unnerved the green "fresh fish" of the 9th New Hampshire who, without fully identifying their targets in the evening haze and smoke, fired directly into the backs of the veteran 48th Pennsylvania as the 4th NCST continued to advance and skirmish. This resulted in a mammoth "chewing out" for their zealous but inexperienced officers by their brigade commander afterward.[37]

General Anderson heard the firing and quickly brought the rest of the brigade forward around 4:30 P.M. The units got into line at a location near Wise's field, close to the base of the western slope of South Mountain. The Federal artillery was now located on the eastern side of the stone wall. They were supported by the 9th, 89th, and 103d New York, who had deployed on the small hill parallel to the 4th NCST position. The 89th New York also had two companies on the extreme right behind the stone wall who had been ordered to wait during the skirmishing. The 4th NCST extended roughly 125 yards into the woods and soon found the 48th Pennsylvania who was positioned along the stone wall on the Wood Road. Company B of the 48th Pennsylvania, who was detached to probe the flank, saw the 4th North Carolina, exchanged a few shots, and then retreated as Anderson's brigade quickly followed them. As darkness approached, Anderson identified advanced toward the stone wall, not knowing Federal infantry lurked behind it. With a Rebel yell which reverberated through the darkness, the 2d and 14th Regiments were ordered forward, the colors of the 2d North Carolina leading the way.[38]

At this time, across the southernmost part of the cornfield adjacent to the south side of the L-shaped woods, the 9th, 89th, and 103d New York Regiments were laying down behind the stone wall, immediately behind the artillery battery on the eastern side. Crossing the cornfield, the 2d and 14th North Carolina were firing in squads at a distance of roughly seventy-five yards, into Clark's federal artillery battery at their front, who were loading deadly double-canister rounds for close range. The 103rd New York then consisted primarily of green troops who quickly broke for the rear and ran into the woods as they realized how close the Tar Heels were. The two companies of the 89th New York could see the 2d North Carolina advancing just a few yards away. Suddenly, the 89th New York was ordered to rise and fire a volley directly into the faces of the 2d and 14th North Carolina Regiments who were now just a few yards away. The artillery peeled off a battery of double-canister which tore into the 2d North Carolina's ranks. One solider later recalled that "an eerie silence" covered the field immediately afterward.

Pvt. David Thompson, Company G, 9th New York Volunteers, recalled advance of the 2d and 4th North Carolina toward their position behind the stone wall. He mentioned that most of the Rebels' guns were unloaded and they did not suspect that the Federals lay just a few feet in their front, "We had been in position but a few minutes when a stir in front advised us of something unusual

129

afoot, and at the next moment the Confederates burst out of the woods and made a dash at the battery. We had just obeyed a hastily given order to lie down, when the bullets whistled over our heads, and fell far down the slope behind us. As the Confederates came out of the woods, their lines touched ours on the left only, and there at an acute angle, their men early treading on those of the 89th, who were on their faces in the corn field, before they discovered them at that instant, the situation just there was ideally, cruelly advantageous to us. The Confederates stood before us not twenty feet away, the full intention of destruction on their faces - but helpless, with empty muskets. The 89th simply rose up and shot them down."[39]

As the smoke from the failed assault cleared, the New York troops realized that mainly dead, wounded, and dying Confederates remained in front of them. Meanwhile, the 4th NCST, who had moved into a position just to the north on Wood Road, spotted the 48th Pennsylvania and opened fire as the 2d and 14th North Carolina Regiments fell back. The fighting pitched, as the 48th Pennsylvanians expended most of their ammunition banging away at the 4th NCST, who stubbornly returned the fire shot-for-shot.[40] Meanwhile, the rest of Anderson's brigade silently withdrew in the darkness and moved west down the mountainside toward the crossroad around 6:30 P.M. Thus, the fighting at Fox's Gap had ended. An unusually detailed description of Confederate uniforms by a Federal soldier, David Thompson of the 9th New York, made note of the North Carolina uniforms found on the dead from Anderson's brigade after that failed charge, "Before the sunlight faded, I walked over to the narrow field. All around lay the confederate dead - undersized men mostly, from the coastal district of North Carolina, with sallow hatchet faces, and clad in "butternut" - a color running all the way from a deep, coffee brown, up to a whitish brown of ordinary dust."[41]

The worst was still to come for the 4th NCST. Note that Brig. Gen. George B. Anderson was not wounded at Boonsboro as Grimes had suggested in his postwar memoirs; but rather would receive a shell fragment wound in his foot during upcoming fighting at the Bloody Lane on 17 September that proved mortal. Casualty statistics for the 4th NCST and in particular Company K at South Mountain are unclear, but it is known Pvt. Alfred Miller was killed on the field, and Daniel Miller was mortally wounded and died that night. Pvt. William Smithdeal, who was wounded in the hand requiring his middle finger to be amputated at Seven Pines, suffered severe pain and contractions of the remaining fingers and stiffening of the hand" after the battle on 14 September and was sent to a Richmond Hospital on 15 September according to service files. Capt. E.A. Osborne anecdotally described the regimental casualties as "…among them some of our best men" and suggested Anderson's brigade suffered "7 killed, 54 wounded, and 29 missing." He further mentioned the regiment's plight at South Mountain, "The men bore themselves with much coolness and courage throughout the entire day…At night the army was withdrawn and moved to the vicinity of Sharpsburg, where we arrived at a 11 o'clock on the 15th and remained in line of battle most of the time until the morning of the 17th. The regiment was now under command of Captain W.T. Marsh, Col Grimes having been compelled to retire from the field on account of an injury received on the morning of the 14th at Boonsboro."[42]

### Sharpsburg: The Bloody Lane

By 17 September, R.E. Lee had drawn his army in a semi-circle along the Hagerstown Pike with his back to the Potomac River. Lee desperately tried to prevent the Federal army from gaining a foothold at South Mountain, but he had to move toward the Potomac River to Sharpsburg in the late evening on 14 September.[43] As Lee began to withdraw toward Sharpsburg, the 4th NCST was heavily involved in skirmishing along the turnpike that night. Anderson's brigade bivouacked on both sides of the road on the evening of 15 September 1862 with skirmishers thrown forward near to the Antietam on the 16th. The next evening, Anderson's brigade again bivouacked on either side of the Boonsboro Turnpike near the end of the Sunken Road. Its skirmishers were engaged with those of the 4th United States infantry.

The brigade remained in this position until early on the morning of 17 September when the battle opened in the Miller farm cornfields along the Hagerstown Pike. By 6 A.M., Jackson's corps was hotly engaged all along this route; and fighting moved into an area known as the West Woods. By 9 A.M., skirmishers from Anderson's and nearby Col. John Gordon's Alabama brigades listened anxiously as they lay near the crest of the small ridge a few yards ahead of Lee's center, awaiting the Federal advance. By mid-morning, Brig. Gen. George B. Anderson's brigade (2d, 4th, 14th, and 30th North Carolina) were located in an old, sunken farm road awaiting the Union advance. The battle was quickly shifting toward the center of Lee's lines, right where they sat. The 4th NCST was about to experience some of the worst fighting they would see throughout the war -- mostly at close range, less than twenty yards away. Anderson's brigade had earlier moved south from the turnpike through a ravine and up a hillside into this lane, just a few feet north of the cornfield. They were on the right of Rodes' brigade next to the rugged Colonel John Gordon's Alabamians. Together they hunkered down in an old farm road that had literally sunken down a few feet from decades of use by wagon wheels, and there they waited with skirmishers posted out in front, just south of the Roulette Farm.

Soon a myriad of glistening Federal bayonets appeared on the crest of the slight ridgeline running parallel to the lane, and the Federal troops presented an immaculate sight with their ranks properly aligned. Anderson's North Carolinians waited until the very last second as the Union soldiers moved within only a few yards of the lane, when they suddenly opened fire. The devastating volley of musketry literally wiped away entire ranks of Federals. Anderson was mortally wounded soon thereafter, opening the way for Stephen D. Ramseur to become the next brigade commander as a brigadier general. The Federals quickly retreated from the initial assault, but the next line to advance were veterans who refused to turn. A melee was quickly underway as the North Carolinians' held their ground. During the assault, elements of the 4th NCST were also dispatched to take a Union battery belonging to Brig. Gen. John C. Caldwell's division, located to the left of the Irish Brigade. Capt. E.A. Osborne later offered his personal recollections of the maelstrom in the sunken road, including his own wounding and mentions that several men from Company K, thirteen in all, were captured when Anderson's lines retreated, who due to the geographical features of the lane were unaware they were left alone. The twelve were quickly returned to the ranks, however, as muster roll data later confirmed they were exchanged by 10 November 1862. Osborne wrote:

"...Anderson's brigade had been on the right of the division from the 14th until the morning of the 17th, when it was moved to the old road, afterwards known as the "Bloody Lane." The 4th Regiment was commanded by Captain Marsh, the 2nd by Col Tew, the 30th by Col Parker, the 14th by Col Bennett, the brigade by General George B. Anderson, General D.H. Hill having command of the division. The 30th was on the right of the brigade, the 4th next, then the 14th, and the 2nd was on the left. About an hour after sunrise the enemy came in sight and began to attack at once. Anderson's brigade was partially protected by the bank of the old road above mentioned, which ran parallel with the line of battle in rear of the crest of a ridge which concealed our men from the enemy's sight until they were within 75 or 80 yards of us.

About 9 o'clock the enemy's line of battle appeared, moving in magnificent style, with mounted officers in full uniforms, swords gleaming, banners, plumes, and sashes waving, and bayonets glistening in the sun. On they came with steady tramp and confidence. They did not see our single line of hungry, jaded and dusty men, who were lying down, until within good musket shot when we rose and delivered our fire with terrible effect. Instantly the air was filled with the cries of wounded and dying and the shouts of brave officers, trying to hold and encourage their men, who recoiled at the awful and stunning shock so unexpectedly received. Soon they rallied and advanced again; this time more cautiously than before.

Our men held their fire until they were within good range again, and again they rose to their feet and mowed them down, so that they were compelled to retire a second time; but they rallied and came again, and the battle now became general all along the line. The roar of musketry was incessant and the booming of cannon almost without intermission. Occasionally the shouts of men could be heard above the awful din, indicating a charge or some advantage gained by one side or the other. Horses without riders were rushing across the field, occasionally a section of artillery could be seen flying from one point to another, seeking shelter from some murderous assault, or securing a more commanding position. Soon Captain Marsh was mortally wounded and borne from the field. The command of the regiment then devolved upon Captain Osborne, who in turn was wounded and borne from the field. One by one the other company officers fell, either killed or wounded, until Second Lieutenant Weaver, of Company H, was in command of the handful of men who were left, and then he was killed bearing the colors of the regiment in his hand. The regiment was left without a commissioned officer; but the men needed none, except for general purposes. There were not more than 150 men for duty, every one of whom seemed to realize his own value, and to act with that cool and determined courage which showed that he understood the emergency, and was determined to do his best. All day long the battle raged with almost unabated fury and with varying results, sometimes one side gaining the advantage and then the other.

As the day worn away the contest seemed to gather new force. The enemy renewed their efforts to gain what they had failed to achieve during the day, while the Confederates were equally determined to defeat their aims. The flower of the two great armies had met in open field, and neither was willing to leave the other in possession. The northern troops displayed wonderful courage and obstinacy during the entire day, while our men held their ground with equal courage and determination. General Anderson and Col Parker were wounded. Col Tew was killed, and Col Bennett had command of the brigade. The men of different regiments became mixed with each other so that all distinct organization of regiments was broken up, and all identity lost-still the men maintained their positions in line, and fought like heros. General Hill was with his men all day long, encouraging and cheering them by his presence and by his cool and fearless bearing. On two occasions the enemy approached to within about 30 yards of our line, but each time they were forced to retire. Late in the day the enemy forced his way beyond the right of the brigade, and Col Bennett found it necessary to retire from the "Bloody Lane."

This he did in good order, and in doing so passed with 60 yards of the right flank of the enemy's line; but they were so hotly engaged with one of our lines in front that they did not observe the Col's movement until he had extricated his men from their dangerous position, and passed some distance to the enemy's front and left. Finding a piece of artillery which had been abandoned, the Col manned it and opened fire upon the enemy's line...In this movement the 4th Regiment lost a number of men from Companies I and K, on the left who were taken prisoners: being separated from the right by a little hillock, they did not know the retreat had taken place until they were in the hands of the enemy. This new position was held during the rest of the day. The command remained on the field until night, when the battle ended. They then bivouacked in a grove nearby. The next day the brigade was commanded by Major Collins, Col Bennett having been disabled. The 4th Regiment was commanded by Orderly Sergeant Thomas W. Stevenson, of Company C. General Hill had the brigade formed and made a little speech to them, calling them the "faithful few," warmly commending their courage and fortitude during the fearful conflict of the day before."[44]

Gen. George B. Anderson was wounded by a shell fragment in one of his feet and removed from the field. Throughout the morning, Anderson's brigade withstood several Federal charges but eventually retreated in the direction of Sharpsburg shortly after noon. A small remnant reformed on the Hagerstown Pike, southwest of the Piper farm house, and assisted in checking the Federal advance in that direction. James Shinn, then the orderly sergeant of Company B, sheds further insight into the events inside the Bloody Lane, including his own frustration with a drunken general officer who wreaked havoc in the lane by giving inconsistent orders to troops who were not under his authority.* Shinn wrote, "Anderson's brigade changed position in a old road early in the morning and soon the enemy was found to be advancing in heavy forces; whilst re-enforcements were coming into us General Wright's brigade came in, Wright was drunk and tried to order our brigade forward, but the commanders chose to await Anderson's orders as we were under cover and preferred to let the enemy come up…".

Shinn also mentions that the 4th NCST had only 80 men available that morning, in contrast to the numbers (150 men) suggested by Osborne, "Another brigade come up and pushed into the road on our brigade and created some confusion. In the mean time, General Wright was wounded and General Anderson too. The command Wt's brigade devolved upon the same comm.; also Anderson's. The Yanks came on but slowly, hesitating. The mini balls, shot and shell rained upon us was coming from every direction except the rear. We were ordered to fall back and weary men took this as a chance (from all Regts') to leave the field entirely. We fell back something over a quarter of a mile and formed and held this position during the day. Made two charges and drove the Yanks back each time; we made this road our main line of defense. In falling back or rather running back the Regts and brigades became mixed up, and was not regularly organized that day.

---

*James Shinn's account of the Sunken Road states that General Wright was drunk although other historic sources do not corroborate such. If Wright was heavily intoxicated, he could not likely ordered the successful bayonet charge while lying on the litter after being wounded. See Report of Col. W. Gibson, 48th Georgia, Commanding Wright's Brigade, Charles H. Andrews' Papers, Southern Historical Collection, University of North Carolina – Chapel Hill, and also OR, Supplement, Part 2, Vol. 3, 570. Shinn, a 27-year old physician at enlistment on 3 June 1861, was promoted to orderly on 20 August 1861. He was commissioned a second lieutenant on 22 July 1862 and a first lieutenant on 11 February 1863. He died of disease on 14 March 1863 at home in Baker's Mills, Rowan County. Jordan, Vol. 4, 26, 738. See also Clark, Vol. 4, 270. Col. George Burgwyn Anderson died on 18 October, and command of his brigade was given to Brig. Gen. Stephen Dodson Ramseur on 6 November 1862. He commanded the brigade until his mortal wounding at Cedar Creek on 19 October 1864, nearly two years to the day after Anderson died. OR Series 1, Vol. 19, Part 1, (1887), 698-699.

Gen' Hill was present reorganizing the men, acting in the utmost fearless manner. Many officers were killed and wounded and some I am very ashamed to say left the field unhurt. The 4th North Carolina went into the fight in the morning with about 80 muskets and was commanded by Captain Marsh. Nearly all the officers were killed or wounded, some slightly, yet they left the field and the Regt was very much scattered, what few there was of us. Some remained on the field at night-long after firing had ceased. Brigade was marched to grove in the rear."[45]

### 4th North Carolina Flag Captured

During the fight at the Sunken Road, the 4th NCST once charged into the 5th New Hampshire, who was led by Col. Edward E. Cross of Brooke's brigade. As the Confederates began to fall back into the cornfield, the 5th New Hampshire was in front of the remnant companies of the 4th NCST, I and K, who were attempting to hold their line not knowing the rest of the regiment was retreating. It is not clear from original sources which company had the colors, although Colonel Cross reported that one of his men captured the 4th NCST flag by executing a, "…change of front to the left and rear, brought his regiment facing the advancing line. Here a spirited contest arose to gain a commanding height, the two opposing forces moving parallel to each other, giving and receiving fire. The 5th, gaining the advantage, faced to the right and delivered its volley. The enemy staggered, but rallied and advanced desperately at a charge. Being re-enforced by the 81st Pennsylvania, these regiments met the advance by a counter-charge. The enemy fled, leaving many killed and wounded, and prisoners, and the colors of the 4th N.C. in our hands."[46*]

Colonel Cross's report states, "We then advanced in line of battle several hundred yards and entered a corn-field. While marching by the right flank…we received a heavy fire of shell and canister-shot…a single shell wounding eight men and passing through the state colors of my regiment I had scarcely reached my position on the left of the first line of battle and opened fire, when it was reported that the enemy were cautiously attempting to out flank the entire division with a strong force concealed behind a ridge, and in the same corn-field in which I was posted. They had, in fact, advanced within 200 yards of the left of our lines, and were preparing to charge. I instantly ordered a change of front to the rear, which was executed in time to confront the advancing line of the enemy in their center with a volley at very short range, which staggered and hurled them back. They rallied and attempted to gain my left, but were again confronted and held, until assistance being received, they were driven back with dreadful loss. In this severe conflict, my regiment captured the State colors of the 4th N.C. Regiment, Corpl. George Nettleton, of Company G, although wounded, bringing them off the field, displaying great bravery and endurance."[47] No accounts filed by 4th NCST officers document the loss of their flag, but Capt. E.A. Osborne earlier mentioned seeing the colors' fall in the hands of "…Second Lieutenant Weaver of Company H" who was "killed bearing the colors of the regiment in his hand."[48]

---

*The North Carolina Museum of History battle flag data also indicates the 4th North Carolina state flag was captured by the 5th New Hampshire Volunteers at Antietam (See NC Archives Document No. 14.86.8, flag collection specifications, 4th N.C. Infantry). This also suggests that the capture of the state flag necessitated the reactivation of another flag issued in 1861 -- a silk, twelve-star, privately made banner akin to the version "First issue" given by the Army of Northern Virginia in fall 1861 at Centerville, later used by Col. Bryan Grimes as a headquarters flag and is how held in the North Carolina Archives' permanent collection.

*North Carolina Casualties at the Bloody Lane, taken 19 September 1862. Courtesy U.S. National Archives.*

*View from North Bank Facing East of NC Casualties at the Bloody Lane.*
*Courtesy U.S. National Archives.*

*North Carolina Casualties on Anderson's Left at the Bloody Lane. Close inspection shows the body lying crossways is decapitated, and many of the others in the top of the image are shoeless. Courtesy U.S. National Archives.*

After Lt. Weaver was killed, Orderly Sergeant James Shinn of Company B tried to organize the remaining men and remove them from the treacherous lane, until he was wounded, leaving Orderly Sergeant Thomas W. Stephenson of Company C to command the remainder of the regiment as they retreated through the cornfields to their rear. Every officer of the 4th NCST present at Sharpsburg was killed or wounded, but Capt. William F. Kelley of Davie County, the former commander of Company D was only slightly wounded, and upon regrouping later that afternoon was placed in command of the 4th NCST.

Company K lost thirteen men captured at Sharpsburg, including privates E.F.M. Carter, Ambrose Casper, Jeremiah Eddleman, Nelson Eller, Milas Holshouser, Otto Holshouser, Calvin Miller, Isaac O'Neil, William Page, William Parker, W.D. Peeler, Henry Severs, George Snuggs, and Noah Troutman who were exposed on the regimental left as the lines started to retreat. Capt. E.A. Osborne noted they were unaware of the lines pulling back, "being separated from the right by a little hillock, they did not know the retreat had taken place until they were in the hands of the enemy."[49]

In the melee ensuing at the Bloody Lane, the Confederates still managed to maintain a facsimile of a line of battle. It is therefore possible that when Lieutenant Weaver fell carrying the regimental colors, this was the same moment described by Colonel Cross of the 5th New Hampshire when the state colors were taken by Corporal Nettle. The *Daily Charlotte Observer* on 8 March 1895 posted an anecdote describing a rather sad incident that several other men of the 4th NCST also witnessed after losing the colors during their retreat out of the sunken road. Although the *Daily Charlotte Observer* does not specify the author of this account, the unidentified correspondent may have been Captain Osborne. The style and detail observed in his other accounts cited herein and he regularly contributed to the *Charlotte Observer* after the war. The author wrote when they left the lane, he saw a little boy near "..six of the dead lying close by...an officer ...was shot through the head and fell close to the road. The little boy rushed up to him. As he did so he was shot through the heart and fell by him, and with a lingering look at the quivering form by his side, gasped and died. Who they were we never learned." Following the battle of Sharpsburg (commonly known as Antietam in the Northern states), voluminous soldier accounts described hardships and privation suffered in Confederate camps, giving us a broader picture of the experiences shared by men in Company K on the Maryland campaign. One was William Adams of Company C wrote home on 30 September from camp near Bunker Hill, Virginia of his venture into Maryland and specifically indicates he is lacking in winter covering and shoes, and bear in mind it was only September when he wrote:

"...I have been in Maryland since I wrote to you and have been in to very hard battles in Maryland and came out unhurt. I see a great deal and could tell you more than I write if I could see you. Our regiment did not have many wounded nor killed but a good many taken prisoners. Frank Sheppard and John Fennster we suppose are taken. We have not heard from them since the fight. They were...left at the camp. The Yankees took them. On their escape they took a good many of our Negroes. That was a great Victory at Harper's Ferry. I would like to have been in that. Our men did not fire a gun. They burned the Yankee's to death and they give up everything and raised a white flag and attacked their army and our men march in. The men say it was the best thing they ever saw. The 7th Regiment N.C. was there and saw it all...I would like to have been there. Pa, I want you to have a pair of boots made. The shoes you had made for me ripped all to pieces. I want you to tell Uncle George about it and not have them made so large as the shoes. They were too large in everyway. Have them number 8 for they are aplenty...Our regiment used everything we had. I have no blanket nor any clothes but what I have on I have got the suit on that you sent me. They came in a good time. I like them very well. If I had a good pair of shoes I would be the best clothed man in the regiment."[50]

On 20 September 1862 the 4th NCST took part in the attack made on the Northern troops who had crossed the Potomac River into Shepardstown, Virginia. This engagement proved disastrous to the enemy -- many were killed in the fighting, but a significant number also drowned in the river as they retreated. Afterward, the command was removed to the neighborhood of Fredericksburg, where it spent the winter doing picket duty and recruiting its members.[51] Colonel Grimes, who was absent during the battle, returned to duty in November and found the regiment reorganized and drilling near Charlestown, Virginia. During these late fall months, the unit was also engaged destroying the Baltimore and Ohio Railroad from Charlestown near Harper's Ferry, Virginia, and according to Grimes, his men were rather adept at the destruction of railroads, which is not surprising considering that former several railroad men had enlisted in the ranks of Company K. Grimes stated, "The work was done effectually at night by tearing up the cross-ties and putting them in large piles of 20-30 and then crossing the iron rails over them and piling a few ties on top of each end of the rails, and just before daylight setting fire to them - the whole at once - the fire so warping the rails as to unfit them for use."[52]

### Uniforms and Supplies in Late 1862

North Carolina troops returning to Virginia suffered immensely following the Maryland campaign, which ended in late September. As was typical on long and arduous campaigns, the men of the 4th NCST entered Maryland carrying backpacks, blanket rolls, and the like, but they quickly dropped all such impedimenta to make their march easier, but the result was misery after the campaign as colder weather sat in. Numerous diaries and original letters from the 4th NCST on the Maryland Campaign contain similar evidence that some companies lost their entire array of bedrolls and knapsacks on 14 September as they were quickly deployed along the National Pike near Fox's Gap during the Battle of South Mountain. Some men and their slaves were left behind to guard their belongings; but when scouts returned afterward to recover their gear, the Federals had taken both. A grim, albeit realistic, description of the general state of the North Carolinians was made by Murdock McSween, a North Carolina attorney who often acted as an unofficial journalist as he visited the troops from his home state in the field.

He wrote to North Carolina Governor Zebulon Vance in November about their plight following the Maryland Campaign. Notice his perception of the dwindled average company size in these units, "Our soldiers in the Army of the Potomac [ANV] need shoes, blankets & clothes very badly—The companies there average probably 30 effective men each. About one third are barefooted or the same as barefooted—I saw many men marching in the snow entirely without shoes or any substitute—there are perhaps 10 men in a company well shod—Very few men are amply supplied with blankets, many have none and others have only one thin blanket apiece...They are of course ragged and dirty, and itch vermin and disease are very prevalent...The articles I think most necessary are shoes, blankets, pants and coats & should be supplied first."[53] Even paper products for officers and non-commissioned officers (sergeants and corporals) to complete their official reports was in short supply, as a "Special Requisition Form 40" completed on 25 October 1862 by Moses Bean indicates. Bean apparently signed for "One Stack of Paper" for Company K Non-Commissioned Officers, but never received it.[54]

Another Special Requisition Form 40 entitled "Co. K 4th NCST," was signed 7 November 1862 by Lieutenant Hofflin reveals that Captain Alexander, acting quartermaster, delivered to Company K "52 Blankets 8 caps" to help re-supply some of their lost items. But it would not be enough, as most of the men were literally without shoes or overcoats and winter was fast approaching.[55] Evidence further points out that commissary sources then supplied a minimal amount of food as well. On an unspecified date in November 1862, Lieutenant Hofflin signed for receipt of "Rations" at their camp near Orange Court House, Virginia. These rations, sent by the quartermaster consisted of "Flour 680 lbs., Beef 735 ½ lbs., Hard Bread 27 lbs., Pork 12 lbs." Considering this amount of foodstuff was to feed roughly eighty four men shown on the most recent muster roll for an indefinite period, (although only fifteen were available for active duty due to many still missing, captured, wounded or dead) we can estimate that each man then received about 8 ounces of flour, 9 ounces of beef, three to four pieces of "hardtack" and about one tenth of a pound of salt pork, was hardly enough to last more than a few days, if that long.[56]

Clothing and other supplies also arrived from Raleigh on 17 November, but were more abundant than food, as evidenced by a handwritten facsimile of a standard requisition Form 40 found in service files. The requisition was written on an unlined scrap of paper by Col. Bryan Grimes, and also signed by Capt. B. Williams, acting quartermaster on the date of receipt. Williams then issued Company K a large supply of clothing, uniforms and blankets.[57] The costs of each individual item was included, as even though the Confederate government had officially abandoned the commutation system in October, company officers still had to account for supply debts incurred against the company budget. The receipts contents are entirely transcribed within the following table, in order to give the reader an idea of costs and specificity found within North Carolina's clothing supply system at this point in the war. Note that not all of the eighty four men then on rolls for Company K (minus roughly 15 who were either on leave, under arrest, or in the hospital) needed a completely new uniform.

| Item: | No. Rec'd: | Cost Each: |
|---|---|---|
| Blankets | 17 | 3.50 |
| Blankets | 14 | 6.00 |
| Overcoats | 3 | 10.00 |
| Overcoats | 1 | 10.50 |
| Overcoats | 13 | 13.00 |
| Knit Shirts | 15 | 2.00 |
| *Morisus Shirts* | 8 | 2.25 |
| Pr Pants | 50 | 7.50 |
| White Shirts | 10 | 1.65 |
| Pr Drawers | 59 | .75 |
| Gray Jackets | 30 | 5.50 |
| Pr Pants | 50 | 6.12 |
| Pr Shoes | 16 | 2.50 |
| Box | 1 | ----- |

An unusual item found in this particular form is "Morisus" shirts. To see this descriptive term on a Confederate supply requisition form is highly unusual. The quartermaster may have been using an unofficial descriptive term, possibly referring to the Island of Mauritius (*môrĭsh'ēəs,–əs*), which is officially known as the Republic of Mauritius. This is a small republic located in the southwestern Indian Ocean, was well-known in the nineteenth-century textile world for exporting a lightweight cloth similar to muslin often used to make clothing. It is unknown whether this material was routinely used for issue shirting from the North Carolina clothing depot or not; but a correlation seems plausible as military shirts made at the North Carolina clothing manufactory were commonly made of various cotton and flannel cloths.58

There were also thirty "gray jackets" received, and since North Carolina did not regularly receive imported English cloth until mid- 863, these garments were likely manufactured of domestic cotton jeans cloth at the North Carolina clothing depot in Raleigh in the revised pattern created by Maj. John Deveraux earlier in 1862, i.e. without a skirt and shoulder stripes. Another point of interest is the presence of three differing varieties of overcoats received by Company K. North Carolina issued 48,093 of these locally-made garments between 1 October 1861 and 30 September 1862, and the state later bought 1,012 ready-made English overcoats in 1863. By 1865 then the Raleigh Clothing manufactory had issued another 13,000 overcoats made of heavy cotton cloth. Although this was obviously not a routine issue item later in the war, evidence interestingly reflects that this company wore state manufactured Overcoats, an item commonly presumed non-existent in Confederate quartermaster inventories.59 Despite receiving some new uniforms and blankets, Company K suffered a shortage of shoes which also plagued their brigade at this point. Pvt. J. W. Bone of the 30th North Carolina wrote that during the march toward Fredericksburg in early December, a number of men wore pieces of rawhide "cut to shoes" that were tied together with strings on their feet, which quickly dried out and fell apart.60

The Company K muster roll completed on 31 October 1862 covered the period from 30 April 1862 is next summarized below. 2d Lt. Marcus Hofflin was promoted to first lieutenant on 31 May 1862 and commanded Company K at South Mountain and Sharpsburg. Lieutenant Hofflin was promoted although he was also listed on sick leave. The Brevet Lieutenant or "Lt" shown in the table was 1st Sergeant Addison Wiseman, who had briefly taken command of the company when so many casualties and illnesses befell the Rowan Rifles following the Seven Days campaign, and while Capt. W.C. Coughenhour was on convalescent leave.61

| Captain | 1 Lt | 2 Lt | Brevet Lt | Sgt | Cpl | Musicians | Privates | Total Enlisted | Aggregate |
|---------|------|------|-----------|-----|-----|-----------|----------|----------------|-----------|
| - | - | - | 1 | 2 | - | 1 | 12 | 15 | 84 |

During the Maryland campaign, Company K was officered by Lieutenants Wiseman and Hamilton Long, with sergeants' W.C. Fraley, M.L. Bean, Michael Hennesy, and Corporal Richard Williams. Bradley Matthews served as musician and stretcher bearer after the battle. Noah Troutman, who was captured in the Bloody Lane, was later released on 20 September at Keedysville, Maryland under parole. Company K also lost Leroy Colley and William Glover mortally wounded in the action at the sunken road. Colley died on 18 September and Glover passed away a day later on 19 September. Julius McDonald was the only private known killed in action at the sunken road from Company K. One man, Ambrose Casper fought through the early morning on 17 September while seriously ill and had to leave the field on due to an illness and was taken to a Richmond hospital. Only fifteen enlisted men from Company K escaped without wounding or capture at Sharpsburg, a marked difference from the eighty-four men aggregate shown on company rolls from April 1862 just before the summer campaigns began.62

Several others missed the Maryland campaign due to previous wounds or illnesses, and were at home in Rowan County on convalesce including Capt. W.C. Coughenhour, and privates George Basinger, John Deaton, John Locket (left the field on 14 September with severe illness), William Lillycross, William Morris, Daniel Moyer, and James Maulden. Other privates including William Buise, John Eddleman, Edward Fulk, and James Roberts were at Richmond hospitals recovering from sicknesses, along with Sgt John Peden. Alexander McQueen, who had earlier returned home to Montgomery County, was still there recovering from wounds received at Seven Pines. His brother Daniel McQueen was wounded on 14 September at Foxes Gap and sent to a Richmond Hospital. Pvt. Robert Beaty continued to serve in the balloon corps, and was not present at Sharpsburg. Lindsey Bryant was detached as a teamster, while John Ketner was detached on an unspecified special duty with brigade staff.[63]

After Sharpsburg when the army was suffering so many hardships due to illnesses, want of clothing and supplies, many men decided they could tolerate the army and its' privations no longer, and deserted. Company K was no exception, as muster rolls indicate brothers John and Henry Castor deserted a few days after Sharpsburg and by 31 December were returned and placed under arrest for court martial. Although Milas Holshouser was eventually proven captured, the officers initially thought he was simply away without leave and arrested him when he returned following his exchange in November. Meanwhile, William Parker and W.D.C. Peeler who were actually captured at Sharpsburg decided to extend their absence a few days after their exchanges. Parker was arrested in Richmond on 20 November and Peeler was arrested on 7 October, and both were taken back to their unit by the provost. On or about December 4, Joseph F. Thompson also deserted, but quickly returned and fought in the battle of Fredericksburg where he would be mortally wounded.[64]

### Brigade Clerk Commission Scandal

In the months previous to Sharpsburg, privates Charles Jones, Jacob Frayley, and William Durrell were assigned as clerks for the brigade staff, and while Fraley showed better judgment, the compiled service files of twenty year old Durrell and twenty two year old Jones show they confabulated a way to relieve their uneventful lives as army privates. Jones and Durrell orchestrated dangerous but entertaining promotions for themselves as officers, which they managed to pursue for several weeks before discovery. The industrious pair were detached to clerkships along with Jacob Fraley of Company K and while in that role, Jones had a friend from another regiment who was also a clerk, pen a fictitious letter to Col. William Parnell recommending a commission on behalf of the Major in charge of the clerks, who supposedly recommended his "esteemed friend" Charles Jones as an officer in the 55th NCT. In reality this occurred without the Major's knowledge of the matter, although Jones received his "commission" as a second lieutenant in Company G, 55th Regiment, NCST, on 12 September 1862 and was actually transferred out of the company! When Jones reported to the 55th NCT, no one knew him, unfortunately, and he was briskly ordered by the Provost Marshall to report for duty with the 4th NCST at Petersburg, Virginia on 2 November 1862. The officers of the 4th NCST did not appear to be aware of the stunt, and it does not appear that he was ever arrested for the act, according to muster rolls which make no mention of any court martial proceedings or arrest.[65]

After the war, Jones became the influential founder of the *Charlotte Observer* newspaper, which remains in operation to this day. Because he was present in 1861 and obviously had a penchant toward reporting the news, it is possible that Jones was "Scribbler"- the anonymous correspondent who provided detailed accounts of the companies' activities throughout the early war period. William Durrell was from the Northern states, and had the respect of officers such as Capt. William Coughenhour, yet, also confabulated commission documents. Not to be outdone by Jones, Durrell took it a step further-his papers said that General R.E. Lee himself had ordered his promotion to 2d Lieutenant, which falsehood was discovered only when he reported to his new unit in 1863 and none of the officers had any knowledge of his alleged orders. The regiment to which he reported is not identified in source documents, but Durrell was hastily returned to Company K. Both he and Jones managed to avoid several hardships that winter by impersonating an officer, although strangely anecdotal accounts and official records do not specify what disciplinary actions were imposed upon them.[66] By 31 December, the companies supply and uniforms had improved, as Captain William F. Kelley inspected them and described the company's discipline, instruction, military appearance, arms, and accoutrements as "Good except as to Clothing."Captain Coughenhour returned from his second convalesce by this time, (which the reader will recall was ironically for a head wound at Seven Pines, but he fell out of a 2d story window in October), and summarized the recent activities of Company K for this period as follows, "The Regiment was last mustered in at Richmond Va. Marched from there to Manassas Sept 14 1862, was in the battle of South Mountain-Sept 17 was engaged at the battle of Sharpsburg. Have been performing camp duty and drilling when not skirmish or more actively engaged"[67]

### Fredericksburg Campaign

Although its role at Fredericksburg was marginal, the 4th NCST participated with D.H. Hill's division, Anderson's brigade. Colonel Grimes was elsewhere assigned as a staff officer in Ramseur's brigade upon returning from convalescence. The regiment was detached as guards for the hundreds of Federal prisoners pouring in from the heavy fighting occurring 13 – 15 December 1862. It was estimated that some 3,000 - 4,000 captured Federals passed through the 4th NCST pickets on those days. Gen. D.H. Hill also reported that most of the casualties in his division were

Sketch of Stone Wall at Marye's Heights. Courtesy NPS.

from Federal artillery which pounded Confederate positions. The 4th NCST suffered 4 killed and 21 wounded in this engagement, mainly from skirmishing in the days following the main battle on 13 December.[68] On that date, Anderson's brigade was posted on the extreme right of Hill's lines behind heavy breastworks and held that position for the next two days.[69] There was constant skirmishing with Federal troops on 14 and 15 December, according to Hill, although the 4th NCST was not engaged. Many Company K men likely saw some skirmishing on rear guard, however, as the regiment was still active in the few days after the battle. On 19 December, 2d Lt. Addison Wiseman was again wounded, this time severely (he had been slightly wounded at Seven Pines), while serving on picket duty near Fredericksburg.[70]

## Supply and Uniforms Winter 1862

Further inspection of supply and other records from this period reveal that after the battle, life for Company K quickly settled into the doldrums of winter camp, but generally they fared well in terms of food and clothing in contrast to the dilapidated state they experienced following the Maryland campaign. On 23 December 1862, Captain Coughenhour signed a receipt for 2 Tent Flies and 1 Fife for Company K; Bradley Matthews was serving a musician at that time according to the muster rolls and received the fife. As noted earlier, overcoats were not uncommon among the North Carolinians in 1862, and another supply form explains how North Carolina's officers acquired overcoats in the field.[71] The government no longer reimbursed enlisted men for clothing purchases, and each unit was given an allotment to buy quartermaster items for enlisted troops. These purchases did not apply to officers, who had use their own funds to buy such goods as overcoats, as evidenced by a form signed by Lieutenant Marcus Hofflin on 31 December 1862 "for my own use" with a cost of $19 for his overcoat. Considering that the frugal Hofflin owned his own clothing mercantile before the war, and was also managing it *in absentia* during his military service, this must have been quite a bargain as he could easily have sent home for one out of his own inventory. On the other hand his garment was much more expensive than those indicated on another supply form; variant costs indicate there were major differences in both style and quality in the officers' garments and those provided for enlisted men. Captain Coughenhour used a plain piece of writing paper to mimic the outline of a supply Form 40 on 31 December, which he entitled "Abstract of Special Requisitions" and it indicates he received several items requested earlier by Lieutenant Marcus Hofflin.[72]

Coughenhour's receipt specifies the items were ordered only two days before delivery from the clothing depot in Raleigh. This is an amazing two-day turnaround time for delivery to a combat unit in the field, and it dispels at least some of the popular myth of a ragged "Johnny Reb" who waited months for new clothing as folklore has often suggested of Confederate troops. The variant price differences observed in this receipt suggest more than one style of both overcoats and shoes were available. The more expensive items were probably for officers. The North Carolina regulation sack coat and pantaloons were out of production by this time, and "Suits" possibly referred to complete sets of pants and jacket. (The form's contents are shown on the next page) Some writers have suggested that the wide range of uniform clothing and costs offered to North Carolina troops is explained by not only the multitudinous regional textile mills producing uniform cloth, but also the advent of imported cloth and supplies from England.

North Carolina sent two state purchasing agents to England in November 1862 with orders to buy up cloth for uniforms, shoes, arms, etc. and ship them back to Wilmington on the state's own steam ship that Governor Vance purchased. The boat was to be employed as a blockade runner, and originally named the *Clyde*, but did not arrive in Wilmington, North Carolina until June 1863. After its arrival, North Carolina's new blockade runner was renamed as the *Advance*. The garments received in December were therefore not likely made from early cargoes of the *Advance* however, as those first shipments of English supplies did not make their way into port until June 1863. North

Carolina uniforms were likely not regularly made of English cloth until mid-1863, so it appears that North Carolina's textile industry was more than adequate to meet supply demands in the winter of 1862, at least in Company K.[73]

| Item: | No. Rec'd: | Date Rec'd: | Cost Per Item: |
|---|---|---|---|
| Overcoats | 2 | 10 Dec | $10.00 |
| Overcoats | 1 | " | $8.50 |
| Pr Shoes | 1 | " | $12.50 |
| Pr Shoes | 2 | " | $10.00 |
| Suits | 10 | 21 Dec | $25.75 |
| Suit | 1 | " | $25.75 |
| Overcoats | 2 | 22 Dec | $25.00 |
| Pr Shoes | 11 | " | $5.00 |
| Shirts | 23 | " | .80 |
| Pr Shoes | 1 | " | $6.50 |
| Pr Drawers | 20 | 23 Dec | .80 |
| Pr Shoes | 1 | " | $5.00 |
| Tent Flies | 2 | " | ------ |
| Axe | 1 | " | ------ |
| Pr Shoes | 9 | 29 Dec | .75 |
| Pr Shoes | 1 | " | $5.00 |
| Pr Pants | 1 | " | $7.00 |
| Overcoat | 1 | " | $19.00 |

The next Company K muster roll covered the period from 31 October to 31 December 1862 and is summarized below:

| Captain | 1 Lt | 2 Lt | Brevet Lt | Sgt | Cpl | Musicians | Privates | Total Enlisted | Aggregate |
|---|---|---|---|---|---|---|---|---|---|
| 1 | 1 | 2 | 0 | 4 | 1 | 1 | 62 | 68 | 72 |

This roll shows that the 4th NCST received pay on 31 December, which was still camped near Fredericksburg, Virginia. Note also that the general outline and structure of the standard muster roll forms changed after this date. The tables included hereafter show the number of Officers, Non-Commissioned Officers, and Private soldiers available for duty in separate categories. The rolls also include data on those who were in hospitals, on leave, Away without Leave (AWOL), or under arrest and confined, which is summarized in the text. The column for "Aggregate" is therefore a summary tabulation of the men listed on the rolls, not those actually present for duty on the morning the roll was completed. The "Total Enlisted" column summarizes the number of privates and non-commissioned officers. The 31 December muster roll firmly shows that Company K had recovered over half of their former numerical strength by this time. Wounded men were beginning to return to camp from hospital convalescence and furloughs, and several men had returned from capture and confinement.[75]

A large exchange of prisoners occurred on 10 November 1861 at Aiken's Landing on the James River, and the thirteen men captured at Sharpsburg were returned to the company shortly afterward, except those who decided to linger in Richmond a few days longer that were counted as deserters when Col. Grimes discovered they had been exchanged. Company K ended the year with sixty-eight enlisted men present for duty, and two officers, Capt. W.C. Coughenhour and 2d Lieutenant Hamilton Long. 1 Lieutenant Marcus Hofflin was sent to an unspecified hospital for an unknown illness, and 2d Lieutenant Addison Wiseman was sent to Salisbury to recover from wounds received at Fredericksburg on 19 December. There were three sergeants present for duty, Jacob Fraley, Moses L. Bean, and Michael Hennesy. Corporal Richard Williams was earlier sent to Richmond to recover from an unhealed wound received at Seven Pines. Several privates became ill after the last muster roll completed 31 October including Charles Hoyer who was hospitalized at Winchester in October, and Wallace Josey who succumbed to a fever on 14 December, and Lewis Mahaley who left camp on 12 December, while Michael Rowland, James Roberts, and Joseph Thompson all left camp together on 4 December with severe fevers. William Page was then counted absent without leave, while Lindsey Bryant remained on teamster duty. There were no new deaths reported between 31 October and 31 December 1862 in Company K.[76]

Regarding the state of supplies during 1862, the issuance of shoes remained poor overall for this company; but it apparently improved some, however, as Company K received forty-one pair between October and December. A review of prices again suggests there were differences in uniform quality available for enlisted men, and in particular there is ample evidence that a typical soldier in Company K could draw state-made winter garments and did not universally rely on items sent from home. This is not surprising as it is well-known that most of their loved ones back at home did not have much to send, although anecdotal letters clearly show that some men, such as Jonathan Shinn, received shoes and clothing from home that were completely worn out on campaign.[77] Summarily, 1862 was a year of first blood and first casualties in battle. It was also a time when the naïve, even cavalier, attitude toward war was quickly changed by the initial contacts with the enemy on the peninsula in April and May. Additionally, the last letter provided by "Scribbler" from Company K was penned in October. Since his identify is unknown, it is not clear whether he died, was wounded, discharged, or simply lost interest in writing. Meanwhile, the Rowan Rifles continued to prepare for the rough times ahead during a long winter encampment hallmarked by chilling weather, useless and redundant marches, and ever present drilling. Desertion from the army increased following brutal campaigns in Virginia and Pennsylvania, as 1863 would be the year that the South had to face a reckoning as to its aspirations for independence.

# Chapter 6

## 1863
## The Tide is Turned

In spite of a bitter cold winter in January 1863 while encamped near Fredericksburg, soldiers found a variety of ways to amuse themselves. Mock snowball battles complete with battalions and officers were common place, but letter writing and looking for food was their primary focus. Many men in Company C of the 4th NCST even sent random letters home to young ladies in hopes of capturing their affection by entertaining them with writing prowess. A young private in Company C, Thomas Gaither, wrote, "We…have quite recently adopted the plan of writing to all the young Ladies we know and to some with whume [whom] we have not the slightest acquaintance. So you may judge from that, that we aim to have all things in hand by the close of the day for a matrimonial change of life."₁ On 28 January, the entire regiment present re-enlisted for the duration of the war and the men were quite proud afterward. On the same day, a deserter from Company E was charged and sentenced to execution on the next day. Gaither alluded to how the incident marred the regiment's reputation and described a sense of dread at having to watch that scene which would occur in front of the entire brigade. Yet, even with occasional desertion and freezing weather, supplies and food was adequate. On 24 January 1863, 1st Lieutenant Marcus Hofflin scribbled what he deemed "Provisions Issued to Troops 4th NCST" on a plain piece of paper, indicating receipt of "792 lbs. pork, 13, 964 lbs. fresh beef, 600 lbs. bacon, 81 barrels of flour, 600 lbs. wheat, 552 lbs. sugar, and 10 bushels, 45 quarts salt" from the commissary department. Hofflin also indicated there were "No Pickles, Dried Apples, Chickens, or Molasses" available.₂

The 31 December 1862 muster roll for Company K stated there were sixty-eight enlisted men available for duty, and with 13,964 pounds of fresh beef, this meant each man in the regiment would have roughly 205 pounds of beef to eat. Not all at once of course, but if distributed across a hundred twenty day period, each soldier could receive around one and a half pounds of meat per day, which is far from the "starving rebel" image so often projected of the Confederate soldiers across the war. It should be understood that actuarial and to some degree, even anecdotal evidence is limited on this issue, but original sources do not reflect that anyone actually drew that full ration of beef every day in this encampment. On the other hand, the generally large body of anecdotal accounts from this period does suggest that the soldiers in the 4th NCST ate reasonably well in the winter of 1863 from beef and pork. As noted earlier, the correspondent "Scribbler" seems to have dropped out of the public eye after October 1862, and never revealed his identity. Muster rolls may offer us some clues as to who this author actually was, however, if we presume that he didn't simply stop writing while remaining in the company, but accept the premise that he either transferred or otherwise left the company as explanation for ceasing to write. We may never know, but it is useful to speculate using available muster rolls showing which men left the company in early 1863.

Bradley Matthews was Absent without Leave from 20 January through August 1863 when he returned to the unit. It was doubtful he was "Scribbler" since his correspondence about Company K stopped after 1862. Another possibility is Charles Heyer, who transferred into the regimental band on 11 February 1863, or John Kenter who was arrested and reduced to ranks for being Absent without Leave in November-December 1862, and afterward sent on a detached detail away from the regiment until October 1864. There were no deaths recorded in the winter 1863 period for the company, so it is likely that "Scribbler" just left the company since he would not have had first hand information to transcribe any longer. Another 4th North Carolina member known as "Nat" was quickly emerging as the premier correspondent, which may also have had something to do with it. "Nat" regularly wrote home to the *Statesville Landmark* newspaper, which was usually also published in the *Carolina Watchman* in Rowan County. Unlike Scribbler, however, "Nat" is easily identified as Jacob Nathaniel Raymer, a private in Company C who was transferred to the regimental brass band in 1863. Raymer literally became a household word in the Iredell and Rowan County areas during the war, as his letters to the editor about the 4th NCST often provided the only reliable details about their loved ones that people back home received for weeks. Locals at home anxiously awaited his next dispatch from the front to hear of how their loved ones and friends fared.₃

Capt. John B. Andrews' younger sister, Ms. Ellie Andrews once had opportunity to meet Raymer while he was back home on leave in Statesville, and was not much impressed with his appearance, but found him quite intellectually appealing. Ms. Andrews recorded their meeting in her diary on 18 March, "…at last, "Nat," our valued Express Correspondent, has been revealed to us--his countenance is bright and active but not handsome--his whole exterior, rather unprepossessing, but he possesses gifts which go far towards making up his deficiencies in appearance. I met him at Dorey's where he had been invited by Dr. Dean--Being fond of vocal music, Dovey and I sang for him "Rock me to sleep Mother" and "all quiet along the Potomac to night," both songs which are just out."₄ Raymer's letter to the *Statesville Landmark* on 23 January, was also published in the *Carolina Watchman* on 2 February, and detailed several camp activities that broke the dull winter routine in the cold encampments near Fredericksburg. Although his writing rarely mentions Company K specifically, his missives described events that the entire regiment experienced or were at least privy to, giving insight into their collective war-time experiences. Raymer penned on this date,

## "From Fourth North Carolina

There is something in the wind; whether or not it proves to be all 'wind' and 'entirely without foundation,' we shall see. For the last two days and nights we have heard occasional firing to the Northeast, the direction of the Rappahannock. Sometimes at the dead hours of midnight, those ominous sounds disturb our slumbers; 'tis then that it makes us feel uneasy.' During the day time we pay no attention to them. The weather has been cold, windy, rainy and every other ugly feature imaginable; and to make ourselves more comfortable, we (my mess) bought us a capital little cooking stove just one week ago, around which we were gathered to-night at eight o'clock, congratulating ourselves on our good fortune and good times generally, then to our utter dismay, a courier stepped to the door of our tent and said, 'Pack up and be ready to march at a moments notice.'

Gracious! How our feathers were clipped! Such a crew of blank countenances and chop fallen faces it is hardly possible to conceive. Our jolly chat was suspended, the smoke ceased to ascend in 'dizzy wreaths' from our pipes, and we sat full three minutes staring at each other as if we had been doomed to perpetual night. "That's the dickens again," says J. as he mechanically took his stumpy pipe stem between his teeth. "Now that we are comfortably fixed and can laugh at stormy winter, we cannot get to enjoy it. It is too bad--too bad! But this war for you, and when shall it be any better?" "There is no necessity for grumbling, boys," I remarked, "and the best we can do is to take it philosophically, make the best of a bad bargain.

It will not always be so, and the day may not be far distant when these hard times will be over, and we can look back with pleasure to the fortitude with which they were borne by us. Cheer up, and let's get to work; cooking rations, packing our knapsacks, (throwing away such articles as we cannot possibly carry, besides being of little service) burning our letters, &c. Now, Nat has one, (a letter of course) no he cannot commit to the flames yet, he don't think it's time has come; at any rate, he will risk 'one eye' on it for a few days. It is now ten o'clock at night, orders to march are not yet issued, but we are momentarily expecting them. We need not conjecture from those pages we can blot nothing, the present, then is all with which we have to do. But, judging from the past, we have reason to look forward with dread forebodings.

Not that our army is not brave, or may be defeated in battle, or any thing of the sort; but the suffering, hardships and the heart rendering scenes incident to battle, all of which we are compelled to witness, these make us quail at the thought of an approaching conflict. I would caution my readers to be prepared for any kind of news; the storm may blow over without a fight, but I do not think it. We can but hope that our cause, under Providence, may be successful as in days past. We are getting pretty well prepared for winter. Though we are but poorly supplied with tents, yet, most of the men have constructed shelters of some kind. Most of them are caves dug in the side of the hill on which we are camped, and covered with sticks, leaves, dirt, & c. But these holes are right dangerous things, as one of our boys found out to his sorry. This is the way of it: A few nights ago we were requested to go serenading some distance from camp. To be sure we went, and a magnificent time we had too. The small hours of midnight were creeping on as we entered camp on our return; but as our quarters were on the opposite side, we had to pass through the entire regiment to get to them.

It was intensely dark, and knowing the hill to be full of uncovered caves, domiholes not finished, we had to be very careful where we set our feet. But with all our caution, my dear friend, John T. made a misstep and tumbled heels over head in a hole about six feet deep. I heard the rumpus and turned to render assistance, but being fearful of a similar fate, I "cooned" it up to the verge of the "hoil," as they are generally termed, and bawled out, "Hello Who's down there?" "Oh Nat," says he "I believe I've broke my leg." "Plague take your leg," I replied, "what about your instrument?" He only have a doleful groan, and handed the instrument up to me. It was enough, if it had been mauled a week, it could not have been mashed flatter. Don't think that my friend was top heavy—not that—but he will run into such places sometimes.

As the winter wore on, the soldiers' perspective on their diet in this regiment seemed to fluctuate between plenty and paucity in spite of the earlier commissary receipt showing they had plenty of meat. A private in Company C wrote about their food, explaining that it was, "tolerable, plenty such as it is. Some of the bacon is so strong that it is impossible to use it. We get plenty of flour, sometimes a little rice." He also indicated that the regiment was largely sleeping in cloth tents with small stone chimneys that were "tolerable comfortable." Typical of soldiers throughout any war, he also despised the drilling they had to do three times a day and roll call each morning. This private reflected the general mood of the encampment by stating, "The boys are desperately tired of this war...Times are very dull at present...".5 Raymer again wrote to the *Statesville Landmark* on 23 February (published in the *Carolina Watchman* on 9 March), telling of bitter cold winter marches and giving examples of how the men dealt with boredom. He also shares an interesting perspective on the practice of "pickets" trading coffee, sugar, etc. with enemy soldiers. In the military tactics of the day, pickets were guards posted on the outskirts of an army to protect it from immediate invasion by an enemy. He entitled this letter,

"From the Fourth North Carolina,

The old fourth is still in the neighborhood of Fredericksburg. This week we made a move which for suffering beats anything we have ever seen. Fortunately for us, it was soon all over. On Tuesday last, at 3 o'clock, P.M., we were ordered to get ready to march immediately. An attempt to describe our feelings would be useless, enough to say we were awfully bored. During the night and day snow had been falling without a moment's intermission, and at the time we began our march the ground was covered six inches deep, and still getting deeper. But there was no use trying to shirk it, (and I am proud to say that but few attempted it) the trip was made. As darkness began to settle on us we set out, loaded like jack mules, and trudging in snow half knee deep. "Good God," thought I as I went half bent against wind and sleet—"this is soldiering in earnest." "How much more could a man endure and live?" "All my philosophy avails but little now. Something uncommonly urgent must be up or they would surely not take us out such a night as this. But if I only knew where we were going; hope we will travel all night, if we don't and have to make our beds in this snow and tempest, besides, some one will freeze sure.' This I sohloquized, and a great deal more.

I verily believe "a preacher would have sworn." I looked around on the desolate hills and plains covered with a vast winding sheet of snow. I could see dark masses of troops moving in front and rear of us, and could not help contrasting ourselves with the French army in Russia. "Can this be America, the boasted land of freedom, or is it the domains of a military despot." "Are these the peaceable citizens of America or the tools of some tyrant." Such reflections were spontaneous, I could not banish them from my mind. I confess that I came nearer "caving in" than I ever did before, but with a mighty effort I was enabled to quell these rising feelings of discontent and, in short succumb.

The labor necessary to get us through the snow soon brought on copious perspiration; mile after mile was slowly counted off as hour after hour of the night wore away. We were not allowed to halt for rest, which was certainly a wise precaution, though it bore dreadfully on us. Finally, we came to a bold running creek with icebound banks, but it proved no obstacle. Without slacking our gait we lunged in, stumbled across and crawled out on the opposite side, considering it a capital thing. What a pity our dear mamas didn't know we could stand water so well; for lack of knowledge they have certainly missed a wonderful chance of rare fun. But wouldn't it have been rich for them to play "mother duck" while we would have seen goslings-ducklings, I should say; if I mistake not, a gosling is a little goose, except when we mean human goslings of which I have seen a few for sartin.

But this is the wrong road; --ah, that is my failing. I hope my kind readers will excuse me, and in the future I will endeavor to stick closer to my text; though a bad one, yet I will expatiate from firstly even unto seventhly--I am sure thcy are at liberty to leave church in case they become wearied. Away we went, (after we got across the creek) not such a breakneck gait either as you might          imagine, but we toddled, I'll say that, for I doubt whether anybody knows how fast that is. Well, we toddled on some two miles further when we were turned into shanties already built, and recently vacated by a portion of Hood's troops.

Footnote:

Nathaniel Jacob Raymer resided in Iredell County, at Statesville, North Carolina before the war. He enlisted in Company C, "The Saltillo Boys" in April 1861. Raymer was well known as a baritone vocalist and musician in the area. He served roughly nine months as a private in the infantry, and transferred to the regimental band in 1862. This image is undated, but was likely taken when the regiment was encamped at Richmond, Virginia. Raymer is wearing the North Carolina state issue uniform, which the regiment received in July 1861. Raymer's pose, weapons and accoutrements are identical to those shown in an identical photo of Private Alfred Turner, another member of Company C who also appears in a rare full length pose taken in the field. See Greg Mast's *State Troops and Volunteers: A photographic record of North Carolina's Civil War Soldiers*, Vol. 1, (Raleigh NC: 1995), 53 (No. 2.77) to view Turner's image. Original held in private collection.

Our surprise was great and agreeable—the move was, after all, decidedly to our advantage. I very readily took back all that I had thought or said during the march, and made a firm resolve never again to be dissatisfied with anything, no matter what, which I did not fully understand. Roaring fires were built from the wood prepared by those who lately occupied the cabins, and in half an hour after our arrival all hands were snoozing comfortable. The next morning we awoke, and at first thought that we had gone home on furlough, or were out visiting, or something of the sort. Things presented such a comfortable appearance that we were right sure that we were dreaming, or the subjects of some trick; but soon we were convinced that all was bona fide, a glance out of doors was sufficient. The snow lay deep on the ground, but the air was milder, and rain was falling on one of your regular drizzle-drozzles. So was it the next day, and the next. The snow disappeared, leaving a world of mud and water, and an hour by sun on Thursday evening, February 19th, the last vestige of a cloud disappeared from the sky, and the atmosphere, through hardly purse, was perfectly transparent.

We could see Fredericksburg, poor Fredericksburg! about a mile distant. We could trace the meanderings of the Rappahannock, and on the bluffs and table lands beyond we can see a forest of tents, occupied by the Grand Army of the North, wondering no doubt whether this is the road to Richmond. Old Burnie tried this rout once, it didn't pay. Fighting Joe Hooker now has a notion of trying it awhile. I should not be surprised if, six months hence, he should exclaim as did the Arkansas belle at the close of a frolic-- Here I've sot, and sot, till I've about tuck root, and nobody didn't come to Richmond I guess, will be like the grapes were to the fox, our, therefore not worth striving for. Our regiment is at this time on picket down on the banks of the river--they will return tomorrow. True, the pickets are not allowed to shoot at each other, but all intercourse is forbidden,--both wise policies.

The former is barbarous in the extreme—the latter can be productive or no good in the long run—none to our enemies at least. A month ago our boys were on picket near the same place; then free intercourse was allowed. As might be guessed, the rebels made it pay, and any quantity of tobacco was swapped off for five times its worth in coffee. Newspapers were exchanged, can-teens and overcoats bought for a trifle, paid in tobacco of course—the yankees are crazy as bedbugs for it. A good many letters were sent across to be mailed; New Yorkers and North Carolinians would discuss "the prospects" for and hour, then shake hands and part mutually well pleased with each other. The Yanks say they are heartily tired of fighting for the d—d negroes and don't care how soon the affair is wound up; and if the privates had the management they would soon wind it up. In a tour from camp, I discovered many traces of the bloody battle recently fought here. The trees are shivered by shells and cannon shot; the saplings in many places are riddled with bullets—some were shot entirely off; fences scattered, houses demolished, and everything looks like it last hastening to ruin.

The most revolting sight of all is the half buried men. These are of the enemy--our own were decently and well buried. There is a place, not very far from our camp, where seventy-seven of the enemy were tumbled into one hole--a few shovelsful of dirt were thrown on them and that is all; their partially decayed bodies now lie exposed to the gaze of passers by. What a shocking thing! If they have been our enemies, they now certainly deserve the respect due to dead men. How many whose bones are bleaching there, not long ago left home full of lusty life, and left there, too, mothers—doating mothers, loving wives, gentle sisters, or little prattling boys and girls, or lisping infants--Harrowing thought! Go, leave me!!

The night is last going, and gusts of wind have caused my candle to melt and run down the bayonet, used for a candle stick, thus depriving me of at least an hour's light. A bright fire is sparkling in the chimney, and as it burns that strange phenomenon, "tramping snow" is going on briskly. I should not be surprised if we should have more snow to tramp before many days, but no matter, we are well prepared for it, provided we get to stay here. We do every thing according to military science out here; we have musket barrels for pokers, (there are not a few scattered over these plains) ramrods for pothooks, parch wheat and pound it in a skillet with the breech of a gun--in fact, a gun has something to with almost every thing we do. No wonder the boys seem so much attached to them, and spend so much time keeping them in order still the time is not more than half occupied with all necessary duties.

The intervals are spent snow balling when there is snow, the "Bull pen," "cat," etc., is the order of the day. I hardly ever hear any one say, "I do wish this war was over"—"When do you think we will have peace;" and such like;we don't bother our brains about it, well knowing that anything that we can do will have but little effect towards shortening or prolonging it. We have an easy time; (except on marches-I must admit that it don't pay to have our feet clogged with snow) we get rations abundant, and good too;--pshaw! if nobody were suffering more than we, why we would consider it a happy time generally. But the trouble is I can't get to see Gemima nor can Gemima get to see me, and I'm afraid she will take a fool notion to pitch into somebody else or somebody else into her."

March was not a good season back at home in Salisbury either as there was trouble brewing for the soldiers' families and friends. Food prices were outrageously high for staple food items such as flour and meat. Many North Carolina merchants simply gouged the public in, often causing several people to do without. On 18 March, a group of women from Salisbury -- largely mothers and wives of Rowan County soldiers, including some whose spouses and brothers were members of the Rowan Rifles -- grew so angry about the price gouging that they took the matter into their own hands. Armed with hatchets, the women marched into the stores of several local merchants whom they deemed "speculators" and demanded the vendors give them flour, bread, and such at lower prices. Some were literally starving, unable to pay the exorbitant prices of $45 for a barrel of flour in Salisbury. This event became known as the Salisbury Bread Riot, and the ladies' aggressive albeit effective action resulted in the price of flour dropping to $25 per barrel. One merchant even gave them ten barrels!6

The ladies were not arrested, but local authorities reported their names to Gov. Zebulon Vance for "plundering." In response, the ladies wrote to Vance to explain their actions. They complained of price gouging for food as well as other problems they faced at home without their husbands. Their letter shows a great trust and confidence in the governor, but more so their expectation that the food crisis be remedied post haste. Their letter also reveals another level of the economic plight in North Carolina. Not only was the government facing price gouging for clothing, but those ladies working at home to assemble the garments also had the short end of the bargain - the very government Vance so ardently defended when he earlier attacked local textile mill proprietors. One example was his letter to the owner of Fries Mills in Winston Salem for refusing to take seventy five percent profit margins on their textile goods sold to the military depot. They were only paying civilian seamstresses fifty cents for a pair of lined pants and seventy five cents to assemble a coat. A careful review of supply forms received by Company K in this period shows that the government charged on average between $5 - $12 for these garments; hardly a fair ratio to the seamstresses. Fed up with the profiteering and greed, the ladies of Salisbury addressed their governor:

"Having from absolute necessity been forced into measures not at all pleasant to obtain something to eat by the cruel and unfeeling Speculators who have been gathering up at enormous prices, not only bread stuffs but every thing even down to eggs Chickens & Vegetables to carry out of our State for the purpose of Speculating them upon them. We feel it our duty Honored and esteemed Governor to inform you truthfully of our proceedings and humbly pray to inform us whether we are justifiable in what we have done-and if not for Heaven's Sake tell us how these evils are to be remedied. We Sir are all Soldiers Wives or Mothers our Husbands & Sons are now separated from us by this cruel War not only to defend our humble homes but the homes and property of the rich man and at the same time that we are grieved at this separation yet we murmur not. God bless them our hearts go with them and our prayers follow them for protection through all the trials and difficulties that may surround them, but...we must live while they are gone...without much or in many cases any assistance from them for how far will eleven dollars go in a family...Meat is from 75 to $100 pr pd flour $ pr bll. Wood from 4 to $5 pr load, meal 4 an 5 dollars per bushel, eggs 50 to 60 cts pr doz chickens $700 pr doz, Molasses $700 pr gal rye 20 cts pr qt...we are willing to do work early and late to keep off starvation which is now staring us in the face, but the government only allows us 50 cts a pr for lined pants and 75 cts for coats and there are a few of us who can make over a dollar a day, and we have upon an average from three to five helpless children to support and still we complain not at Government prices if we can only get bread divided among us meat at a reasonable price... many of us work day after day without a morsel of meat to strengthen for our Labors and often times we are without bread Now Sir we ask you in the name of God how are we to live.

Laboring under all these difficulties Sir as we have told you in the commencement of this letter were from Stern necessity compelled to go in search of foot to sustain life and some forty or more respectable but poor women started out backed by many citizens to get food we took our little money with us and offered to pay Government prices for what we took but the Speculators refused us any thing or even admittance into their premises. We then forced our way in and compelled them to give us something we succeeded in obtaining twenty three blls of flour two sacks of salt about half a bll of molasses and twenty dollars in money, which was equally divided among us...Now Sir this is all we done and necessity compelled us to do it and the reason we have addressed you...we have been reported to you as plunders of the town and disturbing the peace and quiet of the community...we now pray your protection or a remedy for these evils – we as much as any one deplore the necessity of such proceeding and do humbly pray you in behalf of our helpless children to so fix the prices of bread and meat that we can by our own labor gain a honest portion of that which sustains life. To whom can we go but to you our highly esteemed and cherished Gov to redress these evils. You were the choice of our Husbands and Sons and we look up to you Sir with perfect confidence as being able and willing to do something for us-we ask not charity we only ask for fair and reasonable prices for provisions and leather for Sir many of us have been shoeless this whole winter except the cloth shoes we can make for ourselves which are no protection against the cold, in conclusion Sir we humbly beg you after carefully and prayerfully considering our letter to let us hear from you...Soldiers Wives"

The regiment's general morale improved by April, according to Nat Raymer although overall the 4th NCST continued to anticipate the approach of the upcoming spring campaigns with dread, which began in April. Raymer's next letter to the editor started with a brief poem, with an ironic sense of optimism. One of its' more fascinating themes is his discussion of each opposing side's tendency during wartime to attribute divine favor to their side's cause; Raymer admits his own theological biases, but quickly dissuades the reader from the presumptuous view that either side was deserving of such favor. This missive made its way to the *Carolina Watchman* on 20 April although he actually wrote on 8 April 1863 from his camp near Fredericksburg:

"To be happy, and pass life with pleasure
Is a secret 't were well all would treasure:
If the sky be serene, or o'er shaded,
Tho of fortune the Fatex may bereave me
I resolve to be merry and gay,
Time travels too fast
To be sad or o'ercast,
It is wisdom to laugh while we may"

This is our logic-it ought to be of every soldier. What is the use of fretting with things over which we have no control. Contentment is truly the great secret of happiness. Though it is hard for us to bear up under many of the crosses we have here, yet it is undoubtedly best for us to wear a cheerful exterior, and make the best of our lots under all circumstances. Here, if a man is humorously included, he can always find something to laugh at; on the other hand, if he is of a morose and gloomy temperment, rest assured that he can find enough to render him most miserable every day of his life for ten years to come. He will grumble about his rations, consider them not half enough or good enough; he has to perform a great deal of unnecessary duty, his officers use partiality, or neglect him entirely—his company sergeants and corporals are a set of "bigheads" he could do better himself, with a thousand such foolish notions.

All nonsense; they are not to be pitied. It is no wonder that such fellows never have any favors shown them. They do nothing to accommodate their associates are even ill and overbearing in their dealings with them. They are half hypochondriacs, and when they do in fact get sick, the surgeons, disgusted with their former hypocrisy, pay very little attention to them, and to talk of getting a furlough is absurd. These are the men who write those "doleful letters from the army." But the effective portion of the army is composed of such men as think –"Let the wide world wag as it will, We will be gay and happy still."

They are first on duty, always cheerful, popular with their comrades and first when favors are to be shown. Depend upon it, the man who maintains an even temperment in the army will do to be to. Everything still remains quiet on the Rappahannock. True, we have had orders to send all our surplus baggage to Richmond, I.e. call that we cannot carry, and make ready for an arduous campaign. We are expecting marching orders, but where to is impossible for us to tell. The tents of the Yankee army are as thick as ever beyond the river, and almost every afternoon a huge balloon ascends from their midst. The man in the basket takes a peep at the rebels and then descends to communicate some valuable intelligence to Fighting Joe, no doubt. Whether he is pleased or not with all he sees, we can't tell, but he takes good care to keep out of orange of our guns along the river hills.

A storm is gathering evidently, and not here only, but at several other places in the South. Ere another three months roll around, our land will tremble with the terrible shock of mighty armies. Oh, how anxiously we look forward to the results! Our destiny is in the hands of an all wise God—we can but hope that in the future He will favor us as He has done in the past. If our cause, indeed, be just, we will surely come off conquerors in the end, though we may see much tribulation, and "wade through seas of blood." We cannot expect Heaven's blessing on the ground that we are universally a God-fearing people, or even because a majority of us are so, which is certainly not the case: but a certain city was once sparred because of a few righteous persons were found within its limits, so with our nation—our home—may they be spared because of the few pious souls still left in our midst.

I hope to God that not all are gone astray—not all become filthy. God's hand now lies heavy upon us—His chastenings are sore and grievous; but surely we are not all Pharoh's or his descendants that our hearts should grow harder! Our trust lies in the Christian people at home-what if the large majority should be women, our mothers our sisters? On their prayers hangs our salvation. It is now that we can hardly realize our situation. We have so long been in the army that we are almost induced to consider it a necessary part of life; and the wickedness heard and witnessed every day has grown familiar, it does not shock us now like it once did, we pay no attention to it. To say anything about it is folly, instead of doing any good it brings down a cursing on our own heads; the best we can do then is to stand aloof ourselves, hoping that the day is not far distant when we shall be more agreeably situated."

The only Company K muster roll covering the period 31 December 1862 through 30 April 1863 indicates a slight decrease in the total number of enlisted men available for duty until just before the major battles fought at Chancellorsville on 1-3 May 1863, and is summarized below.7

| Captain | 1 Lt | 2 Lt | Brevet Lt | Sgt | Cpl | Musicians | Privates | Total Enlisted | Aggregate |
|---|---|---|---|---|---|---|---|---|---|
| 1 | 1 | 2 | 1 | 2 | 2 | 1 | 49 | 59 | 63 |

The muster roll for this period reveals a great deal of turnover among the company officers. Captain Coughenhour had returned to the regiment from convalescent leave in late 1862, after his wound at Seven Pines, but was quickly transferred to Brigade Staff as acting Brigade Inspector General, leaving command of the company to 1st Lieutenant Marcus Hofflin. However, Hofflin was detached as Regimental Commissary in February, which is not surprising given his propensity for acquiring material goods and supplies evidenced in his successful civilian career. 2d Lieutenant Hamilton Long was company commander for a brief period in February, until he became seriously ill and sent to Richmond for hospitalization 16 March 1863. 2d Lieutenant Addison Wiseman was left in command from February through 3 May when he was wounded at the battle of Chancellorsville. Sergeant Moses Locke Bean was brevetted as a 2d Lieutenant in December 1862, in spite of having a debt to settle with the quartermaster. The roll shows Bean's pay was docked for $3.50 to cover a pair of boots he requested on 8 December 1862, but left unpaid, and he later returned to serve as a non-commissioned officer. Sergeants Otto Holshouser and Michael Hennesy were present, but Sgt. John Peden remained on sick leave since 19 August 1862.

Corporals Richard Williams and Alfred Carter were present but William Parker also remained on sick leave from 19 August 1862. Company K had an unusually high number of enlisted men detailed to serve as clerks for various brigade staff officers in this period, including William

Durrell, Francis Mills, Michael Deaton, James Roberts and Isaac O'Neil. Jacob Fraley, was assigned as a hospital steward on 1 January 1863, and then briefly attached to brigade staff as a clerk. Fraley did not see this as a setback, however, as he was well liked by staff officers, and managed to acquire a post as assistant surgeon in the 7th NCST on 19 February 1863, and later attained an appointment as 2d Lieutenant on 6 April 1863. Jacob Fraley may have also petitioned for his cousin, Wilburn Fraley who was then the company orderly or First Sergeant, to receive a commission as Wilburn was appointed as 1st Lieutenant in February 1863, only to be reduced to the ranks in June following several weeks Away without Leave after the battle of Chancellorsville, and he was unable to explain the absence by capture. Cpl Arnold Friedheim was also detached to serve as orderly to Brig. Gen. Stephen Ramseur, their brigade commander. One can only speculate as to why so many enlisted men were detached as clerks from this company, but a perusal of census data suggests that most were literate who could write well, one of the most stringent requirements for a clerk. Shortly afterward, Alfred Carter was promoted to corporal.

Others did not fare as well, including Milas Holshouser who was still under arrest and confined from November 1862, along with Philip Heilig and W.D.C. Peeler, who had all been identified as Away without Leave. Henry Williams continued to serve with the pioneers where he had been detached since 19 August 1862. John Endie was detailed as a provost guard at Danville, Virginia on 14 February 1863 where he served until 1865. One of the musicians, Bradley Matthews, was also identified as Away without Leave on 31 January 1863 and remained so until after the battle of Chancellorsville. Michael Rowland was identified as Away without Leave on 3 April 1863, and not present at Chancellorsville. Privates John C. Deaton, Richard Fulk, John Lockett, William Lillycross, William Murr, Alexander McQueen, Daniel McQueen, William Morris, John Mauldin, all remained in the hospital or at home in Rowan County on convalescent leave from wounds. Joseph Thompson died in a Richmond hospital on 11 March 1863 from wounds received at Fredericksburg.

The inspecting officer summarized the companies' activities from the time of the last muster roll through early May when the battle of Chancellorsville was fought noting, "The company has been performing heavy duty, they marched to Chancellorsville and was engaged, then to Richmond to camp." The inspector also indicated their arms, supplies, clothing and military bearing were "very good" at this time. It is also useful to note that Nat Raymer reported the regiment received a number of conscripts, or draftees, between February-April 1863, including three in Company K. Those men were Lewis Brady and Joseph Saunders, along with Robert Roberts, the father of James Roberts. James was an antebellum member of the Rowan Rifle Guards and it was doubtless awkward for him to witness the merciless taunting that conscripts received from the veterans, knowing it was also his father. Raymer's letter of 28 April 1863 includes a brief description of the welcome given to the "fresh fish" and was published on 11 May. An excerpt states: "...Yesterday we received thirty-six conscripts in our regiment-and I hope the last installment from the Old North State, the last for a season at least. Like the fellow who got drunk on punch—I say "too much of a good thing is enough at any time." These men are all from the western part of the State, though but two or three from Iredell, and perhaps the same number from Rowan. I am not personally acquainted with a single one of them all. They do not look so hearty and fresh as our soldiers, and from all appearances I fear but few will prove to be of much service. The officer in charge said he started with forty-two, but six escaped from him by jumping from the cars while they were running."

As the winter weather began to clear, the soldiers sensed that the next campaign was looming. One soldier in the 4th NCST wrote to his family and friends on 3 April, again reflecting the inconsistency of food sources, "...We are suffuring at this time & have for some time for something to eat. We get one little mess a day. I am all the time hungry...We are also under marching orders. We are expected to leave at any moment. We know not where we will go...I hope this war can not last much longer...we will certainly suffer badly for something to eat..."[8] Nat Raymer reported to the *Carolina Watchman* on 28 April (published 11 May) that "The old 4th is now on picket five miles below, and near the banks of Rappahannock. They will return tomorrow and re-occupy the same old quarters I presume." He again wrote in a 28 April letter, describing the more leisurely and humorous activities of the regiment at this time. Their recreation was interrupted by an unwanted visit from some Federal guests, indicating that soon spring would bring another campaign:

"Each morning every seventh man in the regiment is allowed to go fishing, and when they return at sunset, the same number are allowed to go for the night if they choose. A few are caught with hook and line but the great mass are caught with dip nets, which are bought from citizens around. The results is fish in super abundance, mostly shad and herring, the former weighing on an average four pounds, the latter about one. We draw from the commissary enough fat bacon to fry them, which being "done up brown," with light bread, rice, coffee made from the same grain parched, and sugar, make a capital meal. We do not fool away time trying to pick the meat from the bones, but swallow all together, if they lodge, an old moldy biscuit (a lot of which are always kept on hand for the purpose) forced down with a ramrod removes all obstructions, besides checking a digestion too vigorous and hereby produces a wonderful sense of relief. Numerous minute fish-bones are protruding all over the surface of our bodies, so much that we look like huge cylinders for music boxes. There is no danger whatever of being "scrounged" at night, (it will be better before we come home on furlough again) but what in the world are we to do about changing our linen? This is a mystery that we cannot solve, and would like to have the advice of sympathizing friends of the momentous subject.

One night last week our camp was thrown into a blaze of excitement about the rumored advance of the enemy below us; it was said that they were crossing the river in heavy force. Orders were issued to be ready to march at a moments notice, (that is the general way of expressing it) upon which the usual consternation was visible. A frightful storm was howling around us which made it almost certain that we would march,--such is invariably our luck. We lay down and slept, well knowing that the long roll would wake us, provided they would wake us to march before day. The wind slashed our old demoralized tent about until it was badly torn as Lou's dress was then a "black racer" chased us in the strawberry patch, but now the consequences were of a more serious nature. The rain dashed on our faces, the little ditch around our tent was overflowed, and if we had not set our feet against small stumps we would have been washed to the foot of the hill; but we pulled the blankets over our hears, turned over for another snooze and when we awoke it was daylight, or as nigh as it could be beneath such black clouds. The rain had not slacked a particle but our suspense was in a measure relieved by orders for the brigade to go on picket, which it did at 9 o'clock a.m., leaving the band in camp; a favor for which we are under obligation to Col. G. the preceding alarm was not altogether false, but greatly exaggerated.

A small force of the enemy had crossed the river and fallen afoul of our fishing parties, scaring them out of their wits, (some I guess hadn't far to go) capturing four wagons, two of which they burned, ok their nets also, and scattered the frightened fellows to the four winds, but took no provisions. After the rascals had done all the mischief, which upon the whole, was rather ludicrous, they beat a hasty retreat to the other side of the river. Since then all is profound quiet; no warlike demonstrations, nor anything indicating a move. Far in the distance beyond the Rappahannock may be seen whole plantations full of yankee tents, and every day that everlasting balloon is up. Our camp is located on a piece of high-lying land, I can hardly term it a hill, but from my tent door I can see over a very large scope of country. Partly because I am somewhat elevated, but more because the timber is swept clean from the surrounding neighborhood. Due North six miles lies Fredericksburg, the spires of which may be seen rising above the intervening pines. In flourishing times the town looks like it might have contained seven or eight thousand inhabitants now not more than two or three hundred of the original denizens can be seen. The lower part was burnt a few days before the late battle, nothing is left but some blackened walls and solitary chimneys. The remainder of the burg is riddled with shot and shells, the upper part especially looks like a ruin, in short, a few words will convey the whole idea, a grave yard and bat roost. The citizens are refugees scattered throughout the Confederacy..."

### "Treading on Sacred Ground" – Chancellorsville

Now battle hardened veterans, as the new spring season brought renewed fighting, the soldiers in Company K were dreading the onslaught they now knew was imminent. They understood the real question was not if, but when, and where the next major engagement would occur. Their questions were answered in late April, as Maj. Gen. Joseph Hooker, a West Pointer known for his fighting spirit, was then commanding the Army of the Potomac. Hooker devised an elegant plan for his spring campaign; he intended to trap the Confederates at Fredericksburg by flanking Lee's Army of Northern Virginia and splitting it in half from the rear on 1 May. Capt. W.C. Coughenhour was returned from his duties as a staff officer in time to command Company K at Chancellorsville, which proved to be a pivotal point in the service of this company, as well as the Confederate army. Historians generally consider the 1-3 May 1863 battles at Chancellorsville to be Robert E. Lee's *coup de' tau* over the Union army, but it also cost the South its premier battlefield leader Lt. Gen. Thomas "Stonewall" Jackson, who although completely surprised the XI Corps when his divisions led by Rodes and Gordon slammed into the unsuspecting Federal right flank, was mortally wounded that night by friendly fire ironically produced by men from North Carolina.

As the armies engaged on the morning of 1 May, Hooker managed to get on Lee's flanks, but could not budge the determined Confederates. Rather than pressing them with his tactical advantage and numerical superiority, Hooker somehow hesitated when he received news the fighting was stalemated. He pulled his army back toward Chancellorsville, and lost precious time, which Lee quickly discerned as a paramount opportunity. Lee later met with Lt. Gen. Thomas "Stonewall" Jackson that night and planned his own scheme in what neither knew would be their last council of war. Lee decided to split his army in two, and ordered Jackson on a bold thirteen mile flank march around the Federal army on 2 May with intentions of attacking Hooker's unsuspecting extreme right flank. Jackson's II Corps consisted of numerous North Carolina regiments, including Brig. Gen. Stephen Dodson Ramseur's brigade (2nd, 4th, 14th, and 30th North Carolina Regiments.), who had acquired a reputation in the Army of Northern Virginia as "shock troops". This was due to having led numerous attacks in some of the heaviest fighting of the war. Ramseur's Brigade was then assigned to Maj. Gen. Daniel H. Hill's Division, who had recently turned his command over to Brig. Gen. Robert E. Rodes when he was ordered back to North Carolina. The battles at Chancellorsville would again prove that Ramseur's reputation was well earned. Hooker's right flank was located just west of Chancellorsville along the rolling countryside that contained the Orange Plank Road. It consisted of Maj. Gen. Oliver Howard's XI Corps, who was unaware that Stonewall Jackson's II Corps was stealthily prodding toward them late in the evening of 2 May; Oliver's XI Corps was wide open to attack. Many of the men were sleeping, playing cards, or otherwise caught unaware as Jackson's men stormed the Union breastworks around dusk.9

Once in position, Jackson ordered his division commanders to direct their brigades to attack quickly. Brig. Gen. Robert E. Rodes had numerous North Carolina regiments in his division, including the 4th NCST who slammed into Howard's XI Corps. The surprise action resulted in a rout, with the Federal lines literally rolled backward some four miles toward Chancellors Crossing running across the rolling hillside and through dense woods eastwardly in chaos. Eventually, Hooker managed to form a new line and his army entrenched themselves around Chancellorsville. Rodes' men now advanced to a point located in a dense wooded area located between Hazel Grove and Plank Road, about one quarter of a mile behind the earth works that Maj. Gen. Henry W. Slocum's XII Corps had just abandoned, where they stopped for the night. A great deal of confusion existed in Lee's army as hundreds of Confederates slowly stumbled their way through the dense wooded areas that lined the Turnpike in total darkness trying to locate their regiments. Many soldiers remained separated from their regiments and simply moved forward with whatever unit was nearby, and then later tried to return to their commands. Later in the evening, just after 10:00 PM on 2 May, Lt. Gen. Thomas "Stonewall" Jackson was mortally wounded while trying to ascertain the location of the new Federal lines.

Ironically, it was a result of friendly fire by soldiers from the 18th NCT, and possibly one or two other nearby North Carolina regiments, (depending upon which scholar one heeds on this subject) who were much confused in the dark, smoky wilderness with hundreds of soldiers moving around. Historic consensus is they thought Jackson and his staff were Federal cavalry troopers, as Jackson had rode in front of Confederate lines about one hundred yards in a deeply wooded area near the Orange Plank Road while attempting to reconnoiter Federal lines. The loss of Jackson caused several high ranking officers to change commands within the II Corps later that night, with the division commanders trying to keep the matter quiet until Lee could sort out what was his next move. Jackson himself even insisted that no one should know of the incident in order to protect the morale of his men. The chaotic scenario in the densely wooded area containing thousands of disenfranchised men trying to locate their regiments, along with the inevitable rumors occurring after Jackson's wounding at both division, brigade and regimental command levels for several hours, produced a general state of confusion and disorganization along Lee's lines into the early morning of 3 May, when several regiments became completely enmeshed in their own lines, making it difficult, if not impossible to distinguish one command from another in some places, especially in Rodes' Division along the Plank Road.

But when Lee chose a replacement for Jackson, the rumors flew even more strongly. Maj. Gen. James Ewell Brown "J.E.B." Stuart, a cavalry officer well known for his aggressive fighting style and skillful reconnaissance tactics, was chosen to replace Jackson as commander of the II Corps. This decision made many officers quite uneasy since Stuart was a cavalry officer and not of the infantry, even though he enjoyed a sterling reputation as a fighter at that point in the war. The 4th

NCST color bearer, Sgt. John Stikeleather of Company C, had born the colors amazingly without a serious wound, until he had a close call at Chancellorsville. Stikeleather was not only brave, but he was also an astute observer of human nature. He recalled, "...Had the sun stood still one hour on Saturday evening on the 2nd of May, Hooker's army would have been reduced to a corporals guard. As Jackson's troops advanced upon Hooker's right, it rolled in volumes over the hills and vales carried dismay into the enemy's ranks, and at the same time the sweet sounds so inspirited our troops as to render them absolutely invincible. Night closing upon us when it did was all that saved Hooker from utter destruction. As we were charging down upon Sickle's corps, through that large and dense forest, so well remembered by those who took part in it, an incident occurred that had much of human nature in it. Many wild turkeys and rabbits were seen by our boys, and most of them were flying or running to the rear. As one of the rabbits passed by us heeling it to the rear, one of our boys called out as it passed him, saying, 'Go it Molly cotton tail, if I had no more character to sustain at home than you have I would go with you.' A little bit of pleasantry, but how much of truth there was in it. How many along that line could have truthfully and heartily endorsed the sentiment? Is it not pride of character after all more than anything else that makes us passable soldiers"[10]

Col. Bryan Grimes was by now known as a rather quick tempered officer, with a propensity for having his subordinates arrested in a rather malicious and self-righteous manner, such as when he had Capt. Thomas Blount arrested and charged with insubordination in 1861 for refusing to move a wagonload of firewood out of his way when passing nearby.[11] By 1863, however, his temper seemed to diminish somewhat as his combat exposure had increased across the previous two years. He rarely showed his frustration in graphic form to his wife, but he regularly wrote her sharing detailed experiences from the front lines. He afforded himself the opportunity to take supper from captured enemy campfires on the evening of 2 May, and penned a quick note to her including an account of the attack and his observations of the chaos occurring following Jackson's wounding. Grimes reflected, "...about 3 o'clock on Saturday evening, the 2nd of May, we were in position with Rodes, Division in front, and unexpectedly to them, fell upon Seigel's Corps that as in reserve, and drove the back for miles upon their lines behind the entrenchments, attacked them, and carried the line of earthworks, took the enemy's camp baggage, the meals, then boiling hot on the fire, which we found very refreshing, and just at dark when we supposed the fighting over, and was in the act of eating my supper, by an enemy's camp-fire and from his larder, then unexpectedly a brisk fire commenced, and in a few minutes cannonading, the enemy raking the woods and plank-road with grape and canister. Fearing the enemy were about to charge, I called upon my troops to occupy the breastwork which we had captured an hour previous, and be prepared for the attack. After getting in position...I went up to the road to see if I could hear anything to account for the sudden firing, when I met a party bearing a litter off the field, and enquired who it was...and upon going a step or two further I encountered Gen. Rodes, who informed me that the wounded officer was none other than Gen. Jackson, but he thought it was advisable that it should be concealed from the troops for fear of disheartening them in view of the serious work ahead of us in the morning. We lay down behind our breastworks, and rested for the night."[12]

Despite the resultant humiliation when rumors circulated afterward that the "Tar Heels" had shot Jackson, the "Old North State" still played a vital role at Chancellorsville, in particular the 4th NCST under the command of fiery tempered Col. Bryan Grimes. Jackson's loss may have started the Confederate army on a downward spiral, but his absence was not so obvious on the morning of 3 May along the Plank Road. In this particular phase of the engagement, the 4th NCST was heavily engaged, and remained with Brig. Gen. Stephen Dodson Ramseur's brigade, consisting of the 2d, 14th, and 30th North Carolina. The brigade was located adjacent to the Plank Road for most of the action on 3 May. There the 4th NCST distinguished itself by participating in several daring assaults on Federal works located on the heights above a small creek which traversed the battlefield, losing over fifty percent of its strength. Daybreak occurred around 6:00 AM, and the Confederates were quickly trying to re-organize their lines after receiving an order from J.E.B. Stuart to renew the attack. Not surprisingly, as many changes in command were hastily executed overnight, there was a series of confusing and misunderstood orders transmitted between corps, division and brigade commanders early that morning, causing delays in the attack.[13]

Brig. Gen. Robert Colston commanded a brigade located near Ramseur on the Plank Road, and he had much uncertainty about which commands the many units entangled behind the earthworks belonged to. He saw some North Carolinian's who after the first two attacks had returned to their former positions, stating, "This was a most critical moment. The troops in the breastworks, belonging mainly (I believe) to General Pender's and General McGowan's brigades, were almost without ammunition, and had become mixed with each other and with fragments of other commands. They were huddled up close to the breastworks 6 and 8 deep...".[14] Rodes' Division was then formed into three lines of battle in the heavily wooded area near a small stream along the southern side of the Plank Road, and Ramseur's Brigade was in a difficult spot from the beginning. Rodes aligned Ramseur in his third rank, just behind Brig. Gen. Samuel McGowan, who was himself located behind the brigade of Brig. Gen. James H. Lane. In his left front was Colonel E.A. O'Neal commanding Rodes' own former brigade.[15] Lane initially struck Brig. Gen. Thomas Ruger's 3d Brigade of Maj. Gen. Alpheus Williams 2d Division, of the XII Corps in their front, with the Third Maryland anchored onto the Plank Road next to the 123d New York, who were ordered to a point slightly behind the Federal earth works after roughly one hour due to running out of ammunition.[16]

## Rodes' Third Attack Stalls

As Lane and McGowan's initial attack slowed, Rodes' second line became engaged around 8:30 AM, which also ended in repulse. Ramseur received orders to move forward at 9:00 AM, but due to the brigades of Anderson, Jones and the infamous "Stonewall" Brigade failing to advance in concert with the rest of Rodes' Division in his front, was about to encounter a dangerous scenario ahead. At 9:00 AM, Rodes ordered his division to advance again, and Ramseur quickly moved his men into line and toward the front up the slope toward the earthworks. As he crossed the small stream traversing the field on the south side of Plank Road, Ramseur encountered the brigades of Brig. Gen. R.H. Anderson, John R. Jones and John H.S. Funk's (Stonewall), and quickly discovered on his immediate front, "...small portion of Paxton's brigade and Jones' brigade, of Trimble's division. Knowing that a general advance had been ordered, I told these troops to move forward. Not a man moved. I then reported the state of things to Major-General Stuart, who directed me to assume command of these troops and compel them to advance. This I assayed to do; and, after fruitless efforts, ascertaining that General Jones was not on the field, and that Colonel [T.S.] Garnett had been killed, I reported again to General Stuart, who was near, and requested permission to run over the troops in my front, which was cheerfully granted..."[17]

Within those confused lines behind the works was the Stonewall Brigade, consisting of the 2d, 4th, 5th 27th and 33d Virginia regiments, under Brig. Gen. E.F. Paxton who was killed when trying to lead his brigade in their advance from behind the works just minutes after they stalled. Col. J.S. Funk of the 5th Virginia could not identify the entangled mass of soldiers from several commands

164

that was hunkering behind the earthworks within his own brigade, whom he blamed for not advancing. Funk recalled, "At this point we found large numbers of men whom fear had taken the most absolute possession. We endeavored to persuade them to go forward, but all we could say was of little avail, As soon as the line was formed once more, having been somewhat deranged by the interminable mass of undergrowth in the woods through which we passed, we moved forward. Here, General Paxton Fell…"[18] Funk immediately took command of the stalled brigade, but to no avail, as they were now demoralized and refused to budge from behind the works. Some apologists have attempted to attribute the Stonewall Brigade's failure to advance to learning of the loss of their beloved Stonewall Jackson the night before, but interestingly Funk did not become aware of the loss until later in the day, suggesting this was not a direct factor among their command breakdown or in delaying the advance by the Virginians. One North Carolina soldier left a somewhat more specific description of whom the 4th NCST encountered as they advanced over the works, as he witnessed the stalled masses of men, "The First Virginia, or "Stonewall brigade" was in front of ours, and on Saturday evening, I am told, did good fighting; but on Sunday morning could not be induced, by threats or promises, to budge out of their position."[19]

In spite of obvious ire and disgust toward the confused masses of stalled infantry entangled behind the earthworks, the hot-tempered Col. Bryan Grimes did not specify which brigade they belonged, but simply testified he witnessed their brigade receive orders to go forward, stating,

"…We rested just in rear of the Brigade, a brigade of previous good reputation, which occupied the breastworks captured by is the day previous. A staff officer rode up and directed by command of Gen. J.E.B. Stuart (who had assumed command after Gen. Jackson was wounded) the officer in command of this brigade to advance and charge the enemy, Gen. Ramseur and myself being on the plank-road and hearing the order given. This brigade commander declined to move forward on his command-except by order of his division commander. Gen. Ramseur then said to his staff officer, "Give me the order and I will charge." I remonstrated with him, saying as we had done the fighting of the previous two days, let this brigade move forward and we would support them. Gen. Ramseur said no, repeated his offer to advance, when this officer said, "Then you make them charge, Gen. Ramseur." Gen. Ramseur then turned to me, saying, "Let us hurry back. Call your men to attention!" which I did upon reaching the command, when he ordered the three regiments of his brigade to advance, the other being detached to our right. The command "Forward!" was given, and we moved up to the earthwork occupied by this brigade, and had to climb over these men now lying down behind it for protection, and over the breastworks, and again form line of battle. Our men were entirely disgusted at their cowardly conduct, and I myself, put my foot on the back and head of an officer of high rank in mounting the work, and through very spite, ground his face into the earth."[20]

It is clear the Stonewall Brigade was one of the units Ramseur's men found inside the earthworks, although many sources show there were other units entangled amongst them behind the same earthworks on the morning of 3 May. If one carefully considers extant research examining the chaos occurring inside the Confederate lines as well as that experienced within the division and brigade commands that day, it seems impossible to know precisely who was ultimately responsible for delaying Rodes' third advance. It is most likely that several commands were involved in the delay, not simply one brigade or regiment. This challenges a popular belief that only the Stonewall (Funk's) Brigade was responsible for the stalled advance. Grimes' behavior on the other hand, is historically interpreted as meaning he was angry at the troops laying behind the earthworks, purposefully stepping one of the high ranking officers in the process of moving over their men. But this may not have been the only thing Grimes was angry about. His own account also states that he was resisting Rodes' order to advance his regiment in the lead, as they had essentially been used up the two days previous. We are left to speculation, but these glimpses into those few intense minutes behind the Confederate earthworks on the morning of 3 May do not suggest that Grimes wanted to charge, and may well have been acting not only from anger toward the stalled troops, but also his own frustration with Rodes' order.

In either case, once Ramseur cleared the chaos behind the earth works, Ramseur's charge began shortly after 9:00 AM as hundreds of North Carolinians, including Company K and the 4th NCST, lunged forward into massive musket and artillery fire. Ramseur reported later that his brigade was then aligned as follows, "...perpendicular to the Plank Road, the left resting on the road...I placed Col. [F.M.] Parker, Thirtieth North Carolina, on the right of my brigade; Colonel [R.T.] Bennett, Fourteenth North Carolina, on right center; Colonel [W.R.] Cox, Second North Carolina, left center, and Colonel [Bryan] Grimes, Fourth North Carolina on left." Once outside the works, Ramseur quickly realigned his ranks into line of battle, and gave them orders to move, "At the command "forward," my brigade with a shout, cleared the breastworks and charged the enemy."[21] Ramseur was quickly ordered to cover Maj. Gen. Richard Anderson's right flank, (located on Ramseur's left) now in their front. This required Ramseur to execute an oblique movement, which was difficult in an open field, much less in a densely wooded area. Nat Raymer was also watching when he noted, "Our [brigade] was then ordered to charge over them which they did without waiting for second orders. The woods through which they ran—literally ran, to the charge, was thickly set with trees of ordinary size, saplings and underbrush, and gently descending to a brook immediately beyond which were the breastworks. As they advanced the roar of artillery and small arms was deafening, and the shower of shells, grape, canister, solid shot and minnie balls that were hurled among our boys was truly appalling. Men were falling on all sides-sometimes whole ranks were swept away, but those who were unhurt rushed on headless of the groans and piercing cries around them. The crash of falling timber could be heard above the combination of unearthly noises; shells bursting in the face did not intimidate men, nor impede their progress..."[22]

Ramseur soon received word to send help to the batteries at Hazel Grove, located about three quarters of a mile on his extreme right. He ordered Col. Parker to take the 30th NCT to a point some six to eight hundred yards south near Hazel Grove, where the 30th NCT discovered a flank attack developing and quickly engaged Brig. Gen. Thomas Ruger's Brigade, (First Division, XII Corps) consisting of the 13th New Jersey, 2d Massachusetts, 107th New York, 3d Wisconsin and 27th Indiana.[23] The 2d Massachusetts was also in that brigade but were detached to another location around this time. As Ruger moved his men into the wooded area on Ramseur's right, his men began to envelop the batteries, where the 27th Indiana found a prime location and poured heavy enfilade fire into Rodes' entire right flank, until the 30th NCT cut off their attack. As a gap had opened on his right, Ramseur realized his predicament, stating later that "I saw the danger threatening my right, and sent several times to Jones' brigade to come to my assistance; and I also went back twice myself and exhorted and ordered it (officers and men) to fill up the gap (some 500 or 600 yards) on my right, but all in vain. I then reported to General Rhodes that unless support was sent to drive the enemy from my right I would have to fall back."[24]

The Federals on Ramseur's right where the gap had formed was Col. Charles Candy's 2d Brigade, (2d Division, XII Corps) consisting of the 5th, 7th, 29th, and 66th Ohio Regiments, and the 28th and 114th Pennsylvania Regiments. Candy was formerly called back to a reserve location near the

Chancellors house earlier that morning, but Maj. Gen. Joseph Hooker appeared and personally ordered him to immediately reoccupy his former position in the earth works near Fairview Cemetery, which the brigade accomplished at the "double quick."[25] The Buckeyes and Pennsylvanians were now facing Ramseur's right-center, and the North Carolinians managed to rake Candy's right with musketry for a few minutes. But, the Buckeyes and Keystone troops returned a terrible direct fire into the right flank of the 14th NCST and thee companies of the 2d NCST, forcing them to halt roughly one-quarter mile from their works during the advance. As the Ohioans pushed the gap on Ramseur's right trying to open it even farther by using their bayonets, killing some of Ramseur's men in close combat. The Tar Heels maintained their fire, however, and stubbornly resisted Candy's exploitive tactics, eventually causing the Federals to withdraw.[26]

Ramseur was also now aware of the flanking movements made by the 7th and 5th New Jersey against the gap on his extreme left, that had opened up on the right wing of the 4th NCST (located along the Plank Road) and the remaining seven companies of the 2d NCST. The decision he earlier made to send the 30th NCT to the right proved to be quite intuitive, since now he could get no support from the brigades of Anderson, Funk (Stonewall) or Jones on his right in spite of repeated requests. Ramseur's right was spared from destruction by the 30th NCT, who soon arrived listening to hundreds of "rebel yells" and intense firing on their left, bolstering their courage. Col. Francis Marion Parker, their commander, tried to align his regiment with the rest of the brigade by moving to their left oblique back toward the Plank Road. Parker's return to his former position on the right of Ramseur's line could not have occurred at a better time. It was described as, In the meantime Col Parker, of the 30th (N.C.), approaching from my position from the battery on the right, suddenly fell upon the flank and handsomely repulsed a heavy column of the enemy who were moving in to get in my rear by my right flank, some 300 or 400 of them surrendering to him as prisoners of war. The enemy still held his strong position in the ravine on my right, so that the 14th (N.C.) and the three companies of the 2nd (N.C.) could not advance. The enemy discovered this situation of affairs, and pushed a brigade to the right and rear of Col. Grimes and seven companies of Col Cox's (2nd N.C.), with the intention of capturing their commands. Col Bennett held his position until ordered to fall back, and, in common with all the others to replenish his empty cartridge-boxes. The enemy did not halt at this position but retired to his battery, from which he .was quickly driven, Col Parker of the 30th (N.C.) sweeping over it with the troops on my right."[27]

Meanwhile, the 14th NCST remained on Ramseur's immediate right flank, along with the 2d NCST in the center and the 4th NCST anchored on the Plank Road on his left. Grimes indicated the 4th NCST quickly put their bayonets into action when they reached the Federal works in the attack, recalling, "The 4th Regiment and three companies of the 2nd Regiment never halted or fired until we had taken the enemy's works in our front and bayoneting the Federal soldiers on the opposite side of the earthwork The hill across the ravine was covered by many batteries of artillery, from forty to fifty guns, which had been scouring the woods through which we just passed with grape and canister. Seeing the infantry driven from their works, they abandoned this artillery."[28] When the 4th NCST, and three companies of the 2d NCST reached the Federal lines, they found Brig. Gen. Gersom Mott's 3d Brigade (2d Division, III Corps) consisting of and aligned in the following order from right to left, facing Ramseur: 8th New Jersey, 115th Pennsylvania, 5th New Jersey, 2d New York, 6th New Jersey. The 7th New Jersey was also in Mott's Brigade, although their position was not behind the earth works, but in a forward spot roughly one hundred yards ahead. Mott had been wounded in earlier attacks, and Col. William J. Sewell took command of the brigade by 9:00 AM when Ramseur attacked. Following Rodes' second assault, Sewell pulled his

167

line back to a point behind the earth works parallel to the Plank Road, in order to re-supply his men with ammunition.

Numerous eyewitness accounts corroborate that the 7th New Jersey had earlier discovered a vantage point roughly one hundred yards in front of the Federal earthworks, apart from the brigade along a heavily wooded knoll overlooking the Plank Road at a right angle earlier that morning, but some writers have suggested they were located further south toward Hazel Grove near the 27th Indiana, but recent scholarship has displaced the latter view. Numerous historians have grappled with the question of whether it was really New Jersey units in front of Ramseur, and this is important to understand because it relates directly with what regiment captured battle flags of the 4th and 2d NCST soon afterward. Original sources consistently indicate the Confederate regiments trying to advance along the Plank Road that morning between 6:00 AM and 8:30 AM were literally terrorized by deadly enfilade fire coming from their left oblique by infantrymen located at an elevation above them. This is an important point to grasp as supporting evidence placing the 7th New Jersey in this location before and after 8:30 AM, because soldier accounts consistently reflect the 7th New Jersey troops reported seeing no rebels in their immediate front, meaning they were in a position enabling them to look down the slope firing at a right oblique angle.[29]

The 7th New Jersey was in that position for over three hours, making numerous flanking movements to redirect their fire upon Lane and McGowan's brigades when they tried to advance during the first two attacks occurring between 6:00 and 9:00 AM, driving them back to their former position behind the earthworks from whence they started. As Lane and McGowan's first two assaults (without Ramseur and the 4th NCST in support at that time) came to a standstill, the old Stonewall Brigade was called to assist them, but their advance stalled after Paxton was killed in front of the brigade, shot through his heart trying to motivate them to advance up the hillside near the small stream known as Scott's Run, which ran through the marshy low ground south of Plank Road. The reader should recall this preceded Ramseur's discovery of the enmeshed brigades hiding behind the Confederate earthworks and refusing to move forward. They may well have received enfilade fire from the 7th New Jersey, whose vantage point allowed them to rake the advancing Confederates along the Plank Road, making this another potential causative factor in the chaos Ramseur found in the earth works. The Virginians hiding behind the works may have not only just lost their beloved General Paxton, but also knew that hot enfilade fire from the heights above awaited them and were avoiding further exposure.

One the other hand, the reader is cautioned, as one historian recently indicated the analysis of troop movements along the Orange Plank Road on the morning of 3 May can defy "…even the most careful analysis of the sources…" showing that even with the best original source accounts of this battle, which are often convoluted at best, there is still much speculation as Confederate lines had become completely entangled in the dense forest and chaos of battle. Their Federal adversaries experienced a similar quandary in the densely wooded area on 2 May, which is precisely what Robert E. Lee desired when he devised his original scheme for the surprise attacks at Chancellorsville.[30] Lee knew that achieving Federal disorganization in heavily wooded terrain would seriously reduce the effects of Hooker's numerically superior army. Recent research on the question has suggested that the "most likely place" for the 7th New Jersey was between the right flank of Ruger's Brigade and the area where the left flank of the 123d New York (Ross's Brigade) had been before they fell back after the initial attack, an advanced location formerly mentioned enabling a right oblique angle of fire down the slope.[31]

Capt. Samuel Hopkins of the 7th New Jersey made a diary entry also supporting their advanced location. He indicated the regiment was located on Graham's right flank as the 3d Maryland and 123d New York retreated, remaining in their advanced location on the wooded knoll above the Plank Road.[32] Col. A.L. McDougal of the 123d New York also mentioned that some troops from Mott's 3d Brigade had moved forward in pursuit of rebels who were falling back, and were interfering with his unit's fire on his retreat.[33] The exact time is unknown, but when Ruger started to run out of ammunition, Brig. Gen. Charles K. Graham's Brigade consisting of the 57th, 63d, 68th, 105th, 114th and 1141st Pennsylvania regiments was ordered to relieve them from their position from behind Fairview Cemetery, some two hundred yards south. Here, the 114th Pennsylvania regiment, known as "Collis' Zouaves" who were clad in their bright red trousers, fired one volley and ran from their place in line backward through the 27th Indiana. A general retreat of Graham's Brigade ensued, except for the 27th Indiana who was ordered to cover the brigade while it retreated, as Ruger's men were nearly out of ammunition.[34]

The 7th New Jersey was still in their advanced position on Ramseur's left as he moved up the wooded slopes along Plank Road shortly after 9:00 AM. They quickly engaged the North Carolinians by firing upon them at the right oblique. The rest of Sewell's (Mott's) Brigade had been refitted with new ammunition in the mean time, and moved back into their former positions in the earth works at the double quick as Ramseur attacked, adding fierce frontal fire as well. Because the 4th NCST and seven companies of the 2d NCST had advanced so quickly at a run, it caused a small gap on Col. Bryan Grimes' right as when the rest of Ramseur's men moved up the hill, they became entangled in the dense foliage. The 7th New Jersey saw this as opportunity, and slipped into the gap formed on the right between the right and left respective flanks of the 2d and 4th NCST as they finally reached the crest of the hill and quickly rushed across the Federal earthworks. The 7th New Jersey was then in the advantageous position of firing into the rear of the North Carolinians who were engaged in hand to hand combat using their bayonets beyond the line of earthworks.

Ramseur further witnessed, "The 4th N.C. and seven companies of the 2nd N.C. drove the enemy before them until they had taken the line of his works, which they held under a severe, direct and enfilading fire, repulsing several units on this portion of our front. The 4th N.C. and three companies of the 2nd were compelled to halt some 150-200 yards in rear of the troops just mentioned, for the reason that the troops on my right had failed to come up, and the enemy was in heavy force on my right flank…"[35] The shock of Ramseur's advance was intense; they smashed into the Federal lines at a full run, throwing them into disarray and quickly drove them back into their last line of works over a hundred yards to their rear. Nat Raymer observed his regiment approach their awaiting enemies, reporting that, "…not until they were within ten paces of the earthworks did the hosts of the enemy turn and flee from them."[36]

# 7th New Jersey Enfilades 4th NCST at Chancellorsville 3 May 1863

## During Ramseur's Final Assault on XII Corps Earth Works

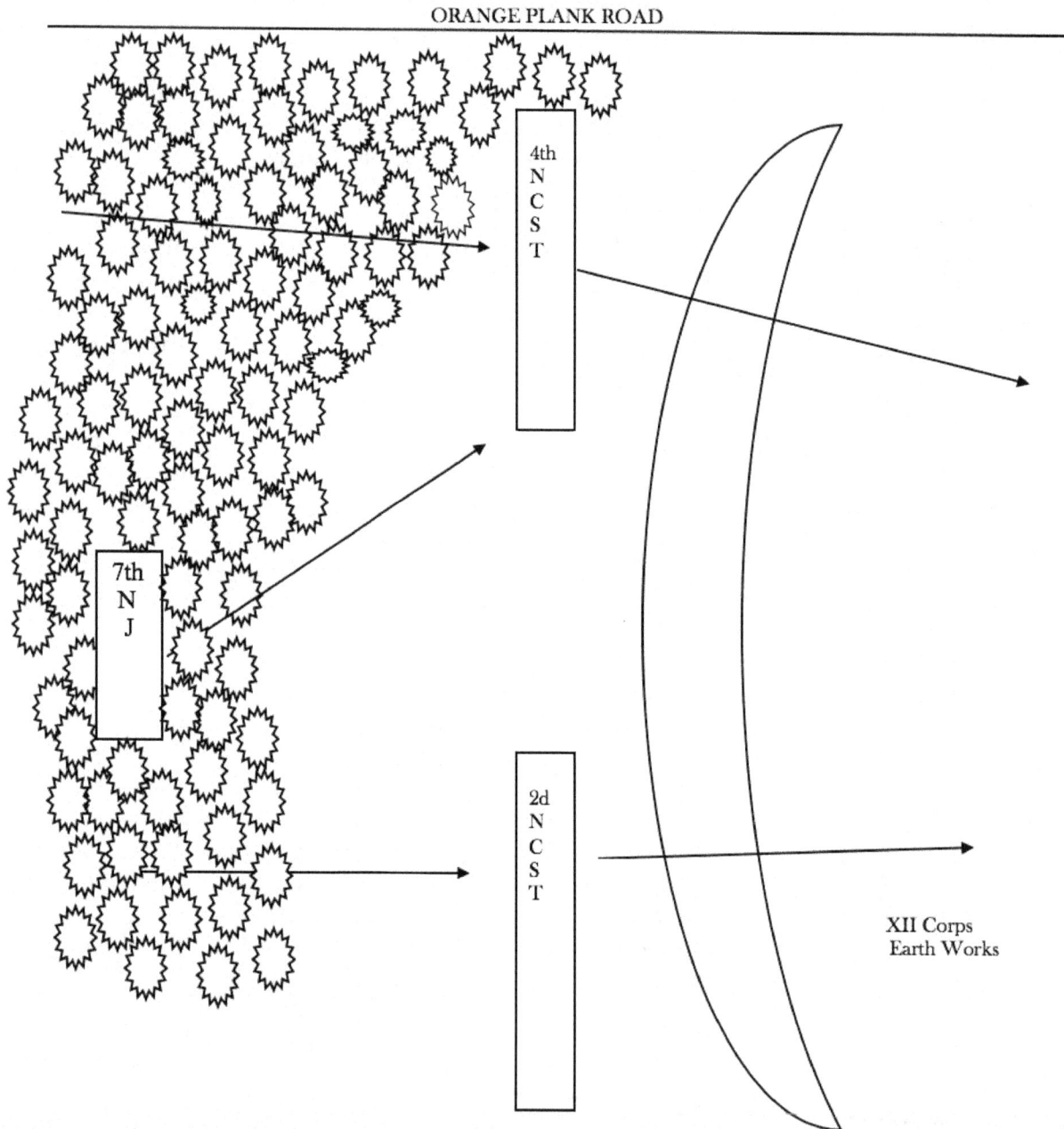

N

ORANGE PLANK ROAD

4th
N
C
S
T

7th
N
J

2d
N
C
S
T

XII Corps
Earth Works

Map Not to Scale. Distance to XII Corps Earth Works from Wood line estimated at 125 yards.
7th New Jersey Position estimated 100 yards forward of XII Corps 6:00-9:15A.M. on 3 May.
Elevation gradient along the wooded slope is roughly 45°

The 7th New Jersey was now behind them, and attempting to get on their right front as fierce hand to hand fighting swirled all around inside of the Federal earthworks. As the fighting pitched, masses of Federals became entangled and disorganized behind the works to the point that regiments were virtually indistinguishable in some places. The 7th New Jersey was holding high carnival that morning, especially when they found the 2d NCST stalled outside of their works for a few minutes. Col. Louis R. Francine commanded the 7th New Jersey, and reported that when the battle escalated behind his works, that his regiment " filled up a gap occurring between Birney's right and our immediate front. After a short time, my regiment advanced into the woods in front of the breastworks, and, by maintaining a flanking position for nearly three hours, captured five stands of colors and over 300 prisoners…The colors were taken from the Twenty first Virginia, Eighteenth North Carolina, First Louisiana, Second North Carolina, and the fifth from some Alabama regiment. The Second North Carolina Regiment we captured almost *in toto*…After this, a regiment having fallen back from our breastworks, and the enemy coming close upon them (the Second North Carolina State Troops), my regiment charged, and captured their colors and themselves almost wholly."[37]

Notice that the 7th New Jersey commander here stated that his regiment had taken not only the flag of the 2d NCST, but also taken the colors of the 18th North Carolina, who had fired the shots mortally wounding "Stonewall" Jackson on the night of 2 May, only adding insult to injury for the beleaguered Tar Heels. After the initial shock, the federals fell back but hastily managed to reform and a maelstrom of violence ensued, with nearly an hour of vicious hand-to-hand combat. Capt. Virgil M. Healy was placed in command of the 5th New Jersey after Brigadier General Mott, his brigade commander, was wounded and Col. William J. Sewell, his regimental commander, was placed in charge of the brigade. Healy having no experience commanding a regiment, was forced to act, and managed to complete several complex evolutions of his lines moving them backward out of the risk of being separated or split into, as his men absorbed the heavy attack by Ramseur's men crossed into their earthworks, amidst fierce hand to hand fighting with bayonets and clubbed muskets. Healy reported, "…during which time our regiment was under…the most severe fire that the regiment ever experienced."[38]

While it may appear obvious who took the 2d NCST flag, there exists a controversy over which regiment actually captured the 4th NCST battle flag. U.S. War Department capture records show that the 7th Ohio Regiment (Candy's Brigade) took the colors on 3 May, but the 7th Ohio wasn't located close to the Tar Heels at this point in the battle. Col. William Creighton commanded those Buckeyes, and his official report makes no mention of capturing any colors. Rather, his regiment was then located further south near the Chancellor house, below the Fredericksburg Road. The remainder of Candy's brigade was earlier ordered to move forward of the rifle pits, and were pressuring Ramseur's right near Fairview Cemetery. Candy soon received orders to withdraw his brigade "across the cleared field" further south, away from the Plank Road vicinity where the 4th and 2d NCST was then engaged with Mott's New Jersey Brigade between 9:30 and 10:00 AM.[39]

Unfortunately, while the 4th NCST was engaged in intense close quarter fighting, the 14th Regiment and three companies of the 2d North Carolina became stalled on Ramseur's right as they tried to move up the hill just southwest of the area known as "Fairview" where several Union artillery pieces were pounding away at their front and right flanks, supported by heavy lines of infantry. This left an even wider gap open on Ramseur's right which the 30th North Carolina, who was making their way back heading north east from Fairview, but was yet unable to attach to Ramseur, who desperately tried to hold that position. But the Federals ultimately exploited the gap on his right flank and even got behind the contentious Grimes, and poured in a heavy enfilade fire, causing many casualties. Numerous men were also captured at this point, including the entire 4th NCST color guard along with their battle flag. Color bearer John Stikeleather of Company A was slightly wounded as a minnie ball passed through his cartridge box and struck him on the hip, seriously bruising him.

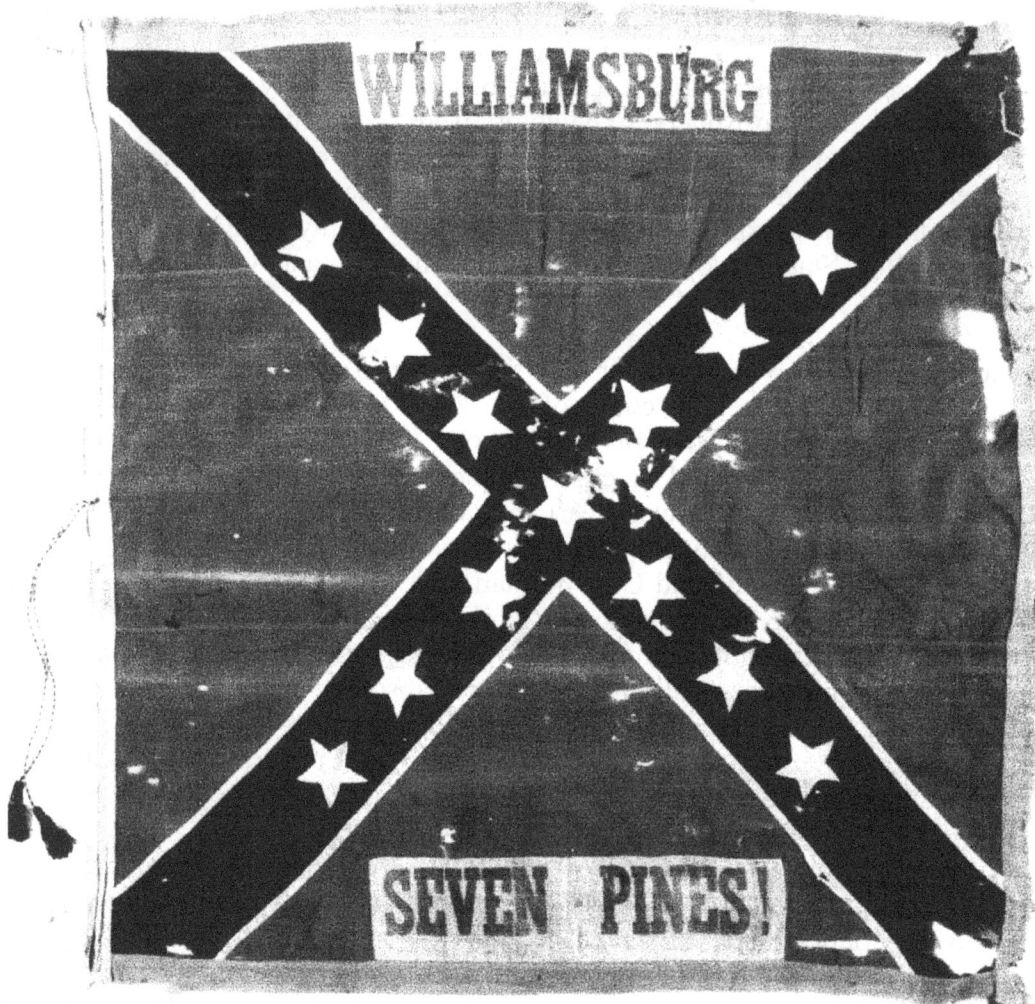

*Courtesy Museum of the Confederacy*

---

Footnote:

The 4th North Carolina battle flag captured at Chancellorsville while in the hands of James Marshborne (Company F) is now held in the Museum of the Confederacy in Richmond, Virginia. It is a cotton and wool bunting, with orange borders and blue silk tassels. The pattern is known as the 1862 Richmond Depot "second issue" or second pattern of battle flag and was authorized by the C.S. government in June 1862. The battle honors were hand sewn on three-inch high strips of polished cotton. Capture History obtained from U.S. War Department Records, File No. 18. Museum of the Confederacy Archives, Richmond, VA.

As he fell, he dropped the colors which were immediately recovered by Pvt. James Marshborne of Company F. Stikeleather wrote about this in a post-war letter: "...But the Fourth Regiment did lose its flag at Chancellorsville on the 3d of May, 1863. I was struck down here by a missile from the enemy, and the flag fell from my hands, and James Marshborne, of Company F, one of the color guard, picked it up and carried it on and was captured with it about one hundred yards from where I fell. Some twenty-five others were captured from the Fourth at the same time...Our loss there (I mean in the Fourth Regiment), was greater than in any other battle in which we were engaged during the war, according to the number taken into the fight. In the midst of such awful carnage not very many knew just what became of the flag, and besides, the ordnance wagons being near, another flag was secured in an hour or two, and my wound was not so severe as to disable me from duty as color-bearer within a few hours. In justice to the gallant (James H.) Marshborne, who was captured with the flag that day at Chancellorsville. I must say that I learned from reliable sources that he never surrendered till he and the few that were with him were flanked, after having gained a position well to the front, on that sanguinary field..."[40]

Assistant Adj. Gen. Seaton Gales confirmed on 13 May in his report to Ramseur that in this portion of the fight, the 4th NCST suffered loss of its entire color guard and battle flag when they were flanked on the right, and that could easily have been either the 5th or 7th New Jersey, as by this time the lines had fallen back behind the works and the 4th NCST had the 7th New Jersey behind it, who was trying to extend itself around Grimes' right flank. The 5th New Jersey was at this point further to their left making them a very unlikely candidate to capture the colors. Gales recorded, "I have regret to report...the loss of the standards of the 2nd and the 4th N.C. troops in the battle of May 3rd. In the 2nd (N.C.) the color-bearer was killed; the corporal who next took the colors was also killed, and all the color-guard (four corporals) present was wounded. The regiment was forced back by the enemy, and most of the officers and men near the colors were captured or disabled. No one witnessed the capture of the standard, but there can be no doubt that the enemy gained possession of it with the captured prisoners. In the 4th (N.C.) the color-bearer and guard were wounded and a portion of taken prisoners. The colors were taken with the guard, the enemy having flanked the regiment on the right."[41]

Thus, Stikeleather and Seaton Gales corroborate the colors were taken by a regiment who flanked the 4th NCST on their right. James Marshborne was carrying the colors at the time of capture, but Stikeleather makes it clear that he did not lose the flag, rather being captured and only surrendering when he and some comrades in the color guard were surrounded, at a location described as in front of the regiment. This position allowed the 7th New Jersey to envelop their right flank and front from behind, as multiple accounts show the 4th NCST had dashed further forward than the rest of their brigade from the earthworks into retreating Federal lines leaving that area open. At that juncture, the 7th New Jersey was firing into both the front and rear of the 4th NCST according to Col. Francine, their commander.[42] It is also important to recognize that none of the other regiments from Mott's Brigade reported taking colors from Ramseur's brigade in their official records, further ruling out other possible units.[43] Stikeleather elsewhere wrote that the 4thNCST battle flag was quickly replaced from a nearby supply wagon on the field shortly after the battle, which he carried until it was also captured at Winchester on 19 September 1864.

Many of John Stikeleather's experiences at Chancellorsville, particularly watching so many of his friends killed, captured, or wounded, led him to reflect on their character as well as his own. Stikeleather viewed the role of color bearers as a highly honored, but potentially lethal service, describing their job as charged to "...protect the colors with their lives, to bear them forward in case the color bearer should fall." When describing these unique soldiers, who would have to take the flag if he were killed or wounded, Stikeleather felt a strong sense of respect and trepidation. Although he was the primary color bearer, he remained humble; he did not esteem himself higher than his friends. He was keenly aware of differences in personalities, and shared common vices and trials that all faced during the war, but somehow Stikeleather struggled deeply to see himself as one of them. After the battle, he felt as if he was "treading on sacred ground", when trying to describe those men whom he considered to be "All heroes of whom any people may well be proud." An example is Pvt. Martin Snow, also in the color guard, and Stikeleather's best friend. Snow was killed in the attack, which deeply grieved Stikeleather afterward. He described Snow in an epitaph as "of humble birth and uneducated," yet "a born gentlemen, and in his make up, was as embodied as much of true and noble manhood as anyone I have ever known."[44]

After the flag was taken, Col. Bryan Grimes soon realized that not only was the Second North Carolina nearly all captured but also that many of this own regiment were captured, along with the regimental colors. He also saw the 7th New Jersey behind and beside of him, attempting to envelop his flank and right front. Grimes attempted to execute a retrograde movement and began to move his regiment back toward their former earthworks, but again stalled as the Federals came at Ramseur's lines once more. Grimes recounted, "The enemy made three distinct attempts to retake this work, forming their men in column by taking advantage of a ravine just beyond the turnpike, but each time were driven back with severe loss…About the same time my attention was called to my right and rear where I saw large numbers of the enemy fast closing up our line for retreat (the right of Ramseur's Brigade having halted to deliver their fire upon encountering the enemy where they were engaged, while we had taken the breast- work). Seeing these Federal troops in my rear, I gave the order to abandon the captured works and fall back to the protection of the earthwork still occupied by this Brigade, through whose cowardice we had suffered so severely. We crossed to the right of the plank road, and got back to our line in the best manner possible."[45]

Meanwhile, the incensed Grimes also had a close call; he was slightly wounded by a spent Minnie ball while resisting the Federals last attack from a spot west of the earthworks along the Plank Road he had managed to acquire, and was in process of retreating further when the Federals again attacked. He wrote afterwards that, "In this charge my sword was severed by a ball, my clothes perforated in many places, and a ball embedded in my sword belt and the scabbard, and I received a very severe contusion on the foot." Grimes soon fell unconscious from pain and exhaustion. While he was being revived by a pouring a canteen over his head, General Rodes approached the scene and questioned one of the officers who had earlier refused to advance, causing much of Grimes frustration that morning. Grimes reacted with his usual frank indignation, as he overheard the officer who had originally refused to move forward deny ever receiving orders to advance earlier that morning as the Stonewall Brigade lay behind the earthworks, "…I was recalled to my senses by the voice of Gen. R. E. Rodes, our Division Commander, inquiring, "What troops are these?" The commanding officer who had refused to advance when ordered by Gen. Stuart's staff officer, said the Brigade. Gen. Rodes said, "Why have you not joined in the charge?" The reply was, "We have had no orders to advance." Under the stimulus of this falsehood, I fully aroused, pronounced it a lie; that I had heard the order given myself, and repeated his reply. Whereupon, Gen. Rodes took out his pistol, rode up to this officer, presented the muzzle to his head, and, with an epithet of odium, told him to forward his men, or he would blow his brains out. He then gave the command, and this Brigade then moved forward, and, without firing a gun, reached the breastworks that we had taken, and found the Federal forces had evacuated the hill…"[46]

Considering the intense fighting in the 3 May assault on the federal earth works at Chancellorsville, the sobriquet "shock troops" continued to apply to Ramseur's Brigade, especially the Fourth North Carolina. Grimes left us a parting comment again expressing his disdain toward the stalled Virginians, whom he saw as responsible for his brigade losing many casualties, in spite of the chaos and many enmeshed regiments laying behind the Confederate earth works that morning, If these troops had moved forward in obedience to orders, and encountered the enemy, we would have advanced quickly to their support, and captured the principal part of Hooker's artillery. As it was, we met with terrific slaughter in my command, and failed to take the artillery. This closed the fighting at Chancellorsville, for the infantry."[47]

## Aftermath and Casualty Reports

The 4th NCST, including Company K, played a key role in the assault and capture of federal works at Chancellorsville, but once again paid dearly for it. Capt. William M. Adams, known as "Bill" among the soldiers who knew him, hailed from Iredell County, North Carolina. He commanded Company C, the "Saltillo Boys" at Chancellorsville. He wrote to his Father a few days afterward telling that many of his friends along with himself were wounded, and called it "…the hardest fight I ever witnessed in my life and hope will never witness another such."[48] Company K deaths shown on muster rolls included privates' E.F.M. Carter and Calvin Miller killed in action, along with Wilson R. Josey. Raymer identifies him only as "R. Josey" who was awarded the Confederate Badge of Distinction posthumously for his deeds at Chancellorsville. Josey was a lifelong resident of School District 34 in Salisbury before the war, and was raised as the second youngest and only male of four children. His father, 34 year old John Josey, is shown in the 1850 census as a farmer with 95 acres of land and no slaves. In 1860 Wilson Josey is found working as a laborer and residing on the farm of John L. Rusher, where his eldest sister, 21 year old Julia, was working as a housekeeper. Available sources do not specify exactly what Josey did to earn this recognition but it is clear that his comrades believed he deserved the honor. A 13 October, 1862, act of the Confederate Congress conferred a "…badge of distinction upon one private or noncommissioned officer of each company…by a majority of their votes…" meaning that the men of Company K posthumously nominated Josey for his heroism.[49]

Company K muster rolls indicate Robert Beaty was mortally wounded on 3 May, and Lewis Holshouser was wounded by gunshot to the right side. Jeremiah Glover was captured by the 12th Illinois Cavalry in the raid on the rear of Lee's army occurring after the main battle on 3 May. Regimental losses were initially reported as six officers and forty one enlisted men killed, fifteen officers and one hundred forty enlisted men wounded, one officer and fifty seven enlisted men captured or missing.[50] Ramseur's brigade began the Battle of Chancellorsville with 129 officers present and 1,380 enlisted soldiers. The brigade also had twelve officers killed in this engagement. In addition, 103 men from the brigade were captured on 3 May, with fifty eight from the 4th NCST, meaning fifty-six percent of the 4th NCST was captured.[51] Col. Bryan Grimes was also wounded at Chancellorsville and left the battlefield, due to the "effects of an old wound received at battle of Sharpsburg." But Grimes was not present at Sharpsburg as a result of having had another horse shot out from under him at South Mountain, Maryland, three days prior, so the circumstances or timing of his departure from the Chancellorsville battle field are not clear. Nat Raymer routinely included casualty lists in his correspondence for the folks at home following major campaigns. His account of casualties at Chancellorsville includes what is to say the least a bizarre event. 2d Lt. Addison Wiseman was wounded at Chancellorsville only one day after returning to the company on 2 May after convalescing from his second wound sustained on picket duty at Fredericksburg earlier in December 1862. Wiseman again was sent to a hospital and did not return to duty until sometime just prior to 1 September 1863.[52] Raymer's casualty report also erroneously lists Pvt. R. Josey as a member of Company C when he was actually in Company K. The account was published in the *Carolina Watchman* on 18 May, and indicates the following privates were wounded: "Holdsouser, Sergt Hennesse."

Another private was mortally wounded but not included in Raymer's early casualty report, Lewis Mahaley of Salisbury. He was sent to Hospital Number 20 in Richmond, where he died on 12 June 1863 of wounds sustained in battle on 3 May. His father, Joseph Mahaley, sought the assistance of the influential Rowan County Clerk of Court, Thomas McNeely, (also father of former Company K officer Capt. Frank McNeely) who wrote to Richmond Hospital Number 20 on 6 July 1863, requesting some personal items belonging to his deceased son be shipped home including a blanket, knife, comb, shoes and clothing along with three or four keys.[53] Like many regiments in the Civil War, the 4th NCST utilized band members to serve as hospital stewards and stretcher bearers during and after battles, ostensibly listed as "non-combatants" in official reports, although many experienced the same gunfire, explosions, etc. as the infantry and as the reader will soon find, often saw worse horrors in field hospitals afterward. Nat Raymer was no exception at Chancellorsville. By now, Raymer's frequent editorials and reports from the front lines had made him literally known as "a household word" in the Iredell and Rowan County areas of North Carolina, where the majority of men in the 4th NCST were from.[54] He gave a gruesome recollection of scenes he observed at the division hospital, far behind the battle lines later that night, which appeared in the *Iredell Express* newspaper in Statesville North Carolina on 15 June 1863:

"After the firing (which lasted about two hours) at that particular point ceased, I went to the hospital three-fourths of a mile back, and by 11 o'clock a.m. the wounded began coming in. Here in where we could see the melancholy fruits of war. Never since the war began have I seen so many men severely wounded, or so many amputations necessary. The work of butchery began about noon on the same day and continued with little intermission until ten o'clock the following day. Arms and legs were scattered and tossed about with the utmost indifference, wounds probed and dressed, balls extracted, and the sufferers made as comfortable as the nature of cause would possibly admit.

Details were sent on the battle field to pick up blankets and yankee tents, overcoats, and in fact anything in the world that would prove useful. Such articles lay scattered in the greatest confusion over the surrounding hills and fields. Our hospital was at "Wilderness Church" around which was a fine grove of pine. Outside these were large fields, cultivated last year, but now fenceless, desolate and torn into great furrows by the maddening wheels of artillery hurrying to and fro, and lying at intervals of a few rods over these fields were dead men and horses slain in the battle on Saturday evening. The few of our own men who had been killed were buried, but those of the enemy (and they were not a few) lay festering in the sun. Half a dozen of these loathsome sights lay within fifty yards of the spring out of which we procured water for the use of our men at the hospital."

On 25 May, Raymer penned an even more lengthy description of a practice that became common among the Confederates during the war-- the pilfering of clothing or other items of dead Union soldiers on the battlefield. The following is excerpted from his letter published in the *Carolina Watchman* in June 1863: "I noticed on the various battle fields that nearly all the enemy's dead were stripped of everything save their underclothes. This is a barbarious practice against which I have ever protested. Sometimes it may be excusable, but certainly not now, since our men are abundantly supplied with the very vest of clothing. This hankering after "yankee blue" is not a good sign by any means...to go farther in the stripping line smacks too much of cannibalism....A sufficient number of portable tents were brought off the field to shelter all our wounded, and blankets enough to make all comfortable." Regarding the death of Lt. Gen. Thomas "Stonewall" Jackson following his wounding at Chancellorsville, Nat Raymer offered a brief observation of a recent encounter when he happened to be in his proximity to see Jackson just before his death. Raymer wrote the missive on 16 May, and it appeared in the *Carolina Watchman* on 1 June. As one may expect of the analytical Raymer, he focused more on describing Jackson's physical appearance and characteristics than eulogizing his military accomplishments or lamenting the loss to the Confederacy:

"The most lamentable event of all is the death of our old hero Jackson. I would not say old either, since he was but thirty-nine, but then his name was familiar to every man in the army of the South as well as the North; to the former a word full of hope and the utmost confidence; to the latter a terror and foreboding some dire calamity. In courage and sagacity few were his equal, none his superior. In his conduct he exhibited these qualities in a wonderful degree of perfection; hence he is called old. The last time I ever saw him was on Friday the first day of the present month, when I perceived that he had bestowed more than usual attention on his dress, a sign of an approaching battle which I never knew to fail.

His coat and pants were of the usual greyish blue, but of the finest quality, and the gold lace fancy work on his sleeve looked as if it might have been put on the day before; his boots were well glossed and his spurs looked like burnished gold. He wore buck gloves with cuffs that came half-way up to his elbows. I barely got a glimpse of his hat since he carried it in his left hand as he galloped past, while I was on his right, but it was black felt, the height usually worn by officers. I would suppose him to be a little over six feet high, or that much at the least; well proportioned, but not corpulent by any means, and would weigh about one hundred and seventy pounds.

He kept his hair and whiskers (very black) neatly trimmed, his mustache nicely curled to the sides of his mouth, but had not made use of a razor for months past. His complexion very fair, blue, restless eyes, in fact quite a restive temperament generally; and a prominent though not a large nose; altogether he was a fine looking man besides being a very good one. He never would have his troops to march or fight on Sunday if it could possibly be avoided; he never failed to attend divine services when an opportunity offered, and on such occasions I have been very near to him, and of course did not fail to scan his features closely."

Raymer's correspondence from Chancellorsville also included a heart wrenching account of watching a young, newlywed soldier literally die in his arms, while trying to minister aid to him. This narrative was published in the *Iredell Express* on 15 June 1863. It reveals a brutal realization of not only his own mortality, but also a natural grief over another realization, the plight of the soldier's newlywed young wife, who was now a widow:

"The night was spent ministering to their wants as best we could, but I could very easily perceive that we were all miserable comforters; sweeter voices, gentler hands, more assiduous attention than ours were needed, and often piteously longed for. How often were my feelings harrowed by such expressions as these: "Oh, if I only were at home;" "I would give all but my life for a soft bed;" "something to eat!-can't you give me something besides meat and crackers to eat." I thought my feelings were thoroughly steeled, and that I could stand anything unmoved, however shocking it might be; but I must confess that our men made me feel awfully bad, and ere I was aware of it I felt a warm tear rolling down my cheek.

This man belonged to the 14th N.C., but by some mistake had been placed in the department of the 4th. I first saw him late on Sunday evening, but was so much engaged with others that I paid no particular attention to him, further than to see that he was resting apparently easy, and to examine his wound. I found the ball had entered an inch below the breast bone, and at a glance I felt convinced that he would die, perhaps before morning. His mind was clear, and he seemed to talk with ease, he did not consider his wound dangerous--said he felt no pain, and ex-pressed a great desire to sleep. I carefully adjusted the blankets around his body and left. During the night I went to see him two or three times, but always found him as I left him at first. Once I drew down the blankets and felt his breast to see whether he still lived. I found that he breathed as calmly as though he was in good health and enjoying a refreshing sleep. Soon after daylight on Monday morning I called on him again, he was awake and in quite a lively humor. Though much weaker than I had ever seen him.

His features struck me as being very peculiar and really handsome. His face was rather long, a fine mustache, close set but short whiskers, and silky hair, all coal black, and last, longer than is usually seen in the army, clustered in curls about his temples, and high forehead now bloodless and white as marble. From appearances I would suppose him to be twenty-three years old-- I made some inquiries about his welfare, and was assured that he was doing finely. After a few jocular remarks, I was called away and did not see him again until two o'clock in the afternoon, when he called me to him as I was passing near. From the moment I first saw him he had been lying on his back with his legs perfectly straight; he had never so much as expressed a wish to change his position, but now to my question. "What will you have?" "Turn me on my side, please," he replied. "No, my friend, you cannot stand it; try and content yourself the way you are. Well then, won't you raise my knees up, and draw my feet towards my body? O yes, I'll do that," and went to work; but I knew from his restlessness that his last hour had come. I put my hands under his left knee and raised it well up; when I released my hold his foot and ankle re-mained stationary, but the remainder of his leg slid away over it and struck the ground beyond. I was perfectly shocked; it was the first intimation I had had of a broken leg besides the other wound.

"Somehow that leg won't stand," said my friend, "try the other." The other sat up very well. After a short pause, he said "Is my left leg broken?" "It is, but don't trouble yourself about it now." He covered his face with his hands and heaved a sigh that seemed to tear his heart strings. A moment afterwards he locked his hands across his breast, and said in a faltering voice, "My leg shattercd-a ball through by breast-I must die-what will Fanny do?-poor Fanny!" "Come now, be quiet; you--"O God! What will Fanny do when I am gone?" I saw that he was fast going, but all I could do to console him was of no avail. He could scarcely speak above his breath. I ventured to ask, "Say, tell me, who is Fanny?" "She is my wife-a a noble woman-I married her last winter --- while I - I- I was at home on furlough - -"He lay as if he were dying--he gasped for breath--then rousing himself, he took my hand, and in a whisper, barely audible, said, "Good by ---you've been my best friend- Tell-tell-her---- Fanny----Fanny"

T'was the last he ever said. I have never learned his name, but he was a whole souled man. His blanket was his winding sheet; we wrapped him in it and the next morning his body was buried beneath a tall pine that grew nearby."

Raymer ended his account of Chancellorsville with a somewhat humorous account laden with veiled hostility toward provost guards who were apparently poaching the hospital liquor supply; one cannot help but wonder if Raymer's motives were entirely altruistic, if not self-serving, gauging by his intense response, "I don't understand how it is that for the last six months provost guards have been stationed at every depot for a hundred miles around Richmond, with instructions to examine every box that passes the roads and take out any liquors which may be found-- ostensibly for the use of hospitals; --and now when the hospitals need it most, scarce half a gallon can be found. The guards did their duty well--scarce a box go through without being ransacked. But who got the liquor, the guards or the Surgeons? How long will the people submit to such outrage? Let the men who bring cargoes to the army go well armed, and if any man dares to open one of your packages, shoot him down--every soldier will back you."[55]

Although Chancellorsville was indeed the South's greatest victory to date, most scholars contend that it was also their greatest loss with the death of Jackson. Although even greater challenges lay ahead, following Chancellorsville the army returned to their previous camp routine for a brief interlude before the next campaign. As Robert E. Lee's invasion of Maryland and Pennsylvania loomed ominously ahead, Raymer described the regiment's encampment and activities on 16 May; an excerpt follows that also includes a flattering but atypical description of Stonewall Jackson, whom was usually described as wearing a rather worn and tattered uniform in the field:

"...Since the excitement and uproar incident to battle have died away here, we have been resting-- and such rest as only soldier knows. We returned to the very same spot which we occupied for six weeks preceding the battle, and remained there four or five days. The sun shone hot on us; not a shade tree, not even a shrub was left standing; the little firewood necessary to cook our rations was hard to find, and worse that all the water which we were obliged to use was getting very bad, as the warm weather drew nearer. For these reasons, Col. Grimes moved us to a beautiful forest about half a mile distant, a favor for which we shall be under lasting obligations. This is indeed a charming place; the regiment is encamped in a romantic valley, through which ripples a sparkling brook, while the field and staff, including the band, are tented on the summit of a hill rising abruptly some hundred feet above, and completely overlooking the regiment.

The little valleys around, and the abrupt round hills are thickly shaded with majestic chestnut oaks, now clad in their richest summer foliage. Twilight is gathering now-- it is already so dark that I can scarcely see to write; but still I keep on. The tree-frogs and whippor-wills have begun their serenade -- we feel like we were at home. No troops save our regiment are in sight, and this Saturday evening everything is so calm, so quiet that we can easily imagine ourselves in a land of peace and plenty, far from the desolating breath of war. Thousands of wild honey-suckles, daisies, blue-bells, and other gayer flowers perfume the evening breeze with their sweet odors;-- we lack but human flowers to make this a paradise.--An hour hence and we will awake the slumbering echoes among these hills with music that for the time will transport us to the happy throng that once assembled in the town hall in Statesville—God bless and spare them."

After the battle, another event transpired revealing more of the men's character who served in Company K and their regiment. The Confederate Adjutant and Inspector General published an order on 22 November, 1862 establishing a "Roll of Honor" containing the names of those considered worthy. Six men were posthumously nominated for this highest award bestowed by the Confederate government.[56] It should be understood that recipients were not chosen by politicians, or generals, but was rather a result of the respect and gratitude of their peers reflected in the nomination process. In spite of this, numerous officers including Robert E. Lee who expressed reservations about each of these honors, on the general grounds that each soldier who did their duty was worthy of such recognition and that many such acts of heroism on the battle field are never known to commanders. Many soldiers declined to cast a vote. The 4th NCST voted to nominate their following comrades for the Confederate Roll of Honor. Whether the Roll of Honor was popular or not, the memory of the Veterans who fought there is clearly sacred ground.

Sgt W. S. Shufford, Company A
Pvt Jacob W. Wilhelm, Company B
Sgt Joseph Leggett, Company E
Pvt G. W. Shivis, Company H
Pvt W. H. Barrow, Company I
Pvt W. R. Josey, Company K

# Chapter Seven

## Summer of 1863
## "Valley of Death..."

## Second Advance into Maryland

As the army began to move, Raymer again provided an update to his readers in Rowan and Iredell counties on 7 June, which he wrote from a make-shift camp near Culpepper, Virginia. His next article appeared in Salisbury in the *Carolina Watchman* on 22 June, specifying the addition of new nickname for the North Carolinians, "Tar Heels," which became popular around this time. Raymer wrote:

"Under circumstances the most favorable than can be imagined, I will briefly and hastily inform you of our whereabouts and how we happened to get there. On last Thursday morning the 4th instant, at half past one o'clock, we were aroused from our profound sleep, not by rattling drums, but quietly, and told to make our way towards Guines's Station as speedily and noiselessly as possible. It was vain for us to grunt and growl, or complain of broken rest, or anything of the sort, but knapsacks were bundled up in a twinkling, strung on our shoulders and away we went. At daylight we were near the station, and leaving it in sight to our left we pushed ahead for Spotsylvania Court House.

As the sun ascended the heat became oppressive, and the dust intolerable. But at 3 P.M., we arrived at our company ground, one and a half miles west of the above mentioned Court House, having traveled about sixteen miles. After taking a cold water bath we lay down for a night's rest with sore joints and aching bones. The next morning we were aroused before the stars ceased to shine, fell into line, and marched in dust and heat worse than the day before, with a rest of ten minutes in every hour, until 4 o'clock P.M. We were moving in the direction of Culpepper and at night found that we had marched about eighteen miles that day, and through A country mostly level, sandy, not exceedingly fertile, but overflowing with pretty girls who stood along the roadside and enthusiastically cheered us.

Of course we had to play occasionally for them, and once a squad of them generously donated to the band a basket of pies, biscuits, and boiled ham. We are called "Tar Heels," and I am proud of the appellation—North Carolina heels, from their adhesive properties, are always put to the most important posts in battle, and they stick or advance; but I am not sure but by-standers would have thought our fingers tarred as well as our heels if they had seen the good things getting out of that basket. It was emptied in the "twinkle of a cat's eye." So, so, we had no time to party, and away we went in a cloud of dust, marching at our fists full of delicacies, and as saney as monkeys with red apples. At night we encamped in a cluster of underbrush, and near a stout creek. Half an hour after arms were stacked hundreds of men were in bathing—it is equal to a night's rest.

Many feet were swollen and blistered, and every muscle in our bodies was aching from the effects of our unusual exertion; but after the refreshing bath our nerves were invigorated, our spirits revived, and at dark we stretched ourselves on the ground, grateful to God for the little shower that was then falling. The following morning, (yesterday) we were up and off at four o' clock. The little rain that fell last night had laid the dust, and made fine walking. We drove rapidly for five miles, when we were very unexpectedly turned into camp to await further orders. Some movement of the enemy caused this, but no matter what brought it about, we got to rest our tired limbs. We remained in that beautiful forest until an hour before day this morning (Sunday), when we took on our line of march anew—two hours brought us to the

Rapidan river, but it was no obstacle, we pitched in and waded across it as though it had been spring branch.

It was about 100 yards wide, and on a average knee deep. Once across, we traveled on without any detention save the usual rest of ten minutes every hour, and at 1 P.M., passed through Culpepper, (town) three miles north of which we are now encamped, having traveled fully eighteen miles today. We have recovered from the soreness felt at first, and are now in good plight to travel. The men march remarkably well, not a straggler is to be seen, and so much cheerfulness I have never seen before on a march. I hear but little complaint of sickness, everybody is eager to see what is up. The campaign is open in earnest, and until its close my readers need not be surprised at anything they hear. Something important is in the wind—I know but little of it, and dare not tell that which I do know.

But if my opportunities for mailing continue the same as now, you shall not lack for information after things have happened-it would not be prudent to tell them before. This country is a perfect ruin, both armies are trying now and have been for the last twelve months to make the destruction complete, and they have well nigh succeeded. He enemy is in strong force beyond the Rappahannock, half a days march from us. A battle is expected to open hourly."

In June, Lee moved his army northward into Maryland and Pennsylvania. Enroute, Ramseur's brigade encountered Federals on the outskirts of Martinsburg, Virginia (now West Virginia); and a brief skirmish followed. Ramseur's North Carolinians, spearheaded by the 14th North Carolina, zealously chased the Federals for two miles over rough ground crisscrossed with stone fences. Five cannon with caissons and horses, 200 prisoners, thousands of bushels of grain, and some small arms and ammunition fell into Confederate hands. Such was the latent action near Winchester on the road to what would be the largest battle ever fought on the North American continent, which the Rowan Rifles were about to experience at Gettysburg, Pennsylvania in a few days. As the march into Federal territory continued, signs of exhaustion and poor supplies were beginning to show by 15 June; Maj. Gen. Robert Rodes, commanding the division to which Ramseur's Brigade was assigned, described his men as they halted after crossing of the Potomac River near Williamsport, Maryland in his official report.

Rodes stated, "Three brigades (Ramseur's, Iverson's, and Doles'), with three batteries of artillery, were ordered across the Potomac at once. It was not until this day that the troops began to exhibit unmistakable signs of exhaustion, and that stragglers could be found in the line of march, and even then none but absolutely worn-out men fell out of line. The whole march from Culpeper Court House to Williamsport, which as an extremely rapid one, was executed in a manner highly creditable to the officers and men of the division. A halt at Williamsport was absolutely necessary from the condition of the feet of the unshod men. Very many of these gallant fellows were still marching in ranks, with feet bruised, and swollen, and withal so cheerfully as to entitle them to be called the heroes of the Pennsylvania Campaign. None but the best of soldiers could have such a march under such circumstances."[1]

When they arrived in Hagerstown, Maryland, Rodes' division camped for a few days before moving on toward Pennsylvania across the Cumberland. Pvt. A.R. Tomlinson of Company H, 4th NCST, provided a post-war anecdote about some useful cherry groves they encountered on a warm summer day in that area, "...My regiment went on provost duty at Hagerstown the first day we arrived there. The town, I think was about fifty-fifty in Northern and Southern sympathy. We cut the Union flag down, and many of the citizens split the flag pole into pieces for souvenirs. When we left Hagerstown the old town hall was full of rations that our regiment had drawn, but our Southern friends there had us do most of our eating at their tables. The hospitality of the people of Hagerstown was equal to that of Virginia, and the ladies of Virginia were the most hospitable on earth, so we did not have to beg them for bread; it they had anything to eat, they gave it freely. Leaving Hagerstown, we marched up the Cumberland Valley to Carlisle and Gettysburg, Pa., and the Valley was full of Dutch ovens, apple butter, cherries, and vegetables. Every fence corner for miles had its cherry tree. The command, Halt, stack arms, cherry trees, charge! would be given, and it was interesting to see hundreds of soldiers climbing the trees at the same time."[2]

John Stikeleather also tells of an incident on the march northward which demonstrates that not only did Col. Bryan Grimes know many of his men personally, but that the men of the 4th NCST, including the Rowan Rifles, were also subject to strict military discipline. The incident occurred in the afternoon one day near Shippensburg, Pennsylvania, a few days before the Gettysburg fight, when the regiment had stopped to rest about noon near the banks of a beautiful stream of clear running water. Stikeleather wrote:

"In Company A was a man quite a character in his way, Hugh H. (Hall). It seems that Hugh was one of a party of foragers that left camp soon after we stopped, and, in a short time returned well supplied with the best the country afforded. Hugh, knowing we were in the enemy's country, seemed to think when he was out foraging that he would be more successful, if he would in speech and manor show himself just a little disloyal to Southern interests. In a farm house near our camp, in the presence of several other soldiers from different regiments in our brigade, he remarked to the lady of the house, "That at Chancellorsville two months back, several of our officers fell, shot by our own men, and if we get into another fight soon, more of them will go the same way." A falsehood out of the whole cloth, and he knew it, but his object was sympathy and rations, both of which he doubtlessly received.

A soldier of the 11th North Carolina Regiment, the gallant Colonel Bennett's regiment, feeling indignant at what he overheard, turned to Hugh, and inquired to what command he belonged; his reply was, Company A 4th North Carolina. The 14th man returned to camp at once, and reported to Colonel Grimes what he had heard from the lips of a man who said, he belonged to Company A of the 4th Regiment. Not knowing Hugh personally, he could not give the Colonel his name, but said he could identify him should he ever see him again. The Colonel sent an order to the Captain of Company A to report with his Company at his headquarters immediately. The order was at once obeyed. Hugh had returned, and was in line when we halted at the Colonel's quarters. The Colonel then turned to the 14th man and said, "Point out the man you heard using that insidious language." The 14th man ran his eye along the line till it reached Hugh, when he said, "There he is." Those acquainted with the noble Grimes, can well imagine what his feelings were at this juncture of affairs. His face turned livid, and for a few moments he could scarcely articulate coherently at all, so great was his anger and indignation, that one of his men should so demean himself in the enemy's country.

Colonel Grimes told Hugh that want of sense was all that saved his life, that, but for the fact he would have him shot right off. The Colonel then turned to Captain McRorie and said "Captain, have two men detailed to dunk this fellow in the creek yonder one dozen times and see that he double quick for two hours around a ring with a sentinel inside of it immediately after his dunking."

185

Captain McRorie at once detailed Pink Smith and Bill Carter to go with Hugh down into the creek to do the dunking. The largest part of the regiment, with numbers from other regiments in the brigade at once repaired to the banks of the creek to witness the scene. The Colonel however, remaining at his quarters. Smith and Carter waded in with Hugh to where the water was waist deep, and dunked him one dozen times, "in due and ancient form." Hugh stood it pretty well, but as he came out of the creek, he looked up towards the Colonel's quarters saying, "George, you brought me into Pennsylvania but you will never take me out again." Hugh was taken up to the Colonel's quarters, and had he shown any signs of penitence, he would have been released at once without further punishment, the Colonel having cooled off very considerably in the meantime.

But, Hugh was still incorrigible as was shown by his answer to the Colonel when asked if he thought he was cured, the answer was, in a half defiant tone, "Well, I don't know whether I am or not." Whereupon, the Colonel had the original order rigidly executed. Hugh made his words good in regard to not being taken out of Pennsylvania again. A few days afterward at the Gettysburg fight, when we fell back one night to straighten our lines, we left Hugh and saw no more of him till after the war, when he came back to North Carolina wearing a suit of blue. There were some reasons why Hugh H. should not have been held to the same accountability for his conduct as other soldiers were, and the above incident was mentioned more, because it was a little out of line of the ordinary in a soldier's life, than to place him in his memory specially under a cloud."[3]

A very unpopular subject with soldiers in the both armies was the ever-present lice, or "gray backs." A. R. Tomlinson of Company H explained how he dealt with the pests, "If I am not mistaken, it was on this march that our raiment was very limited--only one suit of underwear to a man. We came to a creek and the officers told us it was wash day, so we washed our rags--no soap--and hung them on the underbrush to dry out. Now the washing only made the lice bite worse; it takes hot water, fire, and brimstone to exterminate them. We made fires and held our shirts over the embers and, when inflated with steam and smoke, the lice would fall into the fire; and we could hear them thump equal to a corn popper, but not so loud. This is no lie; many old soldiers now living could tell you the same.[4] In spite of the somewhat stoic literary persona Nat Raymer created for himself throughout his correspondence, he apparently had another less obvious side, visible only to those who knew him. The following scenarios occurred when they stopped near Carlisle, Pennsylvania; since the outcome was advantageous to the band members, the following anecdote was written post-war by his close friend and messmate, Pvt. J.C. Steele who witnessed the event:

"Just before the battle of Gettysburg the 4th North Carolina Regiment was on picket duty near Carlisle, Pa. The band of that regiment was encamped near one of those fine Dutch barns, around which were several hog houses about six feet square with a hole in one side just large enough for a hog to go in and out, while a few chickens were scratching for a living. It was suggested that they were contraband of war. Nat said: "This is an enemy's country, and we have a perfect right to confiscate those chickens." Bob by this time had one at full run, and Charley was heading it off form the gate; and as it turned the corner of the barn, Bob was just tipping its tail when it darted into a hog house. Bob didn't take time to see whether a hog was in it or not; but as he started in an old sow started out, and both were in a hurry and they wedged in the door tight.

Bob kicked his heels high to keep them out of the hog's mouth and held his head high to keep her tail out of his mouth. Finally the hog wiggled out and let Bob down. He looked up reproachfully and said: "Charley, why didn't you help me?" Charley replied

186

sympathetically" "I was afraid de old sow'd bite me." But all hands smoked the pipe of peace over the old hen when she was hot and let the old hog go- - for want of a bigger pot. Bob sometimes played pranks. At one time he drew a wool hat, and by pouring hot water in it stretched it out to enormous length, and then folded it up so nicely that it didn't look as if it would hold more than a quart. He then held it up to a sutler, who was selling goobers at enormous prices, and asked him what he would fill it full for. The sutler, supposing it to hold about a quart, priced it accordingly; but as the sutler poured in Bob stretched out the crown, and finally the sutler looked and saw about one and a half gallons and still not full, so he said he would not fill it for that. Bob replied" "Then I will not pay you." So Bob treated the band.",

In spite of their adventures in Pennsylvania, things were about to turn far more deadly and serious for the regiment, however, as soon afterward the army closed in on a small farm town in Pennsylvania where events of the first three days in July would forever alter American history.

### Gettysburg: "I never before saw men so thoroughly worn out..."

Several sources including Col. Bryan Grimes' account and the Official Records both indicate that the 4th Regiment played a vital role in the attack on Union forces at Oak Ridge on 1 July at Gettysburg, and were engaged late in the evening on 2 July along Cemetery Ridge. However, the regiment did not participate in the infamous Pickett's Charge on 3 July. Ramseur's brigade was the first Confederate infantry unit to move into town on 1 July, and the 4th NCST was in the very front as they pushed Federals back through the town of Gettysburg that evening. Company K was mentioned by E.A. Osborne in his regimental history when discussing the events of 1 July at Gettysburg, and he specifically noted "Captain" Moses Locke Bean, who was actually a sergeant at the time of the battle on 1 July.[6]

The latter was most likely a post-war reference when Bean was commonly referred to as captain even though he did not actually hold such rank. Bean was promoted to first sergeant on the battlefield that day, however. Osborne's history was written after the War, and while Bean later attained the rank of captain, on 1 July 1863, Bean was promoted to first sergeant on the battlefield, not a captain. Osborne states, "Captain M.L. Bean, also of Company K, was a true and gallant officer. He and A.C. Carter, of Company K, volunteered to make a bold reconnaissance at Gettysburg to ascertain the enemy' position, and saved the regiment form what might have been a fatal surprise, such as befell one of our brigades the same day."[7] Osborne also mentions a corporal from Company K, "A. Friedheim," described as "steady and reliable." He refers to Arnold Friedheim, whom Col. Bryan Grimes called upon to personally assist him in the night assault of Cemetery Ridge on 2 July, "At Gettysburg, when we started to make the night attack, Colonel Grimes, who could not see very well at night, sent for Corporal Friedheim, of Company K, to guide him and be with him in that trying ordeal. He knew full well that he could trust this man; for there was no braver or truer soldier in the army than A. Friedheim."[8]

John Stikeleather, the regimental color bearer, found that as his regiment encountered the terror-stricken citizens of Gettysburg on the night of 1 July, after the Federals had departed, they were much concerned about more than just the fighting occurring around them, recalling, "The panic among the citizens of Gettysburg was very great the evening of July 1st, as we swept into the town. No men were seen anywhere, they had left home or were concealed somewhere. The panic among the women and children was pitiable to behold; they imagined us to be no better than semi barbarians, and besides during the fight, musket balls had whistled through their houses. Under all the circumstances it is not to be wondered at that they were badly frightened. Our officers used their utmost endeavor to prevent violence of any kind to them in person or property. But in many of their houses were wines and different kinds of liquor, and in all armies there are many men who will drink and will risk a good deal to get liquor and other spoils, such as were easily found that first night in Gettysburg."[9]

The 4th NCST remained in town that night and on 2 July was ordered to engage again. Col. Brian Grimes gave his account of what would have likely been a failed assault on the evening of 2 July at Gettysburg, reporting that his regiment "…remained in line of battle all day with very heavy skirmishing in front. At dark I received an order from Major-General Rhodes to move by the right flank until Brigadier General Dole's troops cleared the town, and then advance in line of battle of the enemy's position on Seminary Hill. Was told the remaining brigade of the division would be governed by my movements. I obeyed this order until within 200 yards of the enemy's position, where batteries were discovered in position to pull up our lines direct, cross and enfilade fires. Two lines of infantry behind stone walls and breastworks were supporting…the strength and position…induced me to halt and confer with General Doles…In answer, received an order to retire quietly to a deep road some 300 yards in rear, and be in readiness to attack at daylight; withdrew accordingly."[10]

Cpl. B.B. Ross of Company C was also a participant in the daring night mission, and described their near miss with disaster on the night of 2 July, when the 4th NCST received orders to be ready to "…move at a moment's notice, and we were informed that we would storm Cemetery Hill that night. About eight or nine o'clock at night the order came to advance, and every man responded with a will to do or die. On the slope of the hill between Chambersburg Road to Cemetery Hill we had to climb a fence. We had been ordered to make as little noise as possible in crossing this fence. We advanced to the crest of the hill, where the Yankees were posted with infantry and artillery. We came so near them that we could hear the Federal officers commanding their men to reserve their fire until we approached nearer, but in the meantime there came an order from our commander to retire as quietly as possible to the Chambersburg Turnpike. On retreating, every soldier seemed to get on the fence at he same time, thus splitting the posts, tearing down rails, and making a considerable noise, which the Federal officers heard, and ordered their men to fire. But the depression of the hill was go great that the balls flew over our heads, and didvery little damage."[11]

The regiment did not actively participate in the legendary "Picket's Charge" on 3 July, but according to Grimes, rather "…remained in line all day with severe and damaging skirmishing and front exposed to the artillery of the enemy and our own short range guns, by the careless use of imperfect ammunition…seven men killed and wounded. Withdrew at night and formed line of battle near Gettysburg, where we remained on July 4th. Commenced retreat with the Army on the night of the 4th instant During the Gettysburg campaign, Colonel Grimes reported the regiment lost 8 killed, 24 wounded and 23 missing or captured."[12] Nat Raymer wrote a stirring recollection of Pickett's Charge, reported in the 27 July *Carolina Watchman*:

"But on the next day, July 3rd, the last desperate effort was made to dislodge the enemy from the mountains on which they had entrenched themselves during the night preceding. The forenoon was taken up deploying troops and giving the various batteries position. About two o'clock in the afternoon everything was ready, and the order given to advance. The firing began, and for three hours hundred cannons thundered their death messengers in the opposing ranks. The best writer in the universe could not give the faintest idea of the horrible conflict. The enemy held their position, though our men rushed upon them in their trenches and cut them down with their swords; bayonets clashed together, but in vain. Our forces were ordered to fall back, they did in good order, but had suffered severely, though at the same time they taught the enemy a terrible lesson concerning the valor of Dixie's boys. The loss I would suppose is almost equal, though Northern papers set down their loss greater than ours. 30,000 I think will cover all, including both parties."

## *Retreat from Gettysburg*

E.A. Osborne sadly recounted few days during Lee's retreat back to Maryland following disaster on 3 July, which they endured in pouring rain, and harassment by Federal cavalry against the rear guard, where Ramseur's Brigade was then serving. Numerous men straggled, and on 4 July, when Lee began his retreat, Company K lost privates W.C. Peeler and Henry Severs to capture. Their circumstance when captured is not recorded, but as hundreds of men were falling out of ranks from exhaustion, it seems plausible to count them amongst those forlorn survivors, or else they simply came to close to the Cavalry and were taken. Osborne reflected, "We were not molested by the enemy during the day except an occasional shot from a sharp shooter, which did no harm except wounding a few men slightly. I myself had a narrow escape from what might have been a serious- if not fatal-wound. We had halted for a rest about noon. Col. Grimes, Lt. Col. James H. Wood and I, with a few others, were reclining on the ground. I was lying on my back, looking toward the rear, with my knees elevated. Soon we heard the sound of a minnie ball pass near. No sound of a gun had been heard by us. But very soon another ball was heard to whistle very near us, and someone suggested that a sharp shooter with a long range rifle had gotten the range of us, and that we should change our location, which we did without delay. I found afterwards that a bullet had passed through the top of one of my high boots, which stood up some three or four inches above my knee, as I was lying on my back with my feet drawn up to my thighs. If I had been sitting up instead of lying down, my body would most likely have been struck by the bullet instead of the top of my boot. For this escape I am profoundly thankful to the merciful Providence that has shielded my through so many dangers, both seen and unseen".[13]

The 4th NCST served as rear guard and was heavily involved with Union cavalry on the entire retreat back into Maryland. On 9 July, just days after the battle, Nat Raymer wrote home again, sharing his views on what all considered a landmark, albeit failed campaign. He found some time to write and recollect while sitting in their temporary camp near Hagerstown, Maryland, allowing us another glimpse of what the Rowan Rifles saw as they rushed into Gettysburg from Oak Hill on 1 July, and also what transpired on 2 July in a letter published in the *Carolina Watchman* on 27 July:

"The last two weeks are big with events of the greatest importance; what the next two may bring to light we cannot even imagine at the present. But of the first I shall attempt to sketch a brief and hastily written outline. I am aware that the readers of the Watchman are waiting impatiently, and in the most painful suspense for news from the bloody battlefields in the North and to relieve the anxiety to some degree I will give at the close of this letter a list of our casualties in our regiment, kindly furnished by my friend, J.E. Steele. On Monday the 22nd of June, we entered Pennsylvania by way of the Cumberland Valley, and a more magnificent country I never saw. It looks like a well cultivated garden, and so thickly settled that we were continually traveling in the suburbs of some city it seemed. The citizens are

German almost universally, and in politics of the copperhead stripe, that is, for peace at any cost.

They live in substantial brick or stone dwellings generally, and on every farm you may see commodious and elegant barns. Small grain is the staple, wheat, rye, barley and oats; but little corn is raised. More luxuriant fields of wheat cannot be imagined, and while we were there it was fully ripe and falling down. The harvesting machines were lying idle in the fields in the very spots from which scouts unhitched the horses and drove them away. Thousands of bushels of small grain will be lost for the lack of means to save it. The horses, mules, wagons, cattle and, in fact, everything that could be of any use to us was pressed for in miles on each side of our line of march. The horses, though are not suitable for cavalry use as general thing. They are too fat and clumsy for any use, but are peculiarly adapted to the farm.

The citizens were frightened out of their wits, whether they had far to go or not, I do not pretend to say. Many fled before us and left all they had in the world at our mercy, and those that remained threw their doors open and told our foraging parties to take what they wanted. The consequence was that we fared sumptuously. Our corps (Ewell's) penetrated the State as far up as Carlisle, and some detachments ventured within a few miles of Harrisburg. It was generally believed that the Capitol was the point that we were aiming at, but on the last day of June we changed direction, and began our march for Gettysburg; that night we encamped near one of the many small towns in that country, and within eight miles of Gettysburg.

During the night some skirmishing was going on, and our troops lay on their arms, ready to move at short notice, but the night passed away and nothing unusual occurred. Early next morning, July 1st we moved forward, and after some maneuvering formed line of battle about noon. By two o'clock, p.m. the ball opened in earnest and lasted until nearly night; the enemy were driven back two miles, through the burg, and up to the base of a small mountain south-east of the town. The next day the fight began early, and raged furiously until dark. The inhabitants of the town, terrified almost to death, fled in confusion in every direction, seeking safety in cellars, in stone houses, behind chimneys, & c.

The windows shuttered, doors, signs and such like in some places were riddled with bullets but the town was not shelled. If it had not been for the sick and wounded Yankees in town, it would have certainly been burned, because union men fired on our boys from the windows. At the close of the second days fight the position of the two armies was precisely the same as in the morning. During the greater portion of the day I was standing on an eminence at one end of the battle line along which I could see for three miles at least. At the points where the fight was hottest dense columns of sulphurous smoke would rise above the tree tops, shutting from view everything beyond. The roar of artillery and small arms was incessant and appalling to one not accustomed to such sights..."

Raymer further wrote that while the regiment had none killed, Otto Holshouser was wounded severely in the arm, and that among the twenty men missing after the battle on 3 July was Hugh Hall (the same man whom Colonel Grimes sorely punished by dunking a few days earlier) and Michael Hennesy. Raymer's assertion that Otto Holshouser was wounded, and Michael Hennesy was captured is further supported by Company K muster rolls covering the period from 30 April to 31 August 1863. This roll contains adequate anecdotal or descriptive information about various soldiers to afford an improved estimate of casualties at Gettysburg than Raymer's or other anecdotal accounts offer. Note the roll includes the number of men present on the latest date, i.e. 31 August 1863.[14]

| Captain | 1 Lt | 2 Lt | Brevet Lt | Sgt | Cpl | Musicians | Privates | Total Enlisted | Aggregate |
|---------|------|------|-----------|-----|-----|-----------|----------|----------------|-----------|
| 1 | 1 | 1 | 1 | 3 | 3 | 1 | 52 | 60 | 63 |

At this time, Capt. W.C. Coughenhour was in Salisbury on furlough, but still serving as company commander, with 1st Lieutenant Marcus Hofflin, who completed this roll, having command in Coughenhour's absence. 2d Lieutenant Hamilton Long and 2d Lieutenant Addison Wiseman were the other two officers. Moses Locke Bean was absent sick, but was appointed as Orderly or First Sergeant during the battle on 1 July. 2d Sergeant Michael Hennesy was captured at Gettysburg, while Otto Holshouser was present as 3d Sergeant. The company had four corporals, not three as shown on the roll, as the names Richard Williams, Alfred Carter, William Parker, and Peter A. Brown are all in the original document. However, only Williams and Carter were present, with Parker at Salisbury on furlough, and Brown in the hospital during this period due to illness. Bradley Matthews continued to serve as a musician but was listed as Absent without Leave. 1st Lt. Hofflin reported that former Orderly/First Sergeant W.C. Fraley was reduced to ranks (private) on 30 June by a regimental Court Martial, and pay records notate he was due six months pay as orderly and two months as a private on 31 August 1863, but circumstances are not specified on the roll. Company K was still missing several privates on that date, including Jeremiah Glover, Daniel McQueen, William Page, Daniel Moyer, and Noah Troutman. Pvt. Michael Rowland was identified as deserted to the enemy at Gettysburg. The company also lacked some men who were in hospital on sick leave, including John Castor, Edward Fulk, Joseph Kelly, and Alexander McQueen who was in a Richmond hospital. William Murr remained in Salisbury on convalescent leave. The muster roll list of wounded conflicts with anecdotal accounts, but concordantly shows Robert Beaty in Richmond from wounds, along with Lewis Holshouser, William Morris, Lewis Mahaley and George Snuggs.

A significant number of privates were also serving on detached duties from this company on 31 August 1863, including George Basinger who was working as a blacksmith in Richmond. John Deaton was assigned as a brigade mail carrier, and John Kenter was serving daily extra duties as brigade forage master. William Lillycross was earlier detailed to serve in Richmond hospitals as a steward, along with Joseph Boone Saunders who was conscripted only a few months earlier in April. Henry Williams remained on detached service with the pioneers. Isaac O'Neil found himself detailed as a clerk to the Confederate Medical Director's office, and James Roberts continued on detail as a clerk for the quartermasters. Francis Mills experienced an unusual duty, when he was detailed as clerk for the Conscription officer located at Salisbury North Carolina after Gettysburg. One of the two privates who had earlier forged commission documents for a lieutenancy while serving as provost clerks, William Durrell (his even proffered that R.E. Lee approved it) was ironically returned to his former duties at the provost clerk's office, along with John Endie who was detailed to serve as a provost guard. One has to wonder what motivated the officers to trust Durrell on the same detail after his earlier shenanigans. On a sad note, the same muster roll indicates 1st Lt. Hofflin had received word from Salisbury that Pvt. Martin Jones, a member of Company K who was wounded at the Battle of Seven Pines, had recently died at home from wounds received in the battle.

This news likely had a heavy effect on his friends still serving in the former Rowan Rifles, who were now acutely aware the war was not going to end anytime soon. In particular, things were looking grim for the Confederacy. Lieutenant Hofflin summarized the activities during the past few months in Company K in the "Record of Events" for the period of 30 April – 31 August 1863 from the camp near Orange Court House, "The Company left Fredericksburg, Va on the 4th of June 1863, and marched to Carlisle PA and was engaged in the Battle of Gettysburg PA, crossed the Potomac on the night of the 13th of July and remain at the resent camp until the 4th of August 1863." Once Lee's army finally encamped following their retreat from Maryland and Pennsylvania, Nat Raymer again had opportunity to reflect and write. He penned on 25 July that "I never before saw men so thoroughly worn out" as he observed the stragglers catching up with the regiment which had stopped to lie down for an hour or two before dawn, indicating "it was nine o' clock the next day before all arrived. Not more than fifty men of our regiment were up with us."72 Raymer's letter from 31 July was printed on 24 August in the *Carolina Watchman*, written from their camp then located near Madison Court House:

“A day's rest affords me an opportunity to write again for the gratification of my numerous friends; hitherto incessant marching has prevented it. After scrambling among mountains and wading creeks and rivers for ten days in succession, we are at last within three miles of Madison Court House, where it is possible that we will see the remainder of Early's Rode's and Johnston's divisions. The remainder of Lee's army is in the vicinity of Culpepper it is said, but I doubt very much whether a single man in our corps knows its exact whereabouts. We have had no fighting since we left front Royal, near which, on the evening of the 23rd inst., we had a sharp skirmish with some Yankees who had the audacity to attempt to cut us off. In the fray we had one sharpshooter out of our regiment killed...The fight took place at the entrance of Manassas gap in the Blue Ridge, and though it was very serious business, yet the scene was something more than ordinary exciting and beautiful. At midnight we were aroused and marched quietly five or six miles up the road to Luray which follows the meanderings of the charming Shenandoah.

The men were exhausted and could go no farther. During the day preceding we had marched upwards of twenty miles, and then the fight in the evening, and the marching at night, was positively more than we could bear. I never before saw men so thoroughly worn out, and it was 9 o'clock the next day before all arrived. When we stopped to lie down it lacked but an hour or two of day break, and not more than fifty men of our regiment were up with us. About 9 a.m. on the 24th we moved up the river, and have been moving ever since until the 29th inst., when we landed here. Our brigade has recently received considerable accessions from home and the hospitals.”

On 5 July, the 4th NCST fell back toward Hagerstown, Maryland, with their brigade. As Lee's army eventually reached a static location, fresh supplies slowly began to trickle in. Lieutenant Hofflin signed another supply form on 3 August showing only a few pairs of shoes and socks were issued to Company K.15 This finding lends more credibility to a popular notion that the North Carolinians were deficient in shoes during the Gettysburg campaign. Considering that the most recent muster roll indicated there were sixty enlisted men present but there were only twenty three pairs of shoes and nineteen pairs of socks received, it could also mean the majority of men had adequate shoes; but we are left to speculate. Hofflin's supply form further states that two pair of $10.00 pants and one pair of $14.00 pants came, probably for officers or non-commissioned officers, as the other nine pair cost $9.00 each. The form reveals four pair drawers, two jackets, and five shirts were drawn. After the loss at Gettysburg, the 4th NCST reacted to the news of the fall of Vicksburg in the west with despair. Raymer succinctly projects his realization of the Southerners' plight was sinking in, writing on 20 July:

"For more than two years the Confederacy has been floating... nothing has impeded our progress save here and there a snag in the shape of Yankee armies, a few gun boats and such like, but all at once we are plunged into a whirlpool from which I fear we shall never be able to extricate ourselves. The news of the fall of Vicksburg and Port Hutson has startled us like a clap of thunder on a cloudless day. We were not prepared for such intelligence. Why have we been told that those places were impregnable, that they were abundantly supplied with rations and ammunition, and that the garrisons were in such splendid trim!

Why have our journalists attempted deception when they knew that the truth must eventually leak out! As yet we have learned none of the particulars; we only know that one of the main pillars under our new government has been removed, and that its removal has caused a mighty tottering among others, the most serious of which is the stagger this slow has given to our currency, it is evidently tumbling, and there is no reason why our officials should shut their eyes to the fact. But it is not expedient for me to proceed further on this subject at present, still I must say that to every observant mind a depreciating currency is a first sign of decay. During the last two weeks a wonderful changes has been effected on our men in ranks,--I did not think it possible in so short a length of time; then, bright hopes and prospects buoyed them up and spurred them on; now, desperation seems to have settled on every countenance and a determination to push affairs to a speedy, perhaps a fearful crisis.

In our department, battle has become quite an every day thing. Fighting does not seem to do a particle of good, for no sooner is one bloody struggle over then preparations are made for another. No strategical points are gained by either party, and this way of standing off and firing into each other for days and nights at a time, or rushing on batteries through a horrid hissing of a thousand death missles don't pay the South; with the North it matters but little; there, armies spring up like Jonah's gourd vine, in one night,--they seem to rise like mushrooms out of the earth. There they have lost near half a million of men, but what of that!

Their places are filled to a great extent by fresh importations from Europe, while we might as well expect reinforcements from the moon as to look beyond the confines of our own territory for help. This morning I heard "intelligent contraband" say that "de whites of de Souf would soon be played out, and de white army was goin' to bust up, den dey would have an army of niggers asn' I's goin to be a major general, yah, yah, yah!" There is no doubt but the negroes in the army hate Yankees just as intensely as our soldiers do. While we were in Pennsylvania if any had desired to do so they could have left us, but instead they were afraid to venture beyond sight of camp for fear they would be kidnapped. What conclusion shall we draw from what has been said above!

Several; first, that our situation is growing alarmingly critical; second, it is high time some method was adopted by which our men might be saved, and not needlessly sacrificed; and third, since butchery and loss of life seems to be doing no good whatever, why is it that the diplomatists are not at work to bring about a settlement. It is folly for the North or any other people to talk about conquering the spirit of the people at the South. We admit that by overwhelming numbers we may be temporarily subjugated; and it is a fact indisputable that those who are laboring to depreciate our currency are doing more for our utter ruin that the whole Yankee armies; but granting that they succeed in establishing their abhorrent rule over us, will it then be a union!

The people of the United States remind me of a man who whips his wife to make her love him. In the even of a failure to establish the Confederacy, allow me to turn prophet for a few moments, and acting in that capacity I would predict no peace for the South for the next twenty years. Our newspapers would be filled with accounts of foul murders, insurrections, plots and rebellions, and the deplorable state of affairs generally would be too horrible to contemplate. But let us turn from the future to the present. It has been said that Gen. Lee's army retired in great confusion from Gettysburg. This is not so because I constituted a mite in that army myself, and I believe that my opportunities for seeing and learning were as good as those of any man in the army. Some of the divisions suffered severe losses, but I can assure my readers that our loss in killed and wounded was no greater than the enemy's while his loss in prisoners was much heavier than ours.

The principal reason for the falling back was that our lines of communication in rear of the army were too long and too much exposed, which we learned to our cost. Another reason was the immense number of prisoners in our hands. They refused paroles on the field or any where else except at Richmond, consequently they had to be guarded back to that place. I saw not less than ten or twelve thousand, and was told that there were other gangs on their way Southward. Instead of confusion the whole retreat was conducted with remarkably good order. We seldom traveled more than eight or ten miles in twenty-four hours, but those marches were made mostly after night.

The main body of the Yankee army attempted to cut us off before we reached Hagerstown, Md., but failed, while small detachments were continually harassing our rear, doing no damage however, but rather a favor, by hurrying up our wagons and the few straggles who were behind. One day while we were yet in Pennsylvania I noticed the road blockaded with wagons for two miles. A pelting rain was making mud and things in general worse every moment. But there were, and had been for two hours waiting for the wagons to get out of the way. The men were getting impatient, wagon masters were galloping about whooping and hallowing, swearing at the drivers and hurrying them up, but it did no good.

Presently a Yankee batter drove in sight, took its position on a hill and began "tossing" shells at the whole train; they bursted and whizzed and sparkled about uncomfortably near, which some how, impressed on the minds of the wagoners the idea that the atmosphere was unhealthy and such an everlasting getting away, never was heard tell of, it is well that the train was not loaded with glass ware. The horses were whipped into a gallop, and the wagons seemed to bounce half a rod without touching the ground. In twenty minutes not one could be seen, but this and similar skedaddles no doubt gave rise to the reported confusion.

The infantry, the bone and sinew of the army, was in no instance hurried or hard pressed. Near Hagerstown we lay in line of battle two days and nights waiting for the enemy to attack us. Instead of advancing on us they crossed the Potomac below us, thus endeavoring to cut us off again. Lee kept his eyes open, and pushing his own army across headed them and beat them at their own game. But armies now confront each other near Bunker Hill, a small town midway between Winchester and Charlestown. We expect and engagement daily."

Supplies again started to arrive again as 1st Lt. Hofflin signed another order from the quartermaster on 1 September 1863 for "1 Pair Shoes @ $6.00" for "my own use."[16] And on 5 September 1863, he received another order from the quartermaster although the number of shoes in the company remained low. The order was for five pair of pants, one shirt, and one pair shoes.[17] Other supplies were gradually beginning to flow back into the company by this time. On the same date, Hofflin also signed for receipt of seven pair paints, seventeen pair socks, three pair shoes, one jacket, eleven shirts and fourteen pair drawers, hardly enough to cover the company.[18] Even firewood ran short during this encampment; on 30 September 1863, a "Fuel Requisition Return" form from the period of July-September was signed by Captain Coughenhour.[19] Company K received five cords of firewood for thirty enlisted men and two officers, which was but half of the monthly allowance required by the sustenance department. It isn't clear why the officers requested firewood, but they were issued cords of firewood.

As in all wars, deserters were never popular with the soldiers who did their duty, but the Rowan Rifles were becoming more outspoken on the matter. The frustrations with what many now perceived to be a "lost cause" and political influences from home were motivating many to take "French Leave", army parlance for being "Away with out Leave." The following quip soon appeared in the *Carolina Watchman* from the field on 7 September: "We have just seen a letter from a private member of Company K, 4th N.C., in which he lays it right and left on those who desert their colors. He says-"The men should watch for them every chance they have, and if need be shoot them." This is the way soldiers in the true sense of the word talk, and it is an honor to the writer. He is a member of the "Rowan Rifle Guards," that every man, woman and child in Rowan may well be proud of—it has been in almost every battle in Northern Virginia, and we have not up to this moment heard that a single man has deserted. Let all our Rowan boys imitate the noble example." As a whole, the regiment remained strong in spirit in spite of poor rations and increasing desertion rates. Nat Raymer's next letter reveals that similar to John Stikeleather, many soldiers turned to the Lord for their strength, and also that things on the front had generally settled down for another brief period. Numerous other soldiers from this regiment document a spiritual revival occurred following their tragic losses at Gettysburg with fervent worship services regularly occurring in the 4th NCST camp. Raymer wrote from near Orange Court House Virginia on 22 August 1863 in a bit of a religious zeal, yet somewhat agitated about their food sources:

"...The only complaint I hear is concerning the quality of our rations. Nothing but corn, meat and beef, with a little bacon once in a while is rather hard diet during the dog days. It might be better, and could be, if we had a brigade commissary worth his room in purgatory; but as it is, he is too hopelessly lazy to make an effort to procure the articles prescribed...brigade commissaries are authorized to purchase green corn, potatoes, & c., from the farmers in the neighborhood...Now, Doles brigade, which lies near us, has been feasting on these things for a week, procured by an energetic commissary, while we have been endeavoring to keep a protracted fast on this loathsome corn bread. As might be expected, the result of this gross mismanagement is stealing; scarce a day or night passes but roasting ears and vegetables are clandestinely brought into camp. The men grumble every where, and some are so bold as to threaten desertion as a last resort to get food appropriate to the season, when such food could be had in abundance if our commissary thought less of his own case and more of the comfort of the soldiers generally.

The officer whose business it is provision the troops, has one of the most arduous and responsible positions in the army; thousands of men feel the least neglect of duty on his part, and bitterly curse him for such neglect; we can see the profusion of luxuries on his table and turn with disgust to our meager diet, yet we are helpless; we have neither money nor credit, and at once our consciences become accommodating and our appetites uncontrollable. The blockade is run, sentinels alluded (which by the way, does not require much shrewdness-- they generally wink at it, or keep both eyes shut) and thus a change of diet finds its way into camp. Place the disgrace or sin whatever it be, where it properly belongs—we are guiltless....Yesterday was fast day, the observance of which was almost a necessity with us.

The camp was profoundly quiet, as much so as any Sunday I have ever witnessed in the army. All labor and duty was suspended, and the men assembled in large congregations to hear and participate in divine service. We have two chaplains in our brigade...both Methodist I believe. They delivered very appropriate and affecting sermons...the solemn ceremonies of the day were concluded with the holy sacrament administered upwards to two hundred communicants. I never saw a scene of the kind more deeply impressing and humbly trust that great good may be the result. The condition of our country was brought vividly before the minds of the hearers, and so eloquently, and touching that tears were seen chasing each other down not a few sun browned cheeks. Our land is waste; bright and smiling farms are trodden under foot; black ruins mark the spots where once stood beautiful cottages with their Thousand pleasant associations; family circles are broken, some of the once happy members lie unburied in foreign land, or fill bloody graves in our own, and the very atmosphere is burdened with the wails and prayers of disconsolate widows and orphaned children.

Such were some of the appeals made to the hearts of the soldiers' who would not be affected? Still scarce a ray of hope sheds its light upon us; reverse after reverse attends our arms, calamity after calamity befalls our nation—all, the just chastisements of a righteous God for our national sins. O!, when will it be said, enough. Peace!—and the same mighty voice, that stilled the ocean's storm, will ere long, still the tumult in our own unhappy land. Let us patiently bide our time, and do our duty faithfully. Let us renounces every evil way, and sincerely follow the dictations of a pure conscience; then let come what will, whether success or misfortune, be assured that in the end all will be for good."

With things relatively calm otherwise in the army for a time, this great revival continued to be the focus of Raymer's thoughts for several weeks. Many men from Rowan County suddenly professed to be Christians. Raymer wrote again from his tent near Orange Court House on 9 September, which ran in the *Carolina Watchman* on 28 September:

"In the absence of all excitement whatever, of military nature, or political either at present, we have nothing to write about unless we light on the great revival again. It seems to be gathering strength daily and nightly, growing wider and deeper, and now I learn from reliable authority that the religious excitement prevails throughout the army of Northern Virginia, and also in some divisions of the army of the West. It is truly encouraging and from its effects we hope ere long to see the welcome dawn of peace. During three weeks past scarce a day or a night has passed in which we have not had divine services in camp. At first a small arbor was constructed, sufficient to accommodate two hundred persons, but from time to time additions and improvements have been made, until now, at least two thousand persons can be comfortably seated; and yet large numbers are obliged to stand around the outside or squat like tailors on the ground.

Some four or five scaffolds have been erected around the hallowed spot on which blazing fires of pine knots are kept burning during night services, and many of the night scenes presented are one of the most affecting and thrilling nature. Soon after sunset squads from other brigades come in—they flock together from every quarter, and by the time the drums are done beating tattoo every seat beneath the arbor is occupied as well as every foot of room about the fire-stands on the outside. And the men listen to what is said, they are not prompted by curiosity or the vain notion of seeing and being seen, a most wonderful motive in some sections. Here we see no gaudy dress or jewelry, no hooting and howling and yelling of fast young men on the outskirts of camp—nor fast young ladies either.

The alter here is not an improvement on the Ancient Roman Amphitheatre, like we have seen in by-gone days, where the gladiators and gladiatoresses made night indeous with unearthly shouts and disgusted every sensible person with their shall I say it?—cavortings. We have no loafers, no pleasure seekers, nor shirkers, nor game making—all feel an interest in the great work now going on, and all alike express themselves as convinced of its thoroughness and sincerity. Notwithstanding, the addition of an equal number of females might bring some evils, yet we painfully miss them, and listen in vain for a lady's voice when a thousand tough soldiers begin to sing a hymn or spiritual song.

And such singing, Oh! It is indescribable! It is overwhelming. It seems like a flood of the most seraphic music is bearing us on. So grand! So sublime! I can not account for it, except it be the feeling with which men sing, and that feeling seems to be imparted to all within hearing distance. The meeting goes on—the interest unabated. Some nights near a hundred penitents come forward to the alter; it does seem that it is going to work a thorough and most happy resolution in the morale of the army, and may we express the hope that the good influences of this revival in the army, may reach the hearts of the massy people at home and work a beneficial change there, where it is certainly as much needed as here. Content reigns supreme among the soldiers—our bill of fare embraces all we can expect once more—we have good health, well shoed and clad, and four months wages in our pockets—I mean what is left of it, after liquidating our debts, and paying for a watermelon at the present."

In the latter days of September 1863 the 4th NCST was located near Raccoon Ford, Virginia. Nat Raymer wrote a letter from his camp on or about 6-8 September that was published a few days later on 16 September in the *Carolina Watchman*. His note provides evidence the desertion rate, which had increased after Gettysburg, was affecting Ramseur's brigade as well as others in the Army of Northern Virginia:

"At early dawn on Monday morning last we bade adieu to our quiet camp, taking up our march for this place where a battle was expected hourly. The enemy in heavy force (we are told) advanced from Culpepper C.H. and, perhaps, would have crossed at this ford, but for the obstructions placed in the way by the rebels. During Monday afternoon sharp skirmishing and pretty hot artillery firing was kept up between the advance of the two armies. Our pickets held the north bank of the Rapidan, while our artillery occupied positions on the heights on this (the south) side.

All day yesterday occasional firing was kept up, and today also at intervals heavy reports jar the stillness of the autumnal air. The casualties, so far as I have been able to learn, have been quite slight on our side, some dozen killed and twenty-five or thirty wounded, principally artillery men. It is hard to tell what will turn up here; some thing we will have a general engagement, others think we will not. From all indications I am inclined to favor the former opinion. For the last six hours a heavy column of Confederate infantry and cavalry have been

197

seen approaching the river, and it would not surprise me at all if they should cross tonight, indeed I think it very probable; and so sure as we cross, that sure will we have a fight, unless the Yankees back down and get out of the way entirely. The enemy no doubt thinks we are weak since Longstreet with his whole corps has left us, but if they engage us they will be apt to find out their mistake.

We expect a rumpus; these grand reviews by Ewell and Lee were infallible signs of a march or a battle; many of us said so then, and now we know it to be a fact. Within the last ten days Gen. Lee, together with Gen. Ewell, has reviewed the entire army of Northern Virginia, and it is said they expressed themselves highly pleased with its discipline and condition. It would be imprudent for me to say anything about our number, but the reader may rest assured that it is sufficiently large to repel any force which the enemy can bring against us. There is no doubt but our army is vastly improved since our return from Maryland, and if we should meet the enemy in battle we confidently hope for a complete triumph—nor need the people at home be surprised to hear of our engagement soon. The sun is now not more than an hour high, and at this moment the cannonading is heavier than it has been at any time during the day; the firing is incessant and betokens a bloody day coming,--who knows but it may be tomorrow?

We are lying bivouacked in a pine thicket within a mile of the Clark's Mountain (which some of my reader's may recall) and about one and a half miles from Raccoon Ford on the Rapidan river, some seven or eight miles below Orange Court House. It is very uncertain whether we remain here till tomorrow's sunrise or not, our movements are frequently sudden and incomprehensible, and I may add very disagreeable sometimes to boot. For instance, if we should be roused at midnight tonight, marched quick time to the river, and then have to pitch in and wade-there would be nothing very romantic in that, especially if the Yankees should amuse themselves by throwing shells at us while we are staggering about in the water or slipping and falling on the banks. But we will not trouble ourselves about the future, self preservation at the present is a soldier's first duty, and one which we never fail to perform. A man was shot today for desertion, he belonged to the 2nd N.C., our brigade. There is no mercy shown to deserters now, so sure as they are caught, that sure will they be executed; their day of grace is past. Let me warn all good citizens against harboring men absent without leave, by so doing they are running a great risk – the law is positive."

The 4th NCST encountered several days of intense skirmishing on picket duty and sustained several casualties in September-October 1863, to the degree that the men spent the much of their time guessing about what was coming next on their outposts. Pvt. Jacob Hanes of Company G stated in a letter to his brother on 16 September, "...on day before yesterday [sic 14 September 1863] there was a right smart little skirmish between the pickets. We lost some 10 or 15 killed and about twenty-five or thirty wounded..."[20] Maj. Frances Shaffner, the regimental surgeon,* mentioned as he penned a note to his brother on 21 September 1963 that the weather was getting colder at night, but the men were well-fed and had adequate shoes, "Still our men are confident, and in most excellent spirits. I have never seen the army to be in better fighting condition. We get splendid beef and good flour, and enough of both. All reports to the contrary are incorrect. Shoes are wanting, but the destitution in this respect is not as great as it was last year this time. Then half the army was barefoot, now seven-eighths are well shod...The weather is very pleasant now. We have had several severe frosts. A few nights ago I got thoroughly drenched. We had left camp to take our position in line, and during the  night  a  rain  came  on,  which  succeeded  in saturating my blankets and drenching me..."[21] The 31 August to 31 October 1863 muster roll demonstrates the effects of two major campaigns on the company thus far, with only twenty five privates available, as most were sick, or still deemed missing or wounded.[22]

| Captain | 1 Lt | 2 Lt | Brevet Lt | Sgt | Cpl | Musicians | Privates | Total Enlisted | Aggregate |
|---------|------|------|-----------|-----|-----|-----------|----------|----------------|-----------|
| 1 | - | - | 1 | 1 | 2 | - | 23 | 26 | 64 |

This roll was completed when E.A. Osborne, now a Major, inspected the 4th NCST while encamped near Kelly's Ford, Virginia. This roll shows the Rowan Rifles with twenty eight men, both officer and enlisted, available for duty this date. In addition to relocating to another camp site, the company underwent a great number of changes among officers in the fall of 1863. Captain Coughenhour reported that Lieutenant Hofflin was on leave and that 2d Lt. Addison Wiseman (whom the reader will recall was wounded twice, once at Fredericksburg and again at Chancellorsville just one day after returning to duty from the hospital) was Away without Leave (AWOL). If Wiseman was truly "AWOL," it had little, if any, repercussion since he was given command of Company K on 27 November after Coughenhour was temporarily assigned to Robert E. Lee's staff as inspector general and assistant adjutant general on 7 November. On 7 December Captain Coughenhour was reassigned to the brigade staff of Brig. Gen. Stephen D. Ramseur.[23] Addison Wiseman was officially promoted to first lieutenant on 9 December.[24] Perhaps his prior history of demonstrated fortitude after twice suffering battle wounds and then returning to his post on both occasions had a positive influence on the opinion of Col. Bryan Grimes, in whose hands his fate ultimately rested. In an uncharacteristic move, the normally litigious Grimes did not press charges against him. At that time, the 4th NCST had but one man, a sergeant, under arrest and in confinement away from camp, so perhaps rank did indeed have its privileges.

2d Lt. Hamilton Long was hospitalized due to illness; he resigned shortly after this roll was taken on 8 November due to poor health. The brevet second lieutenant who replaced him was Moses Locke Bean, who had been serving as first sergeant since 1 July. Bean was promoted to brevet lieutenant on the battlefield at Gettysburg, but his commission date or date of rank was not until 2 November 1863, just two days following Longs' resignation.[25] There were no changes found in status of soldiers listed on previous rolls who were on either detached service, wounded absent in hospitals, or on sick furlough. Company K had several men still sick in camp, however, including Otto Holshouser who was sick in his tent, and five privates under arrest and in confinement in camp for being Away without Leave, and three who were under similar charges and detained elsewhere in the brigade, but oddly, their names are not specified on the roll, as this information was found in the statistical summary. Privates William Buis, W.C. Peeler, Henry Severs were already identified as captured at Gettysburg on 4 July 1863 and Joseph Saunders was identified as Away without Leave. While the company census was low from recent campaigns, their supply situation was also poor at this point in the war. Much of the popular mythology generated regarding the image of a ragged, "Johnny Reb" came from accounts transpiring during this period in the Army of Northern Virginia, as there were in fact several men without blankets, shoes and uniforms.

---

*Maj. (Dr.) John Frances Shaffner became the regimental surgeon of the 4th North Carolina Regiment sometime between March and December 1863. He was formerly the surgeon for the 33d North Carolina State Troops. Shaffner and Col. Bryan Grimes had a great deal of conflict between them as Grimes had charged Shaffner with insubordination in 1864. The allegation was later dismissed. Shaffner was paroled at Appomattox on 9 April 1865. Jordan and Manarin, Vol. 4, 10.

Yet in contrast, evidence doesn't consistently show that all North Carolinians were in a severely deprived state, either. It is understood that while not all soldiers were faring as well, and at this time most men in Company K lacked shoes and needed at least 1-2 pieces of new clothing, with winter settling in, but would soon improve. Supply forms reveal that a steady flow of quartermaster goods began to arrive in late October – November. 1st Lt. Marcus Hofflin received clothing for Company K in camp near Kelly's Ford, Virginia, on 10 November 1863. This supply contained an interesting variation of uniform jacket was issued, identified as two "long jackets," seven overcoats, two wool shirts, fourteen pair paints, six pair of leather shoes and two pair of cloth shoes and two pair of cotton pants. The latter were of a canvas material similar to the cotton drill used to make tents, and did not last long in the field, but North Carolina was then facing a leather shortage. The cotton trousers are likely a variation of the jeans wool uniform items normally given and it is not clear why the Raleigh Quartermasters issued such an item. It is doubtful they were imported from England.[26]

It is not clear what garment pattern or type the phrase "Long Jackets" refers to, but were possibly English "ready-made" garments. There are clearly two types of jacket mentioned on this Form 40. By this point in the war, nearly all uniforms produced by the Raleigh clothing depot were made of imported English cloth, although local mills continued to supply as much gray cotton and wool jeans cloth as possible until the end of the war. North Carolina also received 1,008 English "ready-made" uniforms sometime during 1863, although it is doubtful the 4th NCST received those.[27] After Gettysburg, numerous "ready-made" English trousers and jackets, as well as yards of uniform cloth, was shipped to Wilmington through the blockade that were produced by S. Isaac and Campbell & Co., as well as Alexander & Collie & Co. in London, England via contract arranged with North Carolina's purchasing agents. Hence, after roughly July 1863, Company K likely began to receive the benefit of imported English cloth and their uniform appearance probably reflected a mixture of cotton and wool jeans cloth and English fabric.

Hofflin also procured "Cloth Shoes" – it is not clear precisely what style or pattern this item was, although the clothing depot in Raleigh is known to have manufactured shoes using a heavy, cotton canvas-type material during times of leather shortages throughout the War. Another quartermaster supply receipt signed by Captain Coughenhour on behalf of Company K dated 3 November 1863 contained a larger shipment of clothing and shoes. Recall the latest muster roll included only twenty six enlisted men available in camp, and these data show well over half the company then received new clothing, while the former roll reveals that sixteen men received new trousers and eight had new shoes. The number of new blankets must be interpreted in context of missing information; anecdotal accounts show soldiers frequently received items from home and routinely confiscated blankets, etc. from battle fields, which statistics are impossible to accurately estimate. However, as Coughenhour received sixteen pair pants, ten shirts, twenty five pairs of shoes, twelve jackets, twenty five pair drawers, an nineteen new blankets, there is little credence to the notion of a persistently "ragged rebel."[28]

On 6 November, the morning was clear and bright in camp, and Maj. Frances Shaffner, the regimental surgeon, described it as "pleasant." He was busy working on a report and wrote "...of all men of this Regt. who are absent by reason of sickness, wounds, & c. His summary affords another glimpse into the regimental census at that point, including forty seven men at home on furlough wounded, twenty at home on furlough sick, forty three in hospital sick, ten wounded at hospitals, thirty nine on detailed service "by reason of wounds or disability" and eighteen men still listed as prisoners or war, that were also known sick and wounded, for a total of one hundred and

*Courtesy Rowan County Museum. Photo by R.M. Hatfield.*

This photo is of a frock coat worn by Capt. William C. Coughenhour probably during his tenure as a staff officer due to the garments overall good condition. Made from fine English wool broadcloth, the coat is lined with crème-colored worsted piping. The buttons are a Federal-pattern, staff officer-type made in Waterbury, Connecticut. It is a classic example of a privately purchased and tailored Confederate officer garment in the Civil War. The interior is lined with black polished cotton, and a blue-and-white plaid, heavy cotton cloth is used to line the sleeves. The gold trim on the cuff is of a heavy gold gild and was hand stitched. All top stitching was done by hand. This coat is in good condition but rather fragile and frayed in several interior areas. Perhaps the most unique feature of this coat is the rank insignia on the collar; these are simple brass strips measuring two and a half inches long, attached to the collar with soldiered wire pins. Officers typically had their rank braided. Coughenhour was a cadet at the Statesville Military Academy before the War, where a similar style of officer rank was used by company grade officers. The garment is housed in the Rowan County Museum, Salisbury North Carolina.

seventy-seven men out of ranks for medical reasons.[29] As expected, while commanding Company K, Lieutenant Hofflin stayed very involved in the administrative management of his company, and kept a watchful eye on the flow of supplies, in particular their clothing. On 11 November he signed for several items Captain Coughenhour had requested only eight days earlier in camp near Guinea Station.

While this information shows that officers could then request uniforms from the depot in Raleigh per regulations, (as opposed to privately purchasing uniforms as in the past) what they actually received was often a different story altogether. This issue of new clothing was likely due to an increase of company census, as later muster rolls show that men were beginning to return from leave, hospitals, or missing status during late October-November, and after their arduous campaign into Maryland and Pennsylvania, doubtless needed new clothing. Some may have drawn new uniforms in Richmond hospitals, which was a common practice while on sick leave, but most appear to have simply returned to camp in whatever garments they had when they left. Hofflin next received twelve pair "Gray Pants", thirty five pair drawers, eleven cotton shirts, nine flannel shirts, four "Gray Jackets" at $2.56 each, and twenty five pair pants at $6.12 each, on this shipment. There is evidence of increased uniformity, as the trousers and jackets are both described as gray, although it is impossible to ascertain whether this was English or domestic jeans cloth, or much less what particular variation of hue it contained.[30]

### *Fall Encampment & Skirmishes*

The 4th NCST remained in Ramseur's brigade, and in October there was more fighting occurring near Bristoe Station, Virginia, and while the regiment was present in ranks, it was not actively engaged. On 13-14 October 1863, the regiment participated in an intense skirmish at Warrenton, Virginia, losing two killed and six wounded during what could be considered a Federal rear guard movement, but Company K did not suffer any losses there.[31] Afterward, Gen. Robert E. Lee withdrew the army and crossed the upper Rapidan River to Orange Courthouse and encamped for the winter, although the regiment was also in the brief engagement at Mine Run, Virginia, on 2 December.[32] Some important changes in command and rank were also occurring in the company, as 1st Sergeant Moses Locke Bean was promoted to second lieutenant on 2 November 1863 after serving only four months as orderly sergeant.[33] Another interesting occurrence on 6 November was the resignation of 1st Lieutenant Hamilton Long. Long had served as a junior officer in Company K for roughly one year, and he had only been in service since 17 August 1861, a little over fifteen months. The circumstances surrounding his resignation are yet unknown; but it is clear that Bean and Long had known each other during the antebellum-volunteer era of this company, and their relationship appears to have been without interpersonal conflicts at play that potentially contributed to Longs' resignation. Nat Raymer again sent home his observations of their recent skirmishing and marching, with writing being one of the more lengthy accounts likely due to having more spare time than in previous weeks. He wrote from winter quarters of 24 October and was published in the *Carolina Watchman* on 9 November:

"On the morning of the 9th inst., as the first peep of day reddened the east, we evacuated the banks of the Rapidan and took up our line of march westward. Passing through the suburbs of Orange we crossed the Rapidan (forded of course) at Union Mills; thence bearing a north west we left Madison Court-house half a mile to our left; four miles further brought us to Robeson river, from the north bank of which the enemy's outposts had been driven a few hours before our arrival; heard the firing quite distinctly, and without taking time to undress, or so much as roll up our pants legs, we crossed and pushed on briskly several miles further, hoping to get up in time to engage the enemy that night; but it was useless, he made better time than we, and was entirely out of reach, if not out of hearing before we arrived at the scene of action.

This was on the night of the 10th, the darkness was most intense, and in our exhausted condition it was impossible to go further; in the two days marching we had come about forty-five miles and we literally fell down and slept till daylight the next morning. On Sunday the 11th, we traveled eight miles only, when for some reason best known to Gen. Lee, we went into camp, five miles from Culpepper, and on the Sperryville road; we asked no questions about it, but were glad enough to get rest on any terms. Rations were issued, with orders to have them cooked and everything ready to leave at 3 o'clock in the next morning. When time came we felt the exceeding loathe to get up, but it had to be done and by sunrise we were far on our way towards Warrenton. The fields were covered with a frost that looked like a miniature snow, which made the air so cool that brisk walking was necessary to our comfort. About noon we came to the Hazel river, which besides being a stout stream ordinarily, was now swollen by the late rains in the mountains.

When we arrived in the broad low lands bordering the river we found two or more brigades already congregated which with the addition of ours made several thousand men, all wondering how we were to get across; presently, however, we were relived by the order from Gen. Rodes, or somebody else, to "doff our nether garments," no sooner said than done, and the scene which followed "beggars all description" as the novelist say on more delicate subjects. What we had been dreading all the morning turned out to be a regular frolic, and in the course of an hour all were over safely, and on our way for the next river, which we passed five miles further on at Warrenton (or White Sulphur) springs. This, though not so large as the Hazel, I believe is called the Rappahannock. Here we found the enemy in pretty strong force, holding the north bank and in a bad humor besides.

Their sharpshooters opened on us two miles from the river on the south side, but fell back with considerable loss as we advanced, until they got over the river where they were joined by the reserved. This was somewhat in our way, but measures were taken to clean them out immediately, which was done when fifteen cannons opened simultaneously on them, assisted by a heavy corps of sharpshooters. Their guns replied feebly at first but were soon silenced altogether, and fifteen minutes later we saw a blue column of Yankees on their winding way over the hills beyond the river. "Forward" was shouted from one end of our line to the other.

The cavalry dashed on, leaving a cloud of dust and smoke behind them, through which we groped our way to the river and crossed on the bridge partially destroyed by the enemy. On both sides of the road we saw dead and wounded, men and horses, all, with a few exceptions, belonging to the enemy. The darkness was getting so thick that we could not see objects distinctly, but we could not see enough to convince us that our shells and cavalry together had done but little mischief. Some of the boys were counting the dead Yankees as we were jogging on at a rate little short of double quick, when someone yelled out, "There lies another," pointing at the same time to a dark object lying by an elm not more than eight steps from the road. "Na-rye dead" growled the blue coat, "Are you hurt?" "Yes," he replied. "I'm shot, but not dead by a hornful."

His wound was severe but not mortal I learned afterwards. We traveled on till eight or nine o'clock at night when we "turned in" as we have it out here. The night was right cool, and as soon as our "lodging" was deposited we went to work building fires of such things as we could find. While at this one of our fellows picked up a rail which he thought he would break over a stump and drawing away with all his might hit another dead man. This is the way men are scattered over many portions of northern Virginia – "unwept," no not unwept. I will not say that, for the bare mention of their name years hence will cause tears of agony to flow,-- but I will say "unknelled, uncotlined and unknown."

The next day, Tuesday 13th, we moved through Warrenton, and struck camp three miles beyond the town, without coming in contact with the enemy ourselves, through heavy cannonading was heard in front and on our right flank. Three days rations were prepared that night, and at 4 o'clock on the following morning of the 14th we were hurried up and off at a trot for two miles, when suddenly and very unexpectedly before it was quite light the enemy's sharp-shooters opened a galling fire on us. Some four or five men in our regiment were wounded, and one killed... Skirmishers were sent forward, artillery brought up, and every necessary preparation made for battle, which seemed inevitable. The musketry grew heavier every minute and presently some half dozen brass pieces opened like surly bull dogs, making the calm and frosty atmosphere resound for miles.

The fire was kept up hot during an hour and a half when it ceased entirely and our column was pushed quick time after the fleeing Yankees. The force we had engaged this morning, though pretty strong, was nothing more than the enemy's read guard—his main body was at the time retreating towards Manassas as rapidly as their heels would let them, whither our corps followed to a point eight miles from the Junction, (Manassas). Late this evening, the 14th, Cook's and Kirkland's brigades, of Hill's corps, engaged the enemy on the railroad near Bristo, six miles from Manassas, and a most desperate fight ensured, in which I rather fear, the Confederates lost more than they gained, let those who were present say.

But the enemy had made good his escape, with the loss of some two thousand prisoners, some wagons, and a large quantity of baggage burned up on the railroad, besides a good many killed and wounded. During the 15th of this month we lay idle in a thicket of pines, while around us on almost every side was a vast forest of wagons and artillery, being very neatly the entire crop belonging to both corps, A.P. Hill and Ewell's. At intervals heavy cannonading was heard in the direction of Dunifries, sixteen miles south-east of Manassas, but it occasioned no alarm in camp and the day and night passed off quietly with the exception of a severe drenching form of a thunder shower, which seems to succeed a battle of heavy discharges of artillery invariably.

On the morning of the 16th rain was falling heavily; the cedars, pines and dwarf oaks formed a labyrinth through which it was almost impossible to make our way, and these dripping with water from every leaf and twig, together with the grass and mud shoe mouth deep, soon saturated our garments from head to foot in a way by no means comfortable; but we traveled on slowly in an easterly direction two miles, when we found ourselves on the Orange and Alexander railroad, down which we turned towards Richmond. We made the best of our disagreeable flight, and after following the railroad four or five miles we halted, stacked arms and proceeded to tear up the track. The very elements seemed to conspire against us;

such torrents of rain as fell for two hours, and just while we were at work too, were enough to make us think another flood had broken loose upon us.

By three o'clock p.m. we were done our contract, and about the same time the rain ceased falling, the clouds broke and the bright evening sun chased them far to the east where they were banked up like a huge black pail. For two or three days after this we loitered along the railroad, acting is rear guard for our working parties, working a little ourselves, and so on until we got down to the south side of the Rappahannock, where after destroying the bridge across that stream, the work or destruction ceased, leaving the railroad a wreck, from Manassas to the Rappahannock, a distance of some thirty miles.

At noon on the 19th, the army of Northern Virginia was encamped on the hills between Brandy Station and above the mentioned river, and in that vast multitude scarcely a dry thread of clothing, so incessant and terrible had been the fall of rain and half for the preceding twelve hours. We built large fires, and by them warmed and dried ourselves as best we could till near sunset when the various diversions dispersed "to their respective places of abode." I suppose I know nothing about any save our own, (Rodes) which moved down in the neighborhood of Kelly's Ford on the Rappahannock, five miles below the railroad bridge, where we have been picketing and putting up winter quarters. We have no idea how long we will remain here, perhaps till Christmas, but we would like to stay all winter if possible, since with our sunny shanties we are well prepared for cold weather."

In spite of the privations and hardships of an active campaign, the flow of supplies into camp resumed when they settled into winter quarters. On 20 November 1863, Lieutenant Hofflin purchased one pair of "Pants" for himself, at a cost of $13, specifying they were "absolutely requisite for my own use," again indicating that North Carolina company grade officers serving in the field were then able to purchase uniform items directly from state quartermasters for their own usage.34 Note that the Confederate Government did not officially authorize officers to purchase clothing from government quartermaster's until publication of General Orders Number 28 on 4 March, 1864 which specified that officers could buy clothing at government cost, so long as their privates had already received an adequate supply. This finding further distinguishes the capability of North Carolina's state operated quartermaster system to provide for state troops without reliance upon the central Confederate government, and should dispel any myths of such. On 20 November, Captain Coughenhour signed a receipt for several clothing items including some new hats although he was serving elsewhere on Gen. R.E. Lee's staff.35

Consistent with supply patterns earlier in the war, as winter had sat in, the frequency of clothing delivery increased in contrast to summer months during active campaigning, although here, we do not find evidence of "ragged rebels" as this shipment was only two weeks after the company was amply supplied with clothing. Coughenhour's receipt indicates three pair pants, seven pair drawers, seven shirts, eighteen pair socks, two jackets and ten hats were received. The pattern or style of hats is unknown. Jackets were fifteen dollars each, suggesting higher quality, but again we speculate. They were possibly of imported cloth from England. Afterward, from 21 November to 2 December, Company K found itself out on yet another march, and this time the regiment was again engaged. Pvt. Jacob Hanes of Company G mentioned that his regiment was then "in line of battle" and encountered some Federals near Morton's Ford in a small action.36 Meanwhile, Raymer's next letter was written on 11 November, and printed on 23 November in the *Carolina Watchman*. It is fascinating in that it demonstrates that even in the midst of Christian revival, the war continued to create chaos in the lives of the men. Raymer also provided details of a small but intense action at Morton's Ford, mentioned by Jacob Hanes.

This was not quite the last skirmish of 1863, but required stamina in freezing conditions. Raymer notes many important supplies and some baggage was lost when wagons were left to the rear. Raymer's account, written from camp near the Rapidan River, reveals the earlier Christian revival was not just an emotional reaction to stress, but continued as a genuine change in his comrades' lives, as prayer meetings in camp continued to occur daily. His account is also concordant with supply records, as he shows that the men were generally better clothed, sheltered and shod than they were in October in spite of winter conditions, although some may have lost several items in the baggage train and they went without rations for two days when the wagon trains crossed the Rapidan River without them. This march was apparently unexpected by high command, as the sudden nature of their movement caught Raymer's attention, who quipped he felt someone was caught unawares of the enemy's approach. Raymer begins this account from their now usual church services, which he states were held,

"On Saturday, the 7th inst., at 11 o'clock, a.m. Mr. Rosser, corps Chaplin, preached to a large audience in our camp near Kelly's Ford on the Rappahannock. At the close of the sermon notice was given that on the next day a number of persons would be baptized, some would join the church, and in the evening the sacrament would be administered—all passed off as solemn and systematic as a quarterly meeting, so far as the announcements were concerned, and the congregation assembled; all was quiet and calm; but the benediction was hardly pronounced then all at once and very much to the surprise of everybody a furious bombardment began at the ford,--also above and below it, not more than a mile and a half from camp. Every moment it grew heavier-shells went sparkling and hissing thru' the air in all directions, exploding above and around, scattering fragments uncomfortable near on all sides.

Presently the small arms opened thick and fast down in front; this raised the excitement higher, drums beat, horses were saddled, guns loaded, knapsacks packed, and the command resounded through the entire camp-"fall in." In less time than it takes me to write it, the troops were in line and marching towards the scene of action. From the summit of the hill on which we were encamped we could see what was doing the whole mischief. The enemy had crossed and were advancing. There was no mistake though it hardly seemed possible. We could see a dense column of the blue coats in the low grounds this side of the river, while the hill beyond was glittering full of bayonets.

Several Yankee batteries held very strong as well as advantageous positions on the opposite bluffs from which they raked us "fore and aft" for a distance of two miles or more. It was impossible to hold the place, accordingly the programme was to "fall back" to some safe position, which could not be found north of the Rapidan. The two rivers here are from ten to fifteen miles apart, and the country between them and unbroken and level, or gently rolling, with the exception of Pony and Slaughter mountains, both considerable elevations, the first 3 miles southeast of Culpepper Court House, the last about six or eight miles southwest. On Saturday evening our troops held the enemy at bay until the most of the baggage, camp equipage, & c., was moved to the rear, still some valuable clothing with other camp furniture was lost.

No general engagement as yet had taken place along our portion of the line, and during Saturday night our forces quietly retreated to Pony Mountain, mentioned above, where we formed line of battle before day on Sunday morning, raised temporary breastworks, expecting the enemy to advance rapidly, which, however they did not do, and at 3 o'clock p.m. Sunday, we evacuated again, taking up our line of march for the hills south of the Rapidan, distant eleven miles, which we reached about 12 o'clock the same night after an exhausting march without food or rest. Not even a halt was at Racoon Ford, where our division marched across the river in close columns, and knee deep in water cold as ice itself. Meanwhile the quartermasters and commissaries, together with their wagons, cattle, & c., were scattered to the four winds. When the alarm was given on Saturday evening all struck out pell mell for the Rapidan.

No time was lost making inquires about anybody or anything else, nor was anytime lost asking questions about roads or fords—it was a race for life or death, and by noon on Sunday I presume every wagon belonging to the division trains were saved, so far so good; but by means of the panic the troops, many of them, had to fast for forty-eight hours. I do not think I ever saw a set of men so sorely pitched with hunger. Our rations were left in our camp at Kelley's ford uncooked. We had not had a moments warning, no preparations were made of any sort for a move, and for these and other reasons the convection forces itself on our minds that somebody was caught napping. Not a man in our regiment was hurt, their escape is miraculous—each of the other regiments in our brigade suffered more or less severely...The whole army of Northern Virginia now occupies the same line which it left on the 8th and 9th of October.

The various brigades, so far as I know, are in their same old camps. It is rumored that the enemy is advancing, and that they calculate on giving us battle here, how true I don't pretend to say, but if such a thing is attempted hot work may be expected. We have no quarters, nor shelter of any kind, but fortunately, are abundantly supplied with clothing, shoes and blankets; when once it is settled where we shall remain this winter, why in a week a perfect town of little shanties will spring up. The weather is exceedingly disagreeable. On Monday last we had a regular snow storm though none lay on the ground yet it has reduced the temperature of the atmosphere to the freezing point. Squalls of wind drifts the smoke in our eyes and pierce our clothing to the skin while black clouds scud across the sky spitting a little snow as they go, giving us a rather unpleasant foretaste of what is to come."

Once settled into camp again, excitement continued to abound. On 3 December, there was quite a stir when a large deer, a buck, made his way into camp by accident and received an unexpected chase. The following anecdote appeared in the Statesville newspaper, *The Iredell Express*, a few days later, although its author is not named who wrote, "We are informed that there was quite and exciting time in the Camp of the 4th N.C. Regiment, on the banks of the Rapidan, one day last week; caused by the appearance of a fine large buck among them. The boys gave chase but though fleet enough to catch Yanks, they were compelled to allow the noble animal to escape from their clutches. No such yelling has been heard in that region for a long time, as on that occasion. It was too bad. What nice eating would have been indulged in if he could have been captured and brought to quarters!

John Stikeleather indicated that living conditions in this encampment were generally adequate, and mentioned other forms of entertainment besides chasing deer about camp. Certainly less exciting than the former, Stikeleather seemed content that he and his comrades found good use for the extra time they now had on their hands. He wrote, "Our winter quarters were good, and rations still plenty enough to make life quite bearable under the circumstances. Drilling, picketing snowballing, ball playing, etc. were our out door past time during the winter..."[37] On a clear and cool 4 December morning, surgeon Frances Shaffer wrote in his diary about the health status of the regiment, noting "The total number treated during month 151. One death, Typhoid Fever. To Gen'l Hosp'tl 16 were sent, furloughed, 5, Died 1, Discharged 1, remaining on sick list 32. The remaining 96 have been restored to duty. No news of interest today."[38] In contrast, Raymer's last missive for 1863 details the last military action in which Company K participated that year, which occurred at Mine Run, Virginia. Raymer wrote the letter from their camp on the Rapidan River on 5 December, but it was not published in the *Carolina Watchman* until 21 December:

"We have just been put through another campaign, the results of which, though not what they might have been, are yet more favorable than those which attended our retreat from the Rappahannock. To give a detailed account of our recent operations would require more paper and time than I can appropriate to that purpose; but for the gratification of my numerous readers I will endeavor to give a few brief sketches and outlines, the remainder which is of minor importance, can be supplied from imagination. At 2 o'clock on last Friday morning, the 27th ult, we were quietly aroused from our comfortable bunks and marched briskly in an easterly direction some five miles, when we halted and proceeded to throw up temporary breastworks before the morning star appeared above the horizon.

The ground was frozen and hard, ice was spouted up in wet places, our noses blue (at least they felt so, we couldn't see), our ears frostbitten, hands and feet benumbed, but none of t was taken into consideration; a battle was expected at daylight and preparations must be made for it. I don't think I ever saw men at work with such vim, and when day dawned the work was done, to be left an hour afterwards just as we expected; well, all we could do was hope that other poor rebels (devils) might be benefited by them some day. At sunrise we again took up our line of march eastward, and after many halts we found ourselves, at 10 o'clock a.m., in the vicinity of Locust Grove (I believe they call it), on the turnpike leading from Orange C.H. to Fredericksburg—and in the vicinity of Yankees also, I may add; none of your peaceable sort either, for no sooner were they apprised of our whereabouts than they began pitching minnie balls into the trees around us and sending quartermaster hunters (shells) away over us "the way Ward's ducks went."

Our first corps of sharpshooters were sent forward who were soon hotly engaged and called for reinforcements the second corps was sent to their assistance, which, with the first during the remainder of the day, held the enemy at bay and thus prevented a general engagement, though the fire was kept up with spirit between skirmishers until dark put a stop to it. While this was going on in front, on our left Maj. Gen. Johnson was hard pressed and best on all sides with blue bellies. Ordinarily the old gentleman (Johnson) has his head swamped in a huge black hat, and on this occasions eyes, thus enabling the Yankees to get in his rear; be this as it may the general got his eyes open in time to fight his way out. During two hours battle raged furiously; the woods in which we fought look like they had been visited by a young tornado.

The enemy found they had caught a tartat and were glad enough to let him go. I have never heard a correct account of his loss, but the blow he dealt the Yankees was severe, many of their dead lay on the field unburied last Thursday morning. After the retreat of the enemy and Johnsons deliverance everything became perfectly quiet along the lines. Night had set in, at intervals a picket gun would fire, but with that exception not a sound was heard save the monotonous rumbling of the ambulances over the uneven pike as they bore the wounded off the battle field to the hospitals in the rear. At midnight we (Ramseur's brigade) stopped in the road two hundred yards in read of the line of the battle line; the rebels had fled to parts unknown. I had no idea where they were gone, we could hear of none except the few around us and we had orders to keep very quiet—the enemy's scouts were prowling near, and at any moment a whole column of Yankees might dash on us. Presently we began our march southward, parallel to the enemy's line and but a few hundred yards distant from it; I could hardly call it marching, it was more like creeping, so much caution was necessary to prevent the least possible noise. The stillness was really painful-it made us feel chilly.

The men conversed in tones scarcely above a whisper or were eyed into the most profound silence; no rattling of the cups or canteens was heard; the brown oak leaves lay deep and dry through the woods, but we never set foot outside the road, and when anything rusiled among the bushes on our left every eye was turned in that direction and every soldier instinctively grabbed his firelock. Dim...light was spread over the hills and fields, the effect if the dense clouds between us and the moon nearly full, and by this light we were enabled to pick our way with some degree of comfort and satisfaction. In this manner we traveled about one and a half miles, then falling in the turnpike we turned back towards Orange and on the west side of Mine Run formed a line of battle at 3 o'clock on Saturday morning.

After the arms were stacked we lay down on the rocky hill side and slept soundly until daylight, when we were awakened by sounds of shells falling, assisted by the firing of musketry two or three hundred yards in our front. Upon looking round we discovered the van guard of the enemy deployed on the hill side opposite, shooting into our skirmishers with considerable vengeance. The rain fell thicker and heavier and with it increased firing between the skirmishers, who were now within two hundred yards of each other. We expected the enemy to advance with a rush, but they did not, still we did not know how soon they might and to make ourselves more secure we fell back fifty yards further, to the loot of the hill on which we had bivouacked the preceding night, and screened by the thick underbrush in front, we proceeded to throw up the earth works with all possible haste. By noon the rain had ceased, the clouds broke, partially cleared away, leaving, the air chill and frosty so that our frozen garments rattled like dry raw-hides.

After dark our sharpshooters were relieved by fresh corps. Our boys who came in were well nigh frozen ("gone up the spout" they said) and crouching round the pitiful fires related some amusing incidents. The pickets were so near each other that they could converse with all ease, and an incessant jawing was the consequence. "An faith you reb," said an old Yankee, "wouldn't you like to have a cup of hot coffee this cold morning?"-with a peculiar Irish brogue. "Got plenty Confederate coffee," said reb in reply, "wouldn't you like to have a chew of tobacco?" "Don't care if I do," said yank. "Well, here are some of old Jeff's pills in advance"—and away would go a volley of balls that made the yank dig his nails into the ground trying to be close.

Both parties were lying flat in an old field.—rather an uncomfortable position during a pelting rain of five or six hours, but the slightest move was more to draw a dozen bullets, hence it was to the interest of each that he should keep perfectly still. On another point of the line a few sheep came straggling between the pickets, a Yankee shot one and calling out to a rebel opposite said, "Don't you want to go halvers on some mutton?" "Yes, I wouldn't mind it." "Come on over then," and each threw down his gun and walked up to the sheep, where they had a good, jolly time over their Bowie knives and mutton for an hour. Meantime the pickets on each side were peppering away at each other, careful, however, not to disturb the butchers who were working with might, chatting good humoredly and as much unconcerned...and when done they divided the meat fairly and honestly; each taking his half and bidding the other good-bye, with much good luck, returned to his representative "hoil" and spent the evening amusing themselves with their Enfields. (Too much hurried and mixed up to correct grammatical errors.) Saturday, Sunday, Monday, and Tuesday the aspect of affairs remained unchanged. The two armies lay in sight of each other, while the sharpshooters were incessantly firing between. Our suspense was great, and situation not an enviable one by any means. A little shelling was going on both sides but nothing serious occurred.

On Tuesday night, Dec. 1st, the enemy began to retreat, unknown however to us until 3 o'clock on the next morning, when our division, with Early's also, was marched, quick time, in pursuit. Ramseur's brigade was in the van and picked up several hundred stragglers, broken down &c., as we advanced towards Germana ford, where the Yankees had barely crossed ere we arrived in sight on the south side. In their retreat they destroyed all the property belonging to citizens along the rout. I counted the smoking ruins of five different farm houses, some of which had been costly buildings. For 12 miles scarce a rail, barn or other outhouse, was left. All, or nearly all the stock, and poultry in the whole country had been killed, to feed the starving horde, and yet the prisoners said for lack of rations they retreated; about true I guess, since one of the prisoners offered a silver watch for a dozen of crackers, which unfortunately, could not be raised among the rebels either. People at home can form no idea of the straits to which we are sometimes reduced. When within sight of the river further pursuit was deemed expedient, and the whole column was turned homewards. So many glad fellows I never saw before. A bloodless victory! On Thursday morning last we arrived in the same old shanties we had left..."

### *End of Year Uniforms, Supplies & Muster Roll*

While the reader may conclude that supply and detailed muster roll data often discussed herein is but simple trivia, it is important to realize the level of administrative detail that daily camp life and routine military business required throughout the Civil War. One can easily infer that supplying an army, corps, division, brigade or even a regiment is no small matter, but when one grasps the amount of effort and paperwork involved in managing even one company, we can quickly learn that daily life in the army during the Civil War was much more than large battles or campaigns. To the contrary, these data reviewed in the present study teach us that supplying even one company could at times be a monumental task, much less keeping up with the names of all sick, missing, or wounded from their ranks. Such was the daily business of officers and non-commissioned officers, and this obligation remained the same whether on the march or in a coastal garrison or in a long winter encampment in northern Virginia. Another important event in Company K rank and command occurred when Lieutenant Hofflin was officially promoted to captain on 9 December 1863 although he was already serving as company commander. Captain Hofflin held this post until

2 December 1864 when surgeons forced him to transfer to light duty after he was wounded in the foot.₃₉

On 28 December 1863, Captain Hofflin received another large supply of clothing items, as his men had worn out many items and even lost several blankets etc. during the Mine Run Campaign. Hofflin received one new tent fly for himself, which was a large square piece of canvas duck cloth used in the common practice by enlisted soldiers and officers alike of covering the tops of their mud and stone-based cabin shelters during winter months. They sometimes erected small chimneys out of stone. Only four of the nineteen blankets requested by Captain Coughenhour nearly two months previous had arrived. By this time in the war, most blankets and uniforms issued by North Carolina were of English manufacture.₄₀ Bearing in mind that soldiers could also access their stored winter items from Richmond, or request them from home, Company K likely had several civilian or captured federal blankets as well as the English made blankets. Hofflin's receipt shows he then received two pair pants, four jackets, four pair shoes, six shirts, and four blankets for the company.₄₁

The last quartermaster visit in 1863 occurred on 31 December at the same time when Lieutenant Marcus Hofflin completed their last muster roll of the year. That roll covered the period from 31 October to 31 December 1863, and identifies 1st Lieutenant Marcus Hofflin as company commander, although on a 31 December supply form he signed his name as "Captain Hofflin." Hofflin then received four more pair pants, two pairs of drawers. On 31 December he also received another issue of "pre-cut" firewood, but no coal, in the amount of thirteen cords. This finding begs the question as to why the army was not using the obvious supply of manpower to cut its own firewood. Was it due to security, or fear of desertion? Allowing men to set off in small parties in the forest to gather wood might have provided the opportunity to desert, but one can only speculate.₄₂ This final muster roll of 1863 was completed in the camp near Orange Court House by Hofflin sometime in January 1864, and covered the period of 31 October through 31 December 1863.₄₃

| Captain | 1 Lt | 2 Lt | Brevet Lt | Sgt | Cpl | Musicians | Privates | Total Enlisted | Aggregate |
|---|---|---|---|---|---|---|---|---|---|
| 0 | 1 | 1 | 0 | 3 | 4 | 0 | 37 | 58 | 60 |

It is not unusual to find higher numbers of men on furloughs during winter months when camp life usually consisted of little more than guard duty, occasional drill, and looking for food. Yet, the interested reader can easily imagine the misery of being ill and stuck in camp at one of those primitive shelters in near-freezing temperatures, and pining for home is a common plight expressed in their letters and diaries. For those whose illness did not require hospitalization, this stagnant, frozen environment was a condition generally viewed with more disdain than long, hot marches in warmer weather. Hofflin did not provide much descriptive information on this roll, but in his usual frugal manner, meticulously tracked their pay and expenses in particular he is the only officer throughout the war to document the names of men who lost their equipment in the field. For example, in this roll, Hofflin identified five men, Ambrose Casper, Arnold Friedheim, Jeremiah Glover, James McCanless and Joseph Thompson who lost their bayonets and scabbards in battle. This was a costly item to replace, although other sources from both Chancellorsville and Gettysburg campaigns indicate thousands of Confederates tossed any absolutely non-essential impedimenta such as bayonets, blankets, and even cartridge boxes aside to lighten their loads on foot marches that could last up to eighteen to twenty miles per day in heat often above ninety degrees.₄₄

Hofflin also mentioned that Pvt. Bradley Matthews, who returned from Away without Leave in August 1863, had pay stoppages to account for during that period, including monies he was supposed to be due for commutation clothing. Hofflin had his pay docked for a new uniform upon his return but strangely this was not documented on either of two rolls occurring 31 August and 31 October previous. Another officer present during their inspection described their overall military bearing, appearance, clothing, arms and equipment as "Very Good" at this time. Following Lieutenant Hofflin, the chain of command then consisted of 2d Lieutenant Addison Wiseman, with Moses Locke Bean as Orderly (First Sergeant), then 2d Sergeant Michael Hennesy, who was also missing in action since 3 July, and 3d Sergeant Otto Holshouser, who was then under arrest and placed in confinement within their camp for unspecified reasons. Cpl. Richard Williams remained detached to a Richmond Hospital, while Corporals Alfred Carter and Peter Brown managed the daily duties in the company. Cpl. William Parker remained on sick furlough since 22 December.45

There were several men shown on previous rolls in hospitals as sick or wounded, or at home on leave or medical furlough, who remained in similar status on this roll of 31 December 1863. There were three men still missing and believed captured at Gettysburg, including Pvt. William Buis, W.C. Peeler, and Henry Severs. Daniel McQueen was initially thought Absent without Leave, but was sent home on furlough when it was discovered he was wounded. He was discharged on 23 November 1863 by "reason of disability." Pvt. J.B. Saunders, who was earlier sick in a Richmond hospital, was now identified as Away without Leave where he remained until his capture somewhere in Richmond on 23 April 1865. Pvt. William Page was wounded in skirmishing during the action at Morton's Ford on or about 10 December and sent to the hospitals in Richmond. As usual, several men were also detached for other service, including Privates John Endie who was at Danville, Virginia with the provost guard. Pvt. John Deaton continued as brigade mail carrier, where he had served since August 1863. John Kenter was the brigade forage master, while privates' John Locket and William Lillycross was both assigned to Richmond Hospitals. Privates Isaac O'Neill and Henry Williams were required "extra daily duties" in camp as teamsters under 2d Lieutenant Moses L. Bean. Some other men had only recently became ill and required hospitalization or furlough at home, including Milas Holshouser, Francis Mills, and J.T. Owens, who were all sent to convalesce at home in Rowan County, and Joseph Kelley was sick and forwarded to a Richmond Hospital.46

Previous supply records from September through December demonstrate receipt of at least fifteen uniform jackets, seventy-nine pairs of pants, twenty two shirts, thirty nine pair drawers, nineteen blankets, seven overcoats, and thirty seven pair of shoes, (includes two pair of "cloth shoes" that were unlikely to last in heavy winter marching). Considering the thirty-seven enlisted men shown present on the recent muster roll, if compared against information found in supply forms, we can deduce that while it is true that Company K suffered a period of privation after the Gettysburg campaign in July through mid-October, and probably had a rather haggard appearance, (which was also in generally warmer weather) but over half of Company K was adequately supplied with clothing, particularly pants and undergarments during the cold season. There is evidence of lack of shoes that persistently appears throughout 1863, and certainly there were intermittent days on campaign with lack of food, and wet clothing adding to their misery, but their supply records do not support any notion of a generally deprived, starved soldier extant in this Company for more than brief intervals, as is commonly believed.

A good reason for this is that a steady supply of pants, cotton and flannel shirts and drawers as well as shoes began to arrive from England in June-August 1863. It was later suggested that North

Carolina smuggled an average of 12,000 yards per month of the bluish-gray woolen uniform cloth imported from England through the blockade by mid-war, so it is not clear why Company K did not receive more jackets unless they simply did not need them because doubtless they could have received such. It was also reported that North Carolina received over 10,000 gray blankets and 25,887 pairs of the bluish-gray English military blankets had been delivered along with over 26,096 pairs of army shoes; 1,956 Angola shirts; 7,852 gray flannel shirts; and 1,920 flannel shirts between mid-1863 and 1865, while local North Carolina textile mills were also turning out thousands of yards of cotton and wool jeans cloth to supply the soldiers.[44] The state quartermasters were also making leather reproductions of English military shoes, and some canvas bodied shoes due to a shortage of leather occurring in 1863, as noted earlier, but the quality remains debatable as evidenced by frequent requests for more shoes. By late 1863, North Carolina Governor Zebulon Vance stated his plans were to continue to increase the amount of uniform cloth imported from England so that "I can safely say that the North Carolina Troops will be comfortably clothed to January, 1865."[47]

The primary implications for any discussion of how Company K might have appeared in late 1863 is that following the Gettysburg campaign, they received a mixture of jackets made of local North Carolina textiles and English cloth. Possibly, they also received some of the numerous "ready-made" uniform garments of English manufacture that entered North Carolina, particularly trousers. Supply forms show at least two styles of jackets issued in 1863, including "long jackets" but it is not clear what pattern those actually were. English-made jackets may have been somewhat longer, but as yet, supply records cannot confirm this. Jacket colors were likely both gray and bluish-gray hues the in the latter half of 1863 as a result of mixed issue of locally made cotton and wool jeans cloth and English cloth. By the end of 1863, the predominant uniform cloth was doubtlessly English, as Governor Vance indicated that North Carolina textile mills were struggling to produce adequate amounts of cotton jeans cloth for the state troops by 1864.[48] 1863 was a costly year for the 4th NCST and Company K, with over half of the casualties at Chancellorsville reported by Ramseur's Brigade from the 4th NCST. Although several men objected to such an honor, Company K also had one man, Wallace Josey, nominated for the Badge of Gallantry at Chancellorsville where the regiment lost over one hundred men captured in brutal hand to hand combat behind the Federal XII Corps earth works. The 4th NCST was also heavily involved in the first and second days fighting at Gettysburg 1-3 July, and the 4th NCST Veterans could later boast of being among the first Confederate infantry regiments to enter the town of Gettysburg later on 1 July as Lee's forces pushed Federals back to Cemetery Ridge. The year ended with clear knowledge that in spite of two major defeats the war would not only continue indefinitely following the failed Gettysburg and Vicksburg campaigns. Although Company K was faring well when 1864 arrived in terms of supplies and equipment, their families and friends in Rowan County were not doing as well, as Salisbury experienced a "Bread Riot" when angry soldiers' wives mobbed some downtown merchants who were guilty of price gouging. As difficult as things were, however, 1864 would be a year of even more heartache and privation, even as the Confederacy won more battles at the Wilderness and Spotsylvania.

# Chapter Eight

# 1864 Overland and
# Shenandoah Valley Campaigns

The regiment built winter quarters near Pisgah Church, six miles from Orange Courthouse in the winter of 1863-1864. By now, the men of Company K and the rest of the 4th NCST were jaded by their wartime experiences. The year 1864 would bring little relief, with heavy engagements and more casualties lying ahead. Raymer's first letter reveals a very realistic, albeit embittered, expectation of the coming spring campaigns as he quietly reflected in their winter encampment. One can almost hear the wind whistling outside and smell the pine smoke in the crowded little shelter as his pen scratches his carefully organized thoughts onto paper. Supply documents for this season reviewed later will further indicate a more limited flow of uniforms and shoes than previously, in spite of North Carolina's abundance of cloth and other materials encroached through the blockade from England. Yet by no means were the Rowan Rifles completely ragged and shoeless, and anecdotal sources show they ate well on numerous occasions during active campaigns. Nat Raymer began his first narrative for this year sitting in his winter cabin, working out his thoughts while his comrades slept on the blustery cold night of 18 January. This one quickly made its way to the *Carolina Watchman* but seven days later, on 25 January:

"I have been fortunate as to get a piece of candle, at an enormous cost this time, but that is the way we live in these war times, and feeling indebted to the readers of the "Watchman" I have concluded to spend a few leisure moments discharging that debt by giving my friends and inkling of what is going on with us. Now that it is leap year once again, I think it but just and proper that the ladies ought to be making some advances, at least so much as to "take their seals, pen in hand..." As it is, I don't get a letter once per month...We, our illustrious selves are still alive and kicking vigorously as you could expect men to kick on a quarter pound of meat per day...We are getting along famously; have warm, comfortable cabins, good clothing, warm bedding generally, and enough to eat to keep us from forgetting how to use our jaws, in case we should be so fortunate as to get anything which would require their services.

No conjecturing about the close of the war; all have learned to consider it as something necessary, and consequently, have grown utterly callous. The men have a great deal of duty to perform. They go on picket six days out of the twenty-four, on guard one day of three, fatigue police daily. Our camp looks like a regular garrison; the cabins are alike, each sixteen feet square, with eight or nine occupants, they are built in parallel lines some two hundred yards apart, two fifty long, with the field and staff quarters at one end at the other the guard house. About three acres are enclosed in the square, which is now being cleared off for a drill ground, dress parade, &c. A hospital and church are going up. The former, I trust, may never be needed; at present we have very little sickness of consequence though, within the last ten days we have lost two men by death, both very suddenly...They were buried with military honors, in which the band and a platoon of soldiers were principal actors.

The church, under the direction of...our Chaplin will be a complete success, energy and devotion to a single enterprise are elements of success. There is snow on the ground, and has been for the last month or nearly, though not at all times covering the entire surface. As a general thing, the weather has been extremely cold, but this evening there are some dictations of a thaw. The time passes rapidly with us; we hardly know a day is begun when it is ended. The winter will soon slip away, and then spring will be upon us...instead of such bliss we expect in every sense, but bloody, terrible war. We must face the crisis next summer; and

217

not us only, but every one throughout this scourged land. I would advise all of you to nerve yourselves for the contest. Give us what encouragement you can; bear cheerfully another year, and then if not earlier, may Heaven grant us the reward for which we have been so long and so faithfully struggling—freedom and a home with a jewel."

Assistant regimental surgeon Capt. J.M. Hadley received "1 Tents Fly" on 26 January 1864 at "camp," but the location was not specified.[1] The tent fly was a large, square piece of canvas cloth used to provide shade in summer months and during the winter, was commonly used as a roof for the soldier's wooden shelters. January 1864 was also a difficult month for a former commander of Company K, Capt. William C. Coughenhour. During his tenure as Brigade Inspector General on General Ramseur's staff, he was captured near Winchester by soldiers from the Army of West Virginia according to a report from Brig. Gen. John Echols' 1st Brigade of Cavalry (U.S.). The details of his capture are unknown, but Coughenhour's name reappears when he was promoted to brigade inspector general at Amelia Courthouse, Virginia, on 4 April 1864. Coughenhour was again under Ramseur at the time of his promotion.[2] As Raymer stated in his last missive, supplies and uniforms were abundant during this encampment near Orange Courthouse. 1st Lieutenant Marcus Hofflin signed a receipt for one blanket, three pair shoes, one camp kettle, and two pair pants on 17 February.[3] On 26 February, Hofflin again received supplies, this time thirteen pair shoes, six pair pants, ten shirts, five pair drawers, and two jackets.[4] And again on 3 March, still at camp, he received the following items for Company K, two jackets, nine pair shoes, nine shirts, one "spider" with lid and one axe.[5] A "spider" was a small, three-legged iron cooking kettle of which was a favorite cooking utensil among the soldiers.

The company composition was again changing during this winter encampment, as Pvt. Alexander McQueen was detailed to the Signal Corps in February, but Company K also received six new men that month including privates' Moses Bencini, I.L. Boyle, William Bradley, Daniel Corl, and George Misenheimer. Of this group, only William Bradley was conscripted. Another recruit, Williams Phillips, apparently volunteered, but was enlisted to serve only as a "laundress", and not a combat soldier, as he wasn't ranked as even a private according to a later muster roll of 31 August 1864, but the reason is not recorded. On 12 February, Private Michael Rowland was sentenced to "Hard Labor" at the Salisbury Prison for desertion, having been in confinement since 8 September 1863. Pvt. Milas Holshouser sustained a gunshot wound on picket duty on 9 March, and was sent to a Richmond hospital where he stayed for several months. On 15 March, Hofflin received a shipment for three blankets, two pair socks, one pair pants, and one pair shoes.[6] Another supply form indicates the 4th NCST received seventy pair of shoes on 5 March and two hundred twenty-nine caps of an unknown pattern on 13 March.[7] While the caps imply a hint of uniformity in the regiment's appearance, it is unknown how many of those Company K received, if any. Nat Raymer continued to document camp life and other facets of army life as the spring campaigns opened. On 11 March he wrote of mounting tensions which suggested a major battle was drawing near. This next letter ran in the *Carolina Watchman* on 21 March, following some skirmishing along the Rappahannock River:

"...A little difficulty, which will yet be amicably adjusted, has interfered slightly with my arrangements, and for the time being temporarily impeded my facility—rather my means of correspondence. The trouble is over now, and the excitement incident to the late "On to Richmond," has entirely subsided, and in its stead an unusual calm prevails. But the alarm was sufficient to have our brigade ordered out in the most disagreeable weather we have had since the winter set in, and kept out two days and nights, after all to no purpose whatever.

We have the satisfaction of knowing that the late raid turned out a stupendous failure...The result of the late operations is a standing order in our camp to "hold ourselves in readiness to move at any moment." At present our regiment is on picket at Morton's ford—tomorrow they will be relieved. And a rough time they have had.

Yesterday a sluice of rain fell during the entire day, and today a fine mist keeps everything thoroughly saturated. We are not sorry to see this rain, not by any means. Not that we feel such deep concern in the farms and vegetables around here, but we want to see the mud so deep and the water courses so high as to render all military operations impossible; our armistice for the winter will then last a little while longer for mutual agreement. The campaign will open soon enough at best—not however before we are ready but before we are quite willing. From past experience we can form a pretty good idea of what we may expect this summer, and to confess the truth, we are somewhat loath to enter the arena again...I don't know why it is, but it is none the less certain for that everybody looks forward with glowing anticipations concerning this summer's campaign.

A confidence is felt which I never saw manifested before, and when the terrible ordeal comes, as it will ere long. I don't think there is a soldier in our army but will face the danger boldly and manfully. Last spring we were flushed and sanguine, and now the tale of last summer is easily told and in a few words. Shall it be so again? Ah! the dread, the doubt, the dim uncertainty which veils the future!..."Hope deferred maketh the heart sick," but let us hope on, and struggle on; the end will come, perhaps sooner than any of us imagine. We have no complaints to make—We are blessed with good health almost universally. Our duties are light, and our rations plentiful enough, though of a coarser sort that is quite agreeable. We get barely enough meat to grease our ribs; get flour about twice per week, the balance made up in meal, sugar, coffee and molasses; on the whole, enough to keep us content and in good pork order..."

During this winter encampment, the evangelical revival peaked in the Army of Northern Virginia. Various scholars have estimated there were over 50,000 evangelical Christian conversions in the Confederate army during this period of the War, in contrast to roughly 1,500 occurring after Gettysburg. John Stikeleather, the 4th NCST color bearer, often discussed his own newfound interest in revival, observing with what acceptance that "Many of the soldiers carried with them Bibles and Testaments, gifts of loved ones at home, and along with the gifts were prayers that they might be read and their teachings be heeded. I am satisfied that may were brought to a proper sense of their obligations to their Maker, to their fellows, and to themselves through this instrumentality. Often did the soldiers find comfort from a perusal of God's word. They learned the secret of being alone in the midst of company. Three times a day could a Christian soldier go into his closet and pray, but, in the midst of his comrades, he could open his Bible and read a chapter without embarrassment, and at the close of the reading lesson, with this book open before him, offer up his prayers and none of those present ever suspect but what he was still reading. Many no doubt had these stated occasions of prayer there as well as at home; and, the world knew nothing of it; but the privilege of those who availed themselves of it, was one of much comfort."[8]

Stikeleather also shared a recollection of his own conversion to Christianity which occurred shortly afterward, and his subsequent feelings about the bloody 1864 Spring Campaign then impending. Recall that Stikeleather volunteered to become the regimental color bearer at Seven Pines in 1862, and other than receiving the blunt end of a spent minnie ball at Chancellorsville which knocked him down and tore through his cartridge box, he had thus far survived unharmed in a role many soldiers considered to be the most dangerous position on the battlefield, albeit the most highly honored. Stikeleather opined, "The chances of escape unharmed were fewer than at any time in the past. The contemplation of that which seemed to be lying immediately before us, was to say the least of it, a serious one. With feelings in my breast that such contemplation might inspire, (on the first night of battle) an intense desire took possession of me to re-commit myself then and there into the hands of my divine master. At nine o'clock that night, after most of my comrades had wrapped themselves in their blankets, I went off some hundred paces and was literally alone with God. I kneeled behind a large tree and tried in a spirit of trustfulness to humble myself before him who knoweth the secrets of all hearts. The Lord most graciously looked upon me in my low estate. I scarce had time to give expression and words to the desires that were in my breast, ere I felt that in a most gracious sense that his everlasting arms were around me. My prayer was short, a desire to praise rather than pray filled my breast. Tears of gratitude and joy streamed down my cheeks..."[9] 2d Lieutenant Addison Wiseman likewise had an ominous intuition while home on leave to visit his wife on 3 March. There, he drafted his Last Will and Testament leaving everything to his wife without stipulations should she remarry, in a very unusual act for a Nineteenth Century man who typically left his land to his children.

### Brigade Snowball Fight

The winter encampment was not all piousness, however. In fact, at times these battle scarred veterans showed that they could still be quite boyish and downright playful. 4th NCST Surgeon Frances Schaffer documented the following incident in his diary that nicely illustrates the former. He wrote on 27 March, camping in roughly fifteen inches of fresh snow drifts and heavy winds, "...This heavy fall of snow afforded an excellent opportunity for snow balling, and our boys enjoyed it very much. It was a rare scene, and not frequently witnessed. Battle's Brigade of Alabamians of this Division formed a determination to attack the "Tar Heels." The former having been reinforced, made a successful stand, and in turn we had to toddle. Towards evening of the same day, Johnson's Division attacked Dole's Brigade of Georgians of this Division. Gallantly did the latter repel every assault, and heroically stand their ground against overwhelming odds, until couriers could be dispatched for reinforcements. Very soon Rode's entire Division was out, and at it they went with a hearty good will. First Johnson's men yielded ground, then Rode's in turn, and thus the fight raged with varying success until night. It was a grand sight and cannot be described. In all the engagements "nobody was hurt" seriously, but some received bloody noses, black eyes and sore bruises. Such events tend very much to relieve the monotony of camp and are highly appreciated by every true soldier..."[10]

As spring finally emerged, so did a series of violent campaigns. Sometime in May, Pvt. Robert O. Linster of Company C wrote to his mother. He provided a few details of the regiments latest movements, and hardships from weather and exposure. He also mentions an unpleasant encounter with Gen. Robert E. Lee, who once passed by him briefly. He describes several important details of soldier minutiae, such as the habit of using 'bed rolls' versus carrying the cumbersome knapsacks had become common in the Confederate army. Linster recounted, "We have been on the march through mud, snow and rain. We started last Tuesday from Liberty Mills distance 14 miles. We got here 4 o'clock and commence snowing one of them old big Virginia snows. Our Regiment was left to guard the bridge across the Rapidan River. We threw out sharpshooters-the Yankees 18 hundred strong, caveraly was in 2 miles of us trying to get to the bridge. We form in line of battle stack arms. Orders came to build fires on rocks in the bridge which we did in double quick time and pass the night in fine spirits. In the morning Gen. Lee came along have us a racking for building fires on the bridge. Orders came a few minutes ago for me to go on guard so I will finish at the guard house...We were thrown out yesterday in line of battle, at Union Church to intercept Kilpatrick if he should try to get back to the river up this way...We are having fine times in the way of eatings. We got six boxes and three of our men is home on furlough. We have 3 hams about 60 lbs four bushell meal 1 bushel dried fruit, butter, molasses, coffee, etc greatest plenty. I have been improving finally since coming back. I go on guard about every 3 [sic-weeks] which is very light duty. Our army is in fine health and spirits. I saw Gen.Lee day before yesterday he is the finest looking man I ever saw...We mustered in day before yesterday. I reckon we will get paid off next week if I don't go on picket...The wind is blowing pretty smart but there is a good many fellow drying their shirts by the fire with their coat on. Knapsacks is nearly plaid out in the Army 1 pr pants 2 shirts 2 pr drawers 2 pr socks and 1 blanket and oil cloth is all a soldier has any use of here..."[11]

## *The Wilderness, Spotsylvania and Cold Harbor*

Winter eventually faded into spring, and some of the worst combat of the war lay close ahead for the men of Company K. Ramseur's brigade fought in what has become known as the 1864 Overland Campaign. This series of tough battles included action at the Wilderness, Spotsylvania, North Anna and Cold Harbor from 1 May-14 June 1864. The primary action in which the 4th NCST fought during this campaign was the massive 12 May Confederate counterattack on the "Muleshoe" salient at Spotsylvania. This occurred after Federal II Corps men under Gen. Winfield Hancock overran Confederate lines earlier that morning and occupied the majority of their earthen works. Ramseur was posted at a position just to the left-center of the "Muleshoe," where the center of Lee's line formed an apex. When Rodes ordered him to counterattack and stop the Federal onslaught, Ramseur aligned his brigade with the 14th North Carolina on his left, the 2d North Carolina at left-center, the 4th NCST at right-center, and the 30th NCT on his right. Ramseur ordered his men to hold their fire until they were aligned in the salient. Once given the order to "charge," the men were to push the Federals until the works were theirs again. As he double-quick-timed his men into position, the brigade arrived just in time to stop a flanking movement by Federal troops head on.

Ramseur was wounded just before giving the order to charge, and Col. Bryan Grimes took command and ordered the brigade forward. Lee later credited Ramseur's Tar Heels for saving his lines that day. Their aggressive counterattack pushed the Federals back out of their works, literally fighting for every step in vicious hand-to-hand skirmishing. Ramseur later reported that in that charge, "We drove the enemy back half a mile into his entrenchments."[12] Needless to say, casualties were high in the 4th NCST as they fought their way through the lines to recapture the works. Stikeleather captured in writing what is now an infamous event during the assault, noting that a young private, 14 year old Tysdell Stepp of the 14th North Carolina (located just to the left of the 4th NCST), led the Tar Heels in singing the "Bonnie Blue Flag" in a low, "stentorian" voice as they charged. Stepp was killed just moments later by friendly fire.[13] Raymer's intuition proved correct; the fighting at Spotsylvania was vicious, and he kept close record of what he witnessed in line of battle on the evening of 11 May, continuing his observation as the fighting erupted on 12 May. His vivid account of Ramseur's counter charge (*illustrated on the cover by Don Troiani in the "Bonnie Blue Flag"*) was published in Salisbury by the *Carolina Watchman* on 30 May and includes a subtle reflection of his emotional state. Raymer's reaction to seeing the vicious combat and after-effects of the maelstrom inside the salient with bayonets and rifle butts is numbing, particularly considering all that he had witnessed heretofore. Raymer penned,

"Where shall I begin? That's the question. So great has been, and now is, the excitement, and so much has transpired within the last ten days, that I am utterly at a loss to know where or how to begin the record. This is the eight day of the great battle of the Rapidan, and yet it is not over. And if we are to believe the reports of prisoners, we would suppose the heaviest has not come yet, though for the life of me, I cant imagine how the struggle is to be more sanguine or terrible than it has already been. But we are told that Grant is receiving tremendous reinforcements—where from, it is impossible for me to say—an way they say they are coming.

Morn, May 12th.—My letter was cut abruptly short last evening by a heavy thunder shower; a little rain fell during the night, and this morning dense clouds are sending down an incessant and very cool mist. This is the first rain or unfavorable weather of any kind since the first of this month. It is quite early, not more than 8 a.m., and while I write the thunder of a hundred cannons and the ominous rattle of thousands of muskets tell of bloody work going on in front. Already a number of wounded have been brought in, a list of which you will find appended.

This is the ninth day of the battle, skirmishing began on Wednesday the 4th.—On the 5th a fierce battle was fought by Early and Johnson on our side, in the "Wilderness," some fifteen miles above this point. Our brigade was not engaged; at that time we were on picket at Morton's ford, and had been several days previously. The very air was burthened with rumors of a great battle approaching-of the evacuation by the enemy in our front and of their crossing the river in heavy force below us, all of which has turned out literally true, though at the time we made due allowances for the many extravagant reports which were circulated.

Everything across the river in our front was unusually quiet;--this we regarded as a bad sign—and sure enough, at noon Thursday, we left the river and took up the line of march down towards Chancellorsville, distant about fifteen miles. When half way on our road we received intelligences of the battle in the "Wilderness" and of our victory, which was reported so complete that it made us somewhat dubious. However, I ascertained, by actual observation, that the half had not been told us. Passing the battle ground of "Mine Run" and our fortifications there, on which many remarks were made, we pressed on, and at night we camped on the outskirts of the renowned Wilderness. Thus significant game is applied to a scope of country some ten miles square, extending from Chancellorsville upward on the plank road, and averaging from twenty to thirty miles from Orange Court House.

The face of the country is broken into gentle hills, interspersed with many swamps and marshes; the sod sterile, few farms or habitations are to be seen—large timber is scarce, but the underbrush, brambles and suck like, are so dense as to be almost impenetrable. For this reason very little artillery was used in the various battles, until the contested ground was transferred to this place. On the morning of the 6th, we found ourselves in the vicinity of "blue coats." Skirmishers were sent forward, who soon engaged the enemy, the troops were drawn up in line of battle and the signs generally betokened a battle.

Surgeons and non-combatants were sent to the rear with orders to make ready for the reception of all who might be so unfortunate as to get wounded. Still the day passed without a fight on our position of the line, while at other points the firing was heavy. On the day previous, Early and Johnson had driven the Yankees two miles with great slaughter. Many prisoners as well as the wounded and dead, with all the undescribable debris of the battle field, fell into our hands. On Saturday the 7th, I visited the bloody field. When within half a mile of the enemy's abandoned earthworks signs began to show where the contest was hottest, and soon I found myself standing amidst the congregation of the dead and wounded of the enemy. The few of our own men, who had been killed, were decently buried, and our wounded all cared for.

Besides our own hospitals were filled with Yankee wounded—the latter in proportion of three to one of the former; and yet, many of the enemy's wounded were lying on the field uncared for, as well as all of their dead unburied, (and so the dead remain to this day, I suppose,) and some of them partially burned to cinders by the fearful woods-fire which followed in the wake of our columns. The enemy occupied trenches, out of which they did not retreat until our troops were within 15 steps of them. Indeed, some were actually bayonetted. Finally the enemy could not stand it any longer—no power on earth could have prevented a panic-the advance of the rebels seemed irresistible; the gaps in their ranks were closed as rapidly as they were made, and at last the enemy turned and fled in the greatest confusion, leaving their knapsacks, guns, blankets, canteens, haversacks, and every conceivable sort of plunder in the trenches behind them.

And from the moment they left their works, from that moment the slaughter began in earnest. I saw dead men in every imaginable posture; some with cartridges in their teeth, some with their cartridges or cap boxes, others with ramrods halfway down, and other still on their knees in the act of firing, but the large majority were killed while running for their lives and fell sprawling forward on their faces—or to paraphrase on each, he lay "—With his face to the field And his feet to the foe." The timber was literally torn to splinters—scarce a shrub escaped, and that a single soul should come out living is truly a wonder. Sickened with the many horrible sights, I left the field impressed more deeply than ever with the untold horrors or war-Bloody, terrible war! On Sunday the 8th, the Yankees attempted to outflank us on the right-a corresponding move was made on our part, and during the entire day the two armies marched parallel and within cannon shot of each other. The course was East ward, and at night the van of both armies was near Spotsylvania C. House, where the lines were established and remain to this day. Meantime more or less fighting has been going on every day with variable success on either, but so far as I have been able to learn, no great advantages have been gained by either party.

The reinforcements spoken of by prisoners have arrived, I presume, and today a most terrible battle is raging, regardless of the pelting rain which is now falling incessant and heavily. The cannonading is hardly inferior to that at Gettysburg, while the musketry roars like a furious tornado. The great and decisive battle of this campaign is doubtless in progress now, and while I write I am so much oppressed with anxiety about the results that my hand is really nervous. This cold and constant rain has already made us exceedingly uncomfortable, and to add to our unpleasant situation, shells from the enemy's batteries are hissing through the air and bursting rather near for the good of our health. 4 o'clock, P.M.—The death struggle is over for today, at least, and unless the tide of fortune changes tomorrow, the victory is ours.

The rain has ceased—still lowering clouds hang low over head, and the frightened spring birds are timidly trying to tune up their pipes. Ah! how sad their songs. Instead of joyous carols, as is their wont, their notes are weary and plaintive, fit dirges for the thousands of dead and dying lying on the hills of Spotsylvania.

The roar of battle has ceased for a while; it is said the enemy is retreating-we don't now but it is certain that our troops hold their ground at this time, though lost and won repeatedly during the day. Our loss is heavy, so it is with the enemy, it is impossible to form an estimate at present. Our wounded say the Yankees were drunk this morning—the assertion needs confirmation, and way, they showed uncommon courage. General Daniel is mortally wounded. General Longstreet is severely. Other casualties are reported, but not confirmed. Friday 13th—10 o'clock, A.M.-The battle, for some reason, is not resumed. Quiet reigns this morning. Rain fell constantly last night, adding the greatest misery to many of our wounded, who are uncomfortable enough at best. Blood! blood! It seems that everything we can lay our hands on is clotted with blood.

Two-thirds of our wounded are struck in the head, neck and face-this is the result of fighting behind breastworks, and this is the first great battle since the commencement of the war, where our men were protected by artificial constructions, and it will be observed that casualties, in the aggregate, are not near so great as they usually are. We are not appraised of any movements among the troops this morning. Possibly, the enemy may renew the attack today, or they may be waiting for reinforcements, expecting to fight again tomorrow, or they may be planning a retreat. It is hardly probably that General Lee indulges the remotest idea of falling back-I'm sure his troops do not. Saturday, 14th May.-Can't make out a complete list of killed and wounded. The battle is still in progress, but the enemy is certainly getting worsted, nor should I be surprised if they retreat tonight. It has been raining terribly."

### Casualties

Raymer also included an early list of casualties, including men from Company K:

P.T. Owens, P.A. Helig, Jacob Fraley, and Serg't Otho Holtshouser, Co. K, killed.-Capt. McRorie, N.S. Brawley, killed, Co. A; J.H. Hartners, Pinck Jacobs, Saul Hendren, killed. Co C; Peter Deal, killed. Co. B; Wm. Durell's left arm amputated. A great many are wounded, a complete list of which, will be given at an early day.

Company K indeed lost four reliable men killed in action at Spotsylvania, including 36 year old private J.T. Owen, who had only enlisted in 1863 from Craven County, and 22 year old Pvt. Philip Heilig. Heilig captured a Federal colonel on 8 May, and was given the officer's revolver as a reward. Also, Sgt. Jacob Frayley, who in spite of his previous reduction to ranks as a private after a Court Martial in 1862, was restored and became a trusted non-commissioned officer, and the irascible Sgt. Otto Holshouser, who was captured at Sharpsburg and sent to Fort Delaware, then

---

Footnote:

The names of men Raymer identified as killed from Company K are correct, although Raymer erroneously lists William (Wm.) Durrell as a member of Company B, when he is in fact on muster rolls for Company K. That Raymer listed them first is also important; this is a testimony of Company K participating in some of the most vicious hand to hand fighting of the war on 12 May.

wounded at Gettysburg only to return and die at Spotsylvania while sitting beneath a large tree that was struck by an exploding artillery round. An unidentified eye witness recorded, "Sgt Holshouser…was sitting with his back against a good sized tree, our part of the line not being engaged, when a cannon ball struck the opposite side of the tree, killing him instantly by the shock." Raymer sent another update to the *Carolina Watchman* published on 6 June, then showing Company K losses as eleven including four killed and seven wounded.

To further assess the casualties, recall that the most recent muster roll from 31 December 1863 included twenty nine enlisted men and two officers available for duty, with two more on extra duties in the brigade who could be recalled for battle, making thirty-three men available in camp. In the interim before Spotsylvania, Company K lost Pvt. Michael Rowland who was incarcerated at the Salisbury Prison for desertion, and Milas Holshouser was shot on picket duty on 9 March 1864, and sent to Richmond. The company received six new men in February 1864, including eighteen year old Williams Phillips, the company "Laundress." Some also remained on detached duties elsewhere, sick or wounded and still convalescing. A later muster roll from 31 August 1864, (the last one of the war) indicated all soldiers previously shown as Prisoners of War, on detached service or convalescing were still in those status and therefore not present at Spotsylvania except five who returned to the company in the interim. Therefore two officers and approximately thirty-nine enlisted men were available for duty in Company K on 12 May, (not including the non-combatant).[14]

Nat Raymer's preliminary casualty report was eleven casualties (four killed and seven wounded) for this company. As we have seen earlier, such information is often in accurate. However, Raymer's initial report at Spotsylvania was concordant with Company K muster rolls and hospital records showing Company K lost four killed, including the two senior non-commissioned officers, along with eight men wounded. Among the wounded was 2d Lieutenant Moses L. Bean (gunshot wound right shoulder); Cpl. Peter Brown (flesh wound right leg, bayonet), and privates George Basinger (flesh wound right shoulder, bayonet); James Bean (gunshot, resulting in total disability); Daniel Corl (gunshot wound left toe, severe contusion to chest); William Durrell, whom Raymer erroneously reported as a member of Company B, when in fact he belonged to Company K. Durrell, who had earlier conspired with his friend Pvt. Charles Jones to confabulate commission documents as 2d Lieutenants while serving as provost at Danville, Virginia, was shot in his left arm which required amputation below the elbow. Durrell survived and was retired to the Invalid Corps shortly afterward. Afterward, upon hearing of Durell's plight, General R.E. Lee in fact ordered his discharge from the army, an ironic outcome considering Durrell had earlier forged documents in Lee's name. Other wounded privates were William Johnson (gunshot wound to side); Francis Mills (contusion, left elbow); and Lewis Brady (gunshot). From this, the reader can estimate Company K sustained roughly twenty-seven percent casualties at Spotsylvania. Raymer reported that the 4th NCST had around 300 men present on 12 May, which suggests Company K casualties were about four percent of the total regimental losses. Privates Nelson Eller and James Casper were captured between 19-30 May, with that being Eller's second time as a prisoner of war.

A perusal of the wound types (contusions, bayonet wounds) in not only this company, but also the regiment as a whole provide bitter proof of Nat Raymer's assertion of brutal close range fighting that occurred inside the "Mule Shoe" salient on 12 May when Ramseur's men counter-attacked the Federals, who just minutes earlier had broken through their earthworks. Hand to hand combat was actually a rare occurrence in the Civil War, but there are several instances recorded, which meant the soldiers could effectively use bayonets, pistols, swords, etc. that otherwise rarely found practical use beyond holding candles to write letters by or during dress parade and drill. By this point in the war, the seasoned campaign veteran had learned to toss aside any item not absolutely essential for survival, due to the long marches in unbearably hot weather when carrying anything was difficult.

This habit is often evidenced on regimental muster rolls when several men received pay stoppages for tossing aside their bayonet and scabbard across the war, but it appears Company K had adequate supply of the implement at Spotsylvania, as the 31 August 1864 muster roll identifies only one man charged for losing one in May, Crawford Holshouser and he could have lost it afterward. The reader will doubtless question the soldier's wisdom in tossing aside such a deadly weapon when examining the casualties of this battle. But one must remember the infrequency of such close range fighting during the civil war, and understand the veteran soldier's parsimonious mindset to realize it was an honest, but lethal mistake. Below is Raymer's unofficial report of casualties for the 4th NCST on 12 May 1864. This will aid the reader in building a perspective of the experiences of the Rowan County men in contrast to their comrades in other companies at Spotsylvania. Note that Raymer's account misspelled several names, corrected herein, such as "P.A. Hilery" who was actually Philip Heilig. His description of 2nd Lt. Moses Locke Bean's wound was also underreported, as Bean was shot in his left shoulder, and it was serious enough to require his transfer to Chimborazzo Hospital in Richmond on 15 May 1864. Another example is "P.T. Owens" who is actually J.T. Owens. The high number of flesh wounds to the legs, head and face including saber cuts, along with bone fractures are evidence of the intensity of close range fighting occurring in the salient on 12 May. Raymer wrote:

Co. A-- Lieut F D Carlton flesh wound in right thigh; Sergt W L Thompson, do; private J W Cohen, in left thigh; courter Jas Stinson, do; privates-- Lampey, neck mortal; D Beam, skull fractured, severe; Thos Christie, both thighs, very serious; J W Hobbs, flesh wound right thigh; M S Gilland, flesh wound in left leg; N S Brawley, abdomen, mortal.

Co. B-- Sergt H C Miller, right thigh, flesh wound; Sergt D A Dunaha, right hand flesh; privates N Dunaha, contusion right thigh; J C Hyde, flesh wound right elbow; J A Smith, scalp saber cut; N F Fisher, left thigh flesh wound; J A Barnhardt, right leg amputated; T N Torrence, face; J H Holsclaw, right hip severe; - Overcash, left shoulder, severe; S McLaughlin, right thigh and hand serious.

Co. C-- J A Holmes, chest, flesh wound; Sergt J C Turner, foot slight;   privates A F Lewis, face severe; J F Holmes, contusion left side; Corp'l F A Shuford, left shoulder, very severe; privates G M Locke, flesh wound right leg; S L Wilson, left hand; P Miller, right hip; S Hendren, abdomen mortal.

Co. D-- Capt Thos G Lee, contusion left shoulder; Corp'l D L Howell, flesh wound right groin; Corp'l J Ellis, face very severe; privates M Anderson, right arm broken; Thom Myers, flesh wound scalp and thigh; M Wiggs, left shoulder fractured.

Co. E-- Privates-Jackson, face very severe; J Hawkins, contusion left side.

Co. F-- Sergt Jas Gay, flesh wound face; Corp'l M F Wooten left thigh; privates
J Taylor, right arm; E Flora, neck; J B Woodward, left shoulder; Thos Knight, right hip.

Co. G-- Capt S A Kelly, flesh wound right leg; Lieut D G Smoot, right leg broken; privates H A Wise, flesh wound left shoulder; P S Rose, right arm; Wm Perry, chest mortal; John Cranfield, flesh wound right hand; Monroe Williams, left hand.

Co. H-- Sergt G Powell, abdomen and bowels mortal; Sergt A R Tomlin, flesh wound right foot; Corp' l M Kinder, left hand; privates M L Lambert, left leg; N V Journey, scalp; Jas Mitchel, right foot shattered; C B Parker, flesh wound back; Wm Foreum, bowels mortal (since dead).

Co. I-- Sergt H L Clayton, flesh wound right arm; Sergt Jesse Scott, left hand; privates E J Daniels, right hip severe; W A Johnson, flesh wound chest.

Co. K-- Lieut M L Bean, contusion left shoulder; Corp' l J A Brown, flesh wound right leg; privates F M Mills, contusion left elbow; Geo Basinger, flesh wound left shoulder; Wm Johnson, side; Wm Durell, left arm amputated; D W Corl severely bruised in chest.

KILLED

Co. A-- Capt Wm F Mc Rorie; private N Brawley.
Co. B-- Private Peter Deal.
Co. C-- Privates Jas H Hartness, P Jacobs, G P Arthurs, Solomon Hendren.
Co. D-- None.
Co. E-- Sergt Cuder, Sergt Lugget. private Bowlin.
Co. F-- Sergt Thos Atkinson, Corp'l B Farmer.
Co. G-- Sergt Jas Hanes, privates Jos Shines, and Wm Perry (died of wounds).
Co. H—Corp'l M Walker, privates Sam'l Chamblein, ---- Forcum, Serg't Powell, J Moore.
Co. K-- Sergt Otho Holdshouser, privates P A Hilery, J. Fraley, J T Owens.

Total Killed 23, wounded 70, The Regiment took into battle about 300.

Missing—Sergt's F Morrison and Wm Adams.

### *North Anna, Cold Harbor*

2d Lieutenant Moses L. Bean remained at Chimborazzo hospital until sometime between December 1864 and February 1865 when he returned to the company.[15] Brig. Gen. Stephen D. Ramseur was also wounded at Spotsylvania and taken off the battle field. Afterward, he was recognized by R.E. Lee for his actions there, by promotion to Major General on 1 June 1864 and given command of a division in Maj. Gen. Richard Ewell's corps. Col. Bryan Grimes was promoted to brigadier general on 19 May, but was not placed in command of Ramsuers' former brigade, but rather was given another brigade. Grimes did not receive official word of the promotion until 1 June while in line of battle at Cold Harbor, and Col. James H. Wood was then placed in command of the 4th NCST the same date. Afterward, Ramseur's brigade was then placed under the command of Col. William R. Cox, who was also soon promoted to brigadier general. Cox had been commander of the 2d North Carolina and was highly regarded throughout the brigade as a fierce warrior and expert tactician. Former Company K commander Capt. W.C. Coughenhour, who was then on Ramseur's brigade staff, was re-assigned to Cox's staff. There Coughenhour remained until late 1864. The 4th NCST did not see significant action during the fighting near the North Anna River although was engaged in the trenches at Cold Harbor between 29 May and 2 June. There Rode's division was located on the far left of Lee's line just to the right of Maj. Gen. Henry Heth's division and left of Maj. Gen. John B. Gordon's division near the Shady Grove Road.

On 2 June, Maj. Gen. Thomas L. Crittenden's 1st division, (Wilcox) of the Federal IX Corps advanced in line of battle in the vicinity of Bethesda Church. The 4th NCST was then located just north of Shady Grove Road in the same area. There they faced the 20th Michigan Volunteer Infantry when Rodes attacked, and after a few hours of slugging it out, Rodes line stalled and he ordered his men to begin entrenching. Intense digging continued throughout the night all along the Confederate lines, and by 3 June Lee had established a powerful defensive perimeter. Oddly, soldier accounts from the 4th NCST generally mention little, if anything of the action at Cold Harbor, possibly due to the effects of Spotsylvania still fresh in their memories. Cox's brigade lost about 50 men between 31 May and 3 June. Company K lost four wounded, and two captured. Pvt. Jeremiah Glover received a gunshot to his right hand and was sent to a Richmond Hospital. Also, Pvt. William Parker was shot in his right ankle on either 30 or 31 May. Both were sent to Richmond hospitals, but Glover quickly recovered and was in ranks again by September, while Parker's wound required longer convalescence. Pvt. Levi Turner received a minor gunshot wound, and was hospitalized until 24 August when he was furloughed. Roughly nine days of intense trench warfare ensured when the both sides dug in after Maj. Gen. Ulysses Grant, commanding the Federal army, decided on a fateful charge on 3 June killing and wounding over eight thousand men in roughly thirty minutes. In those nine days, sharpshooters were much dreaded along those lines and many soldiers went for days without food or water simply trying to avoid becoming a target, as they could not move from their dug in position among the earthen works. The lines were so close in some places that even a rifle barrel protruding just a few inches above the trenches resulted in a lethal shower of bullets overhead. On 12 June, the 4th NCST received orders relocating them to the Shenandoah Valley as Grant moved his federal army south toward Petersburg to begin yet another attempt to dislocate Lee from his defenses around Richmond.

### Monocacy - Kernstown

Following a successful spring campaign, R. E. Lee wanted to threaten Washington with another Confederate invasion that summer in hopes of diverting attention from his effort to gain a stronghold in the Shenandoah Valley. Maj. Gen. Jubal Early commanded Confederate forces I the Shenandoah Valley, and went into Maryland during July with orders to intercept the Federal forces intent on capturing Winchester, Virginia. The 4th NCST fought in Brig. Gen. William R. Cox's brigade, with the 2d, 3d, 14th, and 30th North Carolina regiments during this campaign.[16] A number of soldiers in the 4th North Carolina recorded in their letters that they could literally see the spires of churches in Washington, so close were they as they went across Maryland towards Washington. But the circumstances did not allow Early to fully pursue an attack on the United States capital. On 20 July, Early ordered Cox's (Ramseur's) brigade to attack Federal forces at Monocacy, Maryland along the National Turnpike, as the Federals attempted to advance toward Winchester. The Confederates encountered a much larger force there than anticipated, and were forced to retire toward the fortifications around Winchester after several hours of fighting. Cox fought bravely, but lost four cannons and reported a total of 250 men killed, wounded and missing. Muster rolls and service files do not show Company K with losses in either engagement. His brigade was exhausted, and finally arrived at Winchester where they joined General Early, later that night. The next day, Early's men had to fight once more. This time they attacked the roughly

15,000 Federals who had gathered near Kernstown and completely routed them. Early pursued them toward Winchester but, due to the utter exhaustion of his army in the scorching July sun, was compelled to halt about five miles north of the town while only the cavalry continued pursuit.

## Shenandoah Valley Campaign

As Cox's Brigade settled into the earthworks around Winchester, General Ramseur, now commanding their division, was realizing that he was not as popular as a division commander as he had been while heading his former brigade. This was largely due to some events occurring on 20 July at Monocacy, when one of his North Carolina brigades under Brig. Gen. John F. Hoke literally broke in a panic and ran. Ramseur's men largely blamed him, and the debacle nearly ruined his career and prevented him from reaching a higher assignment. Many officers and Richmond politicians sided with the soldiers as well. Yet other officers familiar with Ramseur's abilities and character seemed to believe that his new troops only wanted to cast blame upon him to avoid their own responsibilities.[17] Shortly afterward, Robert E. Lee endeavored to drive the Federals out of the Shenandoah Valley, considered by many in Richmond to be the last true stronghold of the Confederacy after the 1863 losses at Vicksburg and Gettysburg. Nat Raymer again provided detailed accounts of what the 4th NCST did throughout numerous actions taking place in northwestern Virginia that summer, including Stephenson's Depot, Winchester, and later at Fisher's Hill and Rude's Hill. Pvt. Henry Williams was a miner before the war, and was detached on 19 August to work in the mines near Charleston, West Virginia. He remained there until 1865. Other anecdotes from Company K during this period was limited, but Raymer's next letter on the activities of the 4th NCST was written from camp near Charlestown on 24 August. It was published on 5 September in the *Carolina Watchman*, as the Confederates began to anticipate a major engagement near Winchester:

> "Military movements have kept me from writing sooner, and now I have barely time to send a note. I would like to write full particulars of our operations, and will certainly do so at an early day, but for the present a few lines must suffice. I'm anxious to let my good readers know that I am still jogging round on "terra firma," and that everything has worked to my heart's entire satisfaction. Am sorry that I have so long been forced to keep silent, simply because I have not been "at the front," and letters from any other quarter would surely be insipid and irksome. Henceforth I trust no obstacle will be in my way, and at every opportunity to mail I shall endeavor to send the latest news, even though very short it be.

> For the last ten days we have been marching and fighting almost incessantly. The enemy was started at Strasburg on the 17th inst., and up to this time they have kept up a perfect run down the valley, once in a while turning to fight a little, but never slacking the retrograde movement. And now they be in line of battle two miles east of this town and six from Harper's Ferry, having "crawfished" about 50 miles. On their retreat they have committed many depredations. Some dwellings were burnt, and many barns with large quantities of grain, forage, & c., were consumed. They pressed all the bacon and beef killed all the hogs, sheep, cattle, poultry, & c., along their line of march, whether needed or not.

> If needed, they would take them along, if not they were kept lying where they shot. In the many skirmishes along the march a few Confederates were killed, very few not one in our regiment, and but few wounded. Geo Roe, Co. I is, I fear mortally wounded. Andy Thorpe, Co. H, has his left arm broken, Mellargue Co. H, also received a slight wound, and

Geo. Snuggs, Co. K, received a right painful wound in the knee. None but the sharpshooters were engaged. Our corps is faring sumptuously. We get fine new flour and beef of the best quality in abundance, to say nothing of the "roast-neers" and apples, no small item.

I never saw men more gay and cheerful, they evidently have the utmost confidence in Early, who is renowned for his caution and an unexpected flank movements, and more for his incessant marching. This Corps has marched hardly less than 1500 miles since the opening of the campaign, yet the men are hearty, generally well clothed and shod, and so much soiled that the assessor would be perfectly justifiable in putting them down as real estate. Sickness and desertion are two words knocked out of our vocabulary. Possible once in a month a man may take "French leave" of the army around Richmond, but it is certain that none leaves the Valley. I find it here like at other places down South, everybody thinks this is the last year of the war—the yankees themselves think so, and I'm sure that all fondly hope it is. Who wouldn't prefer a camp meeting to a campaign!"

On 31 August, 2d Lieutenant Moses L. Bean completed the last and only muster roll of 1864. This roll was completed while the 4th NCST was encamped near Winchester, Virginia, and is also the final muster roll of the war. While others may have been written, extant archival holdings did not contain them. Capt. Marcus Hofflin was still commanding the company, but he left no anecdotal description of the companies' activities during this time. The roll covers a broad time period of 31 December 1863 through 31 August, and shows the heavy casualties following campaigns at Spotsylvania, and the Wilderness. Although there did not appear to be casualties from Company K at Monocacy or Kernstown, however, the upcoming engagements at Winchester and Cedar Creek would cost them dearly. The last roll shows only seventeen enlisted men available for duty, as the majority were either then wounded or sick on convalesce, or else detached on service elsewhere in the brigade.[18]

| Captain | 1 Lt | 2 Lt | Brevet Lt | Sgt | Cpl | Musicians | Privates | Total Enlisted | Aggregate |
|---------|------|------|-----------|-----|-----|-----------|----------|----------------|-----------|
| 1 | 1 | 1 | 0 | 2 | 3 | 0 | 13 | 17 | 63 |

Capt. Marcus Hofflin remained in command until 2 December 1864 when he was transferred by the surgeons to light duty due to a foot injury.[19] Capt. W.C. Coughenhour was then assigned to the role of Brigade Inspector for General Cox, and described the 4th NCST in general categories of "Discipline, Instruction, Military Appearance, Arms, Accoutrements, and Clothing" as "Very Good." Coughenhour elsewhere stated that most of the regiments in Cox's brigade were lacking overcoats and were generally in poor condition at that time, suggesting Company K was faring reasonably well.[20] Considering the relatively small number of enlisted men available for duty in Company K, supply records show there were adequate shoes available. Receipt of new blankets, uniforms, and shirts were delayed until October; but, clearly, Company K was not ragged or unclothed in contrast to the other regiments in the brigade. General Early earlier devised his strategy in the valley to be based on a series of rapid marches and counter-marches that were basically attempted feigns, hoping to deceive Union commanders into thinking he had more troops than was actually present.

A few days before the last muster roll was taken, Nat Raymer surmised that his comrades were then tolerating the incessant marches and counter-marches in the incredibly humid and hot 'dog days' without telling effects, while men in other regiments repeatedly fell out of formation due to exhaustion although all were now campaign veterans. It was sometime in this period that the famous regimental mascot, a St. Bernard dog named "General" that was captured from a dead

Pennsylvanian colonel by Brig. Gen. Bryan Grimes at Gaines Mill in 1862, succumbed to heat exhaustion and died after faithfully marching beside the Tar Heels for over two years. Food shortages as well as a series of apparently meaningless engagements and skirmishes became the order of the day, but were quickly remedied by the ancient art of foraging in nearby villages and townships along their route. Raymer's ability to keep up with his correspondence is remarkable as the army was constantly on the move from September through October. The Shenandoah Valley campaign in Virginia was about to hit full swing, as General Early planned his next move. Raymer next wrote from a camp located near Bunker Hill, Virginia, on 1 September. His note was published nearly three weeks later on 21 September by the *Carolina Watchman,* informing readers of recent fighting and troop movements involving the 4th NCST as the campaign escalated in skirmishes near Martinsburg and Shepherdstown, West Virginia:

"…on the morning of the 25th ult., we left Charlestown and after an oppressive march of some ten miles in scorching heat and suffocating dust, we came suddenly on a stumbling block at the Baltimore and Ohio Rail Road, four miles Shepardstown, Va. "Bluecoats" were apparently abundant in those parts, and they stoutly resisted our advance…In the coolest manner possible the troops were brought up in battle line, batteries placed in position, skirmishers sent forward and at noon the fight began in earnest. After an hour's vigorous shelling and skirmishing the enemy fell back in disorder…We were pushed in pursuit at once, and not until we landed in Shepardstown was I allowed time enough to stop and take a gravel about the size of a partridge egg out of my shoe… and at sunset we lay down for a little rest. Eight o'clock at night found us again moving back towards Shepardstown… through the town with stirring music at 9 o'clock at night, we were greeted with shouts and yells from all quarters; even the ladies seemed to have lost all control of themselves and went dancing and clapping their hands and waving handkerchiefs as if an universal matrimonial day (or night) had been proclaimed.

Such a joyous welcome is worth six months service at any time. Keeping the road to Martinsburg at midnight we "turned in" three miles from Charlestown. Notwithstanding the men were very tired, yet the arms were scarcely stacked when squads were seen striking out in every direction foraging while a portion of those who remained went to work cooking rations, in all probability, for another expedition tomorrow similar to the one we have had today…Many didn't get further than the apple orchard, others found a cornfield and "oodles" of roast-neers; some happened by the merest accident in the world to stumble into a spring house where it was evident milk and butter were to be had for less than schedule prices; a few bee hives, sheepskins, duck heads, and such like trifling articles, might be found half concealed somewhere in the neighborhood of camp; how they got there is a mystery that has puzzled graver and bolder heads than mine.

Since the affair at Shepardstown things have been comparatively quiet, that is, as quiet as it ever gets in the Valley, by which we mean a march or a "skrimmage" almost every day, but short and easy marches and light fights… The same kind of a fight occurred at Smithfield (six miles below Bunker Hill) on last Monday, and yesterday again our division had a running fight with them from Darksville to some place beyond Martinsburg…we captured a considerable quantity of Quartermaster and commissary stores in and around Martinsburg, such as boots, shoes, clothing, pork, crackers & c. We have no complaints to make. The best of health prevails-plenty to eat and jolly times generally. The weather continues fine, the mornings are cool, almost forty, but the days are oppressively warm…"

While the regiment stood on picket duty north of Winchester on 14 September, Raymer revealed that the weather seemed to be as unpredictable as the movements of the opposing armies whose series of accordion-like movements may be analogized as that of a large serpent. There was more episodic skirmishing, ending in one or the other's retreat without a major engagement for several days. Doubtless, the veterans of the "Rowan Rifles" and their comrades were getting frustrated; but, according to Raymer, the morale of the regiment was very strong. He also reported that Capt. Marcus Hofflin had a horse shot out from under him and bruised his foot while leading the regiment across a river. This explains why Hofflin was removed from command and placed on light duties by the surgeons. There is ample evidence that all were completely exhausted and rather emaciated from the heat and poor food, yet they still held to their duty. Raymer was again published in the *Carolina Watchman* on 26 September:

"It seems that the "weather clerk" has forgotten himself or has made some mistake by sending us chill autumn before the proper time. Indeed each cold blustery gales as we have had during yesterday, last night and today reminds us more of winter than anything else… we are not all prepared for cold weather. It is hardly to be expected that our clothes and shoes partake of the nature of those worn by the children of Israel in the Wilderness; their garments never waxed old, but somehow ours do, and rents patches and fizzles are exhibited accordingly. I doubt very much whether our nearest and dearest friends would recognize us…had rain eight to ten days in succession…the juicy spell closed with a furious hail storm, the whole of which, as well as many soaking showers before it, we had to take patiently as we were marching along the road. The hail stones were, on an average, about the size of large bullets…I have heard of no injury done except a right serious pelting of several thousands of soldiers, and they, I am sure, were thankful for the luxury, ice.

We have been in many skirmishes recently but so far not a man in our regiment has been killed or wounded since the affair at Charlestown on the 21st ult., we were engaged in a hot skirmish at Dulfield Station ( I believe that is the name) on the Baltimore and Ohio Railroad, between Harper's and Martinsburg. At that time Capt. Hofflin, (of Salisbury, N.C.) was in command of our regiment, and while leading his men across a knoll exposed to the enemy's fire his horse was killed under him by a shell. In the fall the Captain's foot was considerably bruised, otherwise he sustained no injury whatsoever. I believe every Confederate soldier in the Valley is glad that his lot is east in Early's Corps…our mode of life is perfect happiness compared the dreadful inactivity around Petersburg…the soldiers there have spent…months in those trenches, scorched with a burning sun, suffering for lack of good water, scarce of palatable rations, exposed every hour to sharpshooters, and…their awful dread of another explosion…we have been skirmishing a little, or marching (which is the life of an army) or luxuriating in the shade, feasting on the finest fruit or other unmentionable luxuries for which this Valley is famous. This is soldiering in the summer of 1864…When one party is ready and shows fight, the other skedaddles out of reach of danger. Consequently and everlasting maneuvering is kept up over an area of some fifty miles in diameter…this interesting game of chase they have up between Strasburg and the Potomac…pleases us extremely well…The best of health is universal, and the spirit of this army is uncommonly buoyant…We are faring sumptuously…that more than anything else is the reason for our liking the valley so well."

With the last wartime harvest sitting in the rich fields of the Shenandoah Valley, Robert E. Lee's hopes for diverting Union pressures on his forces at Petersburg rested on the army under General Jubal Early, who in spite of supply deficits, was earlier showing promise that he could eliminate the Federal threat in that region. That was about to change, although Early erected heavy earthen fortifications around the town of Winchester, which had already changed hands numerous times across the war, sometimes twice on the same day. Early left only one Confederate division to guard his communication lines to Winchester, as the bulk of his army, was out marching in the Valley. Early's adversary would be Maj. Gen. Phil Sheridan, a cavalry officer by profession, who now commanded Union forces known as the Army of the Shenandoah, comprised of the VI, VIII (formerly known as the Army of West Virginia), and XIX Corps. He had earlier distinguished himself in bitter campaigns of Murfreesboro, Chickamauga, and Chattanooga in the western theatre in 1862-1863, but somehow Early underestimated his aggressiveness. Sheridan, in concert with President Abraham Lincoln's goal of making 1864 the last year of the war, decided to take advantage of the situation. Although Early rarely remaining in one place for longer than one or two days, Sheridan wasn't so easily duped, and proved to be a stoic intelligence analyst. He quickly learned from both military and civilian sources on 17 September that Early had moved two of his largest divisions to Martinsburg, making Winchester vulnerable in spite of endless attempts to feign a larger force by the series of counter-marches. Early quickly saw his quandary, and hastily re-concentrated his army along Opequan Creek at Winchester on 18 September, with a major engagement now imminent.

Sheridan's army also concentrated and drew up in line of battle along Opequan Creek outside of Winchester on the 18th of September. Sheridan was gloating over the news that Early had recently complied with General Lee's request to send Kershaw's division and one artillery battalion from his army to reinforce the Army of Northern Virginia then entrenched around Petersburg, who was in dire need of assistance. This reduced Early's army to around 17,000 effective men, but he remained confident he could defend Winchester. Sheridan attacked around dawn on 19 September along the main road running from Berryville. The fighting was heaviest in the morning along that road, where Ramseur's Division was engaged against troops from the Union XIX and VI Corps until well after noon. Sheridan realized that Early's left, which was composed mainly of Rodes and Ramseur's Divisions along the Berryville road, were strong and well placed, and took advantage of a lull occurring just after noon, and quickly re-aligned the VI and XIX Corps into double brigade formations, not unlike a "battering ram" of old Roman military nomenclature. Many of these same regiments had fought in former battles of Spotsylvania, Salem Church and the Wilderness, and were not intimidated by former foes. Sheridan continued his attack, but was unable to break Early's lines, with Federal losses described as severe in early afternoon.

Ramseur's Division, including Cox's Brigade, took heavy losses that morning, and was again engaged in the afternoon in heavy fighting in a densely wooded bottom area known as Ash Hollow, near the Dinkle family farm house, until Ramseur finally withdrew his men roughly two hours later. For unknown reasons, there next appeared a large gap in the Confederate lines after Ramseur pulled back, and the road into Winchester seemed blatantly exposed. Instead of capitalizing, however, Sheridan's men fell into disarray and were unable to take advantage of the opportunity. On the left of Ramseur's Division, Maj. Gen. Robert E. Rodes' division was preparing a massive charge on the exposed gap, where several federal regiments were beginning to pressure Early. Just when Rode's yelled the order to move forward, an artillery shell exploded killing him instantly.

Brig. Gen. Bryan Grime's thought he was ordered to replace Rodes, but when he arrived he found that General Early had in fact placed Rodes' adjutant, who was but a Major, in charge of the division. Rode's charge nearly caused a fatal rout of the XIX Corps at Ash Hollow, but there was another entire division waiting nearby, who quickly reinforced the retreating brigades and bolstered Sheridan's lines. The fighting continued as such until around three o'clock p.m., and the VIII Corps, which had not yet engaged, was next committed to the fight on Sheridan's right.

Also known as the "Army of West Virginia", the VIII Corps was commanded by Brig. Gen. George Crook, and former Indian fighter who captured the legendary chief "Geronimo" after the war, had literally hundreds of rugged, stalwart mountaineers who previously served guarding railroads and chasing bushwhackers with only occasional small engagements occurring in the dangerous mountain terrain of West Virginia. Crook's troops were rough, but generally viewed as green and inexperienced "fresh fish" by hardened eastern veterans who had been in the Army of the Potomac during major campaigns at Richmond, Antietam, Gettysburg and Spotsylvania. Yet Crooks' army endured three harsh winters between 1861 and 1864, and one infantryman in that outfit mentioned that his brigade had marched over seven hundred miles between May and July 1864. Most had previously fought in the 1864 spring campaigns at Piedmont, Lynchburg, Lexington, and Cloyd's Mountain. One regiment in Crook's army now facing the Tar Heels was the 4th West Virginia Infantry, who had served in West Virginia and also with Maj. Gen. William T. Sherman at Vicksburg. They had played a key role in assaulting the Confederate strongholds there, and along with other obviously seasoned combat veterans, they were in no mood to give quarter as they joined in the tenacious contest.

By four o'clock p.m., Sheridan had the VIII Corps posted on his right, the XIX Corps in the middle, and the VI Corps again on his left facing Ramseur and Rode's former command, including Cox's Brigade, and pushed forward en masse, making a general engagement ensuing until around 5:30 p.m., when Early ordered a general retreat back to Winchester. Ramseur's division was on the southern end of town, facing east in the last line of defense at dusk, when there came "a deadly quiet" across the field, as the rest of Early's men shuffled into an L shaped line of battle protecting the outskirts of town for a final stand. Sheridan attacked again at dusk, spearheaded by Maj. Gen. George Custer's cavalrymen, who rushed inside the Confederate defenses, slashing defenders with sabers while dozens were simultaneously knocked off their horses by clubbed muskets. Custer and the rest of Sheridan's army eventually gained the advantage, and pushed the embattled Confederates out of their works. A contagion of rout and panic occurred as Early's men ran back through the streets of Winchester in confusion. Brig. Gen. Bryan Grimes and Maj. Gen. Stephen Ramseur quickly found their commands, and their presence again instilled a sense of discipline.

They quickly established a rear guard in line of battle along a low ridge running across town, extending through the Mt. Hebron cemetery. There, they hoped to offer protection for the remainder of Early's troops trying to escape, which they accomplished as hundreds of exhausted Confederates filed onto the Valley Pike making their getaway. Historians rarely agree on casualty figures at the Third Battle of Winchester, but most have reported Early lost somewhere between 1,800 to 2,000 men, with Rode's Division suffering the worst of it, while Sheridan, who had more troops in his three corps to begin with, lost but around 4,500 men. Company K was heavily engaged in this battle and lost its most popular officer, 1st Lt. Addison Wiseman, who was seen falling in the battle. But as we have seen from Nat Raymer, it was most difficult to obtain accurate casualty information after a large battle. An unidentified officer of the 4th NCST present at the battle of Winchester noted Wiseman was missing and seemed optimistic the lieutenant was yet alive. He wrote from their camp near Strasburg a few days later on 20 September, which was published in the *Carolina Watchman* on 3 October:

"Dear Sir: I am sorry to inform you that Lt. A.N. Wiseman has either been killed or wounded and is in the hands of the enemy. There is but one man in the Regiment who knows anything about him, and he says he saw him fall. I think he was wounded and not able to get off the field. Moses Bencini is also a prisoner, and some of the company say that Lieut. Wiseman and Bencini were together in the fight, and I have no doubt they are prisoners. I feel most certain that Wiseman is not killed, for every man who gets wounded falls, and that is no sign of his being killed. His falling is all that the man who saw him, knows. He thought he was killed, but of course it is not known to be so. Our army got a good whipping yesterday and it goes very hard with us, for we are not used to it. Wm. Murr has a flesh wound above the knee; L. Turner, flesh wound in arm; Henry Castor is missing."

Recall that twenty-seven year old 1st Lt. Addison Wiseman had been wounded three times before and had been with the company since April 1861. He served with Company K at Seven Pines, the Seven Days battles, Chancellorsville, Gettysburg, the Wilderness and Spotsylvania.[21] His story includes a strange irony: wounded in December 1862 at Fredericksburg on picket duty, he returned on 2 May at Chancellorsville and was wounded again one day later on 3 May. This report to the *Carolina Watchman* by the unidentified author was quite hopeful; however, it ultimately turned out to be inaccurate. Lieutenant Wiseman was, in fact, killed at the third battle of Winchester on 19 September 1864 just six months after going home on leave to complete his last will and testament..[22] His death doubtlessly crushed his wife Sarah, of whom Wiseman was extremely fond. In spite of this discrepancy, Nat Raymer provided what he considered to be an accurate summary of casualties from the 4th NCST at Winchester (including Company K) on 19 September. His report of Company K casualties was published on 6 October in the *Carolina Watchman*:

Co. K-- Killed, none. Wounded: Wm Murr, left knee, flesh; Levi Turner, left elbow, flesh. Missing: Lt A N Wiseman (reported killed) Privates Henry Castor and Moses Benceni…Our regiment took 120 muskets into the battle, including non-commissioned officers and sharpshooters. It is certain that some of these reported missing are killed…so long as there is the least ground for hope we will, with others, cling to that hope to the last…Though certainly a reverse to our army, yet, we will hope that something will turn up soon which will turn the scales in our favor…I will say, if our cavalry had held their position on the left, we would not now have the mortification of knowing that we were compelled to double quick to Strasburg, a distance of 18 miles. We are now in our trenches on Fisher's Hill, near Strasburg, waiting an attack, nor do we think we will have to wait long."

An interesting comparison is found in Raymer's statistics against those reported by Rodes' former division on 19 September. Rodes' Division there reported losing 89 Killed and 597 Wounded, while Raymer shows only three killed, and forty wounded.[23] Casualty statistics further reveal something of the character of these men including Pvt. Levi Turner whom he mentioned. He was earlier wounded at Cold Harbor had only returned to the company some few days before the battle at Winchester, only to be again wounded there by gunshot to his left elbow, later causing him to be disabled according to his post-war pension records. A few days before the battle, while skirmishing near Martinsburg on 14 September, Pvt. Michael Davis was wounded, and sent to Richmond. Several men were captured, including Privates Henry Castor, Soloman Tarcroft, and Pembrooke G. Taylor, known as "Pemmie" to his friends, along with Moses Bencini. All were temporarily detained at Harpers Ferry, West Virginia until they were transferred to the military prison at Point Lookout, Maryland on 24 September. It is quite likely that Henry Castor was similarly detained although his service records do not specify where he was taken. While at Point Lookout, James Cameron deserted to the United States Army, and was released after taking the Oath of Allegience. It is not known whether Cameron actually fought with a Union regiment afterward. Bencini was held until 15 March 1865, when he was exchanged and returned to Salisbury.

## *Fisher's Hill*

As Early fell back from Winchester, he gathered his army at Fisher's Hill where he harbored the "hope of arresting Sheridan's progress" albeit unsuccessfully. There Early again engaged Sheridan's three corps, encountering a heavy flanking movement on his left, led by the same West Virginian's under Brig. Gen. George Crook who had troubled his right wing at Winchester. They forced him to withdraw even further to Rude's Hill on 22 September. But his lines once more gave way in a panic when hit with severe enfilade fire on the left, resulting in heavy losses. Early reported he lost 30 killed, 210 wounded, 995 missing, at Fisher's Hill alone. Afterward, he tried to reorganize his shattered army and moved toward Port Republic.[24] Rodes' former division, including Cox's brigade to whom the 4th NCST now belonged, lost 11 Killed and 94 Wounded at Fisher's Hill and during subsequent skirmishing near Rude's Hill.[25]

Company K did not have casualties at Fisher's Hill, but Pvt. Jeremiah Eddleman was captured and taken to Point Lookout, Maryland. A few days later as Early stopped at New Market, over thirty miles to the south Raymer catches up on the regiments late activities which were intense to say the least. His account was published by the *Carolina Watchman* on 24 October, just a few days following their next major engagement which was the battle of Cedar Creek on 22 October. In this letter, Raymer discussed late action at the battle at Fisher's Hill but focused more on his ire over a recent order requiring correspondents to tighten up reports of army strength in their letters back home. Raymer, who was quite used to having *Carte Blanc'* in his work, frankly reveals his chagrin at the prospect in what parallels a modern war correspondent genre. Raymer obviously enjoyed some kind of emotional catharsis and solace in writing freely, but wisely subdued his frustration and cooperated with the order:

> "What next, I wonder? Visions of bayonets, guard houses, bucking ticks and gags for what? all because a poor, wayward "worm of the dust" has been so indiscreet as to let the truth eke out once—just once, and the people got it...I do not intend to be altogether silent, notwithstanding the threatening order recently issued by the War Department:--I have ever been cautious in my correspondence...but in future letters I shall, more than ever, look carefully to my phraseology...the stringent order to which I refer, prohibiting, under severe penalties, army correspondence for the press...Now this smacks of "muzzling" the press and clogging our "quills"...I know it will bear hard upon the thousands at home who are always on the qui vire for latest news relative to military operations...but when we remember that by the suppression of such information, we deprive the enemy (both internal and external) of much valuable foothold, surely no good man will complain.

> This order does not forbid the publication of casualties in battle, nor of anything, that can be of real interest to the wives, daughters, sisters and expectants in the South, whose hearts are kept in painful suspense by reason of the frequent and bloody battles fought during this

campaign, and we assure them that every effort will be made to relieve their minds of that agony...But in spite of every effort to appear otherwise, I feel cramped...laced up in an iron jacket. Accustomed to unbounded freedom in my correspondence ,though having never abused that freedom to my knowledge, yet I am now constantly looking around lest I tread where the crust is thin...Since my last was written nothing of usual interest has transpired. Our loss at Strasburg (or more properly, Fisher's Hill) was not near so great...No one in the 4th N.C. regiment was killed, nor any severely wounded...Some were actually taken prisoners...and were lucky enough to make their escape...others fled for safety to the mountains...among the rugged precipices and dark caves of the Blue Ridge...Numbers of these "mountain refuges" have found their way into camp...whom we supposed killed or captured...had a wonderful effect on the spirits of our men generally...We are still getting on very well. Have been provided with clothing in abundance, paid off and shoes furnished. The weather is getting colder, and last night we had frequent blasts of snow and sleet. We are really glad to see winter coming; we hope to have some rest then, and until that time we expect nothing but marches, hardships and suffering."

The reader will notice that Raymer mentions the regiment received adequate clothing, which had not occurred since the previous summer. Considering the amount of marching and fighting this company had endured, at this point it is reasonable to conclude their appearance was filthy and gaunt, with tattered uniforms at best prior to receiving their new clothing. On 18 October 1864, one day before the battle of Cedar Creek, Col. Bryan Grimes, who was then commanding as separate brigade, received a large shipment of supplies intended for the 4th NCST although he was no longer in command of it.26 This shipment was delivered near Winchester and run to their lines by wagon train. This was the last significant quartermaster issue recorded for Company K in the war, but implies that not only was it more than enough to meet their needs, but also there was uniformity as all had new trousers and jackets. Recall that North Carolina Governor Zebulon Vance later reported that by this time in the war, nearly all uniforms made by the Raleigh Clothing Depot were of the high quality blue-gray tinted English cloth. Co. Grimes' original receipt shows Company K received twenty-seven pair of pants, twenty three flannel shirts, seventeen shirts, thirty-three jackets, nineteen pair drawers, thirty three pair pants, five canteens with straps, and three haversacks. Considering there were roughly seventeen men available for duty at the last muster roll on 31 August 1864, and that Company K lost somewhere between nine to twelve men killed, wounded or captured in fighting occurring during the weeks prior to and at the 19 September battle of Winchester, and on 22 September at Fisher's Hill and Rude's Hill, the number of uniform articles received was doubtless sufficient to carry them into the next phase of their fall campaign. Note that since there were no further Company K muster rolls located at the time of this publication, the actual number of enlisted men available for duty following 22 September is not known, as some may have returned from hospitals or detached service to fill the ranks.

### Cedar Creek

On 19 October, the Battle at Cedar Creek occurred, in a major engagement involving Early's army completely surprising and routing Maj. Gen. Philip Sheridan's three Federal corps (VI, VIII, and XIX Corps) in their camp just before dawn. The battle raged all day, but Sheridan, who was away from the army at Winchester when the battle began, later arrived on the field in time to rally his men, enabling the battered Federals to reorganize and regain their composure, and resist Early to the degree that he eventually retreated toward New Market. The 4th NCST losses at Cedar Creek were summarized in the *Carolina Watchman* on 7 November, when Raymer described his observations of the battle which was ultimately another discouraging rout of the Confederates. Also Maj. Gen. Stephen Ramseur, the regiment's beloved brigade commander for the majority of the war, was mortally wounded and borne from the field. He died a few days later, and Col. Bryan Grimes was promoted to Brigadier General in his stead, and given command of Ramseur's former division. Once again, there is but a paucity of information from Company K for this engagement, but Raymer also happily confirms for his readers that other than occasional skirmishing, fighting in the Valley for 1864 had virtually come to a close, although the Federal army now occupied Winchester:

Co. K. Killed. None. Wounded: B Mathis, musician, right arm, flesh; Serg't W C Fraley, slight; C Holtshouser, right hand slight. Missing: A Friedheim…The entire army regrets the loss of Gen. Ramseur. He was mortally wounded and left in the enemy's hands. Today we hear, upon what seems to be good authority, that he is dead. He was renowned throughout the army in the Valley for his dashing invincible courage as well as for his kind and gentlemanly deportment. We can ill afford to spare such officers…the 19th of October 1864 was one of the most eventful days and Filled with the most remarkable incidents that have ever transpired in any one day since first breaking of this terrible revolution. The morning dawned on us inspired with victory the most complete and decisive; the evening shades gathered on our army broken, dispirited, and – but I feel too sad; --and it might be unwise to say more…in the aggregate, our gains are greater than our losses, and with this, for the present, we must be content."

As military action in the Shenandoah Valley was winding to a close, Early's army was encamped near New Market, where many soldiers in the 4th NCST tried to regain their composure, rest, and tend to routine duties such as picket or guard mounts, and some took time to write home again. Raymer's next feature also displays his eulogy of General Ramseur, and his characteristic wry wit as he recounts a brief chase that took place when a red fox got too close to the hungry Rebels' lines, albeit the fox became a pet to some other regiment in their brigade. Raymer again discussed the weather changes, which was quickly turning into a bitterly cold winter with snow. The *Carolina Watchman* reported Raymer's latest dispatch on 5 December, which he wrote on 21 November:

"Owing to bad weather and constant marching, I have been hindered from writing as frequently as I should like to have done; but…"better late than never"…On the morning of the 10th inst. Our whole army, largely reinforced and in pretty good trim, generally was brought out from their camps in the vicinity of New Market and marched down the Valley. On the evening of the 11th, we "jumped" the yankees in the neighborhood of New Town, eight miles this side of Winchester. Sharpshooters were thrown out, and that night and the day following were spent skirmishing along the lines, and at some points hot and heavy. We thought surely a general engagement would come off Saturday…pickets were incessantly popping away at each other, but on the main line of battle no excitement whatever occurred—except once. About two o'clock in the afternoon a tremendous yell was raised on the extreme left of the line. "Ah, there it is," said some-"That's a charge"—"Didn't I tell you the yankees would endeavor to turn our left flank again"—"Guess they will find an obstacle this time"—"Just listen!" "Boys it's getten' closer!" –said a greasy fellow whose hat I thought was then rising—"What does it mean?" wondered half a dozen at a time as the shouting evidently came nearer—"Strange there is not much stirring;" such and many like them were the remarks made by the men around me, each standing with mouths agape and eyes strained trying to see something as yet invisible.

Presently we saw about half a brigade of hatless men tearing through the thickets at furious gait, some two hundred yards in read of the line of battle and coming up parallel with it, and just ahead of them we discovered as they emerged from the woods into a large open field—What! Not a rabbit I'm sure, else the chase could not have lasted so long, but a fox, a red fox, and one to the largest of his species. Quick as thought hundreds more joined the chase, yelling and hooting like mad men, heading, flanking first on the right then on the left until finally poor Raynard found further effort useless and accordingly "caved in." He was captured without receiving the slightest injury, and is now kept as a pet in one of the brigades in this division. Altogether it was the most exciting chase I ever witnessed.

Soon after dark, we began a "crawfish" movement…in other words we advanced backwards, leaving only our pickets on the line. About 8 o'clock at night the full moon peeped over the snow capped Blue Ridge and poured over us such a flood of bright, mellow light that our column could be seen for a mile moving briskly on the pike damp and black like a huge serpent dragging his unwieldily body over the hills and plains, while a line of the enemy's cavalry like specters in the dim distance…But continuous and accurate firing by the rear guard enabled them to hold off the prowling enemy until the army proper was out of danger, and at 11 o'clock we found ourselves in old camps on Fisher's Hill…having marched fourteen miles in less than five hours.

Apart from the necessity of getting out of danger and reaching a safe position we were compelled to march rapidly to keep from freezing. The wind from the snow covered mountains seemed to pierce to the very marrow, while with all the blankets and handkerchiefs that we could get muffled about our ears and noses we could hardly retain those useful as well as ornamental appendages. I never saw the moon's rays come down with such undimmed lustre. Under other circumstances this would have been very agreeable, but on this occasion it was really annoying…we expected an attack at any moment…when at least we reached Fisher's Hill in safety is it any wonder that we should feel immensely relieved!

Before it was quite light on the morning of the 13th, we set out again, though the blast from the snowy regions was keener and colder than ever. By 9 a.m. furious storms of snow were dashed mercilessly on our faces, but, all unmindful of it the troops marched as lightly, and evinced a spirit as gay and cheerful as though nothing but a gentle breeze from the forests…impeded their progress. At intervals during the day a single beam of sunshine would gleam through the heaviness of black, lowering clouds…the freezing atmosphere would be darkened with the dense showers of snow. At night we pitched camp in the neighborhood of Edenburg—just imagine a camp in a snow storm—I can't describe it—or if I could you could not form an idea of the way we slayed timber and built fires; or how our fingers and toes ached—or how blue our noses got—nor how we lay down, pulled the blankets over our heads and—let it snow. On the next morning (Monday 14th) the bugle aroused us before we got our nap out…My dear reader might have heard a good deal of growling, and perhaps a little "cussin" and threats as to how we'd sleep until we got ready to get up when the war is ended, and such like but it was no use; we found it advisable to make the best of a bad bargain and therefore "simmered" ---

Arose, shook the snow off our heads and blankets, bundled up and set out with as much independence and perfect nonchalance as we intend to show…We were absent five days on three days rations…marched eighty five miles, skirmished one day and night, and what have we gained!… We may conclude then that the fighting in the Valley is virtually ended for this winter. What is going to be done with us? Ay, that is one of the mysteries. Nothing, however, can surprise us…it wouldn't be a matter of wonder if we were specially detailed to plant torpedoes around Salisbury to prevent Kirk's intended raid on the old factory…But laying jokes aside we do hope, sincerely hope, that we may soon get into winter quarters…We are completely run down trying to keep out of the smoke, if beauty causes this attraction I would advise any of my fair readers who are anxious to make a good match to come out here—sure they can be suited, even the most fastidious. Our eyes are red (nary drop of whiskey though) our cheeks look like canvass hams, our whiskers crisped, hair frizzled, and hands, well, just imagine an alligators claw.

Yet not withstanding all these drawbacks (very trifling they are too) our hearts are still as sensitive as ever…,But indeed I have the shivers so badly that I can hardly follow the lines— or ever keep respectfully between them. Rain patters down on my little tent cold, drear, pitiless. Nothing but a column of smoke rises where our fire ought to be—no hopes of thawing there…But if we do have the luck of getting into winter quarters near Staunton, or any where else some distance from Richmond—will those …packages, boxes, &c., for soldiers, come to our portion of the army wherever we may be? This is the question. If we do get luxuries from the old North State this winter (and that is about two-thirds of all we live for now)—if packages, I say, can be sent to this regiment…I do hope I have friends among my readers who will remember me in this the time of my great calamity…"

## *Petersburg*

Without warning, Raymer's musings over a possible upcoming change of venue became something of a reality, when the 4th NCST was ordered to Petersburg, Virginia, on 13 December 1864. Ironically he earlier mentioned going back to Salisbury to protect it from an intended attack; for some of the men in Company K, this would occur before the wars end, but for the regiment, now they found themselves in deadly trench warfare during the siege of Petersburg. Here they would serve the remainder of their time in the army, down to the last days before their service culminated in Robert E. Lee's surrender at Appomattox on 9 April 1865. Aware that anxious family and friends would be shocked by this latest turn of events, Raymer does his best to provide details of their situation and admonishes them to write often.

"Well, this is decidedly an unexpected change of base…On the night of the 13th instant we received orders to move at day light the next morning and as usual all hands proceeded to prepare for the hated task; meanwhile guessing and wondering where we were bound for was the sure topic of conversation…after wading thro snow six inches deep for a distance of a mile and a half to reach the pike, we were agreeable surprised to see the head of the column turn up towards Staunton. The early part of the way intensely cold, and the limestone pike was hard and slick as a frozen mill pond. Towards evening the air grew milder and thawed sufficiently to form a kind of mush through which we trudged vigorously with the most extreme difficulty, and at night struck camp near Mount Crawford having traveled six miles from our starting point. The reader can imagine our condition; but tired and broken down as we were our first duty was to prepare for a cold night, which we did by raking the snow from the spot where we expected to lie and building large fires on them.

The night after all, was spent more comfortable than many might suppose, and on the next morning (15th) we were ready bright and early for the tramp and that evening, at 3 o'clock, we found ourselves at Staunton forty three miles from New Market. By 10 o'clock at night we were jammed aboard the cars like so many market hogs, forty and fifty in a box, half frozen, and particularly out of humor in general. For my part I think it would have been clever had some of the managers divided the whiskey instead of drinking too much themselves, and then by their negligence and mismanagement keep two brigades standing in snow light and ten hours waiting to be put aboard the train.

Without any serious accident we landed near Petersburg on the eve of the 16th and went into camp. The 17th and 18th we "rested our weary bones" and on the 19th went to work putting up winter quarters in earnest. Our camp is located four miles from the city in a healthy atmosphere, that is, out of reach of the shells which frequently pay their unwelcome visits over this way…Since our arrival here we have been on one very disagreeable trip to the lines near Drury's Bluff, enjoying our sunny shanties. Unless something very serious turns up we expect to remain in this vicinity during the winter. Every thing is quiet on the lines except the customary cannonading, which is kept up day and night incessantly. Upon the whole, we are well pleased with our change…"

As the 4th NCST found itself immersed in life inside the trenches surrounding Petersburg, it once again had to adapt to an incredibly dangerous new environment, which Raymer pointed out was due to frequent shells bursting in the vicinity along the Confederate lines. Summarily, 1864 was a violent and demanding year for Company K. Many of the men had not been home in three years, but most held to their post. Desertions became more obvious in late summer, as two privates, Jeremiah Glover and John Locket, were "Absent without Leave" on the last muster roll since 28 August, and supposed to have left together from the picket lines. The major engagements at the Wilderness and Spotsylvania, followed by the Valley Campaign from September to October, nearly left the company without any men available to fight. Such was the plight throughout the Army of Northern Virginia, yet Lee endeavored to hold out his lines in Petersburg as long as possible. The army in the west was likewise facing grim realities of moving toward North Carolina as Maj. Gen. W.T. Sherman's "march to the sea," from Atlanta that culminated in the capture of Savannah in December, where he presented the Key to the City of Savannah to President Lincoln as a Christmas gift. To further illustrate the trials which the soldiers passed through that year, one rather detail oriented private in the 4th NCST stated that during the year 1864, "…I marched 1850 miles, was in 28 battles and skirmishes, helped to build 9 lines of breastworks, received 91 letters, was sick 9 days and received 3 boxes of provisions brought from home."[27]

Other important events occurred in 1864 in regards to command changes; 1st Lieutenant Addison Wiseman was killed at Winchester on 19 September, and 2d Lieutenant Moses L. Bean was given command of the company afterward. Capt. Marcus Hofflin spent most of the year detailed on a fishing party in the Shenandoah Valley, which R.E. Lee had hoped would increase the supply of food for his army. Former Company K commander Capt. W.C. Coughenhour, was again re-assigned from the brigade staff of Brig. Gen. William R. Cox to the staff of Brig. Gen. James Dearing, only to again face reassignment after Cedar Creek to Brig. Gen. William P. Robert's brigade until 1 March 1865.[28] Likewise, Brig. Gen. Bryan Grimes, who was promoted to brigade command following the mortal wounding of General Ramseur at Cedar Creek, was about to be promoted to major general in February 1865, and would be the last major general to be commissioned in the Army of Northern Virginia.[29]

# Chapter Nine

## 1865
## Evacuation of Petersburg, Retreat to Appomattox

There were no supply records or muster rolls found for Company K during 1865, but there are numerous accounts describing activities of the 4th NCST during those final months of the war. As winter crept along, the mail service slowed for several days, causing a great deal of frustration in camp. The delays were in part due to the fact that several important bridges had washed out along the Danville and Piedmont Railway during a series of severe rainstorms in the Petersburg area.[1] In Cox's brigade, the delays were also because several men previously detached on other duties such as Pvt. John Deaton, who was the brigade mail carrier, were returned to their companies to fill numerous gaps in the ranks. Not all available soldiers stayed in the company, however, as Sgt. Peter Brown was detached an unspecified detail in January. Shortly after the company arrived at Petersburg, Pvt. Jeremiah Glover received a gunshot wound on 5 January, but stayed with his unit while attempting to recover. His condition worsened, and he was transferred to a Richmond hospital on 20 February. Glover eventually returned to Salisbury on convalescence, where he remained until captured on 12 April 1865 when the town was raided by Federal cavalry. Pvt. Walter Battle of Company I, 4th NCST described the general state of affairs in the 4th NCST camp in a 12 January letter to his mother:

> "...We draw one third of a pound of meat now and we make out very well. You need not send me any more meat, as you need that more than we do. Send such things as peas, potatoes and such things as you make plenty of and do not have to buy. We are very comfortably fixed up in our winter quarters now. We have been busy cleaning up for the past two weeks...The boys have gone into these quarters with less spirit than any we have ever built. We would not be surprised at any moment to receive marching orders, and none of us have any idea of staying here until spring...a good many say the Confederacy has "gone up" (as they term it) and that we are whipped. I have never seen the men so discouraged before. I hear also that the men are deserting the front lines and going home by large squads. If this is true and it is continued long, the Yankees will whip us certain...The sharpshooters keep everything alive on the lines by day and night. Every dark and cloudy night they keep up such a heavy fire as to resemble a line of battle; although we are some four miles off, we hear every musket that is fired...the batteries on each side take a notion to have a little duel, and for an hour or two there is a cannon shot for every minute, then gradually dies out. It used to make me feel a little uneasy at first, for when we were in the valley and heard a cannon every man would fix up his things, and by the time he got that done marching orders would come, but here we do not mind it any more than if nothing was going on..."[2]

Battle wrote home again on 18 January, stating that their lines were unusually quiet, and that he was aware that "...picket firing has been stopped on the lines. We haven't heard any for several days, neither have we heard any cannonading. The peace question is all the excitement in camp now. From what I saw in the "Examiner" this morning I think myself there is something in the wind. I do hope peace will be made before spring. The men are getting very discouraged, and to tell the truth, they have cause to be. Some of our regiment was down on the lines Sunday, and they say the troops have not had any meat for five days. If the men are not fed they will not stay with the army. They are deserting from the lines every night, and going to the Yankees...We expect to go on picket this coming Sunday, to be gone a week."[3]

January 26 1865 was a clear and cold winter day as the 4th NCST was ordered to go out on picket duty below Petersburg near the Appomattox River, an assignment which everyone seemed to dread.4 Pvt. John Endie, who had been earlier detached as provost guard at Danville, Virginia, returned to the company on 27 January. Walter Battle wrote about the miserable time they had on the picket lines a few days later on 29 January, indicating that several men again took opportunity to desert. This was a problem that became epidemic in the army during the last winter and continue until the end. Battle stated, "...Last week we spent on the front lines doing picket duty in the place of Scales Brigade which has been sent off. We had a awful time; the whole week it rained, and sleeted part of the time, and the rest of the time, it kept up the coldest wind that I ever felt. The men on vidette had to be relieved every half hour, to keep from freezing. One man in our regiment got so cold he could hardly talk when he was relieved. On the right of our brigade, the Yankees were some six of eight hundred yards off, but on the left we were near enough to talk to each other in an ordinary tone of voice, though we were not allowed to speak to them or to communicate with them in any way. We had two men to desert our regiment and go to the enemy. They were two brothers....The Consolidation Bill, which is to be carried into effect shortly will cause a good deal of desertion among our best soldiers. I am afraid our company and regiment will lose their name after all the hard service which we have done since the commencement of the war."5

Battle mentioned his concern over a law recently passed by the Confederate congress, known as the "Consolidation Act" allowing commanders to consolidate state regiments that had been decimated in previous battles who had less than 200 men remaining. The modern reader must understand that other than a few recent conscripts, the typical Tar Heel soldier had survived the War to this point and found great solace in knowing that many of his comrades were also friends and family from their same hometown. Consolidation meant having to serve the remainder of their term of service potentially with strangers, which may have been more convenient for battle tactics, but doubtless would play havoc on morale. After enduring the marches, privations in camp, and horrors of battle together, this new law was offensive to most soldiers because it would potentially separate them from comrades.

Fortunately, it did not affect the 4th NCST in this way, but nonetheless, Battle's concern was quite well-founded. The Consolidation Act resulted in Brig. Gen. William R. Cox's brigade (the 2d NCST under Maj. James T. Scales; the 4th NCST, now led by Capt. John B. Forcum; the 14th NCST, commanded by Lt. Col. William A. Johnston; and the 30th NCT under Capt. David C. Allen was to absorb remnants of the 1st and 3d NCST which were commanded by Maj. Louis C. Latham and Maj. William T. Bennett, respectively. The move was largely due to their decreased size following heavy losses in 1864. The brigade remained so comprised until the end of the War.6 As February dawned, the mother of Robert Linster, Company C, wrote to his captain, John F. Stancill, inquiring as to her son's status. Linster was arrested earlier that winter by General Cox, who ordered him into confinement pending a court martial.

Captain Stancill's response to Linster's mother basically released the soldier of any responsibility for the arrest, stating, "...Robert was placed under arrest by order of Gen Cox & appeared before a court Martial a short time since, but the court being unable to make out a case of it honorably acquitted him and he is now on duty as orderly Sgt. of his company. You may rest assured that he is not at all disgraced by it for he done nothing in the first place to be arrested..."7 On 7 February, the 4th NCST had to form and march "some 10 or 12 miles north of Petersburg" to build some earthworks; but by 10 February they had returned to their camp.8 Nat Raymer, also a band member, did not spend much time in the trenches around Petersburg; but while the regiment was working on the trenches, he managed to get out on the lines and record what he saw on 9 February. This letter was published in the Iredell Express:

in the Trenches near Petersburg

I have always had a great curiosity to see the trenches around Petersburg-I had heard so much said concerning them—such extravagance, almost impossible ___, and incredible stories, that I was determined to see for myself, and accordingly, on the 3rd inst., set out with that object in view. After crossing "Pocahontas Bridge" on the Northern suburbs of the city, I turned directly to the left on the City Point railroad, down which I walked about three quarters of a mile, and after crossing a fine iron bridge, struck the "Covered way" as it is called here, which means simply a ditch sufficiently deep to protect persons from the enemy's shots. From the western terminus of this ditch to the trenches proper the distance is something near three quarters of a mile.--it is from three to eight feet wide, and the backs included from seven to nine feet deep-there is no "covering" at all.

This constitutes the chief thoroughfare through which all men belonging to Ransom's brigade go to and from the city. On nearing the lines I discovered many similar ditches intersecting the main one and thence running in every conceivable direction. It is no wonder I got lost;--a man might as well attempt to explore the Mammoth cave alone and without light,--but by the most indefatigable exertions, and by making all possible inquiries of every one I met, I at last found the headquarters of the 49th N.C. Reg't.--and thence, in company with a competent guide...I continued my observations and explorations with a greater degree of satisfaction. The men I found all burrowed in the earth like so many ground rats,--from four to six to a hole, which is called a "bomb proof"; because, in the first place, it is sunken several feet below the surface, and in the second place, it is covered with logs and earth varying from six to ten feet in thickness.

Still; these "Bomb-proofs" are not altogether a safe retreat; it is no very uncommon thing for a heavy mortar shell to penetrate to the interior--an accident which never fails to cause a general getting out, you may well imagine. The fact is, the men have discovered recently that they are safer in the trenches than in their holes during a shelling spree, which occurs perhaps in twenty-four hours sometimes in daylight, sometimes in night, and lasts one or two hours at a time. There is always a lookout kept, and warning given when there is any danger; and men have become as exploit of dodging in the trenches and around the "traverse," that is seldom anyone is hurt. In daylight the shells may be seen distinctly from the time they leave the enemy's mortars until they explode inside our works, and at night their fiery tails, comet like, indicate their course.

The range is entirely too short to admit the sue of artillery, consequently nothing but mortars are used; and like everything else, they are so far beneath the surface in a kind of pit as to be entirely out of sight--no one could know where they are were it not for the cloud of white smoke produced by a discharge, which always betrays their exact locality. Before leaving that part of the subject, however, I should state that the holes in which the men live are small, and so low that a boy of ten years old would scarcely stand erect;--they are dark and damp and in many instances smoked thoroughly black by the little handful of stone coal and old field pine, their only hope of fire. It is really surprising that such universal good health prevails;--I did not see a single sick man not withstanding their exceedingly disagreeable mode of life. One of the greatest inconveniences to which they are subject is the horrible mud when it rains, or during a thaw.

*Matthew Brady's Photo of Confederate Interior Lines shows "bomb-proofs" at Petersburg VA, 1864.*
*Courtesy US National Archives.*

A ditch leads to every domicile to others, and also to the main trench, the bottom of which, in wet weather, is filled with mud and six inches deep,--yet no man dares attempt to shun it by going over a bank; so sure he risks it he is shot at,--in this way many have been killed by unnecessarily exposing themselves. Really the lines of two armies are not more than two hundred yards apart at the farthest, and in some places the distance is not half so great. The pickets, of course, are much nearer, scarcely fifty yards separate them, yet, there they have lain for the last three or four months, and how much longer they may remain we cannot tell.

The Yankees live like our men, beneath the surface of the earth--it is rare that one shows his head above the breastworks. You might stand on a mound in the center of that wreck of earth (for such it is in reality) and imagine that no living soul dwells within five miles of you, while in truth the very earth beneath and around you is full of living soldiers numbered by hundreds and thousands. I might say a great deal with reference to the defenses, but it might be imprudent--I will only add that so far as I am able to judge I believe them to be impregnable. The men I found cheerful and lively, more so than I could be under the circumstances, unless, like them, I had served a six month's apprenticeship, and then, besides, had the unlimited quantities of good things from home in which they are luxuriating.

I confess to a feeling of squeamishness once or twice when a ponderous mortar shell would light near enough to give one the head ache; and once I was chilled slightly when...I mounted a small bank to take just one peep at the "Pats"--I was really fidgety, and actually could not suppress a desire to see what was going on over there--it may have been a weakness bordering perhaps on a peculiar feminine trait, but so it was--We ventured our heads up barely a second, and the moment after we stepped back in the ditch a minnie cut the dirt immediately above. Well, it is hardly necessary for me to state that I didn't suffer my curiosity to get the better of prudence a second time...Fortunately, on the day I spent in the trenches, the ground was frozen and towards the evening snow fell, through which I felt my way to camp where I landed safely at 9 P.M., thankful that the time is not yet come when it be necessary for me to make my home under the ground.

On 14 February there was more action at Hatcher's Run. The 4th NCST along with Cox's brigade were called out, although not engaged, but the men were exposed to the harsh Virginia winter conditions, causing some to become ill. Pvt. Walter Battle mentioned the brief hiatus, which he did not experience, due to his having been detailed to guard supply wagons, "...Our division was ordered down on the extreme right last Sunday a week ago, to meet the Yankees at Hatcher's Run. Our division was not engaged; the other two divisions of our corps did some fighting before we got there. The troops were gone about a week, and they suffered considerably from the cold. It was snowing and sleeting when they left. I missed the pleasure of that trip. I have been permanently detailed at brigade headquarters in charge of a guard, to guard quartermaster's stores, and things generally among the wagon yards... Our brigade goes on picket this morning, Saturday..."9 Private John F. Thompson was in a Richmond Hospital since 1862, but released sometime before February 1865 as he was paroled between 14-17 February at Burkeville Junction, Virginia, and did not return to Company K.

*Sketch of Petersburg Trenches. Courtesy NPS*

Their division was located near Swift Creek until 17 February 1865 when three of its brigades were moved to Sutherland's Depot on the right of the Confederate lines. Two soldiers from Company K previously captured and sent to the Federal prison at Point Lookout, Maryland, Henry Severs and W.D. Peeler, were paroled and exchanged on 18 February, although neither made it back to the lines to engage the enemy again. Cox's brigade covered the division front at Swift Creek during the movement and afterward went back to meet the division at Sutherland's Depot. They again faced skirmishing there, and Pvt. William Murr sustained a gunshot wound in the knee on 23 February and was sent to a Richmond Hospital. Another man from Company K, Pvt. Michael Rowland, who had only recently returned from incarceration at Salisbury Prison for desertion on 1 December 1864, but he quickly took "French Leave" and deserted again on 24 February while the regiment was near Sutherland's Depot. Pvt. Milas Holshouser had already been captured and wounded once each in the war, and returned to the ranks in 1864. He deserted on 28 February, but later returned to the ranks before April. The regiment did not stay at Sutherland's Depot for very long -- on 25 February the division moved eleven miles to Sutherland Station on the right of Petersburg, where they again encamped in the trenches once more until at least 10 March.10

In the interim, Pvt. William Buis who was captured at Gettysburg in 1863, was paroled from Federal prison at Elmira, New York on 2 March and sent to Richmond for exchange but did not return to the company. Maj. Frances Shaffner reported on 10 March in his diary on that day that conditions were still wet and muddy, but the overall health of the regiment was good, as was his perception of their morale, "Yesterday and last night rain fell abundantly, and to-day, the weather being much colder, and quantity of hail has been falling…The health of the troops is very good, and they are in better cheer than I had anticipate.--The feeling is much better than it was when I left a month ago, and the discipline enforced very rigidly. The rations now issued are enough to sustain the life of any reasonable man notwithstanding the many reports to the contrary.--Our Brigade is at present on our right about 12 miles beyond Petersburg.--We occupy a front position at the trenches, in full view of the enemy, and within hearing of his drums. Everything is remarkably quiet to-day. Yesterday there was a little cannonading on our left, but none in this immediate neighborhood..."[11]

Dr. Shaffner again opined on 12 March that the improving weather conditions made a new campaign inevitable even though the regiment was still in trenches, "...We still occupy the same position on the front lines which we did a week ago. Comparatively speaking everything remains quiet. There is a continual warfare between the pickets on our right, and occasionally the sullen boom of artillery chimes in. Immediately in front there has been no interchange of shots. The hostile picquets [sic - pickets] are within 100 yards of each other, and on open ground, but by mutual consent, there is no firing. The roads are drying rapidly, and very soon a heavy engagement must ensue. Rations are ample, and with a blind confidence in the wisdom and skill of our noble commander, they are ready to do anything at his bidding..."[12] On 15 March, former company commander Capt. Francis McNeely, who resigned after the battle of Seven Pines due to health problems to serve as a drillmaster at the Camp of Instruction in Greensboro, North Carolina, requested to have his commission reinstated. Because McNeely was suffering from "tuberculosis of lung with haemopthisis, " instead of returning to the front lines with Company K, he was promoted to major and reassigned to the 63d Regiment North Carolina Militia in Rowan County, the former nemesis of the Rowan Rifle Guards during the antebellum era.[13]

Meanwhile, in Company K, 2d Lt. Moses Locke Bean was promoted to first lieutenant on 16 March, although he had been in command of Company K nearly four months since Captain Hofflin was wounded and removed from command. Bean was appointed to serve as acting regimental adjutant also.[14] Bean was earlier wounded at the battle of Spotsylvania by an artillery shell fragment in his shoulder, and tried to continued in the ranks but was removed by the surgeon when it became evident he could not tolerate campaigning. He was sent to a hospital, but in typical form, was not yet fully recovered when he managed to return to the company sometime between December 1864 and February 1865. A weekly report from General Hospital No. 3 in Lynchburg, Virginia shows his diagnosis as "*febris intermittent tertiana*" indicating he developed an infection from his wound.[15] Bean had another interesting characteristic, in that he had long advocated for enlisting slaves as soldiers.

With ranks dwindling from casualties and illnesses late in the war, Bean used his authority as an officer to solicit a plan he had earlier devised to recruit a company of slaves from his home town of Salisbury. Bean wrote to his district state representative, A.G. Ramsey, on 11 March 1865 requesting authority to recruit at least one, possibly more companies, referring to a recent act by the Confederate congress enabling the army to replenish its heavily depleted ranks with slave recruits. In an effort to persuade the representative, he stated that he was one of his constituents from Salisbury, and "…could serve my country to a greater advantage against our enemies" with such companies, and argued his strong belief they would be effective soldiers.27 Ramsey agreed, and wrote to the Confederate Secretary of War, J.C. Breckenridge, on 16 March stating he hoped Bean's request would be approved, but did not feel he or anyone else in his county had authority to make such a decision. Breckenridge wrote back on 8 April that he wanted to pursue Bean's plan. This would have been a significant landmark in history, but it was in fact too little too late, as the Army of Northern Virginia soon surrendered. Bean was unaware that his request was approved at the time of Lee's surrender, however.16

In spite of a common dread of impending action, Shaffner also reveals a typical soldier's wit, telling of unwanted visitors in his shelter within the trenches, "…I wish (for my own amusement) you could spend one day in my cabin. The mice are here by dozens, and occasionally a large rat exhibits himself. Last night these creatures kept up a great carousal. They rumbled over everything, neither did they spare my blankets. It would do you no good to mount a stool       here and scream! The mice would only stare at you in amazement and probably hitherto unseen, one would drop upon you from the roof. Last night one shared pillow, but soon disappeared at the stroke of my hand. Of course my scanty commissariat suffers in supporting this large addition to my Mess, and I am almost tempted to hunt a Tom cat for boon companion. Something must be done, and that speedily, or I shall be without breakfast every morning..."17

Another man was paroled from Point Lookout Maryland on 18 March, Pvt. Jeremiah Eddleman who was previously captured at Fisher's Hill on 22 September 1864. Similar to other soldiers recently paroled, available evidence suggests he as well failed to return to the company for unknown reasons. Only three days later, Pvt. Wallace Josey who was incarcerated at Point Lookout, died of scurvy further attesting to the tribulations found in Civil War military prisons. Meanwhile, Pvt. Walter Battle wrote his last letter home on 23 March. He described the regiment's most recent movements and reveals there was a ban on correspondents' reporting war news. This ban explains the relative silence of Nat Raymer during this period, who, based on his earlier reactions to what he perceived as censorship in 1864, must have been furious that he could no longer report his unit's activities to folks at home. Battle penned, "…We have moved twice since I wrote that letter. After the first move, we were temporarily attached to Mahone's Division, the last move we made we joined our own division, which is in the entrenchments in front of Petersburg. Our Brigade is on the extreme left of it, between the Appomattox River and Swift Creek, with the river between us and the Yankees…The papers are not allowed to publish any war news, so we are as completely ignorant as you are as to what is going on..."18

Tactically, Lee found himself in a bind as the month of March 1865 drew to an end. As Grant was closing in on him, the Confederates would have to abandon Petersburg and Richmond when Sherman crossed the Roanoke River. Meanwhile, in North Carolina, Johnston's army had become so small it could no longer slow down Sherman. Lee did not want to abandon Petersburg and Richmond before the roads dried, however; and he realized his need for all possible advantages in order for his army to escape Grant and unite with Johnston in North Carolina. Lee decided to stall, in a plan he devised with input from Gen. John B. Gordon, the flinty Alabamian who had thus far been wounded five times and survived. Gordon thought he could succeed in an assault on Fort Stedman, a large earthen fort located on the Union lines roughly one mile south of the Appomattox River. Lee agreed, and the assault proceeded on 25 March, just after midnight. However, the 4th NCST did not participate in this attack.19

Former regimental commander Brig. Gen. Bryan Grimes was commissioned as a major general on 23 February and placed in command of Rodes' old division which included Cox's Brigade. He described the layout of his lines as the last days of the War began to unfold, "On the night of Sunday, April 1, 1865, my division occupied a portion of the defenses around the city of Petersburg, my left resting on Otey's Battery, near the memorable Crater, my right extending to the dam on a creek beyond Battery Forty-five, Ramseur's old Brigade of North Carolinians, being commanded by Colonel W.R. Cox, Second North Carolina, holding appointment as temporary brigadier; on their right Archer's Brigade of Virginia Junior Reserves; Grimes' old Brigade of North Carolinians, commanded by Colonel D.G. Gowan, of the thirty-second North Carolina; Battle's Brigade of Alabamians, commanded by Colonel Hobson, of Fifth Alabamians; Cook's Brigade of Georgians, commanded by Colonel Nash, extending to the left in the order above named, numbering for duty about two thousand two hundred muskets, covering at least three and a half miles of the trenches around Petersburg, with one-third of my men constantly on picket duty in our front, one-third kept awake at the breastworks during the night, with one-third only off duty at a time, and they required always to sleep with their accouterments on and upon their arms, ready to repel an attack at a moment's warning."[20]

### *Appomattox Court House-Last Days of the Confederacy*

On 2 April, Lee knew it had to be done; he ordered the evacuation of Petersburg and sent word to Richmond to President Davis he could no longer protect them. One soldier in the 4th NCST wrote of the movement away from Petersburg, "About five o'clock a.m. the enemy captured a part of our works in two places - one near Petersburg, another near Hatcher's Run. Hard fighting all day. The enemy pressed through to the Appomattox River above Petersburg. About ten p.m. we evacuated Richmond and Petersburg. We fell back across the Appomattox River across the Pocahantas Bridge, then marched up the river. Marched slowly all night."[21] Company K lost one man captured on 2 April at Petersburg, Pvt. John Locket who was taken to Hart's Island, New York for incarceration until after the war. Some other men from Company K would soon join him there, as Privates L.M. Brady, John Kenter, and Milas Holshouser was all captured there on 3 April and likewise sent to Hart's Island. Holshouser had only recently returned to the lines from deserter status, but consistent with the earlier trend in this regiment for soldiers who had done honorable service in past engagements, no charges were pressed. It may also have stemmed from a lack of manpower as well, but Holshouser had a sterling record before deserting. As Federal soldiers entered Richmond on 3 April after Lee abandoned Petersburg and ordered the army to retreat toward Appomattox Court House. One Company K man, William Murr, was left in a hospital there and later captured. He was turned over to the Union provost guards.

Lee continued to retreat until he encountered Federal cavalry at Sailor's Creek on 6 April. The 4th NCST remained in Cox's brigade, Grimes' division, when the following events occurred, "...Grimes Division was covering Lee's retreat, when a determined stand was made at Sailor's Creek and the enemy held in check until both flanks of the division were turned by superior numbers, and the command was saved from capture by a rapid retreat. Grimes stayed with his men until all were over the creek and the bridge destroyed, then plunging his horse Warren, into the water, crossed under a perfect storm of bullets and made his escape."[22] The 4th NCST was heavily engaged that day, and according to one private, were "...attacked early in the morning while near Burkeville Junction [17 miles SW of Amelia Court House].We fought all day, falling back slowly until about sunset when the enemy massed their forces and attacked us with great vigor. Broke our lines which caused our troops to retreat in great confusion, leaving near a hundred wagons in the enemy's hands. Our loss pretty heavy in prisoners. We then fell back to the High Rail Bridge across the Dan River and rested during the night."[23]

After the war, U.S. Army Maj. John Moore asked former General Bryan Grimes to draft an account of his experiences during the last few days before Lee surrendered the Army of Northern Virginia to Maj. Gen. Ulysses Grant. Grimes agreed, and wrote more of the action on 7 April, "The next morning (Friday) we continued our march down the railroad and formed line of battle on the "impediment of Caesar's'--the wagon train—marching by the left flank through the woods parallel to the road traveled by the wagon train, and about one hundred or so yards distant from the road. Upon reaching the road and point that turns towards Lynchburg from the Cumberland road, three of my brigades, Cook's, Cox's and Cowand's, had crossed the Cumberland road and were in line of battle, and at right angles with Battle's and Archer's Brigades, who were still parallel with the Cumberland road. Heavy firing was going on at this point, when General Mahone came rushing up and reported that the enemy had charged, turning his flank and driving his men from their guns and the works which he had erected early in the day for the protection of these cross roads."

Grimes continued, "I then ordered my three brigades, Cook's, Cox's and Cowand's, at a double-quick on the line, with Battle and Archer, charging the enemy and driving them well off from Mahone's works, recapturing the artillery taken by them and capturing a large number of prisoners, and holding this position until sent for by General Lee, who complimented the troops of the division upon the charge made and the service rendered, ordering me to leave a skirmish line in my front, and that Fields' Division would occupy my position; to hurry with all possible dispatch to the road which intersected the Lynchburg road, as the enemy's cavalry were reported to be approaching by that road. We reached the road, halting and keeping the enemy in check until the wagons had passed, and then continued the march parallel with the road traveled by the wagon train, continuing thus to march until night, when we took the road following to protect the trains."[24] E.A. Osborne later recalled that "a charge was made and the enemy driven back and a large number of prisoners captured. General Lee complimented the men in person for their gallantry on this occasion..."[25]

Beginning very early on the morning of Saturday, 8 April, Grimes' division marched all day along the Lynchburg Road but found no contact with the Federals. This was a welcome relief to the men, who were "much jaded" from want of food over the past few weeks. Later that evening, Grimes allowed them to stop long enough to draw rations but quickly resumed their march after dark. Even with a brief meal, the men were still "hungry, tired and sore, but cheerful and brave. About 9 o'clock that night heavy firing was heard in front, and the men were ordered forward, marching most of the night, passing through the town of Appomattox Court House before day..."[26] Grimes' division came into camp about eight miles from Appomattox Court House on the morning of 9 April. Just after dawn, they joined Gordon's 2d division and formed in line of battle. Almost immediately, the Federals attacked and attempted to flank the left wing. Federal artillery completely "enveloped" the area in smoke as incoming rounds tore the earth around the 4th NCST. Grimes ordered an advance, and his troops struck the hastily erected federal works, pushing the enemy back some three-quarters of a mile to a small range of hills before reforming.[27] Cox's brigade was at a right angle to the rest of the division on the extreme right of Grimes' lines, with orders to guard his flank. General Gordon sent repeated messages to Grimes ordering him to withdraw "now." Grimes refused, thinking Gordon failed to grasp the excellent position his men held, commanding the only safe exit route along the Lynchburg road. Eventually, the stoic Grimes received a message from Lee himself, directing him to withdraw immediately. Grimes reluctantly complied and ordered his skirmishers to withdraw by the left flank. As he did, Cox's men were ordered to maintain their position in line of battle until the rear of the division had passed at least "100 yards" in order to screen their movement on his right flank and rear. No one realized it at the time, but the Tar Heels had just executed their last tactical formation of the War.[28] One private remarked, "we had no idea we were so close to the end…"[29]

## *The Last Volley*

When the Federals realized Grimes was moving back, they cheered loudly and charged out in front of the division from behind their earthworks, firing and threatening to disrupt the retreat. Cox immediately ordered his brigade, still lying unnoticed at the brow of a small hill, to stand and fire a volley directly into the stunned Federals, who could only fall back into the woods. Although this event became the subject of quite a debate in post-war accounts, it is now generally known as the Last Volley of the Confederacy, and the survivors from Company K participated. Lieutenant Bean was commanding the company when Grimes ordered Cox's North Carolinians to fire the last volley.[30] Cox's men quickly rejoined the division which marched to a spot near the position outside Appomattox it had held just before dawn that day. Grimes eventually caught up with Gordon and hastily inquired where he should post his division in line of battle. Gordon retorted "anywhere you choose" which offended Grimes. Gordon promptly informed him that the army was to be surrendered, and Grimes indignantly told Gordon that he should have told him earlier, that he could have "…escaped with my division to North Carolina." Grimes also said he planned to "…inform my men of the purpose of surrender, and that whomsoever desired to escape that calamity could go with me."[31]

The determined Grimes then turned his horse, who he had named "Warren" (who, incidentally, had managed to survive thus far without wound and would remain with Grimes for several years afterward, suggesting his fare with horses had improved). Gordon followed after him and, when he caught up, simply put his hand on Grimes' shoulder, and calmly asked him if he really wanted to "desert the army, and tarnish his honor as a soldier." Gordon also mentioned that desertion would be a negative reflection on General Lee as well.[32] Grimes wisely reconsidered and purposed not to inform his men. However, rumors were already spreading of surrender; and when Grimes told them he feared it was "fact," a soldier in the 4th NCST reacted by "tossing down his rifle, raising his hands and crying out 'Blow Gabriel, Blow! My God, let him blow, I am ready to die!'"[33] Pvt. Sumpter A. Hoover of Company C reflected in a letter home that when he saw Maj. Gen. Ulysses S. Grant coming into the Rebel camp under a flag of truce, he knew it wasn't long until the end, "There we were surrounded by the Union soldiers and Lee surrendered on the 9th of April, 1865. I saw Grant and his staff come over into our camp carrying a white flag, hunting General Lee…Then and there we were ordered to stack arms, then we knew what was up."[34] The next two days were spent preparing parole documents and eating rations given by the Federal army. There was a great deal of fraternizing between the armies in spite of orders to the contrary. Some Federals even offered money to the Rebels who had none for their journey home, but not all reacted positively to the gesture. One Confederate was quite offended, noting that unlike the "yankees" who only thought of getting something for themselves, Southern people were generous and would help their own during their journey home.[35]

# The Surrender

The tattered veterans of the 4th NCST were under command of Capt. John B. Forcum of Company C* and stood on the brigade's right when the division was formed to formally surrender and stack arms on 12 April. Grimes looked at them a few moments and finally ordered them to stack arms. Amidst "bitter tears" the men came to the grim reality that the war was lost.[36] As the remnant of Company K stacked their arms, E.A. Osborne overheard the following bittersweet remark from one of the men, "...a member of Company K, Fourth Regiment, whose name I cannot remember, set his gun down at the surrender with a sigh, saying, "Sit there, Betsy, you've made many of them bite the dust."[37] When this was done, General Grimes called the North Carolinians to "attention" for the last time and had them to file past him in order that he might shake hands with each man. As he did so, with streaming eyes and faltering voice, he said: "Go home, boys, and act like men, as you have always done during the war." From the ranks, one grizzled and barefooted veteran looked at Grimes as he passed, and remarked, "Good bye, General; God bless you; we will go home, make three more crops, and try them again."[38] Company K surrendered fourteen enlisted men and one officer, 1st Lt. Moses Bean on the morning of 12 April 1865. Bean somehow managed to get home to Salisbury only a few days afterward and took the Oath of Allegiance at Salisbury on 30 May 1865.[39] The names of Company K men present at the surrender on 12 April 1865 were as follows:

1st Lt. Moses Locke Bean
2nd Sgt. Alfred C. Carter
Cpl. Andrew Mowrey
Pvt. George Basinger
Pvt. Wilburn C. Frayley
Pvt. James McCanless
Pvt. William McQueen
Pvt. Frances M. Mills
Pvt. George A. Misenheimer
Pvt. George D. Snuggs

Muster roll data further shows that Company K had five other men on detached duties at the time of Lee's surrender, including privates Lindsey Bryant; J.L. Bogle; James W. Bean, who was also listed as "disabled"; Alexander M. McQueen, who was working as a teamster; and Michael Beaver, who was detached to the ambulance corps. Each of the latter soldiers mentioned was paroled on 12 April but it is doubtful they were present with the other ten men in the company for the surrender ceremonies and the final stacking of arms. Of the ten men stacking arms on the morning of 12 April, only 1st Lt. Moses Locke Bean, 2nd Sgt. Alfred C. Carter, Cpl. Andrew Mowrey, Pvt. George Basinger, Pvt. Wilburn C. Frayley, Pvt. William McQueen, Pvt. Frances M. Mills were present with the original Rowan Rifle Guards at Fort Johnston at Smithville, North Carolina on 30 May 1861 at Fort Johnston. Likewise, Pvt. Lindsey Bryant, who was on detached duties on 9 April 1865, was also an original member of the Rowan Rifle Guards present on 30 May 1861.[40]

---

*The war was equally as difficult for Jesse Forcum's cousins of Iredell County. In one family of four brothers serving in the 4th Regiment of North Carolina Infantry, Bazel Forcum was killed in mid-1862; William Forcum was killed at Spotsylvania Court House on 12 May 1864; and John B. Forcum (who had received a fractured skull at Gettysburg, recovered, and attained the rank of captain) was in command of the 4th Regiment with General Lee at the surrender at Appomattox in 1865. (Forcum Family files, Iredell County Public Library, Statesville, North Carolina).

This reflects that Among the 115 men present in Company K during 1861, there was a .06 percent survival rate across the war. This implies a 94 percent casualty rate in Company K, including those wounded or killed in action, captured/prisoner or war, desertion, medical disability, and death due to illness.[41] Comparatively, Cox's brigade surrendered 51 officers and 521 enlisted men for a total of 572, roughly 30 percent of the remaining troops in Grimes' division. Grimes surrendered 172 officers (including staff) and 1,727 enlisted soldiers for a total of 1,899 men in his division at Appomattox. Comparatively, Grimes commanded about 6 percent of the 28,231 men reported for the Army of Northern Virginia on 9 April. A review of statistical data associated with the surrender suggests that with six regiments in Cox's brigade, there were an average of 95 men in each regiment. Hence, the number of survivors in Company K may be slightly lower than average for their division due to having less men available at the time of surrender.[42]

On 10 April, the men gathered their composure; and Grant ordered the confederates be provided with rations. Many started their journey home and had plenty of time now to remember where they had been. On 11 April, another incident is supposed to have occurred involving the 4th NCST regimental band, led by William Neave. Neave and his younger brother Edward were former members of the Salisbury Brass Band, and Edward served in Company K. Although one of the band members wrote about it in their diary, J.C. Steele, the story may be apocryphal as no other documentation of the incident existed and the last days of Lee's command have literally been examined and accounted for minute by minute. William Neave, then leader of the Army of Northern Virginia Band, supposedly led them in a final musical tribute to the defeated leader. The story was described as follows:

"Both General Lee and General Grimes had their headquarters on the opposite side of the road from our camp and about four hundred yards distant. Late in the night I was sent to General Grimes' camp for the last batch of our paroles. While standing waiting for them a band came up and serenaded General Lee. I joined the crowd near his tent, while the band played that beautiful air, "Parting is Pain," also known as "When the Swallows Homeward Fly." There was light in the tent, and the General stepped outside and asked to whom he was indebted for such sweet music, and was told the band of the 4th North Carolina Regiment. He took a step forward as though about to say something, but he could not. He just raised his hands like a benediction and almost sobbed out: "God bless you, men, God bless you! I can say no more."[43] The war was over for The Rowan Rifles.

# Chapter Ten

# After Lee's Surrender:
# The Road Home

*"...everything we had was gone"*

One can only imagine what those exhausted and tainted men felt as they spent their last bivouac trying to organize their thoughts, which for most were anxiously turned to their return home. Once they received their last army rations and paroles from the Union army, the Company K survivors started making their way back to the Old North State. The following incident took place on 13 April and involved some veterans of the 4th NCST who lend a lighter perspective to what was likely a common scenario in those final days. The eyewitness wrote, "...it was the next day we reached a little country store, where we found congregated about a hundred pardoned men and a number of women from the neighborhood. The store was a tithing station and a place where rations were issued to the needy soldiers' wives, and it was ration day, which accounted for the presence of the women. There was a small lot of meat to be given to the women. The storekeeper said the rest of the meat had been sent to Danville a few days before. He also had a lot of cowpeas. As General Grimes rode up some men from his old regiment, the 4th North Carolina, told him of the situation, saying that they did not wish to take the meat from the women, but that the man had refused to let them have the peas. The man stated that he could not let the peas go, for his bond would be responsible. General Grimes said that he would be responsible and give a receipt for the peas. The man still resisted, until Grimes finally told him that he would use force sufficient to take them, then he gave up the peas. Some of the women then said they would cook the peas for the men, and all went off satisfied. Most of the men had haversacks, but one stepped behind the house, pulled off his drawers, and made a sack by tying the legs at the ankles and off he marched with the peas in the forked sack around his neck."[1]

Two of the 4th NCST band members, correspondent Nat Raymer and his former tent-mate J.C. Steele, traveled together. Steele described their journey in his diary, "On Wednesday the 12th, [April] we were up early and started for home on foot. Nat Raymer who had been the war correspondent of the home papers during the war, and myself who had been room mates and bed fellows during the war planned that we would make the trip home together, and take the most direct route we could find. We would have to depend on the country for a living as we had neither rations nor money, but we found the same hospitality for which Virginia was noted, still existed. On our way home we crossed Dan River a few miles above Danville and came through Leaksville, N.C., and spent the last night at Mocksville. The war was over and I was back home, and everything we had was gone..."[2] On the same day, the town of Salisbury in Rowan County received a visit from Union cavalry under Maj. Gen. George Stoneman, who was quickly moving toward the town from Statesville on his search to destroy government facilities to destroy them.

### Stoneman's Raid – *"Look out the window, the Yankees are burning Salisbury"*

By February 1865, citizens of Salisbury were terrified by rumors that Federal Cavalry raiders under Maj. Gen. George Stoneman were moving from Columbia, South Carolina to Charlotte. Residents began to stash their valuables in anticipation of a raid, and some went as far as to have large trenches dug near their dwellings where they buried fine goods such as silver or even clothing wrapped in cloth.[3] Several former members of the Rowan Rifles had already returned to Salisbury due to wounds or illnesses by the time some 4,000 troopers from Maj. Gen. George Stoneman's Federal cavalry raided the town on 12 April, including privates' Moses Bencini and Jeremiah Glover. At this time Salisbury was host to a several Confederate government-run facilities, including the Salisbury Prison which contained both Southern political prisoners and Union soldiers; a distillery making liquor for hospital use; and the Salisbury Supply Depot, headquarters for the Commissary of Subsistence of the Fifth District which was comprised of nine surrounding counties, and several hospitals, including Murphy's Hall where during antebellum numerous conscription balls were held, Barkers Factory near the railroad depot and a hospital, in addition to at least a dozen other buildings including churches that were converted for medical use. Because the town was a transportation hub with excellent roadway access and railroads, it was quickly pressed into service by the Confederate Medical Department and by 1865 hundreds of wounded and invalids were pouring into town each month.4

There was also an Ordnance Depot containing uniforms, blankets, small arms ammunition and artillery rounds. Maj. Abraham Myers was chief of commissary, whose primary duty was to procure pork, flour, meal, salt and such for the troops. Myers was the same merchant who provided his wife and other ladies of Salisbury with silken cloth for the Rowan Rifles new flag in 1861. In 1865, the Salisbury Depot also had a foundry which turned out numerous types of weapons and ammunition. In addition, Salisbury was also the site of the government-run Nitre and Mining Bureau, which manufactured chemicals needed for gunpowder.5 On the morning of 12 April, General Stoneman was well-aware of Confederate operations in Salisbury and was bent on their destruction. Stoneman was well aware of its importance but for some reason nearly decided to bypass the town in favor of moving his troops eastward where Maj. Gen. William T. Sherman's army recently defeated the remnants of Maj. Gen. Joseph Johnston's western Confederate army at Bentonville in March 1865 and were moving on toward the capital city of Raleigh. Rumors intensified that "the Yankees" were coming from the western counties several weeks before the raid, but on 3 April Confederate authorities in the town received credible word that Stoneman's cavalry was in fact near Charlotte and also in the western counties headed east toward Salisbury.

The militia force in Rowan County was small in 1865, and composed largely of men too old or medically unable to tolerate active campaigning, although it still had a few able-bodied men to attempt a temporary defense when the veteran Federal troopers came thrashing through the streets of Salisbury. When convalescing wounded soldiers staying in local hospitals heard, many volunteered to assist and hastily organized several small companies to man the fourteen artillery pieces held by the undermanned militia.6 Often referred to as the Home Guards, this haphazard band who assembled to defend the town was closer to the legendary desperate and "ragged Johnny Rebel" stereotype than any other unit discussed thus far, but it problems that had little to do with adequate supplies. The force was about 800 strong, with fourteen cannons. In addition to the groups already mentioned, it also included several armed citizens with no military training, and at least one hundred Virginian soldiers who had stopped at the railroad depot enroute to another location, and several companies of Union soldiers described as "foreigners...Irishmen" who had finagled their way out of the Salisbury prison by agreeing to "galvanize" and assist the home guards by taking an oath.7

Maj. Frances McNeely, the former Rowan Rifles commander, was commanding the militia artillery, in spite of his poor health.8 There have also circulated numerous stories that Capt. William C. Coughenhour was in Salisbury during the raid, although there is only anecdotal evidence. Coughenhour served on the staff of Brig. Gen. James Dearing until 1 March 1865, when he was assigned to Brig. Gen. William P. Robert's brigade just before being paroled at Appomattox on 9 April. However, there is a discrepancy in records regarding what Coughenhour actually did after being transferred to Robert's brigade staff for the remainder of the war. His name does not appear on the Appomattox surrender rolls although other records of staff officers suggest he was at Appomattox on 9 April. Captain Coughenhour had presumably just returned home following his surrender at Appomattox and was reportedly nominated for mayor shortly afterward. Further confounding the story, another source suggested that Coughenhour was serving as a militia officer when Stoneman's cavalry raided Salisbury, only three days after Appomattox. As Stoneman's cavalry raiders attacked and burned several important buildings on 12 April including the Salisbury Prison, clothing depot and ordnance stores, Coughenhour reportedly negotiated with Stoneman to prevent the burning of several additional buildings. It is most likely he was still with the army, as there is more supporting evidence for that notion, although his role in the raid on Salisbury is unclear.9

Before dawn on 12 April, Major McNeely had his cannons positioned on the hill located above Grant's Creek near modern Catawba College, waiting for Stoneman's men. As the Cavalrymen approached the town from the west, they could hear trains departing from the railroad depot in town along roads to Charlotte and Morganton as dozens of citizens had recognize the danger and tried to flee. Major McNeely also posted artillery pieces throughout town and along the roads approaching Salisbury from the south and west, supported by the various infantry companies of the make-shift defense force. Just after daybreak, Stoneman sent about 200 troopers from the 11th Kentucky Cavalry and the 13th Tennessee Cavalry regiments (Union) to create a diversion along the Grant's Creek area, approaching from the west.10 Maj. McNeely's artillery opened fire when they saw the troopers. A short skirmish ensued and waking residents realized their imminent danger as they saw the long lines of Union cavalry approaching Salisbury from the west while the artillery was thundering away and small arms began to pop and rattle. Citizens panicked and terror stricken women and children began running house to house seeking a hiding spot until "every door was closed, the inmates were in a momentary expectation of a demand to render up their houses to the flames."11

Stoneman had ordered a "general charge along the entire line" and his troopers rushed the defending Home Guards and artillery, who quickly fell back toward town. In this early phase of the raid, Major McNeely was killed near his battery as they opened fire on the cavalry during the charge up the hill from Grant's Creek. It seems ironic that he survived the rugged campaigns of 1861 and 1862 in the Army of Northern Virginia only to be killed as a militia officer during a small firefight defending his hometown. As Stoneman's columns entered Salisbury, they "rode into the public square with drawn swords in their hands and oaths in their mouths."12 Their oaths were the only ones Union soldiers kept in this raid, however, several of the clever "galvanized Yankees" who were earlier released from the Salisbury Prison to help the Home Guards man the artillery simply fired over their heads, while many abandoned their cannons altogether and ran to meet the Federal troopers while singing praises of the "old flag." Most easily discerned the overwhelming odds, and recognized that resistance was "to no avail," gladly surrendering to their comrades in the Union who were blistering their way across town.13

Stoneman's scheme had called for his troopers to split into a two-pronged force with the main body approaching from the west along modern Jackson Street toward the center of town and the smaller diversionary force that had breached McNeely's artillery at Grant's Creek. Privates Moses Bencini and Jeremiah Glover were both captured while fighting in the streets of Salisbury. Bencini was earlier captured at the third battle of Winchester on 19 September 1864 and confined at Point Lookout, Maryland, until recently exchanged on 15 March 1865. Glover had been wounded three times already, but this was his first capture. They were taken with other prisoners to the military prison at Louisville, Kentucky, and later transferred to Camp Chase, Ohio. Bencini took the Oath of Allegiance on 13 June 1865 and once more returned to Salisbury, but where he remained.

Meanwhile, after crossing Grant's Creek and entering town, Federal troopers from 11th Kentucky cavalry captured a train attempting to depart on the outskirts of town. This particular train contained the widow of former Confederate General Leonidas Polk and his daughters, who were not harmed but their trunks were burned containing all of their clothing. One of the cavalrymen discovered the general's sword in one of the boxes, and kept it for himself as a souvenir.[14]

The small militia force gave a brief resistance, with a few minutes of intense close-quarter firing around houses and trees occurring in town, until the Federal troopers were ordered to burn several houses and other structures. The "destruction of property was immense" according to the Salisbury Banner newspaper. Citizens were horrified, and one shocked woman told her cowering children in amazement, "look out the window, the Yankee's are burning Salisbury." Eventually, the arsenal caught fire and the stored ammunitions began to explode, which reportedly could be seen some fifteen to twenty miles away.[15] The Federal troopers eventually drove the militia out of town, and they encamped in Salisbury for the night. A "feverish state of the public mind" gripped inhabitants of the town afterward, who prayed their homes would not be burned. Stoneman took the large, genteel home of Dr. Josephus Hall as his temporary headquarters, and soldiers camped on its manicured lawns as well as those of other homes throughout town. Stoneman's initial raid on 12 April resulted in capture of fourteen pieces of artillery, and 1,364 prisoners including hundreds of soldiers convalescing in hospitals.[16]

The destruction of Confederate government facilities at Salisbury lost 75,000 suits of uniforms, 250,00 high quality imported English blankets, 10,000 stands of arms, 1,000,000,000 rounds of small arms ammunition, 6,000 lbs. of gunpowder, 10,000 lbs. of artillery ammunition, and three magazines. In addition, the losses included over 15,000,000 in Confederate money, and medical stores valued at $100,000.[17] As always, war yields a plethora of bitter-sweet humor, and Salisbury was no different. Many local legends arose from this scenario, including one suggesting that Stoneman's horse ate some of the boxwood trees located along the front of the Halls' home, which greatly upset Dr. Hall's wife. The story goes that she quickly approached General Stoneman and scolded him, demanding to know why he had allowed his horse to eat her boxwood sprigs. The woman's ardor so tickled him, that he immediately ordered his soldiers not to disturb the ladies horticulture. While it is not certain the incident occurred, the story is an integral part of the oral tradition at the Hall House, now an historic site in Salisbury.

The next morning, 13 April, Stoneman sent a detachment of cavalry toward the Yadkin River in pursuit of the fleeing militia, only to discover they had entrenched themselves on the bluffs just above on the Davidson County bank of the Yadkin River. The militia was commanded by Capt. Zebulon York, and they had named their position "Fort York" in his honor. As the troopers came into view, they suffered heavy musket and cannon fire from the embankments for several minutes. The Federals were unable to scale the heights and withdrew to Salisbury. Stoneman moved west to Statesville shortly afterward, abandoning the town which was now largely in ruins. Even as the Confederates realized their victory, no one celebrated. In a solemn mood, the Home Guards returned to Salisbury only to witness dozens of stunned citizens, many who were now homeless, along with several former slaves who one observer noted were "...at a loss to know what to do with themselves now that they had no masters to look after them." Most simply wandered the streets with an air of "indifference and unconcern" as to their condition.[18]

Accounts of 4th North Carolina members returning to Rowan County indicates some traveled as late as 18 April, only to find Salisbury burned-out and most citizens impoverished. Many discovered they had lost everything they had.[19] Pvt. Nelson Eller, who was earlier captured and near Spotsylvania on 19 May 1864 and incarcerated at Fort Delaware, took the Oath Of Allegience on 15 June 1864, and was released on 19 June 1865. Eller started for home with "nothing but a shirt, an old army blanket serving as trousers and shoes made by a friend from the uppers of an old boot."[20] The next few weeks were arduous and tense at best, while the town was occupied by a Federal garrison commanded by Col. Charles A. Butterfield on 9 May 1865, whose force was comprised of troops from Ohio, Indiana, Illinois and Pennsylvania. Citizens gradually reestablished a sense of order, but the tensions ran high. Although there is no record of unprovoked assaults or other violence occurring toward unarmed citizens, a number of verbal altercations occurred and few fraternized with the Union soldiers.

The youth of Salisbury seemed to take it harder than even the veterans, as their behavior toward the Federal troops was "haughty" and the young women deemed it a "symbol of status" to openly declare to their antagonists that they were "still a rebel."[21] In spite of the animosity both given and received, the Federal troops occupying Salisbury eventually helped rebuild many of the homes and other buildings that were destroyed in the raid. The war was finally over, and those idealistic, enthusiastic youth of 1861 had well proven they could fight, but the humble survivors now had to face the reality that the war was in fact a "lost cause." Many were quite bitter for several years afterward, although most seemed to absorb the loss and continue their civilian lives. The veterans and Rowan County residents who survived the war there gradually realized they had made an indelible mark on Southern culture and United States history and the wounds seemed to heal for many.

### *In the Company of Veterans*

One hundred fifty years later, there remains as much myth as truth about those fabled men known as Confederate Veterans. Much of this had to do with literally thousands of printed stories that emerged after the war, some which have not always been supported with historic evidence, but nonetheless are a part of American culture. As most volunteer companies extant before the Civil War in North Carolina served their communities in many ways beyond simply providing a military presence at formal ceremonial functions, the Rowan Rifles continued to operate long after the civil war as an independent company as well as part of larger Veteran's organizations. It is unknown how long they waited to begin meeting again after the war ended but newspaper advertisements from the *Carolina Watchman* indicate they were meeting on 22 June 1876. The company provided an honor guard for the Fourth of July parade and festivities, along with the Silver Coronet Band of Salisbury which was led by Edward Neave.[21] On 12 October 1876, Capt. Williams Brown was once more commanding the company according to a newspaper advertisement announcing, "All members and everybody else interested in the Rowan Rifle Guard, are requested to meet at headquarters next Monday night. Every member is ordered to bring his gun and equipments."[22] Thus we see the company not only continued to exist, but Capt. Brown was again the leader. This is most likely due to the death of Capt. McNeely during Stoneman's raid on 12 April 1865. The announcement also shows that the Rowan Rifles were also again armed, which seems odd given the restrictions imposed on former Confederate soldiers during the reconstruction period. It is not known how many veterans participated in the Rowan Rifle's post war meetings.

A number of Civil War Veterans from Rowan County indicated they wanted their stories told correctly, and with the authenticity and humility that only men who have "borne the battle" can share, Salisbury's Confederate Veterans quickly organized themselves into an organization known as the "Veteran Regiment" in 1886 which was the core of what eventually became the modern Sons of Confederate Veteran's camp known as the Rowan Rifles. Several former Company K members held offices in the organization, including James R. Crawford who was its first commander. Its purpose was to see that their history was accurately preserved and to honor the memories of their fallen comrades. The precise number of men reportedly belonging to this organization varied into the twentieth century when the last members eventually passed away, but in September 1893, they had over three hundred members. In the decades following the Civil War, they regularly held formations and appeared at parades, ceremonies and other civil events where they were held in highest regard, and often bestowed honors on their fallen comrades. One such contingent even traveled to Richmond Virginia to a national Confederate Veteran's Reunion in 1893.[23]

Salisbury witnessed a large Veteran's Reunion on 14 September 1893, when the Charles F. Fisher camp of veterans met at the Old Court House, where former United States President and General George Washington once visited, and where the Rowan Rifles held their regular meetings both before and after the war. On this day the old soldiers again met there at eleven o'clock a.m. when they were ordered into formation by Col. James R. Crawford. At this event, many Confederates who had never attended a reunion came out, and one observed stated there were "...incidents of the war recalled and camp life lived over" throughout the day. Veterans often held their meetings in the Old County Courthouse, and their speaker, Mr. J.H. Boyden addressed the group stating that their mission was to become a "non-partisan and non-political" unit, solely to preserve their history. Some other former Company K members played important roles in this organization, including Capt. W. C. Coughenhour and Edward Neave, who served as members of their advisory board. On this date, the veterans were also treated to a lively speech by Dr. W.H. Leith whose oratory filled "the hearts of the veterans... with enthusiasm." Afterward, they formed ranks and marched over to an old brick warehouse near the Railroad depot, where they were given an elaborate meal prepared by the ladies of Salisbury.[24]

The Rowan Rifles' activities were not limited to Rowan County after the war, either. On 13 August, 1893, the *Salisbury Daily Sun* newspaper ran a brief article (shown below) indicating the had been to Greensboro on a recent trip. The reader will recall that during the antebellum period the Rowan Rifle Guards made numerous trips to Greensboro to drill or participate in other formal ceremonies, and apparently that tradition continued near the turn of the century. Notice also that the newsprint indicates they were cited as "Company A" rather than Company K. It is not clear if this was an error, or whether they may have been designated as such by the larger Veteran's organization as those records are not available. It is possible they may have been aligned with another such company or more to form a larger group such as a battalion for services such as the parades and other civic events and simply re-designated as Company A.

## COMPANY A'S DISTINCTION.

### The Very Best in Camp at Greensboro.

The Rowan Rifles, which returned yesterday from Greensboro, made a splendid showing in the recent State encampment at Greensboro.

First of all, the quiet, orderly conduct of the boys was so noticeable as to call attention of the colonel to them and gain his praise for their behavior. Col. J. N. Craig was especially complimentary to this feature of Company A.

That this company made an excellent impression, cannot be doubted when it is known that three out of the five days, it had orderly. The orderly-officer's work, it will be remembered, is to remain on duty for 24 hours, to superintend the cleanliness of the camp, appear on dress parade and attend upon superior offices. Salisbury's company enjoyed a distinction in this respect.

Extreme modesty prevents the claiming of superior merit by the boys, themselves, but they showed it all the same.

The former band leader, Edward Neave, was the last known Company K Veteran to attend a reunion, which was held in Statesville, North Carolina on 18 May 1920, with only three men from the former 4th NCST regimental band present, including himself and J.P. Gillespe, and Nat Raymer's former tentmate, J.C. Steele, who stated he thought they were the "only ones known to be living."[25] However, David Lewis Holshouser was long believed to be the last surviving member of the company, who died on 20 June 1930 at age 86, as cited in his obituary published in the Salisbury Daily news on 23 June 1930 (shown below). However, Pvt. Nelson Eller, one of the original members of the Rowan Rifle Guards, outlived Holshouser by thirty two days, passing away at age 89 years on 25 July 1930. Hence, to date, Eller, not Holshouser, was the last member of the Rowan Rifles to pass away.[26]

Eller was from Iredell County, and relocated to Montgomery County, Illinois shortly after the war, where he married Nancy C. McClain of Hillsboro, Indiana, and had six children and was active in the Baptist Church. Apparently Eller did not establish contact with the Salisbury Veteran's Regiment, or they would have likely publicized his death in Rowan County as they did for William Durell, another Rowan Rifle Guard who similarly relocated to Illinois after the war. (Durrell was one of two pranksters who confabulated commissions as 2d Lieutenants for themselves in the 55th NCT while serving as provost, but were never punished) The *Carolina Watchman* published his obituary on 23 September 1886, indicating he died in Chicago on 4 August 1886. It is likely that he was friends with Pvt. Nelson Eller, as they were both original members of the Rowan Rifle Guards, but whether their friendship is connected with their dual relocation to Illinois after the war is unknown.

Eller is buried in Liberty Cemetery near Bingham, Illinois, along with three other North Carolina soldiers, Pvt. Joseph Pinkney, 2d North Carolina Cavalry, Pvt. Martin Dempsey Cavin, Company I, 7th NCST, and Capt. Franklin Guy, Company D, 4th NCST. As they served in the same regiment, Eller was doubtless familiar with Captain Guy, but it remains unknown whether their connection had anything to do with his or the other "Tar Heels" who are buried there. There are also fourteen other Confederate Veterans from other states buried in that cemetery, so it is doubtful a coincidence. Eller spent nearly three years in northern prisons, and while possibly apocryphal, he may have formed ties to Union soldiers from that state while incarcerated, or else had ties there before the war. Salisbury was occupied after 9 May 1865, who were predominantly troops from Ohio, Illinois, Indiana and Pennsylvania, and while William Durell is believed to have returned to Salisbury for a period prior to relocating to Illinois, it is unknown whether he or Eller knew them.

Two other men from Company K survived to witness the advent of the First World War, including John Endie who died in 1914 at age seventy five; Arnold Friedheim, who passed away on 31 May 1915, at age seventy-six. This was ironically the 53d anniversary of the battle of Seven Pines where the 4th NCST over half of its men. His conduct in the war earned the respect of peers and officers, and even Gen. Bryan Grimes later mentioned that there was no "braver or truer soldier in the army." Milas Holshouser also passed away in 1915 at the age of eighty-four years, along with George Snuggs. Ambrose Casper did not live to witness the onset of World War I, but survived until 1912 when he died at age seventy-one years. Among other groups to emerge after the Civil War dedicated to preserving and honoring the memories of Confederate Soldiers was the United Daughters of the Confederacy, which were originally comprised of actual daughters of living

Confederate Veterans. At one of the reunions on 25 September 1902, they presented Crosses of Honor to numerous Confederates, and one of their number, Ms. Francis C. Tierman, left us a fitting epithet that has proven prophetic, describing the soldiers as, "*...men such as the world is not likely to behold soon again!*"[27]

# References

## Chapter One

1. United States Bureau of Census, 1860 and Census Slave Index. (Hereafter US Census)
2. Bradley, Stephen. *North Carolina Militia Officers Roster as Contained in the Adjutant General's Officers Roster*. (Wilmington, NC: Broadfoot Publishing,1992), 1. (Hereafter Bradley)
3. Governor's Office Record Book, Vol. 5, 1841-1855, No.1349, Cited in Abstracts of Letters of Resignation of Militia Officers In North Carolina 1779-1840. Compiled and Abstracted by Tim Kearney. (Raleigh, NC: Walsworth Printing Company, 1992), iv-xiii.
4. Brawley, James S. Rowan County: A Brief History. (Raleigh, NC: NC Department of Archives and History, 1974), 57. (Hereafter Brawley, Brief History)
5. Troop Returns from Military Collection. Box 7. Militia Records, NC Archives.
6. Heath, Raymond A. Jr. "The North Carolina Militia on the Eve of Civil War." (Master's thesis, University of North Carolina, 1974). (Hereafter Heath)
7. Brawley, Brief History, 57.
8. Ibid., 60-61.
9. Ibid., 61.
10. Ibid., 58.
11. Governor's Office Record Book, Volume 5, 1841-1855; Numbers: 1237, 1238, 1320, 1292 and 1349. NC Archives, Adjutant General Files.
12. Brawley, 57.
13. Governor John Ellis Papers, (GP 146), NC Archives.
14. Heath, "Antebellum Militia".
15. Bradley, vi.
16. Brawley, Brief History, 55.
17. Raby, Roy S. "The Fayetteville Independent Light Infantry: Citizen Soldiers of Cumberland County 1793-1997." (Masters' thesis, Fayetteville State University, 1997), 23.
18. Brawley, M. (Transcriber). Indexed Summary of *Carolina Watchman*, Brawley Collection, No. NCAAA 39. Rowan County Library, Salisbury, NC, 1858-1861. (Hereafter Brawley's Index).
19. *North Carolina Population Data Series*, March 1969, "County Population Trends in North Carolina 1790-1960: State, Region and County," 1, 85.
20. Brown, Louis A. *The Salisbury Prison: A Case Study of Confederate Military Prisons 1861-1865*. rev. ed. (Wilmington, NC: Broadfoot Publishing, 1992), 1-5. (Hereafter Brown)
21. Rumple, Jethro, Rev. *History of Rowan County Containing Sketches of Prominent Families and Distinguished Men*. Bi-Centennial ed. (Edith M. Clark, Ed.). Reprinted by Elizabeth M. Steele Chapter of the United Daughters of the Confederacy. Baltimore: Regional Publishers, 1974, 174. First published 1881 by J.J. Bruner, Salisbury, NC. (Hereafter Rumple)
22 Harris, William C. *North Carolina and the Coming of the Civil War*. (Raleigh, NC: Division of Archives and History, Third printing, 2000), 5-6.
23. Rumple, 252.
24. Ibid.

25. Brawley, J.S. The Rowan Story 1753-1953: *A Narrative History of Rowan County, North Carolina.* (Salisbury, NC: Rowan Printing Company, 1953), 178-181. (Hereafter Brawley, Narrative History)

26. Ibid., 140.

27. Jordan, Weymouth T. and Manarin, Louis, H. *North Carolina Troops 1861-1865: A Roster.* Second printing, Vol. 4 (Raleigh, NC: 1988), 110. (Hereafter Jordan and Manarin)

28. Company K, 4th NCST Muster Roll 31 December 1861 to 28 February 1862. Private Collections, Bryan Grimes Papers, PC 3.8. (Hereafter Grimes Papers)

29. Compiled Confederate Military Service Records, Microfilm Group 109, M230, Roll 140. North Carolina Soldiers. 4th North Carolina Infantry. Rowan County Public Library, Edith M. Clark History Room, Salisbury, North Carolina, F.M.Y. McNeely. (All Company K references are in Group 109, M230, Rolls 136-142 and hereafter cited as CSR).

30. Jordan and Manarin, Vol. 4, 103-104.

31. Iobst, Richard W. *The Bloody Sixth: The Sixth North Carolina Regiment, CSA.* NC Archives and History (1965), Reprinted by Olde Soldier Books, Gaithersburg, MD, 1987, 9.

32. Jordan and Manarin, Vol. 4, 103-104.

33. The Heritage of Rowan County, North Carolina, Vol. 1. (The Genealogical Society of Rowan County, Inc., 1991), 370. (Hereafter Rowan Genealogical)

34. Andrews, Elle M. *Elle's Book, Being the Journal Kept by Elle M. Andrews from January 1862 through May 1865.* Transcribed and annotated by Ann Campbell MacBryde. (Davidson, NC, Briar Patch Press, 1998), 42. (Hereafter Andrews).

35. *Salisbury Banner,* 1 December 1858. University of North Carolina Chapel Hill Special Collections, Microfilm No. C071-S16b-1858-1862.

36. CSR, Hofflin.

37. Davidson County NC Wills, 1810-1970, I. N. Wiseman, 1836, CR.032.801.92, NC Archives.

38. Jordan and Manarin, Vol. 4, 104.

39. Rowan Genealogical, 292.

40. CSR, Eddleman.

41. US Census Slave Schedules, 1860.

42. Grimes Papers, Co. K Muster Roll 31 December 1861 to 28 February 1862.

43. Jordan and Manarin, Vol. 1, 76. See also Vol. 11, 148.

44. Powell, William, (Ed.). *Dictionary of North Carolina Biography.* (Raleigh, NC: University of North Carolina Press, 1979), 286-287.

45. Ibid.

46. Rayner, George. *Famous Families of 19th Century Rowan County.* Piedmont Passages Series, Vol. 4, (Salisbury, NC: Salisbury Printing Co., 1991), 57. (Hereafter Rayner)

47. Ibid., 53.

48. Ibid., 54.

49. United States National Archives, *Records of the Office of the Chief of Ordnance, Deliveries to the Militia Under the Act of 1808,* Entry No. 118. Record Group 156, Vols. 2, 3, 4, 13, 62, 66, 104.

50. Murphy, John M. & Madaus, Howard M. *Small Arms of the Confederacy.* (Newport Beach, CA: Graphic Publishers, 1996), 71-82, 187-189, 409-418.

51. Huntington, R.T. *Hall's Breechloaders.* (Baltimore: Johns Hopkins Press, 1984).

52. Jones, Victor T. Internet website: www.ancestory.com

53. Brawley's Index, 131.

54. Tolbert, Noble J. (Ed.). *The Papers of John Willis Ellis*. Vol. 1, 1841-1859. (Raleigh, NC: NC Archives, 1964), 332. (Hereafter Tolbert)
55. Coates, Earl J. and Thomas, Dean S. *An Introduction to Civil War Small Arms,* (Gettysburg, PA: Thomas Publications. 1996), 177.
56. Troop Returns, Military Collection, Box 7. North Carolina Militia Records, North Carolina Archives. (Hereafter Troop Returns).
57. Sandburg, Carl. *Abraham Lincoln: The Prairie Years and the War Years*. New York, (New York: Harcourt Brace), 137-145.
58. Brawley's Index, 136.
59. Ibid., 139.
60. Ibid., 136.
61. Ibid., 142.
62. Ibid., 144-145.
63. Troop Returns, Military Collection, Box 7, NC Militia Records, NC Archives. (Hereafter Troop Returns)
64. Tolbert, 238.
65. Ibid., 257.
66. OR, Series 1, Part 1, Vol. 3, (1898); 46.
67. Brawley's Index, 150.
68. Ibid.
69. Ibid.
70. Ibid., 155.
71. Ibid., 160.
72. Ibid., 160-162.
73. Ibid., 164.
74. *Proceedings of the Military Conventions – Held at Goldsboro and Salisbury, July 11, 1860 and Dec. 14. 1860*. Salisbury, N.C. J.J. Bruner, Editor and Printer. 1860, North Carolina Collection, University of North Carolina Library, Chapel Hill, North Carolina. (Hereafter Proceedings)
75. Proceedings, 14 December 1860.
76. Ibid.
77. Ibid.

## Chapter Two

1. Tolbert, Vol. 2, 885-887.
2. Sprunt, James. Chronicles of the Cape Fear River: 1600-1916. (Spartanburg, SC, 1974; reprint, Wilmington, NC: Broadfoot Publishing, 1992, 276-280.
3. Herring, Ethel and Carole Williams. Fort Caswell in War and Peace. (Wendell, NC: Broadfoot Publishing, 1983), 25-54. (Hereafter Herring and Williams,1983)
4. Herring, Ethel and Carole Williams. Fort Caswell in War and Peace. (Wendell, NC: Broadfoot Publishing, Revised edition, 1999), 10. (Hereafter Herring and Williams, 1999)
5. Clark, Vol. 5, 24.
6. Herring and Williams, 1999, 18.
7. Angley, Wilson. "A History of Fort Johnson on the Lower Cape Fear," (Southport, NC: Southport Historical Society, 1996), 68-76. (Hereafter Angley)

8. Herring and Williams, 1999, 21-22.
9. OR, Ser. 1, Vol. 51(3), (1891); 6.
10. Clark, Volume 5, 24.
11. Ibid.
12. OR, Ser. 1, Vol. 1, (1880-1901); 476.
13. Ibid., 476.
14. Tolbert, Vol. 2, 563.
15. Ibid., 555.
16. OR, Ser. 1, Vol. 3, (1889); 39.
17. Angley, 70.
18. Tolbert, Vol. 2, 553. See also OR, Ser. 1, Vol. 1, (1901), 474.
19. OR, Ser. 1, Vol. 3, (1889), 39.
20. Tolbert, Vol. 2, 257.
21. Brawley's Index, 166.
22. The *Carolina Watchman*, 19 March 1861. Salisbury, NC: Rowan County Public Library, Microfilm held in The Edith M. Clark History Room. (Hereafter *Carolina Watchman*)
23. *Frances M.Y. McNeely Papers*, No. 737, Private Manuscripts Collection, NC Archives. (Hereafter McNeely). See also Jordan and Manarin, Vol. 4, 103.
24. Burton Alva Conkle. *John Motley Morehead and The Development of North Carolina 1796-1866*. (Philadelphia, PA: 1922. Original held in Harvard University Library, Boston, MA.), 386-387.
25. Jordan and Manarin, Vol. 4, 104.
26. Rumple, 351.
27. *Carolina Watchman*, 23 April 1861.
28. OR Ser. 1, Vol. 51(3), (1891), 12.
29. Clark, Vol. 5, 27.
30. Ibid.
31. Herring and Williams, 1999, 24.
32. *Statesville Landmark*, 6 June 1911.
33. *Carolina Watchman*, 16 April 1861.
34. CSR, Roll 140, McNeely.
35. Brawley, 91.
36. *Carolina Watchman* 9 May 61.
37 Jordan and Manarin, Vol. 6, 446.
38. Stikeleather, John A. Recollections of the Civil War in the United States 1861-1865. (Olin, N.C. 27 May 1909. University of North Carolina Chapel Hill, Southern Historical Collection), 2. (Hereafter Stikeleather)
39. Andrews, April 1861.
40. Tolbert, Vol. 2, 775.
41. Iobst, Richard W. "North Carolina Mobilizes: Nine Crucial Months, December, 1860-August, 1861." Doctoral Dissertation, University of North Carolina at Chapel Hill, 1968, 38-39.
42. Lilly, James. 4 May 1861. Lilly Collection, 1785-1863. NC Archives. (Hereafter Lilly)
43. Ibid.
44. Ibid.
45. North Carolina Convention & Military Board (1861-1862), North Carolina. Original held at North Carolina Collection, University of North Carolina at Chapel Hill. (Raleigh

NC: Syme & Hall, Printers to the Convention, 1861). Call No. VC342.2 1861d Vol. 1, 30-31. (Hereafter NC Convention, 1861)

46. Brown, 3-4.

47. Brawley, 93.

48. Foard, Fred C. Civil War Remembrances. NC Archives, Private Manuscript Collection, 11-12.

49. Stikeleather, 2-3.

50. Wilmington Daily Journal, 18 July 1861.

51. NC Convention 1861, Vol. 1, Schedule C, 27 May 1861. See also Iobst, 36.

52. Ibid., Vol. 1, 24 May 1861 Letter from Warren Winslow to Weldon Edwards.

53. Ibid., Vol. 1, 14.

54. Ibid.

55. Civil War Collection: Regimental Records, Muster Rolls of North Carolina State Troops 1861-1865, Company K, 4th North Carolina State Troops. Adjutant Generals Office. Adjutant General Files (AG-16-22), Boxes 48, folder 29, Company K Muster Roll, 31 December 1861 to 28 February 1862. North Carolina Archives. (Hereafter Co. K Muster Rolls).

56. CSR, Roll 140, McNeely.

57. Brawley, 93.

58. Brawley's Index, 168-169.

59. Clark, Vol. 1, 234.


## Chapter Three

1. NC Convention, Vol. 1, 24 May 1861 Letter from Warren Winslow to Weldon Edwards.

2. CSR, Roll 140, McNeely.

3. Grimes Papers, Company K, 4th NCST Muster Roll 31 December 1861 to 28 February 1862.

4. Jordan and Manarin, Vol. 3, xi-xii. See also Clark, Vol. 1, 3-7.

5. Adjutant General Records, (AG 23, No. 159.5), Undated document, from North Carolina Ordnance Department Record of Issues 1861; North Carolina Archives, 316-333.

6. North Carolina Adjutant General Records of Military Boards and Letter Books (AG-16, No. G435), July 1-August 19 1861, Letter from Warren Winslow to Col Bradford. (Hereafter NC Military Board)

7. Company K Muster Roll 31 December 1861 to 28 February 1862 and CSR, 4th NCST.

8. U. S. National Archives, Records of the Office of the Chief of Ordnance, *Deliveries to the Militia Under the Act of 1808*, Entry 118, Record Group 156.

9. OR Series 3, Vol. 1, (1889); 39.

10. Ibid., 1.

11. OR, Series 3, Vol. 1, (1889); 43.

12. OR, Series I, Vol. 51, Part 2, (1897); 158-160.

13. Military Boards Miscellaneous Correspondence, 22 August 1861, Warren Winslow, NC Archives, Military Collection, Civil War Collection, Box 36, File 16, Raleigh NC.

14. Adjutant General, Letter Books, May 1861-July 1862, AG-22, 308. Also see Adjutant General's Letter Book 16 Dec 1861-1 June 1863, 27, 44, 52, 70, 88, 122, 132, 142, and 147. (Hereafter Adjutant General Letter Books)

15. Clark, Vol. 1, 5-6.
16. Ibid., 6.
17. Adjutant General Letter Books, 16 December 1861-1 June 1863.
18. Clark, Vol. 5, 466-471. Vance's discussion of how North Carolina supplied her troops reveals not only did they quickly exhaust weapons supplies in 1861, but also uniforms and other necessities, leading to procurement of supplies from England.
19. Brawley, 173.
20. *Patrick H. Cain Collection*. Letter, 30 June 1862. Perkins Library, Duke University. J.C. Turner Letter to Miss Emily Cain. (Hereafter Cain)
21. Craig, Joel and Baker, Sharlene (Ed.). *As You May Never See Us Again: The Civil War Letters of George and Walter Battle, 4th North Carolina Infantry*: Coming of Age on the Front Lines of the War Between the States 1861 – 1865. (Wake Forest NC: The Scupperong Press. 2004), 3. (Hereafter Battle)
22. William A. Adams, Sergeant Company A, 4th North Carolina Infantry. William A. Adams Collection. McClelland Family Papers. Southern Historical Collection. Chapel Hill, NC: Perkins Library, University of North Carolina at Chapel Hill. No. 3869. (Hereafter Adams)
23. Clark, Vol. 5, Index, 28.
24. Hanes, Jacob H. Private, Company G, 4th North Carolina Infantry. Letters. The Catherine E. Hanes Collection. Southern Historical Collection. Chapel Hill, NC: Perkins Library, University of North Carolina at Chapel Hill. (Hereafter Hanes).
25. Jordan and Manarin, Vol. 4, 1.
26. Battle, W., 44.
27. Adams, 22 July 1861.
28. William England Family Papers. 10 December 1862. North Carolina Archives. See also "*Depots for the Deposit of Supplies for the Army from the different States*. The City Intelligencer: Strangers Guide. (Richmond, VA: Macfarlane and Ferguson, 1862), 12. (Hereafter England)
29. Mast, Greg. *State Troops and Volunteers: A photographic record of North Carolina's Civil War Soldiers*, Vol. 1, (Raleigh NC: 1995), 1. (Hereafter Mast)
30. Fraley, Ashbel S. 2d Lieutenant, Company A, 4th North Carolina Infantry. "Incidents of the War," diary entry from 25 July 1861; Southern Historical Collection, University of North Carolina, Chapel Hill. (Hereafter Fraley)
31. Stikeleather, 4.
32. Marshbourne, Samuel Daniel. Diary; Private Manuscripts Collection. North Carolina Archives, 1-2. (Hereafter Marshbourne)
33. Manarin, Vol. 4, 104.
34. North Carolina Confederate Militia Officers Rosters as Contained in the Adjutant General's Official Rosters. (Wilmington, NC: Broadfoot Publishers, 1992), 1.
35. CSR, Roll 136, Blount.
36. Young, John A. Colonel. Diary entry from Sunday, 8 September 1861. Iredell County Library, History Room, Statesville, North Carolina. (Hereafter Young).
37. Adams, 1 Oct 1861.
38. CSR, Roll 136, Anderson.
39. Battle, W., 51-52.
40. Letter from Pvt. William Lillycross to Capt. Frances M.Y. McNeely; Frances M.Y. McNeely Papers, No. 737, Private Manuscripts Collection, North Carolina Archives.

41. Jordan and Manarin, Vol. 4, 104.
42. Brian Grimes Private Collection, Box 3.8, 8 December, 1862. NC Archives. (Hereafter Grimes)
43. OR, Series I, Vol. 5, (1898); 990.
44. Chambers, Capt. Henry A. Diary of Captain Henry A. Chambers. (Wendell, NC: Broadfoot's Bookmark, 1983), 44.
45. Jordan and Manarin, Vol. 4, 104.
46. Battle, W., 55-56.
47. Clark, Vol. 1, 235.
48. Ibid, 82.
49. Stikeleather, 6-7.
50. Grimes, Bryan. Private Collection. 4th North Carolina State Troops, Muster Roll, 1 December 1861-2 February 1862. Box 3.8, North Carolina Archives. (Hereafter Grimes, Co. K Muster Roll)

## Chapter Four

1. Battle, G., 22-23.
2.. Adjutant General Records, (AG 23, #159.5), Undated document from North Carolina Ordnance Department Record of Issues 1861; NC Archives, bound volume, 326.
3. Wheat, Dr. Thomas A. A Guide to Civil War Yorktown. (Knoxville, TN: Bohemian Brigade Books and Publishers, 1997), 5, 21.
4. Grimes, 16 March 1862 and 18 April,1862.
5. Ibid., 18 April 1862.
6. Grimes, Co. K Muster Roll, 28 February-30 April 1862.
7. Holcombe, Brent H. (Ed.). Marriages of Rowan County 1753-1868. (Baltimore, MD: Genealogical Publishing Company, 1981), 432. (Hereafter Holcombe)
8. Grimes, Co. K Muster Roll, 28 February-30 April 1862.
9. Cowper, Pulaski. *Extracts of Letters of Major General Bryan Grimes to His Wife, Written while on active service in the Army of Northern Virginia. Together with some personal recollections of the War, written by him at it's close, etc.* Ed. Gary Gallagher. (Wilmington, NC: Broadfoot Publishing. 1986), 13. (Hereafter Cowper)
10. Letter from Pvt. Arthur Evans to his wife Rebecca, 11 May 1862. 4th North Carolina Files, Museum of the Confederacy, Richmond, Virginia. (Hereafter Evans)
11. Gibson, Joseph F. Co. C, 4th NCST, letter to his brother John A. Gibson in Catawba County, 24 May 1862. Catawba County Historical Association, Transcribed by Mrs. Addie Cloninger.
12. Fraley, 22 May 1862.
13. Ibid.
14. Strelow, Derrick J. *Daniel F. Carpenter, 4th North Carolina Infantry in the War for Southern Independence.* 1995. Unpublished monograph held at Rowan County Public Library, Salisbury North Carolina. Contains typescript of article from Statesville Landmark newspaper, "Mr. J.C. Steele and Capt T.M.C. Davidson spend a day with Comrade Carpenter at Catawba – Talked of War Days". Appendix C, 16.
15. Clark, Vol. 1, 237.
16. Rumple, 351.
17. OR Series 1, Vol. 11, Part I, (1884); 951.

18. Hoover, Sumpter A. *Reminiscence of S. A. Hoover, 1861-1865*, Co. C, 4th Regiment, North Carolina State Troops. Iredell County Library, History Room. Statesville, North Carolina. (Hereafter Hoover)

19. Clark, Vol. 1, 238.

20. Ibid.

21. Newton, Steven H. *The Battle of Seven Pines*, (Lynchburg,Virginia, H.E. Howard Publishing, 1993), 53. (Hereafter Newton)

22. Clark, Vol. 1, 238.

23. OR Series 1, Vol. 11, Part I, (1884); 955-956.

24. Ibid., 952.

25. Ibid., 956.

26. Ibid.

27. Funkhouser, R.D. Southern Historical Society Papers, (William Jones, Ed.), (New York, 1876-1959 original printing, 1977-1980 reprinted), Vol. 35, 368-369. See also Clark, Vol. 1, 238-239.

28. OR Series 1, Vol. 11, Part I, (1884); 956.

29. Ross, B. B., Corporal, Company I, 4th North Carolina Infantry. *Experiences During the War 1861-1865*. Southern Historical Collection, Wilson Library, University of North Carolina at Chapel Hill. G Portion, 5-6. (Hereafter Ross)

30. David Carter Collection, Southern Historical Collection, University of North Carolina, Chapel Hill.

31. Cowper, 15.

32. Stikeleather, 7-8.

33. CSR, Roll 140, McNeely.

34. OR, Series I, Vol. 11, Part I, (1884); 953.

35. Ibid., 955-956.

36. Allen, Harrell T. Lee's Last Major General: Bryan Grimes of North Carolina. (Mason City IA: Savas Publishing. 1999), 60-61. (Hereafter Allen)

37. Grimes Papers, NC Archives, Commission as lieutenant colonel, 1 May 1862.

38. CSR, Roll 140, McNeely.

39. Jordan and Manarin, Vol. 4, 104.

40. Fraley, 2 July 1862.

41. Battle, W., 29.

42. Fraley, June 1862.

43. CSR, Roll 140, Kyle, Letter from Capt. F.M.Y. McNeely to Kyle's mother, 18 June 1862.

44. Jordan and Manarin, Vol. 4, 108. See also 1880 US Census for Rowan County, NC.

45. Jordan and Manarin, Vol. 10, 212. See also Grimes Papers, Co. K Muster Rolls, after 30 April 1862 indicating Lowrence died at Seven Pines.

*Chapter Five*

1. Allen, 60-61.

2. Grimes, 5 July 1862.

3. Fraley, 26 June 1862.

4. Allen, 65.

5. Cowper, 16.

6. Cowper, 6-17

7. Stikeleather, 8-9.
8. Clark, Vol. 1, 242.
9. Cowper, 17.
10. Shinn, James W. First Sergeant, Company B, 4th North Carolina Infantry. Osborne Papers. Southern Historical Collection. Wilson Library, University of North Carolina at Chapel Hill. No. 567. Notes compiled by James W. Osborne. (Hereafter Shinn)
11. Gorman, William R. Our Living and Our Dead. (Perkins Library, Duke University. 1898), 21-22. (Hereafter Gorman)
12. Strelow, 16.
13. Capsule History of the 4th NCST, Antietam National Battlefield Park Archives.
14. Evans, 19 July 1862.
15. Adjutant General Records, AG 23, No.159.5. North Carolina Ordnance Department Record of Issues 1861, (bound volume), NC State Archives, 323.
16. Mast, Greg. "Tar Heels." *Military Images*, Vol. 11(2). Nov-Dec. 1989, 6-31.
17. Warren, Richard. Uniforms of the Confederacy, Plate 72. "North Carolina State Issue Uniforms 1861-1865." *Journal of Confederate Historical Society*. Vol. 28(2), Summer 1990, 45-52. (Hereafter Warren)
18. Clark, Vol. I, 25-26.
19. Warren, 45-52.
20. Vance, Gov. Zebulon. Governor's Letter Book. 10 October 1862. North Carolina Archives. (Hereafter Vance)
21. England, 10 Dec. 1862.
22. Battle, W., 30.
23. Cowper, 18.
24. Priest, Michael. Before Antietam: The Battle for South Mountain. (Shippensburg, PA: White Mane Publishing Company, 1992), 178-180. (Hereafter Priest)
25. Cain, undated, 1862.
26. Priest, 35.
27. Shinn, 11 September 1862.
28. Andrews, 47.
29. Ibid., 47-48.
30. Shinn, 14 September 1862.
31. Priest, 177.
32. Cowper, 19.
33. Priest, 177.
34. Ibid., 197.
35. Clark, Vol. 1, 245.
36. Priest, 204.
37. Ibid.
38. *Wren, James: Diary*, Antietam National Battlefield Archives, 103.
39. Thompson, Pvt. David. "In the Ranks to Antietam, by Private David Thompson, 9th New York Volunteers," in *Battles and Leaders of the Civil War*, Vol. 2., edited by Robert U. Johnson, 556-558. Eaton, NJ: Stackpole Books, 1990. (Hereafter Thompson)
40. Clark, Vol. 1, 245.
41. Thompson, 558.
42. Clark, Vol. 1, 246.
43. Ibid.
44. OR, Series 1, Vol. 19, Part. I, (1887), 284-287.

45. Shinn, 18 September 1862.
46. OR, Series 1, Vol. 19, Part 1, (1887), 59.
47. Ibid., 288.
48. Clark, Vol.1, 247.
49. Ibid., 249.
50. Adams, 30 September 1862.
51. Clark, Vol. 1, 250.
52. Cowper, .22.
53. Murdock J. McSween letter to Governor Zebulon Vance, 17 November 1862.
    Cited in *The Papers of Zebulon B. Vance*, Vol. 1, 1842-1862. (Raleigh: NC Archives
    1963), 258-260. (Hereafter Vance)
54. CSR, Roll 136, Bean.
55. CSR, Roll 138, Hofflin.
56. CSR, Roll 138, Blount.
57. CSR, Roll 136, Williams.
58. Vance, undated letter, 1862.
59. Clark, Vol. 1, 27.
60. Bone, J.W. Record of JW Bone's Service in the Civil War. Co. I, 30th Regiment North
    Carolina Troops. Typewritten manuscript. Stanly County Public Library, Albemarle,
    NC. (Hereafter Bone)
61. Grimes, Company K Muster Roll, 30 April – 31 October 1862.
62. Ibid.
63. Ibid.
64. Ibid.
65. CSR, Roll 138, Jones.
66. CSR, Roll 138, Durrell.
67. Civil War Collection: Regimental Records, Muster Rolls of North Carolina State Troops
    1861-1865, Company K, 4th North Carolina State Troops. Adjutant Generals Office.
    Adjutant General Files (AG-16-22), Boxes 48, Company K Muster Roll, 31 December
    1862. North Carolina Archives. (Hereafter Co. K Muster Rolls). See Summary of
    Principal Events by Capt. W.C. Coughenhour.
68. OR, Series 1, Vol.21(1), (1888), 561, 644.
69. Clark, Vol.1, 259.
70. Company K Muster Roll 31 December 1862.
71. CSR, Roll 138, Hofflin.
72. Ibid.
73. Clark, Vol. 1, 26-35. There is much detail regarding imported English army supplies in this
    citation, including discussion of how North Carolina purchased cloth for uniforms.
74. Company K Muster Roll 31 December 1862.
75. Ibid.
76. Ibid.
77. Shinn, October 1862 letter to his father.

*Chapter Six*

1. Gaither, Thomas W. Undated letter from Winter 1863 contained in *The Civil War Letters
    of Thomas W. Gaither, John Burgess Gaither, And Mollie D. Gaither of Iredell*

*County, North Carolina*. Transcribed and edited by Jessie D. Hardy; Gaither Family
  Papers, N. 3517. Southern Historical Collection, University of North Carolina at Chapel
  Hill. (Hereafter Gaither)

2. CSR, Roll 138 Hofflin.
3. Statesville Landmark, 19 December 1917.
4. Andrews, 77.
5. Gaither, 8 March 1863.
6. Brawley, 103-104.
7. Company K Muster Roll, 31 December 1862 – 30 April 1863.
8, Gaither, 3 April 1863.
9. OR, Series I, Vol. 25(1), (1889), 994-995.
10. Stikeleather, 10.
11. Brian Grimes Private Collection, Box 3.8, N.C. Archives.
12. Gary W. Gallagher, Ed. Extracts of Letters of Major Gen'l Bryan Grimes to his Wife.
    Compiled from Original Manuscripts by Pulaski Cowper, (Wilmington, NC:
    Broadfoot Publishing, 1986), 17.
13. OR, Series 1, Vol. 25(1), (1889), 1006.
14. Ibid.
15. Ibid., 943.
16. Ibid., 473, 698, 705.
17. Ibid., 995.
18. Ibid., 996.
19. Ibid., 711-713.
20. Cowper, 32.
21. OR, Series 1, Vol. 25(1), (1889), 711.
22. Raymer, *Iredell Express*, Statesville NC 15 June 1863.
23. OR, Series 1, Vol. 25(1), (1889), 712.
24. OR Series 1, Vol. 21(1), (1988), 996.
25. Ibid., 734-735.
26. Ibid., 996.
27. Ibid.
28. Cowper, 32.
29. Michael W. Taylor, *To Drive The Enemy From Southern Soil: The Letters of Colonel
    Frances Marion Parker and the History of the 30th Regiment North Carolina
    State Troops.* (Dayton OH: Morningside House Books,1998), 260-262.
30. Ibid., 254, Footnote 65.
31. Ibid., 260-261, Footnote 83.
32. Ibid., 261, Samuel Hopkins Diary cited in Footnote 83.
33. OR, Series 1, Vol. 25(1), 705, (1889).
34. Ibid., 414.
35. Ibid., 996
36. Raymer, *Iredell Express*, Statesville NC 15 June 1863.
37. OR, Series 1, Vol. 21(1), (1888), 478.
38. Ibid., 475.
39. OR Ser. 1, Vol. 25(1), (1888), 738.
40. Stikeleather, John, Post-war letter. Statesville Landmark, 20 December 1897.
41. OR Series 1, Vol. 25(1), (1889), 998.
42. Ibid., 478.

43. OR, Series 1, Vol. 25(1), (1889), 473-482.
44. Stikeleather, 31-32.
45. Cowper, 38.
46. Ibid., 33. Grime's sword belt and buckle are now in the NC Museum of History.
47. Cowper, 40.
48. Adams, William M. Southern Historical Collection, University of North Carolina Chapel
      Hill, NC No. 3869. McClellan Family Papers.
49. Journal of the Confederate Congress 1861-1865. Vol. VI, (Washington, DC: U.S.
      War Department, U.S. Government Printing Office, 1905), 479.
50. OR, Series I, Vol. 25(1), (1889), 996-998.
51. Ibid., 949.
52. Jordan, Vol. 4, 104.
53. CSR, Roll 140, McNeely. Letter from Thomas McNeely to Richmond Hospital Number 20
      Clerk F. Foard on behalf of Lewis Mahaley's father, Thomas Mahaley, 6 July 1863.
54. *The Statesville Landmark*, 20 and 23 December, 1897.
55. *Iredell Express*, NC 15 June 1863.
56. General Orders No. 64. Adjutant and Inspector General's Office. Richmond, VA. 10 August
      1864. North Carolina Division of Archives and History, Raleigh, NC

*Chapter Seven*

1. OR Series I, Vol. 27, Part 2, (1889), 550.
2. Confederate Veteran, (30), 141.
3. Stikeleather, 12-13.
4. Confederate Veteran, (30), 141.
5. Ibid., (14), 107.
6. CSR, Roll 136, M.L. Bean.
7. Clark, Vol. 1, 272.
8. Ibid., 275.
9. Stikeleather, 15.
10. Grimes, 2 July 1863.
11. Ross, 6.
12. Grimes, 3 July 1863.
13. Clark, Vol. 1, 97.
14. Company K Muster Roll, 30 April to 31 August 1863.
15. CSR, Roll 138, Hofflin.
16. Ibid.
17. Ibid.
18. Ibid.
19. CSR, Roll 132, Coughenhour.
20. Hanes, 16 September 1863.
21. Shaffner, John Frances. Diary entry from 6 November 1863. Shaffner Papers, Private
      Manuscripts Collection, North Carolina Division of Archives and History. (Hereafter
      Shaffner)
22. Company K Muster Roll, 31 August - 31 October 1863.
23. Crute, Joseph L. Jr. *Confederate Staff Officers*. (Powhatan, VA: Derwent Books, 1982),
      115, 161. (Hereafter Crute)

24. Rumple, 351.
25. Jordan and Manarin, Vol. 4, 104.
26. CSR Roll 138, Hofflin.
27. Wise, Stephen. Lifeline of the Confederacy: Blockade Running During the Civil War. (Columbia, SC: University of South Carolina Press, 1988), 46-73, 105-106. See also Clark, Vol. 1, 23-28 for a discussion of English imported supplies and uniforms in North Carolina.
28. CSR, Roll 132, Coughenhour.
29. Shaffner, 6 November 1863.
30. CSR, Roll 138, Hofflin.
31. Clark, Vol. 1, 32-34.
32. Company K Muster Roll 31 October - 31 December1863.
33. Ibid.
34. CSR, Roll 138, Hofflin.
35. CSR, Roll 132, Coughenhour.
36. Hanes, 2 December 1863.
37. Stikeleather, 12-13.
38. Shaffner, 4 December 1863.
39. CSR, Roll 138, Hofflin.
40. Clark, Vol.1, 34.
41. CSR, Roll 138, Hofflin.
42. Ibid.
43. Company K Muster Roll 31 December 1863.
44. Ibid.
45. Ibid.
46. Ibid.
47. Clark, Vol.1, 32-33.
48. Ibid., 26-27, 33-35.

### Chapter Eight

1. CSR, Roll 138, Hadley.
2. Crute, 161.
3. CSR, Roll 138, Hofflin.
4. Ibid.
5. Ibid.
6. Ibid.
7. Ibid.
8. Stikeleather, 17.
9. Ibid.
10. Shaffner, 27 March 1864.
11. Linster, Robert O. Private, Company C, 4th North Carolina Infantry. Letters. Special Collections, Perkins Library, Duke University. Durham, NC (Hereafter Linster).
12. OR, Series I, Vol. 36, Part I, (1891), 1081.
13. Stikeleather, 19.
14. Company K Muster Roll, 31 October - 31 December 1863.
15. Jordan and Manarin, Vol. 4, 104.

16. OR, Series I, Vol. 36, Part I, (1891), 347, 564.
17. Ibid., 353.
18. Company K Muster Roll, 31 December 1863 - 31 August 1864.
19. Brigade Inspection Report, Cox's Brigade, 30 September 1864. Washington DC: US National
    Archives, Record Group 109, M935, Roll 10, 33-P-24. (Hereafter Cox's Brigade Returns)
20. Ibid.
21. Jordan and Manarin, Vol. 4, 104.
22. Ibid.
23. OR, Series I, Vol. 36, Part I, (1891), 557.
24. OR, Series I, Vol. 43, Part I, (1893), 556.
25. OR, Series I, Vol. 36, Part I, (1896), 557.
26. CSR, Roll 138, Grimes.
27. Swan, Thomas Belt. "A Memorandum of My Travels in the Year of 1864, by Thomas Belt
    Swan, Co C, 4th North Carolina State Troops." Unpublished original manuscript held in
    private collection. 31 Dec 1864. (Hereafter Swan)
28. Crute, 48, 165.
29. Jordan and Manarin, Vol. 4, 9.

### Chapter Nine

1. Shaffner, 12 January 1865.
2. Battle, W., 85.
3. Ibid., 127.
4. Swan, 26 January 1865.
5. Battle, W., 128.
6. OR, Series I, Vol. 46, Part I, (1894-1895), 1270.
7. Linster. Undated letter, February 1865.
8. Swan, 7 February 1865.
9. Battle, W., 130.
10. Mast, 320-321
11. Shaffner, 10 March 65
12. Ibid, 12 March 1865
13. CSR, Sworn Affidavit for Pension, F. McNeely
14. Jordan and Manarin, Vol. 4, 104.
15. CSR, Bean.
16. Ibid., Letter to A.G. Ramsey, District Representative to State Assembly, 11 March 1865.
17. Shaffner, 19 March 1865.
18. Battle, W., 131-132.
19. Clark, Vol. 1, 264.
20. Cowper, 104-105.
21. Swan, 2 April 1865.
22. Clark, Vol. 1, 265.
23. Swan, 6 April 1865.
24. Cowper, 112-113.
25. Clark, Vol. 1, 265.
26. Ibid.
27. Cowper, 115.

28. Ibid., 117.
29. Bone, 46.
30. Rumple, 351.
31. Cowper, 119.
32. Ibid.
33. Cowper, 119.
34. Hoover, 9 April 1865.
35. Calkins, Chris. The Final Bivouac: The Surrender Parade at Appomattox and the Disbanding of the Armies April 10-May 20 1865. (Lynchburg, VA: H.H Howard, 1988), 1-2.
36. Clark, Vol. 1, 27.
37. Ibid., Vol. 5, 256.
38. CSR, Roll 136, Bean.
39. Nine, William G. and Wilson, Ronald G. *The Appomattox Paroles April 9 -15, 1865.* (Lynchburg, VA: H.E. Howard Publishing.4th ed., 1989), 53, 54, 58, 71, 102, 159, 161, 162, 166. (Hereafter Nine and Wilson)
40. Grimes, Company K Muster Roll 31 December 1861. See also Jordan and Manarin Vol. 4, 103-106 to estimate casualty rates in Company K against Appomattox paroles.
41. Cox's Brigade Returns, M935, Roll 10, 11.
42. Steele, James Columbus. *Sketches of the Civil War Especially Cos. A, C and H from Iredell County, N.C. and the Fourth Regimental Band.* (Statesville, NC: Brady Printing Company, 1921). (Hereafter Steele), 62. See also *Confederate Veteran* (22), 260.

## Chapter Ten

1. *Confederate Veteran* (22), 260.
2. Steele, 62.
3. Van Noppen, I.W. *Stoneman's Last Raid.* (Raleigh, NC: NC State Press, 1961), 57-58. (Hereafter Van Noppen)
4. Van Noppen, 48-49.
5. Brawley, 106.
6. Van Noppen, 107.
7. Ibid., 63.
8. CSR, Roll 140, McNeely.
9. Crute, 165.
10. Van Noppen, 63.
11. Brawley, Brief History, 106-107.
12. Van Noppen, 63
13. Ibid., 64.
14. Ibid.
15. Brawley, Brief History, 107.
16. OR, Series 1, Vol. 49, Part 1. (1891), 324.
17. Ibid., 334.
18. Brawley, Brief History, 109.
19. Swan, undated entry, April 1865.
20. 4 June 2009, *Ramsey News-Journal, To Remember Civil War Soldier Nelson Eller.* Vol. 128(22), 16, Ramsey, IL. (hereafter Ramsey News-Journal)

21. Brawley, Brief History, 109.
22. *Carolina Watchman*, 12 October, 1876. University of North Carolina Library.
23. *Confederate Veteran*, Vol. 1(1), 177, (1893, 1988 reprint).
24. Ibid., Vol.1(10), 301, (1893, 1988 reprint).
25. Ibid., Vol. 10(11), 394, (1902, 1988 reprint).
26. *Ramsey News-Journal*. 4 June 2009.
27. Van Noppen, 63.

## *Appendix A*

### Company K, 4th Regiment North Carolina State Troops
### Compiled Muster Roll & Biographical Data
### Enlisted Men, 1861-1865

The following is a synoptic roll of men serving in Company K not identified as original members of the Rowan Rifle Guards before April 1861. (The original members are discussed in Chapter One.) This roll includes volunteers and conscripts alike, and lists each by the highest rank attained during the war. All references are cited *a priori* in lieu of a lengthy list of end notes because each name contains data from various primary sources including Company K muster rolls and the papers of Maj. Gen. Bryan Grimes, both held in the North Carolina Archives, and the 1850, 1860 and 1870 U.S. Census for Rowan, Davie, Davidson and Iredell counties, North Carolina from whence the majority of soldiers resided before they enlisted. In cases where the soldier came from another state or outside of the Rowan area, the census counties are referenced in text. Note that in some cases, the soldiers were identified only by their first initials and last name, or in other cases, their identifying information such as name, initials or age conflict in census, muster roll or other data making it difficult to consistently identify them. In such cases, the soldier is listed herein by the most common moniker, with variant spellings included as they appeared in original sources.

Secondary sources include the work of Louis Manarin ad Weymouth Jordan, *A Roster of North Carolina State Troops 1861-1865*, Vol. 4, 104-113, and their Addenda, as well as the Appomattox Paroles, (4th Ed.) compiled by William G. Nine and Ronald G. Wilson, published by H.E. Howard, Inc. in 1989. There is also a significant amount of genealogical information drawn from the "*Heritage of Rowan County*" published in 1999 by the Rowan Genealogical Society in Salisbury, North Carolina. Marriage data is cited from *Rowan Marriages 1753-1868*, compiled by Brent H. Holcomb, (Baltimore, MD: Genealogical Publishing Co., 1981), as well as the work of R.H. Knotts, (Ed.). *Rowan County Marriages 1868-1900*. Last, there is a group of soldiers whose Compiled Service Records are held within the same group as men who are well documented as members of Company K but either their names did not appear on muster rolls, or their information identified them with another regiment or company. These men are listed separately in Appendix B, as they are not clearly linked to this company.

### *Pvt. George H. Basinger*

In the 1850 census, George Basinger was 7 years old, the second oldest of five children and attended school district 23 in Rowan County. His father, John Basinger, was a farmer who held 110 acres of farmland valued at $110.00 and no slaves. His cousin and boyhood next door neighbor, John Basinger, later served together with George in Company K. By 1860, his mother Mary had died, and his father remarried. During that census, the farm was valued at $510.00. George was then working as a day laborer, and still single, and no slaves. Military records show that he was 5 feet, 8 inches tall and worked as a farmer. H was sworn into Confederate service by Lt. Marcus Hofflin at Salisbury on 9 March 1862 at age 19. The Roll of Honor indicates he was captured at Sharpsburg on 17 September 1862 in the Bloody Lane. After Gettysburg, Basinger was detailed as a blacksmith at the Richmond armory, but returned to the company in 1864. He was wounded at Spotsylvania on 13 May 1864 by gunshot wound to left shoulder and admitted to Wayside Hospital Number 9 in Richmond the same date. It is not known how long he was in the hospital, and his name also appears on a list of POW from Maj. Gen. Joseph Johnston's army, although the list was undated. Pvt. Basinger was one of the sixteen men remaining in Company K who surrendered at Appomattox 9 April 1865. He returned to Salisbury and took the Oath of Allegiance on 23 May 1865. Basinger married Lydia Moose on 16 December 1885 in Salisbury. Basinger applied for a pension on 4 June 1907 due to gunshot wound "through the shoulder blade" sustained at Spotsylvania Court House on 13 May 1864, and his doctor described him as "disabled one half."

### Pvt. James W. Bean

39 year old James Bean enlisted in Company K on12 April 1863, exactly two years before be would be paroled at Appomattox in 1865. Bean was married to Hetty Beaver on 16 February 1850 when he was age 23 and she was 19 years old. The 1850 census reflects that they had no children, and owned their own home with one slave. Bean was wounded at the battle of Spotsylvania on 12 May 1864 and admitted to Wayside Hospital Number 9 at Richmond a few days later. He was given sixty days leave to Salisbury on 16 July 1864. Bean returned and was still absent in hospital recovering in August 1864. He soon transferred to Staunton General Hospital where he remained for several months. Bean drew a new uniform suit there on 14 December 1864. He eventually returned to the company, and surrendered at Appomattox on 9 April 1865. The last Company K muster roll indicates he was listed as "disabled" through 1864, and he was not likely present in ranks on the morning of 12 April for the surrender ceremony, because he was then detached on lighter duty.

### Pvt. Moses Anthony Bencini

Moses Bencini was born in 1846. In 1864, he was 5 feet, 8 inches tall, with blue eyes and dark hair and a light complexion. In the 1860 census he was 14 years old and an orphan. He resided with his sister, Maria at the home of their legal guardian Luke Blackmer, an attorney from New York who practiced in Salisbury. Bencini and his sister then held $7,000.00 in financial assets each, and the Blackmer family had $28,976.00 assets and nine slaves. Bencini originally enlisted in Company G, 6th NCST but was discharged for unknown circumstances, possibly due to his age, in 1862. He later volunteered at age 18 in Company K on 21 April 1864 for duration of the war. He was captured at the third battle of Winchester on 19 September 1864 and confined at Point Lookout, Maryland, until 15 March 1865 when he was exchanged. Bencini returned to Salisbury and fought in Stoneman's Raid with the Home Guards on 12 April 1865, where he was again captured and taken to a prison at Louisville, Kentucky. He transferred to Camp Chase, Ohio, on 2 May 1865 where he stayed until he took the Oath of Allegiance on 13 June 1865. The 1870 census indicates he still resided at the Mansion House Hotel owned by Mr. Rowzee, and was then unemployed. He married Nancy Eleanora Price on 28 August 1878 in Rowan County. The 1880 census identifies him at age 34, married to Nancy, and employed as a salesman in Salisbury, with a six month old child, and seven year old William W. Price.

### Pvt. David, M.L. or J.L. Bogle

This name is surrounded by a cloud of ambiguity. The Roll of Honor identifies a Pvt. David Bogle in Company K, but gives no other information about him. Compiled service records show that J.L. Bogle was conscripted into Company K on 24 February 1864 for the war, and was then a resident of Rowan County. There was no census information found for M.L., J.L., or David Bogle in 1850 or 1860. Likewise, there are no marriage records from 1735-1868, or 1868-1900 for M.L, J.L. or David Bogle. The Appomattox surrender rolls show a Pvt. J.L. Bogle from Company K, 4th NCST who surrendered on the morning of 9 April 1865. He was detached on an unspecified duty on the morning of 9 April 1865 according to service records, and was therefore not in the ranks at the surrender. He may have been one of the men assigned to the commissary detail led by Capt. Marcus Hofflin, which was actually a fishing party created to help supply the army with food.

*Pvt. I. L. Boyle*

This name is found in the Complied Service Records as a member of Company K. Neither the 1850 nor 1860 census included this named in Rowan or surrounding counties. His only appears on a Company K muster roll on 15 March 1864. The place and date of enlistment is not known. Neither the Roll of Honor nor Appomattox surrender rolls from 9-12 April 1865 mention this name. It is most likely the initials and surname "I.L. Boyle" is a misspelling of "J.L. Bogle" and it was somehow erroneously included as a separate name in service records.

*Pvt. Lewis M. Brady*

Lewis Brady was 5 feet, 7 inches tall with brown eyes, dark hair, and a dark complexion. In 1860, he lived in Gold Hill with his parents. He was then age 15, and working as a day laborer. His father was a farmer, and reported $545.00 in assets and no slaves. Brady turned 18 in 1863, and was conscripted into Company K on 26 February that year at age 19. He was illiterate, and could only sign his name by a mark on the company muster roll. Brady contracted an illness on 1 June 1863, "debility of emaciation bilious remittent fever…" just one month before the battle of Gettysburg. He was admitted to the General Hospital at Farmville, Virginia on 3 June 1863, where he remained until 12 August when he was given a 60 day furlough to Gold Hill. Brady returned in October, and continued to convalesce in the hospital until 21 May 1864 when he was transferred to Wayside Hospital Number 9 in Richmond. Brady is simultaneously reported in the work of Louis Manarin as wounded at Spotsylvania although neither company muster rolls nor his service files support that assertion. Brady returned to the company, albeit against his will, in time to serve at Petersburg, and was captured on 3 April 1865 at City Point by Captain Jackson of the 68th Pennsylvania Volunteers. He was confined at Hart's Island, New York Harbor, and assigned to POW Company 14. When he was in processing at the prison, Brady told the clerk he was from Rowan County North Carolina, who recorded it in his prison documents. Brady was released on 18 June 1865 after taking the Oath of Allegiance.

*Sgt. Peter Alexander Brown*

Brown was 5 feet, 10 inches tall. He was married, 23 years old and living in Salisbury with his wife, 26 year old wife Elisa and their 2 year old son in 1860. Brown was a farmer, and reported $1,300.00 in assets and no slaves in the census. He enlisted in Company K on 14 June 1861. His service records contain an admission record from Winder General Hospital in Richmond dated 30 April 1864 which reflects he was mustered in for the duration of the war on 16 June 1861 at Smithville, North Carolina by Capt. Frances McNeely. The Rowan Rifles were then deployed to Fort Johnston since 22 April 1861 and because of the later enlistment date it is doubtful he was an original member of the antebellum company. The 31 December 1861 Company K muster roll indicates Brown was one of six privates absent due to illness in November-December 1861 at Camp Pickens near Manassas, Virginia, although his records do not identify the illness or where he was hospitalized. He returned, however and served in all major campaigns of 1862. He was promoted to corporal sometime between January-April 1863, and served in the Chancellorsville and Gettysburg campaigns. He was also in the 1864 Overland Campaign, and wounded in the leg at Spotsylvania 12 May 1864. He was admitted to Camp Winder General Hospital on 17 May 1864, and given a 60 day furlough on 3 June. He was promoted to Sergeant in August 1864 while still in the hospital. He returned to the company, and was detailed to serve with the Confederate Inspector General's Office on 20 January 1865. Brown served in that capacity until the end of the war, and took the Oath of Allegiance at Salisbury on 3 July 1865 in Salisbury.

*Pvt. Stephen Alexander Brown*

Known as "Alex" this 23 year old man was 5 feet, 10 inches tall in 1860. He was living with his parents and worked as a laborer on their farm in Salisbury. He was raised as the second oldest of seven children. His father, Alexander Brown was one of the wealthier men in the county, reporting $32, 839.00 in assets and eleven slaves. Brown mustered into service on 18 July 1861 at Camp Hill near Garysburg. He was reported sick from 25 July through 31 August 1861 at Camp Pickens. Brown recovered, although was wounded in the foot and shoulder at the battle of Seven Pines on 31 May 1862. He was sent home to convalesce, but did not survive. He died of wounds "at home" in Rowan County 28 June 1862. His father filed a claim for a settlement of pay due his son from the Confederate government on 3 March 1863, and received $82.26.

*Pvt. William A. Buis*

28 year old "Bill" stood 5 feet, 6 inches tall, and had dark hair, dark eyes and a dark complexion in 1860. He was then a blacksmith, and his financial assets are unknown but he was not identified as a slaveholder. Buis enlisted in Company K at Garysburg, North Carolina on 14 June 1861. Muster rolls show Buis present during the Penninsula campaign, Seven Days, and Maryland and Fredericksburg campaigns of 1862. He was also engaged at Chancellorsville 1-4 May 1863 and at Gettysburg on 3 July 1863 where he was captured. He was incarcerated at Fort Delaware, Delaware, until transferred to Point Lookout, Maryland, sometime in 15-18 October 1863. Buis was later transferred to the military prison at Elmira, New York, on 12 July 1864. He was ultimately paroled at Elmira on 2 March 1865 and transferred to Aiken's Landing on the James River, Virginia and awaited his exchange. Buis returned home to Salisbury and took the Oath of Allegiance there on 6 June 1865.

*Pvt. John Alston Campbell*

John Campbell was born in 1835. He was 25 years old in 1860, and then resided with his parents in the area north of the railroad near Salisbury. He was the oldest of five children, and his father, George S. Campbell, was a farmer with no slaves and had $770.00 in assets. Campbell's date and location of enlistment in Company K are not shown but his name first appears on muster rolls on 28 February 1862. He contracted pneumonia in March 1864, and was admitted to Wayside Hospital Number 9 in Richmond on 1 April. He remained there, and died on 17 April 1864. His uniform must have been in good condition, as it was later given to a quartermaster agent identified as "A. Rankin" on 26 October 1864. His personal effects contained $7.50.

*Pvt. Ephraim Frances M. Carter*

In July 1860, 27 year old Ephraim was living with his wife, 20 year old Sarah E. in their own home. Carter had $178.00 in assets, and was working as a farmer with no slaves. His service files reported his age as 30 years when he was mustered in by Lt. William Brown on 6 September 1861 in Rowan County. Carter was assigned extra duty as a nurse in the regimental field hospital in January-February 1862 but he served at Seven Pines, the Seven Days battles and was reportedly captured at or near Sharpsburg, Maryland, on or about 15 September 1862 according to muster rolls. However, his service file reflects that he was admitted to Winder Hospital Number 5 in Richmond on 9 October 1862 but does not specify whether he was wounded or sick. Hospital records also show he deserted from 16 October 1862. Later Company K muster rolls indicate Carter was confined at Fort Delaware, Delaware, until paroled and transferred to Aiken's Landing, James River, Virginia, on 2 October 1862 for exchange. Carter was declared exchanged on 10 November 1862 and was present until killed in action at Chancellorsville on 3 May 1863.

*Pvt. Ambrose Casper*

Ambrose was born in Rowan County on 19 March 1841. He was 5 feet, 5 inches tall, with hazel eyes, dark hair, and a dark complexion at age 19 in 1860, and living with his parents and working as a laborer on their farm. Ambrose was a religious man, and was baptized at the Organ Lutheran Church in Rowan County on 22 August 1841 according to church records. His father, Andrew was a farmer with $2050.00 in assets and no slaves. His brother James C Casper was also in Company K, but their elder brother Milas "Miles" Casper enlisted in the 57th NCST in 1861. All three brothers were later captured and held in Northern prisons, with Ambrose supposedly twice captured. However, he enlisted in Company K at age 20 on 9 March 1862 and served in the Penninsula and Richmond campaigns of 1862, and then listed as captured at Sharpsburg, Maryland, on 17 September 1862.

He was supposed to have been confined at Fort Delaware, Delaware until exchanged on 10 November 1862 at Aiken's Landing in Richmond. However, hospital records from Winder Division 5 in Richmond suggest he was there instead, with an admission date in September and a 30 day furlough from 30 October 1862. Casper returned to the company, however and was present until captured at Old Church, Virginia, on 30-31 May 1864 after the Spotsylvania campaign. This time records did not conflict, and he was confined at Point Lookout, Maryland, until transferred to Elmira, New York, on 9 July 1864, during the same time his brother James was there. They took the Oath of Allegiance together on 11 or 12 June 1865 and were released afterward. Ambrose died at home in Salisbury on 15 August 1912, at age 71 years.

*Pvt. James C. Casper*

James was 5 feet, 7 inches tall with dark hair, hazel eyes, and a dark complexion and 23 years old in 1861. He was illiterate, unmarried and living alone, and working as a blacksmith. He was also the elder brother of Ambrose Casper. James lived with R. John Klutz in 1860. Klutz was a farmer with several hundred acres of land but no slaves. Two other Company K members, William Peeler and Williams Phillips also resided and worked there. Casper served in all major campaigns of 1862, and was wounded slightly in the arm at Seven Pines. He was at Chancellorsville when his former next door neighbor Wallace Josey was killed in action and later awarded the Badge of Gallantry. Casper also fought at Gettysburg in 1863 and was captured at Spotsylvania on 12 May

1864, just 2 weeks before his brother Ambrose. James was taken to Belle Plains, Virginia initially, but soon removed to Point Lookout, Maryland, until he was again transferred to Elmira, New York, on 3 July 1864 where his brother Ambrose was also held. Casper was released from Elmira on 11-12 June 1865 after taking Oath of Allegiance with his brother. He returned to Salisbury. He married Mary Jane Corriher on 31 December 1884.

*Pvt. Henry M. Caster (Castor)*

Henry Caster was born in 1835, and his great-grandparents immigrated to the United States at New Bern, North Carolina from Switzerland in the early 18th century where a Swiss colony was established. In the 1860 census he was age 25, residing with his widowed Father John. He had earlier attended Rowan School District 24. His father then held $650.00 in assets and no slaves. Caster was age 26 when sworn in by 1 Lt W.C. Coughenhour on 3 July 1861. He became ill with an unrecorded disease, and was admitted to Winder Hospital Number 4 in Richmond on 9 October, 1862 but quickly recovered. Caster was a carpenter, and was detailed to help build winter quarters in camp between November-December 1861. Caster was assigned extra duty 15 March through 1 September 1864, although it is not known what those duties were. He was captured at the third battle of Winchester on 19 September, but his activities after that time were not recorded beyond a mention in an anonymous casualty report by an officer of the 4th NCST published in the Carolina Watchman on 20 September 1864, that listed him missing to 1865.

*Pvt. John A. Caster*

John was born in 1831 in Rowan County. In 1850 he was age 19, married and living in School District 24 in Rowan County with his wife, Mary Elizabeth House, whom he married on 7 November 1847. They had four children in 1860, and when Caster enlisted in Company K on 16 March 1862 he was 32 years old. He was absent sick much of the time he was in service. The date of admission is not recorded, but he was identified as a deserter from Winder Hospital on 2 November 1862. He was again found in a hospital at Lynchburg, Virginia for unspecified reasons on 14 September 1863. His condition improved by 26 September and he was detailed to work with the quartermasters in both I and III Corps. Little else is known of his service except that he was again at Winder Hospital in January 1865. He was given a 60 day furlough to Salisbury but it was remanded on 14 January because "transportation could not be found." Arrangements were finally made, and he left for Salisbury on 26 January, but he simply remained there until he took the Oath of Allegiance there on either 16 May or 10 June 1865. The 1870 census shows he remarried to Bertha Stirewalt and worked as a farmer in Rowan County.

*Pvt. George A. Cauble*

George Cauble was born in 1840 at Rowan County, and in 1850 was attending School District 32 there. His father, George Lyerly, was a farmer with $1,000.00 in assets and no slaves in the 1850 census. In 1860, George was 21 years old and apprenticed as a carpenter to Michael Davis on the south side of Salisbury. Davis had a 15 year old son, Michael, who also later enlisted in Company K in 1864. Davis had $2,150.00 in assets and no slaves. Muster rolls show Cauble enlisted on or about 12 July 1861 at age 21. He was reported absent sick from their camp at Plains Station Virginia September through October 10 1861. He returned to duties, and served at the battle of Seven Pines on 31 May 1862, and was also engaged at battle of Gaines Mill on 27 June 1862 where he was killed in action.

*Pvt. Noah N. Church*

Noah Church was born in 1842 in Watauga County. In 1860 he was unmarried and residing near Lower Forks in Wilkes County, and had no slaves or assets in the census. Church enlisted in Company K at age 19 on 9 September 1861, and was sworn in by 1st Lieutenant Williams Brown at Salisbury. He contracted Typhoid in camp near Danville Virginia, and was admitted to Moore Hospital there on 11 January 1862. He transferred to Hospital Number 5 in Richmond on 12 January 1862, where he stayed until 16 March 1862 then he returned to Company K. He was wounded in the right hand at Seven Pines on 31 May 1862 but records do not specify whether he was hospitalized. His name appears on muster rolls until 1864. The 1870 census located him as age 28 and working as a farmer in Watauga County. He was then married to 28 year old Rachael, and they had two daughters, ages 3 and 6 months.

*Pvt. Daniel W. Corl (Dannal Caral, Correll)*

24 year old Daniel was living with his mother Margaret and two older sisters on the South Side of Salisbury in the 1860 census. Daniel worked then as a day laborer and his mother reported $125.00 in assets, and Daniel owned three slaves. Corl was a Conscript, and reported to Greensboro in Guilford County where there was a Camp of Instruction for Conscripts to initially muster into service. He was sworn in by 1 Lt. Marcus Hofflin (who kept meticulous company records) on 20 January 1864 after arriving in the company. Corl was wounded in the "left great toe" at Spotsylvania on 19 May 1864 and muster rolls show him reported absent wounded until 26 July 1864 when he was recommended by the surgeon for a detail as a machinist due to his wound remaining unhealed. Although his company commander, 1 Lt. Hofflin approved the transfer, the division commander Maj. Gen. Robert Rodes also had to approve it, but apparently had reservations about his condition because he insisted that the transfer would not occur unless Corl's doctor provided a "certificate of his condition" each month to 1 Lt. Hofflin throughout his tenure as a machinist. Effective 1 September 1864 the transfer occurred, and Corl was detailed out of the company as a machinist. He took the Oath of Allegiance at Salisbury on 31 May 1865. Corl married Mary Ann Barcum on 9 November 1872, who died shortly afterward. He remarried Mary C. Brown on 4 November 1875, and he died in Salisbury in 1896 at the age of 56.

*Pvt. John T. Crowell*

In 1860 John Crowell was 18 years old and working as a clerk. He was single, and resided with the family of M.L. Holmes, a wealthy farmer in Gold Hill who reported $90,800.00 in assets and nineteen slaves. Crowell was sworn in by 1 Lt. William Brown in Rowan County on 19 July 1861 at age 19. He quickly became ill when he arrived at Camp Pickens, Virginia in the midst of a typhoid and measles epidemic. Crowell barely unpacked his bags when he was reported sick in quarters from July through November 1861. He was later sent to Hospital Number 13 in Richmond, and returned to the company before the 31 May 1862 battle of Seven Pines. He was wounded in the breast there and died in an unspecified Richmond Hospital on 3 June 1862.

*Pvt. Michael Davis*

Michael Davis was 15 years old in 1860 and resided with his parents in Salisbury. His father was a carpenter with two apprentices and held no slaves. The other apprentices were George Cauble, who later enlisted in Company K, and Rufus Miller, who later enlisted in Company C of the 4th

NCST. He enlisted in Company K on 8 February 1864 at age 18. His pension records show he was wounded in June 1864, and later admitted to Winder Hospital at Richmond, Virginia, on 14 September 1864. He did not stay in hospital long, and returned to the company by 26 December 1864 when he is reported present on the muster roll. He was paroled at Salisbury on 2 May 1865.

*Pvt. James Frank Dorsett*

The 1860 census of Davidson County shows 14 year old "Frank" Dorsett living with his father, S.M. Dorsett, who was a master carpenter, and his mother, Athalia. Frank was the second oldest of six children and there were five carpenter apprentices living with them. No financial assets were reported but his father had three slaves. Frank enlisted in Company K on 16 March 1862 at age 16 and deserted from Yorktown exactly one month later on 16 April 1862. His name does not appear on original muster rolls afterward, and he forfeited any pay due according to muster roll data.

*Cpl. Jeremiah A. Eddleman*

Jeremiah Eddleman was 19 years old and living with his parents in South Salisbury in 1860. His father Daniel Eddleman was a farmer with $8,500.00 in assets and seven slaves. There is a discrepancy in his age found in service files, which reflect 23 years at enlistment on 15 March 1862. He was present during the battles of Seven Pines, the Seven Days and was captured at Sharpsburg, Maryland on 17 September 1862. He was confined at Fort Delaware, Delaware, until transferred to Aiken's Landing, James River, Virginia, for exchange on 2 October 1862. He was declared exchanged 10 November 1862 and released to his regiment. Eddleman was found seriously ill with diarrhea when he returned, and sent to Windsor Hospital Number 5 in Richmond where he was admitted on 7 October 1862. He was granted a 20 day furlough on 6 November 1862 and returned to the company afterward. He did not fully recover, and although fought at the battles of Gettysburg in1863, and was promoted to corporal between January and June 1864. He was present at the battles of Spotsylvania and Cold Harbor in May and June 1864, respectively. Eddleman still found himself in poor health due to chronic diarrhea, and was re-admitted to the General Hospital on 17 June at Charlottesville, Virginia where he remained until 2 August 1864. He managed to return to the company while they were in the Shenandoah Valley, and fought at the battles of Winchester and Fisher's Hill. He was captured a second time at the Fisher's Hill on 22 September, and confined at Point Lookout, Maryland, until he was paroled and transferred to Boulware's Wharf, James River, Virginia. There, he was received on 19 March 1865 to be exchanged. However, it is doubtful he returned to the company as his name is not found among the sixteen survivors at Appomattox in April 1865.

*Pvt. John J. Endie*

John Endie was born at Rowan County in 1839, although resided in Iredell County in the 1860 census. He worked as a carpenter, and was not a slaveholder, although his assets are not reported. He enlisted at Rowan County on 29 June 1861 at age 22. While stationed at Camp Pickens near Manassas, Virginia, he was detailed to build winter quarters in November-December 1861. Endie was detailed as a nurse to Winder Hospital's Third Division on 15 February 1862. He later became ill and was admitted to Chimborazo Hospital Number 3 on 10 May 1862, with an unspecified diagnosis. He remained there until 16 June and returned to the company. He was wounded in the arm while the company was on picket duty on or about 2 February 1863, and afterward Gen. R.E. Lee ordered him detailed "to light duty" as a provost guard at Danville, Virginia on 14 February

1863. His service records note that he was never paid for extra wages owed him for carpentry work his performed, much of it on staff officer quarters. This may explain why Gen. Lee was involved in his transfer to light duty. He served there until 27 January 1865. Nothing else of his active service is known, as Endie was not identified as one of the sixteen survivors of Company K at Appomattox. His name appears on the Roll of Honor. After the war, he married Mary Temple of Salisbury in 1865. His daughter Laura was born in 1867. Endie died in 1914 at the age of 75.

*Pvt. Jesse Fraley*

Born at Salisbury in 1839, Jesse Fraley was a physician, age 24 and living with his widowed mother in Salisbury in 1860. His mother owned the farm bequeathed by Jesse's father. Neither Fraley nor his mother's financial assets are reported but his mother had six slaves. Fraley was the youngest of four children. In spite of his profession, he enlisted in Company K as a private on 8 September 1861 at age 25. His medical training was recognized and he was detailed as a nurse on 10 October 1861 to Division Hospital near Plains Station, Virginia where he worked until again detailed for extra duty as a clerk in the Adjutant General's office in February 1862. He was transferred to the 4th NCST Field and Staff as a hospital steward on 1 January 1863. It is not known why he was not appointed surgeon earlier, but Dr. Fraley was finally appointed an assistant surgeon on 17 February 1863 and transferred into the 7th NCST where he served until the end of the war. He was paroled at Greensboro, North Carolina on 1 May 1865.

*Cpl. Arnold Friedheim*

Arnold Friedheim was born 17 November 1838 in Minder, Germany, where he was raised in the Jewish faith. Friedheim was age 20 when he immigrated to the United States, arriving in New York with his brother Albert on 24 May 1858 according to a passenger ship index. He came to Rowan County where he had several relatives, and worked as a merchant until he enlisted in Company K at Rowan County on 15 June 1861. He was promoted to corporal sometime between January-August 1864. He was paroled at Appomattox 9 April 1865, and returned to Rowan County. There, he took the Oath of Allegiance in Salisbury 6 June 1865. "There was no braver or truer soldier in the army..." according to Col. Bryan Grimes, who mentions Friedheim in his post-war ad hoc notes of significant members of the 4th NCST. It should be noted that the several men named on the Colonel's list were generally noted for heroic or otherwise gallant deeds on the field of battle, or their stoic, resilient character as soldiers. After the war, he moved to York, South Carolina with his wife Sophie. She died before him, and Arnold passed away a widow on 31 May, 1915 (ironically the 53rd anniversary of the battle of Seven Pines) at age 76.

*Pvt. Edward Fulk*

Edward Fulk was 23 years old when he enlisted on 15 March 1862 at Rowan County. Muster rolls indicate he was sick from 4 April 1862 through August 1864, and although his service file states he died in service, it is not clear when or what caused it. He was buried on 18 May 1862 at an unrecorded location.

*Pvt. Samuel Frank Gardner*

Sam Gardner was 5 feet, 5 inches tall, married and had three children in 1860. He enlisted at age 23 in Salisbury on 19 March 1862, and was known as "Frank". His time in service was brief. He was severely wounded in the side at Seven Pines on 31 May 1862. Reports conflict as to the date of his death; the Carolina Watchman posted an obituary of his death on 18 August 1862, noting the he was ill for several weeks, but started to improve and decide to take a walk one day, when he suddenly fell dead from "heart dropsy." Muster rolls note that he died in Richmond on 28 July 1862, however. His widow, Margaret, filed a claim for settlement of pay due him at the time of his death on 26 February 1863 and was paid $103.16. Capt. William Coughenhour provided testimony for Widow Gardner, and indicated Frank had worked as a farmer before the war.

*Pvt. Jeremiah "Jerry" Glover*

Jerry Glover was 6 feet tall, with light hair, gray eyes, and a medium complexion. In 1860 he was living with his parents in Salisbury on their farm located on the Old Concord Road adjacent to the modern "Old Rowan County Home" property some three miles south of Salisbury. He was then identified as age 16, and working as a day laborer. His father John was a farmer and a shoemaker, who reported $1,600.00 in assets and no slaves. His elder brother was William Henry Glover who was also in Company K. The Glover family had ancestors who migrated to the United States from Ireland in the mid-1700. Jerry's grandfather was Brig. Gen. John Glover in the Revolutionary War. Family lore holds that the general provided the boats that General George Washington used to take his army cross the Delaware River in his famous surprise attack on the British. Jerry Glover enlisted in Rowan County and reported his age as 18 on 29 June 1861. His service file contains much conflicting information as to his medical and service status. One document states he was captured by the 12th Illinois Cavalry in May, 1863 during the "raid on the rear of Lee's army" and paroled on or about 24 May 1863, while another states he was wounded by gunshot on 6 July 1863.

However, hospital records from Chimborazo Number Three complicate the picture even further. Those records show he was admitted there upon his parole from capture in May 1863 from Danville Virginia with a diagnosis of Syphilis. He transferred to the General Hospital at Danville, Virginia on 3 July 1863 through 15 July 1863. He was given a 30 day furlough from Windsor Hospital on 6 September, 1863 to Salisbury, but records simultaneously show he was detailed as a cook at Baker Hospital on 11 September 1863. He rejoined the company before 1 January 1864 as his name appears on the muster roll as present. Glover is again shown as wounded on 3 June 1864, with a gunshot wound to the right hand when he was admitted to a hospital at Petersburg that day.

He was transferred to Pettigrew Hospital in Raleigh a day later, and on 10 June 1864 was again transferred to the hospital at Salisbury where he stayed until 28 August 1864 when he is shown absent without leave. Glover returned to the company but he was sent back to the hospital by the regimental commander on 25 December 1864 due to his wound not healing. It appears the stoic Glover returned to the company again, as he was re-admitted to Winder Hospital Number 9 in Petersburg on 25 February 1865 with a gunshot wound to the left knee sustained on 5 January 1865. He was furloughed to Salisbury on 28 March 1865, but still refused to stay out of the fight. He was captured by Federal troops in Stoneman's Raid on Salisbury on 12 April 1865. He was then confined at Louisville, Kentucky, until transferred to Camp Chase, Ohio, on 2 May 1865. He was released on 13 June 1865 after taking Oath of Allegiance.

*Pvt. William Henry Glover*

William Glover was the elder brother of Jerry Glover. He is reported as age 25 in the 1860 census. He and his wife, 20 year old Malvina, had a 2 year old son David and owned their own home in South Salisbury with no slaves or financial assets reported. William worked as a farmer/laborer, and was next door neighbors to Michael Beaver and his wife Sarah. Service files state William was age 25 when he enlisted in Company K on 26 June 1861 in Rowan County. Glover was assigned extra duty as a nurse in the regimental field hospital in July to August 1861. He participated in the 1862 campaigns on the Penninsula, and distinguished himself at the battle of Seven Pines. He subsequently fought in the battle at Gaines Mill during the Seven Days battles around Richmond, and was also at Sharpsburg where he was mortally wounded. He died on 19 September 1862, but records do not indicate where he died. Afterward, his widow filed a claim with the Confederate government for pay due him and received $169.96 on 26 January 1963. Malvina remained friends with the Beaver family. When she remarried in 1865, William's former comrade Michael was their bondsman.

*Pvt. Philip A. Heilig (Heilick)*

In 1860, Philip Heilig was 19 years old and living with his mother who was identified as a farmer in the census with $19,000.00 in assets and no slaves. Philip was the oldest of 6 children, who each held $3,000.00 in assets from an inheritance from their father. He enlisted on 30 June 1861 in Rowan County at age 19. He was reported sick in an unspecified hospital shortly after arriving at Camp Pickens near Manassas, Virginia in July and August 1861, for an unspecified illness although there was a typhoid outbreak during that encampment. He was severely wounded in the leg at Seven Pines, on 31 May 1862 but survived and returned to duty in time to be captured at Sharpsburg, Maryland, on 17 September 1862. He was confined at Fort Delaware, until transferred to Aiken's Landing, James River, Virginia, on 2 October 1862 for exchange. Pvt. Helig was declared exchanged on 10 November 1862 and returned to the company. He was on leave in March 1864, to serve as best man in the wedding of his comrade Otto Holshouser on 8 March in Salisbury. He returned to the company, and shortly afterward captured a Federal colonel on 8 May according to *Clark's Regiments of North Carolina*. As a reward for his courage, he was given the colonel's revolver, but he didn't carry it for long because he was killed at the battle of Spotsylvania on 12 May 1864. His mother filed a claim with the Confederate government for pay due him on 20 October 1864, but the claim document in his service file does not specify the amount.

*Pvt. David Heim*

There was no census data found for David Heim in Rowan or surrounding counties in 1850 or 1860. He was age 30 at enlistment on 4 July 1861 in Salisbury. His service was brief, as he died at Plains Station Virginia in an unspecified hospital of cholera morbus. This was a nineteenth-century medical term for a broad category of non-epidemic cholera and other gastrointestinal diseases, hallmarked by intense manifestations of vomiting, diarrhea, fatigue, and weakness, usually resulting in death. Such a condition is now referred to as gastroenteritis. (See antiquusmorbus.com for a useful reference on antiquated eighteenth- and nineteenth-century medical terminology).

*Pvt. John L. Hendricks*

John Hendricks was 22 years old, unmarried, and lived in the area of Rowan County north of the railroad in 1860. He had four slaves according to the census. Hendricks enlisted on the same date as Pvt. David Heim on 4 July 1861, and was then age 22. His service was also brief, as he died at Camp Pickens near Manassas, Virginia, 19 August 1861 of typhoid fever.

*Sgt. Michael Hennesey (Henesee)*

Known as "Mike" to friends and family, he was 5 feet, 8 inches tall with blue eyes, dark hair, and a dark complexion. He immigrated to the United States from Ireland in the 1850's and came to Rowan County via New York. He was age 25 in 1860 and living with the family of John Shuman in Salisbury, to whom he was apprenticed as a carpenter. Shuman reported $2,025.00 in assets and 8 slaves. He enlisted at "Garrett's Store" in Rowan County at age 26 on 16 July 1861 for the war. Oddly, he mustered in as a private but was promoted to sergeant on the same day he enlisted. Sgt. Hennesey is erroneously reported as "missing, thought deserted" at Gettysburg between 3-5 July 1863 on muster rolls but was rather captured according to a prison ledger with his signature found in his service file. He was confined at Fort Delaware, Delaware, until released May 1865 after taking Oath of Allegiance.

*Pvt. Charles Heyer*

There was no census data from Rowan or surrounding counties in 1850 or 1860. He enlisted at age 25 in Rowan County on 4 July 1861. Company K muster roll data shows him present until September 1864 when he was detail as a musician in the 4th NCST regimental band. Heyer was an original member of the Salisbury Brass Band during antebellum. He was quickly appointed as a musician, and permanently assigned to the band on 11 February 1863.

*Pvt. Wiley Holshouser*

There were no census records from Rowan or surrounding counties in 1860 or 1850 for this soldier. His service files show he reported his age as 21 on 29 June 1861 when he volunteered for the duration of the war. Company K muster rolls show him present through 1864 but his fate is unknown, as he was not present at Appomattox in April 1865.

*Pvt. Crawford Holshouser*

Crawford Holshouser was born in 1844 at Rowan County. He was the 2d eldest of six children by Jacob and Deliah Holshouser, who immigrated to Rowan County from Germany in the 18th Century. In 1860 he was age 16 and residing on his parents' farm at Gold Hill. His father reported $1730.00 in assets with no slaves. His older brother Miles was also in Company K, as was his cousin, Otto Holshouser. Crawford was illiterate, signing his name only with a mark on muster rolls. Prior to enlisting in Company K, he was an officer in the Rowan County militia. He was commissioned as a 1st Lieutenant on 30 December 1861 in Company E, 76th North Carolina Militia Regiment, which was assigned to the 19th Brigade. He first appears on muster rolls in 1862, and the Roll of Honor states he was captured at Sharpsburg on 17 September 1862, but his service file erroneously indicates his enlistment date was not until 10 February 1864. He was wounded in the hand at Cedar Creek on 19 October, 1864. His service files notate that he was present or accounted for until 19 January 1865. Records from Appomattox do not indicate he was present at the time of surrender. He apparently returned to Rowan County, however, as he was paroled at Salisbury 16 May 1865 and took Oath of Allegiance there on 27 June 1865. He married Elizabeth Harkey on 6 November 1865.

*Pvt. David Lewis Holshouser (Lewis D.)*

There was no census data found in Rowan or surrounding counties in 1850 or 1860 for David Lewis Holshouser. He was born to David Holshouser and Louise Agner in 1844 at Rowan County. He supposedly enlisted at age 21 in Rowan County on 7 March 1862. His death certificate indicates he was 86 years old in 1930, however, suggesting Holshouser exaggerated his age to enlist. He did not serve long before being severely wounded in the breast at the battle of Seven Pines on 31 May 1862. It is not known whether he was hospitalized then. He survived, and was with the company at the battle of Chancellorsville on 3 May 1863 where he was again wounded. There he suffered a gunshot to the right side. The surgeon indicated the wound was "cut near the crest of the Illium, and passed out of the rear…" He was admitted to Greaner's Hospital Ward Eighteen in Richmond and reported as absent-wounded by Company K through August 1864. He was given a 60 day furlough shortly after entering the hospital, and returned there where he remained until the end of the war. He returned to Salisbury and took Oath of Allegiance there on 10 June 1865. Holshouser was married at some point, but was widowed when he died from cancer on 20 June 1930. He had the distinction of being the last surviving member of the Rowan Rifles.

*Pvt. Milas Monroe Holshouser "Miles"*

Miles was 5 feet, 7 inches tall, with blue eyes, dark hair and a light complexion. He was born on 19 March 1841 and was the eldest of their six children. The 1860 census shows him at age 19 and residing with his parents and siblings on their farm in Gold Hill. His father Jacob reported $1,730.00 in assets but did not own slaves. Miles was then employed as a day laborer. Crawford Holshouser, also a member of Company K was his younger brother, and Otto Holshouser, also a member, was his cousin. In 1861 21 year old Miles was a resident of Iredell County in Statesville when he came to Salisbury to volunteer for Company K on 29 June 1861. He was reported sick in quarters while stationed at Camp Pickens near Manassas, Virginia in July-August 1861. Although his service records did not support this, a family anecdote suggests that he was wounded in the left leg at Seven Pines on 31 May 1862. Muster rolls show him present until the battle of Sharpsburg when he was captured near Boonsboro, Maryland on or about 17 September 1862, and confined at Fort Delaware, Delaware, until he was transferred on 2 October 1862 to Aiken's Landing, James River, Virginia, for exchange. He was declared exchanged there on 10 November 1862 and returned to the company.

Rowan County marriage records indicate he returned home to marry 18 year old Dela Troutman on 11 November 1863. Miles returned to the field shortly afterward and was present until he was wounded in the right leg on or about 13 February 1864. The details are not found in his records, but his records suggest that General R.E. Lee ordered him to serve as a "sentinel" (guard) when he was admitted to the unspecified Richmond hospital. He was transferred to Jackson Hospital in Richmond on 9 March 1864, and remained there detailed as a hospital guard. During his tenure as a guard while convalescing, Miles was accused of Forgery and arrested. Records show that he was sent to the Provost Marshall, Maj. J.H. Harris in Richmond although the outcome is not clear. Although entirely speculative, he may have forged the order from Lee to prevent himself from returning to the line of battle by serving as a hospital guard. If true, this may also lend some insight into the severity (or lack of it) of his wound. The charges must have been dropped, as he was given a furlough to Salisbury on 11 August 1864. He returned to the hospital as he received another 30 day furlough to Gold Hill on 5 January 1865.

Miles is reported as deserted from the hospital on 28 February 1865. He may have went back to the company without authorization from the doctors, however, as he rejoined the company prior to 3 April 1865 when he was captured at Petersburg. Prison documents show he was taken to Hart's Island, New York Harbor and confined there until 8 June 1865. On that day he was released after taking the Oath of Allegiance. His first wife Dela died on 25 April 1881, leaving their three children. Miles remarried Dela's sister, Rosanna Lee Troutman on 25 September 1881. He died on 14 January 1915. He is buried at St. Peters Church cemetery in Rowan County beside of Dela.

*Sgt. Otho (Otto) Holshouser*

Known as Otto to friends and family, he was born in 1837 to Jacob Jr. and Rachel Brown Holshouser of Rockwell. Jacob was the illiterate postmaster of that district, and the Rev. Samuel Rothrock, a well known Lutheran minister of the area, recorded in his diary that he regularly visited Jacob to help him complete his monthly reports at the post office. The minister was also close friends with Otto's grandfather, Jacob Sr., as his diary further mentions they often visited and exchanged meat, shoes and other dry goods, many of which Jacob was believed to have made himself. Otto's great, great, great, great grandfather was Casper Holzhauzen who migrated to Pennsylvania from the Palatinate area of Western Germany in the early 1730's. The 1860 census shows Otto working in Gold Hill as an overseer for eleven slaves on the farm of Mary Heilig, a widow, who was the aunt of his close friend Philip Heilig. Otto was then reported to be age 23. Mary Heilig was wealthy and reported assets of $19,000.00. Each of her six children held $3,000.00 in property willed to them by their father before his death.

Otto enlisted in Gold Hill on 3 July 1861 as a private, and indicated his age was 25. He was captured at or near Boonsboro, Maryland, on or about 17 September 1862 and confined at Fort Delaware, Delaware, until transferred to Aiken's Landing, James River, Virginia, on 2 October 1862 for exchange. He was declared exchanged 10 November 1862 and returned to duty. Holshouser was promoted to sergeant between January–April 1863. He fought at Gettysburg, and was wounded in left elbow on either 2 or 3 July, but rejoined the company prior to 1 September 1863. He was present through 6 March 1864, when he received a furlough to go home and marry Laura M. Brown on 8 March. Philip Heilig of Company K went with him, and is shown on the marriage records as his bondsman (best man) in the ceremony. Otto was killed near Spotsylvania Court House, Virginia, on 10 or 11 May 1864, just before the massive Federal assault on Confederate "Muleshoe" salient on 12 May (see front cover of this book for illustration). An unidentified eyewitness reported that "Sgt Holshouser…was sitting with his back against a good sized tree, our part of the line not being engaged, when a cannon ball struck the opposite side of the tree, killing him instantly by the shock."

*Pvt. Joseph C. Irvin*

The 1860 census identifies 22 year old Joseph as a clerk working at the establishment of T.C. McNeely, a merchant in Salisbury. He reported $125.00 in assets. Little else is known of his life before the war. He enlisted at age 23 on 21 June 1861 at Rowan County. Muster rolls show he was present through December 1861, but afterward his name does not appear and nothing is mentioned of his fate afterward.

*Pvt. John C. Jenkins*

32 John was married in 1860 at the time of the census, and resided with his 28 year old wife Margaret in their own home. His occupation is unknown, but his birthplace is shown as Ireland in the census. No financial data was reported and his name does not appear as a slave holder in the 1860 slave index. His name is not found on early muster rolls for Company K, although he appears in 1864 as a conscript. He was paroled at Salisbury on 2 May 1865. His first wife died, and he remarried Ellen Heilig on 6 January 1869.

*Pvt. Charles R. Jones*

Charles Jones was a resident of Rowan County, without assets or slaves when volunteered for Company K at age 21 on 21 June 1861. He was present until he ostensibly received a commission as a second lieutenant in Company G, 55th Regiment, NCST, on 12 September 1862 and transferred out of the company. A document in his service file indicates that his commission was confabulated, probably as a prank along with another private from Company K, William Durrell. A third friend of his identified as Jack Connelly was then detailed as a clerk, who fraudulently penned a letter to a Col. William Parnell recommending the commission on behalf of a Major Myers, who supposedly recommended his "esteemed friend" Charles for a commission. Yet this occurred without the Major's knowledge of the matter, and when Jones reported to the 55th NCT, no one knew him. He was ordered by the Provost Marshall to report for duty in the 4th NCST at Petersburg, Virginia on 2 November 1862. The officers of the 4th NCST did not appear to be aware of the stunt, and it does not appear that he was ever arrested for the act, as muster rolls continue to report him present through 31 August 1864 and make no mention of any court martial proceedings or arrest. After the war, Jones became the influential founder of the *Charlotte Observer* newspaper, which remains in operation to this day. Because he was present in 1861 and obviously had a penchant toward reporting the news, it is likely that Jones was "Scribbler"- the anonymous correspondent who provided detailed accounts of the companies' activities in 1861 through part of 1862.

*Pvt. Wallace Josey*

The 1860 census identifies Wallace as age 16, and residing on his widowed mother's farm in Gold Hill. His mother, Sarah, reported assets of $810.00and no slaves. He reported his age as 20 years old when he enlisted in Company K on 29 March 1862. Muster rolls show he was present until 3 June 1864 when he was wounded in the face at Cold Harbor, Virginia when the regiment was stationed in the trenches. Nothing else is recorded about his service.

*Pvt. Wilson R. Josey (William R.)*

The only son of John Josey, Jr. who was a farmer owning 90 acres of land and no slaves, 16 year old Wilson was living with the John Rusher family in 1860 according to the census. Rusher was a farmer with $1,800.00 in assets reported. Wilson was illiterate as he could only sign muster rolls with a mark. He enlisted in Company K at age 18 on 29 June 1861 in Salisbury. He was present in all major campaigns of 1862 including the Penninsula, and distinguished himself at the battle of

Seven Pines. He was also in ranks during the Seven Days battles, South Mountain and Sharpsburg. He was killed in the fierce early morning assaults led by his regiment as part of Ramseur's Brigade against the Federal XII Corps on 3 May 1863 at the battle of Chancellorsville. His personal valor in this battle earned him a nomination for the Confederate Badge of Distinction for Gallantry, an honor considered akin to the Medal of Honor by Confederates after the Civil War. It is not known whether his family was made aware of the award or not.

*Pvt. Joseph Kelly*

25 year old "Joe" was working as a bartender in Salisbury in 1860, unmarried, and reported no financial assets or slaves. He is reported as age 35 on 14 April 1863 when he enlisted in Company K. The age discrepancy likely reflects an error on part of the recorder in muster records as it would not be logical for a man already of age who was volunteering to report himself 10 years older, especially since he was still within conscription range and volunteered. Muster rolls indicate he was present until 1 December 1864. However, Kelly was absent on sick status during much of that time. His illness or condition is not recorded in service files. He was detailed as nurse at the Confederate Hospital in Salisbury on 1 December 1864 where he remained until the end of the war. He was paroled there on 2 May 1865.

*Pvt. Rego Landcherry (Lancherry)*

Rego Lancherry was born in Italy, and it is not known when he migrated to Rowan County. There is no census information on him from 1850 or 1860, although marriage records show he married Jane Johnson on 7 April 1860. When he enlisted in Company K on or about 12 March 1862, he was living in Salisbury, and was 30 years old. He quickly became ill with pneumonia in the bitter rains the regiment suffered on the Virginia Penninsula at Yorktown, and died almost one month later in the hospital at Richmond, Virginia, on 11 April 1862.

*Sgt. Hamilton C. Long*

Hamilton Long, nicknamed "Ham" by his friends, was reported as 25 years old when he enlisted as a private in Company K, 4th NCST at Manassas, Virginia, on 17 August 1861. He was the son of wealthy physician Dr. Alexander Long, who was well known in Salisbury. Dr. Long had six slaves and financial assets of $3,300.00 in the 1860 census. Long was 22 years old and working as an Agent at the Salisbury railroad depot in 1861. In antebellum North Carolina, the local rail agent was a very influential person; they had access to a telegraph, and controlled information flow of news and information regarding the status of departing and inbound passengers, as well as receiving mail and other important deliveries from the rail road. Long grew up as the youngest of three children. Long was appointed second lieutenant on 23 November 1861 and fought at the 1862 battles of Seven Pines, Seven Days battles around Richmond, South Mountain and Sharpsburg and witnessed the killing fields of Fredericksburg. In 1863 Long participated in the major actions of Chancellorsville and Gettysburg before resigning on 6 November due to "chronic diarrhea." Long eventually returned to Salisbury, where he regained his health. Long was present as part of the militia on 12 April 1865 when Federal cavalry raided and burned the government facilities in the town, but he was not wounded or captured. The 1870 census indicates he was living with a woman indentified only as "M" and had a seven and a half year old female child living with them, but it is not clear they were his wife or daughter. A review of post war marriage records 1868-1870 in Rowan County did not identify him as married, but he could have married outside of the county. In the 1870 census Long was still working as an Express Agent at the Salisbury Railroad depot, as he had done before the war.

*Pvt. James Clayton McCanless (McCanlas)*

James McCanless was born in 1841, and named after a paternal uncle who had moved to Colorado in the 1850's that was shot and killed by outlaw gunslinger "Wild Bill" Hickok. On 7 July 1860, 18 year old James was living with his parents on their farm in Gold Hill. His father Joseph was a miner with financial assets of $3,550.00 and no slaves. McCanless lived only two doors away from John T. Crowell, who also enlisted in Company K. His elder brother William worked as a bookkeeper, in contrast to James who worked as a day laborer. Note the census spelled his last name as "McCanlas." 19 year old James enlisted as a private in Company K on 29 June 1861 in Rowan County for the duration of the war. He was admitted to hospital in Richmond, Virginia, on 28 June 1862 with gunshot wound to right hand, resulting in loss of "little finger." The location and date of his wounding were not recorded in his service records or on the company muster roll for this period. James rejoined the company prior to 1 January 1864 and was present as a private with the sixteen survivors of Company K at Appomattox on 9 April 1865. He was paroled on the same date, and returned to Salisbury afterward. James took the Oath of Allegiance at Salisbury on 13 June 1865, and his name appears on the Roll of Honor for Company K. He married Elizabeth Steidfor on 4 July 1886.

*Pvt. Julius A. McDonald*

Julius McDonald was born in Ireland in 1841. It is not known when he came to Rowan County. There was no census data found for 1850 or 1860 in Rowan or surrounding counties. He enlisted as a private in Rowan County at age 20 sometime during 20-22 September 1861 for the war. Julius was present in the 1862 campaigns including Yorktown, Williamsburg, Seven Pines, the Seven Days, and he was wounded at Sharpsburg, Maryland, on 17 September 1862 fighting in the Bloody Lane and died on 21 September at an unnamed location.

*Pvt. Alexander M. McQueen*

26 year old "Alex" was a resident of H.M. Sossaman's boarding house in Salisbury on 5 June 1860. He was a former resident of Montgomery County, where his father, Alexander McQueen was a farmer with seven slaves. His brother William was an original member of the antebellum Rowan Rifle Guards and later served in Company K, along with his other brother Daniel who also enlisted in Company K. Alex was unmarried and worked as a millwright in 1861. He lived a few blocks away from William Buis, another member of Co. K whose father owned the Mansion House Hotel in Salisbury. McQueen's personal assets are not shown, but his name does not appear as a slave holder in 1860. He enlisted at age 27 at Orange Court House, Virginia, on 20 March 1862 for the war. He was severely wounded in the thigh at the battle of Seven Pines on 31 May 1862. McQueen was again wounded on 15 December 1862 at Fredericksburg according to the Roll of Honor. The latter erroneously identified him as later dying from that wound however. Yet, he was absent-wounded until February 1864, when he returned but was detailed for lighter duty in the Signal Corps. He remained there and was reported present in August 1864. Likely due to subsequent problems with his health from the wounds, McQueen was next detailed as a teamster, where he served as a private until the end of the war. He was present among the sixteen survivors

of Company K at Appomattox on 9 April 1865, although his detached duty precluded participation in the final surrender ceremony.

*Pvt. Daniel McQueen (McQucan)*

Daniel McQueen was the oldest brother of Alex McQueen. In 1860 he resided with his father on their farm in Montgomery County, North Carolina where he worked as a laborer. Daniel and Alex attended public school in 1850, and their mother was deaf according to the census. Daniel enlisted in Company K on 21 March 1862 in Rowan County. He was present at Seven Pines, the Seven Days battles, and was wounded in heavy fighting at Fox's Gap along the National Turnpike at South Mountain on 14 September 1862. Muster rolls show him absent wounded in an unspecified hospital until he was discharged on 23 November 1863.

*Pvt. Bradley Matthews*

The 1860 census reflects Bradley Matthews lived alone in Surry County but the original document was illegible that described his financial assets. He was not a slaveholder. He traveled to Garysburg when the regiment was in camp of instruction to enlist on 18 July 1861 at age 22. He was present in all major campaigns in 1862 according to muster rolls, and reported as Absent without leave (AWOL) from 20 January 1863 through August 1863. He did not face court martial for unknown reasons and returned to the company in August 1864 when they were in the Shenandoah Valley. His post-war pension records show that he was wounded in the right side at Minute Town, Virginia, on 19 October 1864 after the Battle at Cedar Creek. There is no other information as to his whereabouts or further service.

*Pvt. James Mauldin*

James Mauldin did not appear in the 1860 census as a slaveholder but his financial assets were not recorded. Service files show he enlisted in Rowan County at age 18 on either 9 or 24 March 1862 for the war. Mauldin was wounded at Seven Pines on 31 May 1862, sustaining a fracture of his thigh, and reported absent wounded through 10 August 1863, when he died of wounds received at Seven Pines. The location of his death is not reported.

*Pvt. Alfred W. Miller*

Alfred Miller was 5 feet, 10 inches tall, and was 23 years old and unmarried in 1860. The census identifies no financial assets. He was then living with his parents, Peter and Sophia Miller who reported assets of $2,100.00 and no slaves. Miller enlisted on 3 July 1861 at age 22 years. He was present in all major battles of 1862 in which the regiment participated, and distinguished himself at the battle of Seven Pines. He was mortally wounded at the Battle of South Mountain on 14 September and died in the hospital at Frederick City Maryland although the date was not recorded. He was buried on 24 September 1862 in a cemetery at Frederick City, Maryland. His father filed a claim for settlement of pay due after Alfred's death, and Capt. W.C. Coughenhour testified on his behalf that Pvt. Miller died in battle and had worked as a farmer before the war.

*Pvt. Calvin M. Miller*

Calvin Miller was 21 years old and living with his wife Jane and two children (under the age of 2) at Gold Hill in 1860. He was then employed as a day laborer with $280.00 in assets and no slaves. Miller enlisted at age 22 in Rowan County on 3 July 1861 for the war. He was slightly wounded in the head at Seven Pines on 31 May 1862, and was captured at Sharpsburg, Maryland, on 17 September 1862 and confined at Fort Delaware, Delaware, until he was transferred to Aiken's Landing, James River, Virginia, and declared exchanged on 10 November 1862. He was killed in action at the battle of Chancellorsville, on the morning 3 May 1863 along the Orange Plank Road as Ramseur's Brigade assaulted the Federal XII Corps earth works.

*Pvt. Daniel Miller*

Daniel Miller was 35 years old in 1860, and lived with his wife Nancy and three children ages 3-7 years on their farm. His financial assets were $10,000.00 in 1860 and he co-owned eight slaves who were leased to a mining company as laborers. Daniel was also the legal guardian of two orphans, David and James Reid, ages 5 and 3 years respectively, who resided with him. His enlistment is not recorded but it was in August 1862 when his name appears on muster rolls. He was wounded and captured at South Mountain, Maryland, on 14 September 1862. He died a few days later in an unspecified hospital at Frederick, Maryland, on 23 September 1862 of the wound.

*Pvt. George A. Misenheimer*

George Misenheimer enlisted in Rowan County, where he resided, on 29 February 1864 supposedly at age 32. However, that is likely in accurate as the 1860 census reflects that 16 year old George Misenheimer was living with his mother, Sarah, who was a boarder at the farm of a J. Miller where George worked as a farmer. J. Miller's financial assets were not recorded but he had three slaves in 1860. There is no evidence that Misenheimer or his family owned slaves. The Roll of Honor states that he was captured at Sharpsburg on 17 September 1862, although his service files and muster rolls do not corroborate it. Misenheimer became ill with chronic diarrhea, following a sever case of Rubella occurring on or about 15 April 1864. He was admitted to Jackson Hospital in Richmond on 21 April 1864. He was next transferred to the General Hospital at Farmville, Virginia on 29 April 1864, and furloughed for 40 days on 30 April. He eventually recovered and was present at Appomattox on 9 April and participated in the surrender ceremony on 12 April, when he was paroled. After the war, as he married Mary Temperance Turner on 25 July 1874 in Salisbury.

*Pvt. John Mowrey*

The 1860 census identifies 36 year old John as a laborer and resident on the farm of Jacob Koontz in China Grove. Koontz's assets were $1,541.00 with no slaves. John Mowrey had no assets or slaves. He enlisted in Company K on 14 June 1861, and is listed as age 24. He is found on the 30 December 1861 muster roll as present but this is the only time his name appears on Company K rolls; he died at Yorktown from wounds received during the siege there in April 1862.

*Pvt. William A. Murr*

William Murr was 5 feet, 9 inches tall, with dark eyes, dark hair, and a fair complexion according to records from Libby Prison where he was incarcerated after being captured in a Richmond hospital on 3 April 1865. In 1860 Murr was living with Capt. William Brown of the Rowan Rifle Guards to whom he was apprenticed as a tinnier, although his widowed father, Julian Murr, also reported William was then residing with him in Salisbury on the same census. Murr's father reported $1,200.00 in assets and neither he nor Brown had slaves. Murr enlisted on 22 June 1861 in Rowan County, and became ill while stationed at Camp Pickens near Manassas, Virginia in October 1861. He was detailed to a Richmond hospital on 2 October 1861, and remained there until April 1864 when he was released to his company. He was at the battles of Spotsylvania and Cold Harbor, and in the Shenandoah Valley campaign, and endured the miserable fall and winter encampments that year, only to become ill again in February 1865 requiring hospitalization. He was captured at Richmond on 3 April 1865 when Federal troops entered the city. He was sent to Libby Prison until transferred to Newport News, Virginia, on 23 April 1865 and released on 30 June 1865 after taking the Oath of Allegiance.

*Sgt. Edward B. Neave, Musician*

Edward Neave was born in Scotland. His father came to the United States to establish a textile mill, which unfortunately failed. Instead of taking the trade himself, he became a "professional" musician, but in 1860 was employed as a tinsmith. He lived in a small room at the Baker and Owens Tin ware Store in Salisbury where he also worked. Neither Neave nor the store owner, Alfred Owen, had no slaves or assets recorded in the census. Owen also boarded 24 year old William R. Gorman of Cabarrus County, who was then employed as a carpenter. Gorman was also a member of the Salisbury Brass Band. He left a detailed correspondence of his war experiences until his death in May 1864. Edward was also life-long friends with William C. Coughenhour, who became 1st Lieutenant of the Rowan Rifle Guards in March 1861, and was later captain. Neave enlisted as a private in Company K on 23 December 1862 at Rowan County. He was appointed chief musician (sergeant) on 11 February 1863 and transferred permanently to the 4th NCST regimental brass band, where he was quickly promoted to Chief Musician.

Edward's half-brother William Neave did not serve in the Rowan Rifle Guards or Company K. He was also known as an expert musician, primarily a trombonist, and was a master of many instruments. After the Civil War he ran a music school tutoring primarily for piano and violin. He was a circus musician when he first came to Salisbury to perform, and he was known as a strong pro-Union supporter. The 1860 census indicates 34 year old William Neave was earning a living teaching music and performing, and resided at the Boyden House Hotel on South Main Street, where William C. Coughenhour resided. William struggled for weeks trying to decide which side to support when the War erupted in 1861, but ultimately decided to support his state and enlisted in the 11th North Carolina Regiment. It is not known why William chose to enlist in another company besides the Rowan Rifles. It seems odd because not only were many of his friends and neighbors members of the Rowan Rifles, but also his brother Edward joined the company. Edward attended a Veterans Reunion in Statesville in September, 1920, with only two other band members, J.C. Steele and A. Gillespe. Neave died shortly afterward making him the longest living member of Company K.

*Pvt. J.T. Owen*

This soldier was a conscript, and resided in Granville County, North Carolina before the war. He was conscripted into service there on 20 July 1863 at age 36. His father David Owen was a farmer in the 1860 census with no assets or slaves reported. Owen's service records state he was a "replacement" for another conscripted that purchased their way out of being drafted in 1863. Owen is reported as present in the company from August 1863, and during much of that period he was detailed to Division Headquarters as a teamster. He returned to the company in April or May 1864, and was engaged at the battle of Spotsylvania on 12 May 1864 where he was killed in action.

*Pvt. William H Page*

William was born in New Brunswick, New Jersey, and relocated to Rowan County before the war. He does not appear in the 1850 or 1860 census there as a slaveholder, and he worked as a Railroad Engineer prior to enlistment. He was age 24 when he volunteered for Company K on 22 June 1861. William was engaged in all campaigns of 1862, and was wounded slightly in the shoulder at Seven Pines on 31 May 1862. He was also engaged in the Seven Days battles in Richmond and was captured in the Bloody Lane at Sharpsburg, Maryland, on 17 September 1862. He was quickly paroled on 21 September 1862 and returned to the company. He apparently had enough of army life, and deserted in November 1862. He is reported absent without leave (AWOL) from 10 November 1862 through August 1864.

*Pvt. William D.C. Peeler*

At age 17, William Peeler resided and worked on R. John Klutz's farm as a day laborer in Gold Hill according to the 1860 census. His assets are not reported but his name did not appear as a slaveholder. Klutz reported his own assets as $592.00 and no slaves. James Casper and Williams Phillips, both of whom also served in Company K, and were employed by Klutz. Peeler enlisted at Rowan County on 7 March 1862 when he was 18 years old. He distinguished himself during the battle of Seven Pines, and was later captured at Sharpsburg, Maryland, on 17 September 1862 and confined at Fort Delaware, Delaware, until transferred to Aiken's Landing, James River, Virginia, for exchange on 2 October 1862. He was declared exchanged 10 November 1862 and returned to the company. He fought at Chancellorsville on 1-3 May 1863, and Gettysburg where he was wounded and captured on 1 July 1863. Pvt. Peeler was hospitalized at the U.S. General Hospital, West Building, in Baltimore, Maryland, and records notate that he had his left arm and left leg missing, suggesting he was wounded by a close range artillery explosion. He was there from 14 October 1863 through 2 March 1864 when he was transferred to Fort McHenry, Maryland. He was later transferred to the prison at Point Look Out, Maryland, on 21 July 1864 where he remained until he was paroled on 18 February 1865. Upon parole, he was transferred to Boulware's and Cox's Wharf, James River, Virginia, where he was received 20-21 February 1865 for exchange. He was reported present with a detachment of paroled and exchanged prisoners identified at Camp Lee near Richmond on 23 February 1865, but did not see any further action. He returned to Salisbury later and was paroled there on 15 May 1865.

*Pvt. Robert S. Roberts*

Robert Roberts was 43 years old in 1860, and owned a farm in Davidson County, near Lexington, North Carolina. He was not a slaveholder but his financial status was not recorded. His son, James

Roberts, was a member of the antebellum Rowan Rifle Guards and later served in Company K also. James was in the company when his father was conscripted (drafted) in April 1863. Both were present for the battles of Chancellorsville and Gettysburg, although James was detailed as a clerk for much of his time in service, and also placed on medical disability lists so it is doubtful they ever fought together in the ranks. Robert was engaged at Spotsylvania and Cold Harbor in 1864, and is reported present through August 1864, but was not identified at Appomattox in April 1865. He was paroled at Salisbury on 20 May 1865.

*Pvt. Thomas Ryan*

Thomas Ryan was 31 years old, and stood 5 feet, 8 inches tall, with gray eyes, light hair, and a "ruddy" complexion in 1864. His date of enlistment and financial assets were not recorded. He is identified as a volunteer in service records, but his name appears on 1864 muster rolls as a Conscript. Ryan deserted at New Berry, Virginia, on or about 2 May 1864 and was released on 3 May 1864 under an Oath of Amnesty, with orders to "...remain north of the Ohio River during the war." He did so, and took the Oath of Allegiance in Louisville, Kentucky, on 5 May 1864.

*Pvt. Joseph Boone Saunders*

Joseph Saunders was born in White Water Arkansas in 1834. He was married and had six children in 1861. Saunders was then employed as a school teacher in Rowan County, and had no slaves or financial assets reported. He was conscripted at age 20 in Rowan County on 1 April 1863 and fought at both Chancellorsville and Gettysburg. He was detailed as a hospital steward at Richmond in July, where he remained until contracting Rubella in 1864. He was admitted to Jackson Hospital in Richmond, Virginia on 10 February 1864, and was reported absent – sick on the muster rolls throughout much of 1864 and was eventually detailed to work as a hospital steward in Richmond. Like many Confederate soldiers in the Richmond hospitals, when Saunders realized the Federals had captured the city he left the hospital trying to evade capture. He was reported absent without leave (AWOL) from the hospital until he was captured by Federal troops on 23 April 1865.

*Pvt. Henry C. Severs (Seavers)*

Henry Severs was born in 1842 at South Carolina, and was the eldest of seven children. His father migrated to the United States from Germany in the 1850's. His family spoke both English and German languages, yet Severs was illiterate. Severs was industrious, as at age 17 he was self-employed as a Brewer of alcoholic beverages in Charlotte, North Carolina with $6,800.00 in financial assets reported. Severs did not own slaves. His date of enlistment is not recorded, but it was in early 1862 at age 19. He was present at the battles of Yorktown and Williamsburg, and wounded in the thigh at the battle of Seven Pines. He was not hospitalized, however, and continued in action during the Seven Days campaign, where he was again wounded. His name appears on a list of wounded at Gen. Kershaw's Brigade infirmary on 29 June 1862, but he was reported "healed and returned to Richmond." Note that Kershaw's Brigade was comprised of South Carolinians, and Severs was born there so he may have been in contact with people he knew from home. Severs was captured at or near Sharpsburg, Maryland, on 17 September 1862 but was quickly paroled on 21 September 1862. Henry returned to the company and fought at Chancellorsville 1-3 May 1863. He was also at Gettysburg, and captured there on 4 July as the army retreated toward Maryland. He was confined at Fort McHenry Maryland. The next event in his service records is unusual to say the least; he was admitted to the U.S. Army General Hospital in Baltimore, Maryland, on 14

October 1863 with a diagnosis of Gonorrhea. One can only speculate as to where he may have contracted the illness, but the notion that he did so during the retreat from Gettysburg, or while in prison, raises complex questions regarding Civil War prison life. He was next transferred to Point Look Out, Maryland, on 21 July 1864. He was paroled at Point Look Out on 18 February 1865 and again transferred to Boulware's and Cox's Wharf, James River, Virginia, where he was received 20-21 February 1865 for exchange. Severs was present with a detachment of paroled and exchanged prisoners found at Camp Lee near Richmond on 23 February 1865.

*Pvt. George D. Snuggs*

There was no census information located for this soldier in 1850, 1860 or 1870 from Rowan or surrounding counties, but his name did not appear on the index of slaveholders in 1860. The Company K muster roll for 30 December 1860 shows that age 25 he enlisted at Gold Hill in Rowan County on 27 June 1861 for the duration of the war, and was sworn in by Capt. W.C. Coughenhour. Snuggs was wounded slightly in the arm at the battle of Seven Pines on 31 May 1862 but not hospitalized. His service records indicate that he was captured at Sharpsburg, Maryland, on 17 September 1862 and confined at Fort Delaware, Delaware. He was held there until transferred to Aiken's Landing, James River, Virginia, for exchange on 2 October 1862. George was declared exchanged 10 November 1862, and returned to Company K. At the battle of Chancellorsville on 3 May 1863, he was wounded and taken to an unspecified hospital. He rejoined the company sometime between November-December 1863 and was present until 9 April 1865, when he was reported among the 16 survivors of Company K, and was one of the eleven men present on line the morning of 12 April 1865 when the formal surrender ceremony occurred. He took Oath of Allegiance at Salisbury on 29 May 1865. After the war, Snuggs moved to Stanly County and was a resident of Albemarle. At age 73, the 1910 census reported he was married to Effie Ann with two children and three grandchildren. He passed away in 1915.

George Snuggs was one of a group of veterans from the Stanly County, North Carolina present in the town of Albemarle (the county seat of Stanly County) on the morning of 11 May 1910, when the new Confederate Monument was unveiled by the United Daughters of the Confederacy. In May 1998, there was a memorial service held there by several local Civil War re-enactors and the Sons of Confederate Veterans as well as United Daughters. One elderly lady was present stated she was age 97, and informed the author that she was present on that historic morning and was friends with some of the Confederate veterans. She described them as the "...proudest and happiest men I ever saw" and felt they deserved to be remembered with honor. Her name has escaped the author across the years, but she insisted that we should persist in perpetuating such memorials. She also asked the author to promise that he wouldn't "forget them." The kind elderly lady passed away not long afterward. This simple anecdote is included to bear witness that the author kept his word, and as a reminder that we daily lose important links to our common past, and should make effort to protect it.

*Pvt. James A. Solomon*

James Solomon first appears on Company K muster rolls in 1862. He enlisted in Rowan County on or about 1 March 1862 at age 21. His financial assets or slaveholding status are not recorded in the 1860 census. He was present at the siege of Yorktown, the battles of Williamsburg and distinguished himself at the battle of Seven Pines, only to be killed a few weeks later on 27 June 1862 at the battle of Gaines Mill during the Seven Days battles around Richmond.

*Pvt. Solomon F. Tarcroft*

Solomon Tarcroft was a conscript but his service does not state a date of enlistment. The 1860 census did not record his financial or slaveholding status. His name appears on company muster rolls in 1864, and he was captured at the third battle of Winchester, Virginia, on 19 September 1864 and confined at Harpers Ferry, West Virginia, until transferred to Point Look Out, Maryland, on 24 September 1864.

*Sgt. Pembrooke Giles Taylor*

Known as "Pemmie" to his friends, Taylor is mentioned in the correspondence of Nat Raymer of Company C as a member of Company K, 4th NCST. He was a resident of Davie County in the 1860 census, then age 30, married with three children, and employed as a laborer with no slaves. His date of enlistment is not recorded, and his service files indicate only that he was captured at the third battle of Winchester, Virginia, on 19 September 1864 and confined at Harpers Ferry, West Virginia, until transferred to Point Look Out, Maryland, on 24 September 1864.

*Pvt. Fletcher Thompson*

Fletcher Thompson's date of enlistment is not recorded in his service records, nor was financial assets or slaveholding status recorded in the 1860 census. He appears on the 31 December 1861 to 28 February 1862 Company K muster roll on a detached detail as a courier during January-February 1862. His name does not appear on later rolls, and service records do not indicate any further evidence of service.

*Pvt. Nelson Augustus Thompson*

16 year old Nelson Thompson resided with his parents in 1860 working as a laborer. He and his twin brother Sylvester was the second eldest of nine children. His father Wiley Thompson reported financial assets at $2,200.00 and no slaves. Thompson enlisted at Rowan County on 19 June 1861, when he was 18 years old. He died at Camp Pickens near Manassas, Virginia, on 22 September 1861 of typhoid fever.

*Pvt. Noah Benjamin Troutman*

Noah Troutman volunteered on 11 March 1862 in Salisbury at age 27. The 1860 census did not record financial assets or slaveholding status. Troutman was captured at Sharpsburg, Maryland, on 17 September 1862 and paroled a few days later at Keedysville, Maryland, on 20 September 1862. He was ordered to face court martial on 23 February 1863, by General Orders No. 26, Headquarters, Army of Northern Virginia, but was cleared of charges and released to the company. His service files did not specify the nature of charges. He was engaged at the battle of Chancellorsville on 1-3 May 1863, where he was wounded in left leg requiring amputation in the field. He survived, but was discharged later in 1863 and returned home. He was living in Rowan County after his discharge, when he took the Oath of Allegiance at Salisbury on 4 July 1865.

*Pvt. Levi Turner*

In 1860 Levi Turner was 16 years old, residing with his parents, and illiterate. He worked as a day laborer. His father James Turner was also a laborer with $50.00 in financial assets and no slaves. Turner enlisted in Rowan County at age 21 on 7 March 1862. Turner was present until he was wounded in left knee at Seven Pines on 31 May 1862 according to pension records. He returned to the company in 1862, and served at Chancellorsville and Gettysburg in 1863. He was admitted to hospital in Richmond on 1 June 1864 with a second gunshot wound; the location and date of wound are not recorded in his service files. He was released on 3 July 1864, and given a 30 day furlough on 25 August 1864. He returned to the company, only to be wounded a third time, this time in the left elbow, at the third battle of Winchester, Virginia, on 19 September 1864 according to his pension application. He must not have returned to the company afterward, although is not identified as a deserter, because he was paroled at Troy, North Carolina, on 22 May 1865. He took the Oath of Allegiance at Salisbury on 10 July 1865.

*Pvt. Henry Williams*

Henry Williams was 5 feet, 11 inches tall, with hazel eyes, fair hair and fair complexion at age 24 years. He lived in Cabarrus County near Gold Hill where he worked as a miner, and had eight slaves in 1860. He volunteered on 20 September 1862 at Rowan County. He was present in the major campaigns of 1863, including the battles of Chancellorsville and Gettysburg. He was later detailed as a Pioneer, which was akin to modern Combat Engineer service in the Civil War, from 19 August 1862 through 15 August 1864. Then, he was again detailed "on detached service at the mines" making use of his former trade. He remained on detached service and did not likely see further action. He took the Oath of Allegiance at Charleston, West Virginia, on 9 April 1865. The latter suggests that he may have been working in the salt mines in the Saltville, Virginia area or other location in West Virginia as the region was rich with mining activity for salt, coal and copper during the war.

*Cpl. Richard D. Williams*

Richard Williams was 24 years old at enlistment in Rowan County on 30 May 1861. Note the date of his enlistment was the same day the Rowan Rifles mustered in for the duration of the war at Fort Johnson, but service records reflect Williams was still in Rowan County and not with the antebellum company. Williams lived in Gold Hill and worked as a miner, but financial assets or slaveholding status did not appear in the 1860 census. He was promoted to corporal prior to 1 September 1861, and later wounded by an artillery round exploding near him at the battle of Seven Pines on 31 May 1862. He was hit in the face and right hand, causing the loss of his left eye, right thumb, and second finger on his right hand. He was reported absent-wounded on detail as a guard and cook in a Richmond hospital until ordered to rejoin the company on 21 October 1864. Although he tried to return to the ranks, Williams never recovered fully, and on 4 November 1864 he was retired to the Invalid Corps by "reason of disability."

*Pvt. George S. Winters*

George Winters enlisted in Company K at age 18 years on 18 June 1861. The 1860 census did not record his financial assets or slaveholding status. Company K muster rolls indicate he served until killed in action at the battle of Seven Pines on 31 May 1862.

*Pvt. Henry Wise*

Henry Wise was 35 years old, and married to a widow when he volunteered to enlist on 9 March 1862. He was the younger brother of Tobias Wise, who also served in Company K. His financial assets are not recorded in the 1860 census, and he did not appear in the index of slave holders. He was severely wounded in the shoulder and leg at Seven Pines on 31 May 1862, and died in an unspecified hospital in Richmond, Virginia, on or about 22 June 1862 from wounds. His personal effects were given to his wife there by a clerk on 22 June 1862.

*Pvt. Tobias Wise*

Tobias Wise was 47 years old, and married to 38 year old Sarah Smith in 1860. He then owned his own home located in the area of the county "North of the Railroad" near Davidson County, with $3,312.00 in financial assets and no slaves. Wise was the elder brother of Henry Wise, who also served in Company K. Tobias enlisted at Rowan County on 9 March 1862, although his age was then recorded as 40 years. Wise was engaged at all major battles in 1862, including Yorktown, Seven Pines, the Seven Days, South Mountain, and Sharpsburg. He became ill during the early winter of 1863 and was sent to an unspecified Richmond Hospital, where he died on or about 19 April 1863.

*The Company "Laundref"*
*Williams Phillips*

This man first appears on the 31 August 1864 muster roll completed by 1st Lieutenant Marcus Hofflin, who did not rank Phillips as a private, but rather a "Laundref." This word is a variant of the term "Laundress" and was commonly used by Europeans, and has a Welsh origin, and describes a person who simply washes laundry. Williams Phillips was in the 1860 Rowan County census, as 14 years old and residing and working as a laborer on the farm of R. John Klutz in Gold Hill with no financial assets or slaves. Two other Company K men, James Casper and William Peeler also lived and worked there. Phillips became affiliated with Company K on 29 February 1864 at age 18 in Rowan County, but why he was not enlisted or conscripted as a soldier is unknown. The muster roll indicates it was his friend "Private Casper" who recruited him into the organization, and pay records show he received pay due from his date of enlistment as the soldiers did. Phillips accompanied Company K through the battles of Spotsylvania, North Anna and Cold Harbor, and also fought in the arduous Shenandoah Valley campaign August-October 1864. Phillips did not appear in the 1870 census in Rowan County, and there were no marriage records located after the war.

# Appendix B

## Soldiers Erroneously Affiliated with Company K in Compiled Service Records

Both Compiled Service Records and a popular reference work by Louis Manarin and Jordan have suggested these men were members of this company, but upon review of the original documents, were not clearly linked to Company K. Some of their service records are contained in the same files as known Company K members, but the War Department Clerks did not include clear documentation of their connection to this company beyond including their files in the same groups. None of these men appear on Company K Muster rolls. Some were identified as a member of a different company in the 4th NCST or another regiment, and their records may have been filed under Company K in error.

### Pvt. E. Bright

There is no E. Bright found on Company K muster rolls 1861-1864. He may have been a conscript. His service file shows that he deserted to the enemy near City Point Virginia, and was taken into custody by the 1st New York Mounted Rifles at Rich Square on 6 April 1865. He was taken to Portsmouth, Virginia and reported to the provost marshal there. Bright was confined at Washington, D.C. and took the Oath of Allegiance on 9 April 1865. He was reported as present at Washington D.C. on 12 April 1865.

### Pvt. James H. Cameron

The Compiled Service Records for North Carolina associate this man as a member of Company C, 21st NCST although his service file is located in the same group as Company K. There is a lengthy document included in his service file from the Adjutant General's office indicating the clerk was unable to link him to Company K, suggesting his inclusion was an error. Cameron was captured at Winchester on 19 September 1864, and was taken to Point Lookout, Maryland. He eventually took the Oath of Allegience there and joined the Union Army but records did not specify what regiment. A review of the *Roster of Union Soldiers* (Janet B. Hewett, Ed., Wilmington, NC: Broadfoot Press, 1977) identified four Union regiments having a man with the same name, Company I, 8th Kentucky Cavalry, Company G, 53d, Ohio Volunteer Infantry, Company D, 3d New Jersey Cavalry and the 5th Wisconsin Infantry Regiment but this author was unable to confirm to which regiment he joined at the time of this publication.

### Pvt. D.F. Hallhouse

D. Hallhouse was a conscript. His name does not appear on Company K muster rolls and his service file notes only that he was paroled at Salisbury on 11 May 1865.

### Pvt. William H. Marr

This soldier's was actually a member of Company B, 4th NCST and not Company K. His service files were erroneously included amongst a large group of documents for Company K, which may have led to his inclusion in as a Company K member in the work of Manarin and Jordan.

*Pvt. John Murphy*

John Murphy was a resident of Craven County, North Carolina before enlisting, and his connection to Company K is doubtful. His service files are located with the group containing Company K but this may be an error as his name does not appear on any muster rolls. He deserted to enemy at or near Mumfordsville, Kentucky, on 2 May 1864 and took the Oath of Allegiance at Louisville, Kentucky, on 5 May 1864. It is not clear what he was doing in Kentucky. One possible scenario is that Murphy was one of the Company K men detached to work in the mines in western Virginia during 1864, which would explain how he got into Kentucky, but this is unlikely since his name does not appear on muster rolls.

*Pvt. T.J. Oldham*

Oldham's connection to Company K is not clear, as his service files notate only that he was captured in an unspecified hospital in Richmond on 3 April 1865, and transferred into custody of the United States Army Provost Marshall on 20 April 1865. There are no further records indicating whether he took the Oath of Allegience or other outcome. His name does not appear on Company K muster rolls so it is doubtful he was actually a member of the company.

*Pvt. R.A. Robinson*

R.A. Robinson does not appear on Company K muster rolls. The only document located in his service file stated simply that he took the Oath of Allegiance at Charlotte, North Carolina, on 15 May 1865.

*Pvt. R.M. Ruth*

There is no census data located for this soldier in Rowan or surrounding counties in 1850 or 1860. His name does not appear on any muster rolls, but he is identified as a member of Company K who is buried in the Confederate Cemetery in Winchester, Virginia.

*Pvt. James L Wallace*

James Wallace was identified by the author as a member of Company A 4th NCST although his service documents are located in the same group as Company K. His name does not appear on Company K muster rolls. He died at Point Lookout, Maryland, on 21 March 1865 of Scurvy.

*Pvt. George Wright*

George Wright's date of enlistment is not recorded, although he was conscripted sometime in 1864. Wright's financial assets or slaveholder status was not recorded in the 1860 census. He was present during Lee's retreat from Petersburg in April 1865, and was captured near Appomattox during the engagement there on 9 April 1865 prior to Lee's surrender. He was paroled on 14 or 17 April 1865 at Burkeville Junction, Virginia. Rowan County marriage records indicate he married Ellen M. Miller on 14 December 1880 and was residing in Salisbury at the time.

# *Appendix C*

## *Company K Mortality & Discharge Table 1861-1865*

### Deaths by Disease

|                                      | 1861 | 1862 | 1863 | 1864 | 1865 |
|--------------------------------------|------|------|------|------|------|
| Number Lost:                         | 8    | 2    | 3    | 1    | 0    |
| Discharged:<br>(Not to Invalid Corps) | 3    | 2    | 1    | 2    | 0    |

## *Appendix D*

### *Co. K Desertions 1861-1865*

|                    | 1861 | 1862 | 1863 | 1864 | 1865 |
|--------------------|------|------|------|------|------|
| Rowan Rifle Guards | 0    | 2    | 0    | 3    | 0    |
| 1861 Volunteers    | 0    | 1    | 0    | 0    | 0    |
| Conscripts         | 1    | 1    | 0    | 2    | 0    |

Note: Includes all Rowan Rifle Guards who remained in Co. K, Volunteers who enlisted during or after June 1861 and Conscripts 1862-1864.

## Appendix E

### Ordnance Items Issued 4th Regiment, North Carolina State Troops
### June - December 1861

| Captain: | Simonton | Wood | Andrews | - | Carter | Barnes | Kelley | Osborne | Marsh | McNeely |
|---|---|---|---|---|---|---|---|---|---|---|
| Co. | A | B | C | D | E | F | G | H | I | K |
| **Item:** | | | | | | | | | | |
| Muskets, or Rifles | 111 | 80 | 88 | 78 | 79* | 89 | 78** | 64** | 80 | 90 |
| Bayonets | 111 | 80 | 88 | 78 | 79* | 89 | 78** | 64** | 80 | 80 |
| Ball Screws | 10 | 4 | 4 | 5 | 0 | 5 | 6 | 5 | 4 | 4 |
| Spring Vices | 5 | 4 | 4 | 0 | 5 | 5 | 5 | 5 | 4 | 4 |
| Screwdrivers | 92 | 80 | 88 | 78 | 79 | 89 | 78 | 64 | 80 | 80 |
| Wipers | 92 | 80 | 88 | 78 | 79 | 89 | 78 | 64 | 80 | 80 |
| Cones | 130 | 80 | 0 | 5 | 0 | 24 | 25 | 20 | 80 | 20 |
| Cart. Boxes | 93 | 80 | 88 | 78 | 80 | 89 | 78 | 64 | 80 | 80 |
| Cap Boxes | 93 | 80 | 88 | 78 | 80 | 89 | 78 | 64 | 80 | 80 |
| Scabbards | 93 | 80 | 88 | 78 | 80 | 80 | 78 | 64 | 80 | 80 |
| Waist Belt | 93 | 80 | 88 | 78 | 80 | 80 | 78 | 64 | 80 | 80 |
| Cartridges | 800 | 4,500 | 3,300 | 3,390 | 4,500 | 4,560 | 800 | 2,300 | 0 | 3,000 |
| Caps | 1,000 | 4,500 | 3,300 | 4,400 | 5,000 | 4,278 | 900 | 200 | 0 | 5,000 |

Source: Adjutant General Records, (AG 23, #159.5), North Carolina Ordnance Department Record of Issues 1861, 316-333. North Carolina State Archives. Records show Capt. J. Whittaker's Company D transferred to the 45th NCST in June 1861 and did not receive further ordnance as part of the 4th NCST.

Key:

The term "muskets" most likely refers to U.S. M1842 .69 Percussion Muskets as this pattern is commonly associated with the same phrase in ordnance receipts. There were also other descriptive terms in ordnance records denoting other patterns that are indicated by asterisk above, explained as follows:

\* "Rifles" – Refers to M1841 .54 Mississippi Rifles. The Fayetteville Arsenal held roughly 9,000 in April 1861.

\*\* "Guns" – Refers to Muskets Altered to Percussion of the older M1816/1822 pattern, as inferred by .69 caliber notation.

# Index

## A

Adams, William 81, 82, 83, 87, 138,175,227
Allen, David C. 246
Anderson, George B. 81
Andrews, Elle 39, 79, 127, 150
Andrews, John Barr 39, 79, 81, 127, 150
Austin, Greene 37

## B

Bailey, Guilford D. 101
Barber, John Y. 37
Barger, Paul 31, 121
Barnes, Jesse 79
Barrow, W.H. 180
Basinger, George 32, 97, 142, 191, 225, 227, 255, 285, 286
Basinger, John W. 32, 285
Basinger, Sene 32
Battle, George 81,82, 90
Battle, Walter 82, 88, 109, 125, 245, 246, 249, 251
Bean, James W. 225, 255, 286
Bean, Moses Locke 19, 23, 108, 139, 141, 146, 158, 187, 191, 199, 202, 212, 225, 226, 227, 230, 241, 250, 255
Beaty, Robert D. 25, 92, 97, 142, 175, 191
Beauregard, P.G.T. 86, 87, 90
Beaver, Hetty 288
Beaver, Michael W. 32, 257, 297
Beaver, R.E. 32
Beaver, Robinson L. 32
Beaver, Sarah 32, 297
Bell, John J. 22
Bencini, Lueco 14
Bencini, Moses L. 220, 237, 238, 261, 263, 288
Bennett, Resden T. 133, 134, 135, 168, 169, 187
Bennett, William T. 248
Best, R.A. 105
Blackwell, Ben 34
Blount, Thomas M. 85, 90, 165
Bogle, J.L. 255, 286, 287
Bone, J.W. 141
Booth, John C. 77

Boyden, J.H. 264
Boyle, I.L. 218, 287
Bowers, James John 11, 24, 57, 101, 102, 108
Bradford, Colonel (first name not cited) 76
Bradley, William 218
Bradshaw, John A. 85
Brady, Lewis M. 159, 225, 252, 287
Bragg, Thomas 40, 41
Braun, Michael 98
Brawley, N.S. 224, 226, 227
Brawley, R. 37
Breckenridge, J.C. 251
Brown, Ann B.G. 20
Brown, Catherine Miller 98
Brown, J.A. 227
Brown, Jeremiah M. 14, 24
Brown, John 98
Brown, Laura M. 298
Brown, Mary C. 291
Brown, Peter Alexander 191, 212, 225, 245, 287, 288
Brown, Sarah Antionette 98
Brown, Stephen Alexander 288
Brown, William(s) 16, 19, 20, 23, 29, 31, 42, 43, 45, 53, 67, 75, 89, 263, 289, 291, 304
Brunner, Anna 11
Brunner, Charles H. 11
Brunner, Clarissa 11
Brunner, John J. 11, 24, 38, 39, 40, 42, 43, 44, 45, 52, 55, 70, 74, 80, 83, 102
Brunner, Mary B. 11
Brunner, Mary Kincaid 11
Brunner, Thomas K.11
Brunner, William 11
Bryant, Anna 25
Bryant, Lindsey 25, 142, 146, 255
Bryant, William L. 25
Buchanan, James 1, 51, 54
Buis, William 142, 199, 212, 250, 288, 301
Butterfield, Charles A. 263

## C

Cain, Emily 78
Caldwell, John C. 131
Cameron, James 236, 311

319

Candy, Charles 166, 167, 171
Cantwell, John L. 50, 51, 54
Campbell, George S. 288
Campbell, John 97, 288
Carpenter, Daniel 100, 121
Carter, Alfred 25, 108, 158, 159, 187, 191, 212, 255
Carter, Bill 185
Carter, David 79, 81, 90
Carter, E.F.M. 138, 175, 289
Carter, James 107
Casey, Silas 101
Casper, Ambrose 97, 138, 141, 211, 266, 289
Casper, James 225, 289, 290, 305, 310
Castor, Henry 142, 235, 236, 290
Castor, John 142, 191
Cauble, George 25, 290, 291
Cauble, Greene 26
Chambers, Henry A. 90
Chipley, Colonel (first name not cited) 88
Clark, D. P. 32
Clark, James 97
Colley, Leroy Carter 25, 141
Colston, Robert 164
Connelly, Jack 299
Cotton, Florida 35
Coughenhour, Christian 21
Coughenhour, Christina Rodgers Brandon 21
Coughenhour, Jacob C. 21
Coughenhour, Mary Caroline Monroe 22
Coughenhour, Thomas Adam 22, 29, 30
Coughenhour, William Chambers 19, 21, 23, 26, 29, 30, 34, 53, 59, 107, 108, 109, 122, 123, 141, 142, 143, 144, 145, 158, 161, 191, 199, 200, 201, 202, 205, 211, 218, 227, 230, 241, 260, 261, 264, 290, 294, 302, 304, 307
Corl, Daniel 218, 225, 227, 291
Cowan, John 50
Cox, Jacob Dolson 128
Cox, William R. 166, 167, 227, 228, 230, 241, 246, 252
Craig, Henry K. 42
Crawford, James Reid 24, 97, 264
Crawford, William Dunlap 24
Crawford, William Henderson 25, 97
Creighton, William 171
Crittenden, Thomas L. 228
Crook, George 234, 236

Crooks, Henry W. 32, 85
Crooks, John 32
Cross, Edward E. 134
Cummings, William W. 26
Custer, George A. 234

**D**

Dalton, Captain (first name not cited) 81
Darby, W.R. 38
Darlingkiller, Frederick 50, 54
Davidson, T.M.C. 100, 121
Davis, Jefferson 40, 100, 108, 117, 252
Davis, Michael 67, 235, 290, 291
Davis, Samuel 82
Dearing, James 241, 260
Deaton, John C. 26, 142, 159, 191, 212, 245
Deaton, Michael 159
Dennison, Captain (first name not cited)
DeRossett, W.L.
Doles, George P. 184, 188, 195
Douglass, Stephen A. 41, 43
Dorsett, James F. 97, 292
Durham, Seaton G. 124
Durham, John R. 124
Durrell, William 26, 142, 143, 158, 191, 224, 225, 266, 299

**E**

Early, Jubal 228, 233
Edwards, Weldon N. 68
Echols, John 218
Eddleman, Jacob Adam 26
Eddleman, Jeremiah 97, 138, 236, 251, 292
Eddleman, John 142
Edney, Bates M. 12
Eller, Nelson 26, 138, 225, 263, 265, 266
Elliason, William A.
Ellis, John W. 1, 2, 14, 21, 35, 40, 41, 42, 43, 48, 49, 50, 51, 54, 55, 59, 67, 68, 75
Endie, John 159, 191, 212, 245, 266, 292, 293
Evans, Arthur 98, 122
Ewell, Richard 118, 198, 227

**F**

Featherston, Winfield 100, 102

File, Tobias 26
Fisher, Charles F. 37, 81, 264
Fisher, N.F. 226
Floyd, John B. 2, 42, 43, 51, 52, 77
Foard, Fred 62
Francine, Louis R. 171
Frayley, Wilburn C. 23, 35, 163, 181, 255, 285, 325, 331
Frayley, Jacob L. 27, 142, 224
Frayley, Jesse 293, 350
Friedheim, Arnold 159, 187, 211, 238, 266, 293
Fries, Henry 124
Fulk, Edward 97, 142, 191, 293
Fulk, Richard 159
Funk, John H.S. 164, 165, 167
Funkhouser, R.D. 104

## G

Gaither, Thomas 149
Gales, Seaton 173
Garland, Samuel 100, 118, 126, 127, 128
Garnett, T.S. 164
Gallimore, Barbara C. 28
Gardner, Samuel F. 97, 122, 293
Gibson, John 99
Gibson, W. 133
Gibson, Joseph 99
Gillespe, A. 304
Gillespe, J.P. 265
Glover, Jeremiah 175, 191, 211, 228, 241, 245, 259, 261, 294
Glover, Malvina E. 32
Glover, W.A. 108
Glover, William H. 32, 141, 294, 295
Goodman, John T. 37
Gordon, John B. 131, 161, 228, 251, 253, 254
Gorman, William A. 121
Gorman, William R. 304
Graham, Charles K. 169
Graham, William A. 13
Grant, Ulysses S. 222, 228, 251, 253, 254, 256
Grimes, Bryan 90, 96, 98, 100, 101, 102, 103, 104, 107, 108, 109, 113, 117, 119, 120, 122, 125, 126, 127, 128, 130, 134, 139, 140, 143, 145, 163, 165, 166, 167, 169, 172, 173, 174, 175, 179, 185, 187, 188, 189, 190, 199, 221,

227, 231, 234, 237, 238, 241, 252, 253, 254, 255, 256, 259, 266, 285, 293

## H

Hadley, J.M. 218
Hall, Hugh H. 185, 190
Hall, Josephus W. 38, 262
Halton, Reuben J. 98
Hancock, Winfield Scott 221
Hanes, Jacob 82, 198, 205, 206, 227
Hardee, William 58
Harris, J.H. 297
Harris, William C. 17
Hayes, Rutherford B. 128
Healy, Virgil M. 171
Hedrick, John J. 50, 51, 54
Heilig, Ellen 299
Heilig, Mary 298
Heim, David 295
Helig, Philip 159, 224, 226, 295, 298
Hendricks, John L. 27, 85, 296
Hennesy, Michael 141, 146, 158, 190, 191, 212
Heyer, Charles 37, 149, 296
Hill, Ambrose Powell 117, 118, 119, 204
Hill, Captain (last name not cited) 39
Hill, Daniel Harvey 98, 100, 117, 118, 119, 120, 121, 122, 125, 126, 127, 128, 131, 143
Hobson, E.L. 252
Hooker, Joseph 98, 154, 161, 162, 163, 167, 168, 175
Hofflin, Marcus 17, 19, 22, 23, 29, 31, 59, 92, 140, 141, 144, 145, 149, 158, 191, 192, 195, 199, 200, 202, 205, 210, 211, 212, 218, 230, 232, 241, 250, 285, 287, 291, 310
Hoke, John F. 67, 68, 75, 82, 229
Holshouser, Crawford 97, 226, 296, 297
Holshouser, David Lewis (Lewis D.) 97, 175, 191, 265, 266, 297
Holshouser, Milas 138, 142, 159, 212, 218, 225, 249, 252, 266, 297
Holshouser, Otto 138, 158, 190, 191, 199, 212, 224, 225, 295, 297, 298
Holshouser, Wiley 296
Hoover, Sumpter A. 102, 254
Hopkins, Samuel 169
Horah, George 27
Horah, W.M.H., Sr. 27

McNeely, Francis M.Y. 21, 52, 60, 61, 62, 70, 75, 76, 85, 86, 89, 91, 97, 98, 107, 109, 260, 261, 263, 287

McNeely, Thomas 21

McNeely, Margaret 21

McRorie, William A. 185, 186, 224

McQueen, Alexander 28, 142, 159, 191, 218, 255, 301, 302

McQueen, Daniel 97, 142, 159, 191, 212, 302

McQueen, William 28

Miller, Alfred W. 108, 130, 302

Miller, Calvin 138, 175, 303

Miller, Daniel 130, 303

Miller, H.C. 226

Miller, P. 226

Miller, Rev. Captain (first name not cited) 80

Miller, Rufus 291

Mills, Francis 28, 97, 159, 191, 212, 225, 227, 255

Mills, W.J. 28

Minor, Mary 34

Misenheimer, George 218, 255, 303

Misenheimer, Paul 26

Moore, B.R. 43, 60

Moore, James 227

Moore, John 253

Moose, William A. 28

Morris, William 28, 122, 142, 159, 191

Morrison, F. 227

Mott, Gersham 167, 171

Moyer, Daniel 28, 30, 142, 191

Mowrey, Andrew 28, 29, 255

Mowrey, John 28, 97, 303

Mowrey, Sarah Ann 32

Mowrey, William George (William C.) 28, 29

Mull, Lucretia Christine 24

Murr, William 29, 31, 159, 191, 235, 249, 252, 304

Myers, Abraham 55, 260, 299

Myers, E. 38

Myers, Thom. 226

## N

Naglee, Henry M. 101

Neave, Edward 22, 23, 37, 92, 256, 263, 264, 265, 304

Neave, William 37, 87, 256, 304

Neeley, James W. 41, 335

Nettleton, George 134

## O

O'Neal, Isaac P. 34, 49, 158, 179, 212, 214, 236, 335, 341

Orr, A.J. 86

Osborne, Edwin A. 26, 70, 79, 90, 101, 102, 103, 104, 107, 119, 120, 129, 130, 131, 132, 133, 134, 138, 187, 189, 199, 253, 255

Owens, J.T. 212, 224, 226, 227

## P

Page, William 138, 146, 191, 212

Palmer, George S. 120

Palmer, Innis N. 101

Parker, C.B. 227

Parker, Francis Marion 131, 132, 166, 167

Parker, William 23, 29, 31, 142, 158, 191, 212, 228

Parnell, William 142, 299

Patterson, Edward 29

Patterson, R.E. (Bob) 121

Patterson, R.L. 37

Paxton, Elisha F. 164, 165, 168

Peden, John T. 29, 142, 158

Peeler, William (W.D.C.) 97, 108, 138, 142, 159, 189, 199, 212, 249, 289, 305, 310

Pender, Dorsey 164

Pendleton, William N. 89

Phillips, Williams 218, 225, 289, 305, 310

Pierce, W.W. 82

Plowman, Solomon 34

Polk, Leonidas 262

Pope, John 122

Porter, Fitz Hugh 117, 119

## R

Rand, I. 86

Ramseur, Stephen Dodson 131, 133, 159, 161, 164, 165, 166, 167, 168, 169, 171, 173, 184, 189, 199, 218, 221, 227, 229, 233, 234, 238

Ramsey, John A. 54

Raymer, Nathaniel Jacob (Nat) 37, 149, 150, 151, 153, 157, 159, 160, 166, 169, 175, 176,

Verble, John 14

## About the Author

Philip Hatfield, Ph.D. is a member of the Company of Military Historians, and holds a doctorate in psychology from Fielding University; a master's degree in psychology from Marshall University; and a bachelor's degree in psychology and history from the University of Charleston. Dr. Hatfield is a veteran of the U.S. Air Force, and has written five books and numerous scholarly articles related to the Civil War.

IN MEMORY OF
ROWAN'S
CONFEDERATE SOLDIERS
THAT THEIR HEROIC DEEDS
SUBLIME SELF-SACRIFICE
AND UNDYING DEVOTION
TO DUTY AND COUNTRY
MAY NEVER BE FORGOTTEN
1861-1865

35th Star Publishing
www.35thstar.com